Hamilton versus Jefferson in the Washington Administration
Completing the Founding or Betraying the Founding?

By the middle of 1792, just a little more than three years after America's new government under the Constitution had been set in motion, Alexander Hamilton and Thomas Jefferson – President George Washington's two most important cabinet secretaries and two of the most eminent men among the American founders – had become open and bitter political enemies. Their dispute was not personal but political in the highest sense. Each believed that the debate between them was over regime principles. Each believed that he was protecting the newly established republic, and that the other was laboring to destroy it. Carson Holloway's *Hamilton versus Jefferson in the Washington Administration* examines Hamilton and Jefferson's differences, seeking to explain why these great founders came to disagree so profoundly and vehemently about the political project to which both were committed and had dedicated so much thought and effort.

Carson Holloway is an associate professor of political science at the University of Nebraska at Omaha and the author of several works of political philosophy. He has been a Visiting Fellow in Princeton University's James Madison Program in American Ideals and Institutions and a Visiting Fellow in American Political Thought at the Heritage Foundation. His scholarly articles have appeared in the *Review of Politics*, *Interpretation: A Journal of Political Philosophy*, and *Perspectives on Political Science*, and he has written more popular articles for *First Things*, *Public Discourse*, and *National Review*.

Hamilton versus Jefferson in the Washington Administration

Completing the Founding or Betraying the Founding?

CARSON HOLLOWAY
University of Nebraska, Omaha

CAMBRIDGE
UNIVERSITY PRESS

32 Avenue of the Americas, New York, NY 10013-2473, USA

Cambridge University Press is part of the University of Cambridge.

It furthers the University's mission by disseminating knowledge in the pursuit of education, learning, and research at the highest international levels of excellence.

www.cambridge.org
Information on this title: www.cambridge.org/9781107521117

First published 2015

Printed by Sheridan Books, Inc., USA

A catalog record for this publication is available from the British Library.

Library of Congress Cataloging in Publication Data
Holloway, Carson, 1969–
Hamilton versus Jefferson in the Washington administration : completing the founding or betraying the founding? / Carson Holloway.
    pages cm
ISBN 978-1-107-10905-6 (hardback) – ISBN 978-1-107-52111-7 (paperback)
    1. United States – Politics and government – 1789–1797.   2. Hamilton, Alexander, 1757–1804 – Political and social views.   3. Jefferson, Thomas, 1743–1826 – Political and social views.   4. Federal government – United States – Philosophy.   I. Title.
E311.H65   2015
973.4'1–dc23   2015021271

ISBN 978-1-107-10905-6 Hardback
ISBN 978-1-107-52111-7 Paperback

To Gary Glenn, Larry Arnhart, and the memory of Morton Frisch

Contents

Acknowledgments

I would like to express my appreciation to Cambridge University Press for publishing this work. I must particularly thank my editor, Robert Dreesen, for shepherding the book – and me – through the process. My thanks are also due to the anonymous reviewers of the manuscript for their helpful and insightful suggestions.

I also owe a considerable debt of gratitude to the Earhart Foundation for supporting my work over the years, especially during the summers of 2009 and 2011 as I did the research that would lead to the present book. I would also like to thank the University of Nebraska at Omaha for a faculty development fellowship in the spring of 2010 that supported my work on this project. In addition, I am deeply grateful for the support of the Heritage Foundation. During the 2014–2015 academic year I held a fellowship in American political thought at Heritage's B. Kenneth Simon Center for Principles and Politics. By releasing me from the classroom for a year the fellowship provided me with much needed time to complete the manuscript. Here I must also thank the Center's director, David Azerrad, and its assistant director, Arthur Milikh, for their excellent intellectual companionship and friendship.

I also wish to thank my colleagues and friends in the profession who have given me much appreciated encouragement and advice. Brad Wilson and Matt Franck have generously shared their time, knowledge, and judgment with me in numberless conversations and e-mail exchanges about Hamilton and Jefferson's approaches to constitutional questions. I am also very grateful to Alan Gibson for the many discussions we have shared, from which I have always learned a great deal about the founding in general and James Madison in particular. I must also thank Jim Ceaser, Jim Stoner, Darren Staloff, Michael Zuckert, Jeff Morrison, Clement Fatovic, and Paul Carrese for their encouragement. Finally, I am grateful for the support of my colleagues in the Political Science

Department of the University of Nebraska at Omaha, and particularly that of Randy Adkins, my department chair.

Writing a book requires not only professional but also familial support. For patiently putting up with my prolonged time in the office, and for listening to my almost daily musings on Hamilton and Jefferson, I am grateful to my excellent wife, Shari, and my wonderful daughters, Maria, Anna, Elizabeth, Catherine, Jane, and Emily.

Finally, I wish to thank my graduate school teachers, Gary Glenn, Larry Arnhart, and Morton Frisch, to whom this book is dedicated. I can never repay them for introducing me to the study of political philosophy and statesmanship.

Any merit this book possesses could not have been achieved without the help of the people and institutions I have mentioned. Any faults in it are my own.

1

Introduction

By the middle of 1792, just a little more than three years after America's new government under the Constitution had been set in motion, Alexander Hamilton and Thomas Jefferson – President George Washington's two most important cabinet secretaries and two of the most eminent men among the American founders – had become open and bitter political enemies. According to Jefferson, Hamilton was "a man whose history, from the moment at which history can stoop to notice him, is a tissue of machinations against the liberty of the country which has not only received him and given him bread, but heaped its honors on his head."[1] According to Hamilton, Jefferson, who had taken such pains to present himself "as the quiet, modest, retiring philosopher," was in reality an "intriguing incendiary," an "aspiring turbulent competitor," and "a man who is continually machinating against the public happiness."[2]

As these remarks indicate, the dispute was not personal but political. It was, moreover, political not in the ordinary sense but in the highest sense of the word. Hamilton and Jefferson may have felt a personal political rivalry over who would exert the greatest influence over administration policy, but this was neither man's deepest concern. Rather, each believed that the debate between them was over regime principles. Each believed that he was protecting the newly established republic, and that the other was laboring to destroy it.

As secretary of the treasury, Hamilton devised and promoted an ambitious policy agenda that began with a plan to provide not only for the Revolutionary War debt of the national government but also for much of the state debt as well; proceeded to call for the creation of a national bank; and concluded

---

[1] Thomas Jefferson, *The Papers of Thomas Jefferson*, ed. John Catanzariti, Volume 24 (Princeton, NJ: Princeton University Press, 1961), 357.

[2] Alexander Hamilton, *The Papers of Alexander Hamilton*, ed. Harold C. Syrett, Volume 12 (New York: Columbia University Press, 1967): 504 and 196.

by proposing a system of government support for American manufacturing. Hamilton regarded these policies as essential to completing the American founding by delivering on the Constitution's promise of energetic government, which Hamilton believed was necessary to safeguard the Union.

For his part, Jefferson believed that Hamilton's treasury program was not only ill advised but positively (and, indeed, intentionally) dangerous to the character of the American regime itself. Jefferson contended that Hamilton's system of funding the nation's debt was in fact primarily intended as a tool by which the secretary of the treasury could corrupt the Congress with a view to destroying the Constitution's limits on the powers of the national government and, ultimately, replacing America's new republic with a monarchy modeled on the British Constitution. Where Hamilton thought he was completing the founding, Jefferson thought he was betraying the founding. In addition, Hamilton believed that the constitutional and political principles on which Jefferson opposed him were so dangerously erroneous, and had been pressed with so much fanaticism, that Jefferson and Jeffersonianism were the real threat to the republic.

The appearance in 1793 of grave problems of foreign policy did not ease but instead exacerbated the differences between Washington's two chief ministers. Hamilton believed that Jefferson's partiality to France threatened to drag America into the French revolutionary wars, something that could not be in America's interests and would in fact be very dangerous for the newly established North American republic. For Jefferson, Hamilton's lack of enthusiasm for the French cause was further evidence of his opposition to republican government, and Hamilton's public defense of Washington's neutrality proclamation put forward heretical interpretations of the executive power that threatened further damage to American constitutionalism.

We are compelled to ask how such deep differences about the very meaning of American constitutionalism and American republicanism could emerge so soon after the work of the founding had apparently been crowned by the writing and ratification of the Constitution. What led Hamilton and Jefferson to disagree so profoundly and so vehemently about the nature of the larger project to which both were committed and had dedicated so much thought and effort? How could they believe so much to be at stake in the political and constitutional questions raised by Hamilton's treasury program and by the foreign policy challenges that confronted the young nation? This book seeks to shed light on these questions by examining in detail the great debates between Hamilton and Jefferson while both served in Washington's administration.

These questions have admittedly been asked and answered by other scholars in other books. There are many excellent biographies of Hamilton and Jefferson, many superb studies of their thought, and many admirable accounts of the politics of the 1790s. None of these treatments, however, has offered the intensive examination of the Hamilton-Jefferson debates attempted here. The epic scale of each man's life, the impressive range of each man's thought, and the variety of issues at play during the first Washington administration prevent more general studies from giving the detailed account of Hamilton and Jefferson's arguments and counterarguments that the present study aims to provide.[3] I hope that by pursuing a more precise understanding of Hamilton and Jefferson's cabinet clashes, this book will enrich our understanding of the American founding, and particularly of the different interpretations these leading founders put forward of common American principles.

Such an undertaking promises not only to help us understand the founding better but also to understand ourselves – or our own political situation – better. This is the case because so many of the issues that Americans debate today are the same as, or at least very similar to, the ones that divided Hamilton and Jefferson as the American regime was just setting sail. Then as now, the country carried a large public debt, the payment of which raised serious questions of prudence and respect for public faith. Jefferson regarded Hamilton's plan to assume the war debts of the states as unjust because it benefited states that had not paid their debts at the expense of those who had – an argument that prefigures contemporary complaints about federal "bailouts" of improvident institutions. Similarly, present-day charges that government financial policy is made primarily in the interest of the wealthy echo Jefferson's criticisms of Hamilton's funding system, the bank, and his proposal to subsidize American manufacturing. Above all, Hamilton and Jefferson's disagreements about the meaning of the Constitution – about the scope of the power of the national government in relation to domestic affairs and the scope of the executive power in relation to foreign affairs – are reenacted almost daily in contemporary American politics.

Moreover, by helping us understand the founding better, and by helping us understand our own disputes better, such a study can also help us understand better our own relationship to the founding. Americans of all political persuasions desire – although in different ways and in relation to different issues – to live in some kind of continuity with the founding and indeed to turn to the founders for answers to the questions that divide us now. This impulse is strongest and most understandable in relation to questions that touch on the correct approach to the Constitution, which the founders after all wrote and ratified, and on the basic character of the regime, which after all the founders established. This examination of Hamilton and Jefferson's disputes certainly does not discredit such an impulse, but it does challenge it because in turning to the founders for answers to the questions we dispute, we find that in some important cases the founders have no unequivocal answer because they were just as divided as we are. This does not mean that we cannot live in continuity

---

[3] This is true even of John Ferling's comparative biography, *Jefferson and Hamilton: The Rivalry that Forged a Nation* (New York: Bloomsbury Press, 2013), which, because it covers the entirety of each man's life, cannot focus the same amount of attention on the Washington administration as I give in the subsequent chapters of this book.

with the founding or be guided by its principles in confronting our own problems, but it does mean that this guidance cannot always take the form of a simple appeal to what the founders would have said about this or that contemporary political question. We must instead immerse ourselves in their arguments and try to learn from their seriousness about the need for political reasoning to be informed not only by expediency but also by constitutional and moral principle.

In what follows, I have tried to give as full an account as I could of Hamilton and Jefferson's arguments that touched on such principles during their time together in Washington's cabinet. I have not attempted a comprehensive evaluation of the merits of each man's arguments, but I have tried to clarify them where I thought I could, and I have pointed out their strengths and weaknesses where I thought I perceived them. The reader may sense that I am generally more inclined to Hamilton's positions than to Jefferson's. This is true. Candor requires that I confess I began this project expecting that I would find Hamilton more persuasive, and that this expectation was fulfilled. Nevertheless, I have tried to be fair to Jefferson and to present his arguments as completely and as accurately as possible, so that the reader will have sufficient information to draw different conclusions from my own.

The book is divided into three parts. Part I covers the disagreements between Hamilton and Jefferson early in Washington's presidency over the first steps of Hamilton's treasury program. Chapter 2 examines the argument of Hamilton's *Report on Public Credit*, emphasizing his belief in the centrality of sound public credit to energetic government, as well as his understanding of the principles of justice that informed his plan for a provision for the public debt. Chapter 3 considers Jefferson's reservations about, but also the grounds of his ultimate decision to support, Hamilton's plan to assume some of the state Revolutionary War debt. It also presents the first direct clash between Hamilton and Jefferson over a matter of policy: their opposed advice to Washington over resolutions passed by Congress to protect the back pay of some American soldiers. Hamilton's *Report on a National Bank* is the subject of Chapter 4, which seeks to explain his argument that a public bank is necessary to realize the Constitution's promise of energetic government, as well as his understanding of the principles by which such a bank should be organized. Chapters 5 and 6 then turn to Hamilton and Jefferson's most famous constitutional debate, contained in their opposed opinions for Washington on the constitutionality of the national bank. Chapter 5 presents Jefferson's argument that the bank is unconstitutional and his claim that the constitutional interpretation on which it rested would destroy the Constitution as a charter of limited government. Chapter 6 presents Hamilton's defense of the constitutionality of the bank and his counterargument that Jefferson's approach to the national powers would effectively render the government unworkable.

In the year following the debate over the bank, the disagreements between Hamilton and Jefferson gave way to a complete political break between the two men, with each believing that the other posed a dire threat to the Constitution and the republic. Part II traces the arguments involved in this rupture. Chapter 7 gives an account of Hamilton's *Report on Manufactures*, the political and constitutional principles that informed its argument, and Hamilton's belief that national support for manufacturing was necessary to fostering the kind of energetic government that could successfully defend America. Chapter 8 examines some minor but nevertheless instructive exchanges between Hamilton and Jefferson over how to understand the American Revolution, the power of the national government to alienate territory, and the apportionment bill of 1792. Then Chapters 9 and 10 turn to Hamilton and Jefferson's comprehensive and damning mutual critiques. Chapter 9 covers Jefferson's argument that Hamilton's policies aimed to corrupt Congress and that his approach to the Constitution aimed to destroy its limits on the national power, all with a view ultimately to overthrowing the republic and establishing in its place a monarchy on the British model. Chapter 10 presents Hamilton's response to Jefferson's charges, as well as his counter-critique that Jeffersonianism, by weakening the government and undermining public faith, threatened to create the kind of chaos that would give a popular demagogue the chance to make himself king.

Part III examines the debates of 1793, Hamilton and Jefferson's final year in the cabinet together, when issues of foreign policy took center stage. Because those issues arose primarily from the French Revolution and its international consequences, Chapter 11 presents the differing views of that revolution that Hamilton and Jefferson expressed while serving under Washington. Chapters 12 and 13 examine the conflicting lines of advice that Jefferson and Hamilton gave President Washington on the status of America's treaties with France in the wake of the French Revolution and the war arising out of it. In a meeting of the cabinet to discuss America's posture toward France and its enemies, Hamilton suggested that America might be able to hold its French treaties to be temporarily suspended or even permanently discontinued. Chapter 12 offers an account of Jefferson's written rejection of Hamilton's suggestion, and Chapter 13 examines Hamilton's written opinion in support of it. While Washington did not take Hamilton's advice and declare the treaties suspended, he did, on the advice of the whole cabinet, issue a proclamation of American neutrality. The final chapters of this section follow the arguments over the character of foreign policy and the scope of the executive power that arose as a result of the proclamation. Chapter 14 recounts Hamilton's arguments in his *Pacificus* series, focusing on his claims about the constitutional role of the executive in foreign policy, the proper understanding of the French treaties, and the role of gratitude in foreign policy. Chapter 15 takes up James Madison's rejoinder to Hamilton in his *Helvidius* articles, which were written at Jefferson's urging. Finally, a brief concluding chapter offers some reflections on what lessons we might draw for ourselves from the Hamilton-Jefferson debates.

Some readers may wish to consult for themselves the Hamiltonian and Jeffersonian writings to which I refer throughout the book. Many of the more famous ones are conveniently available in the Library of America collections of Hamilton's and Jefferson's writings, edited by Joanne B. Freeman and Merrill D. Peterson, respectively. Everything else can be found in the massive compilations of Hamilton's papers, edited by Harold C. Syrett and published by Columbia University Press, and Jefferson's papers, edited by Julian P. Boyd, Charles T. Cullen, John Catanzariti, and Barbara B. Oberg and published by Princeton University Press. The hard-copy editions of these multivolume works are not so readily available, at least not to those who do not have easy access to a university library. Their contents, however, have been made available online by the National Archives. Interested readers can browse and search their contents by volume number at the following websites:

- http://founders.archives.gov/content/volumes#Hamilton
- http://founders.archives.gov/content/volumes#Jefferson

In the chapters that follow, when quoting from Hamilton and Jefferson (and other founders), I have modernized their spelling, capitalization, and punctuation but have kept their use of italics.

PART I

A DEBATE BETWEEN CABINET COLLEAGUES

2

Establishing the Public Faith

Hamilton's Report on Public Credit

According to one account, George Washington, having been elected America's first president, and pondering the challenges his administration would confront, asked revolutionary financier Robert Morris what the new government should do about the nation's considerable debts. Said Morris: "There is but one man in the United States who can tell you; that is, Alexander Hamilton."[1]

If Morris exaggerated, it was not by much. And if the story is apocryphal – in relating it, Hamilton biographer Forrest McDonald admits that it is based on "secondhand recollections" – it still points to an important truth: Hamilton was probably as uniquely prepared to be the nation's first secretary of the treasury as Washington was to be its first president.[2] Hamilton certainly knew more about finance than any of the leading founders, and it is probably not an overstatement to say that among that crowd of very able men he was singularly qualified to confront the infant republic's daunting financial difficulties. He had taken special pains to acquire the knowledge he would need for such a task. While serving as Washington's aide de camp during the Revolution, Hamilton had used his spare moments to study texts such as Malachy Postlewayt's *Universal Dictionary of Trade and Commerce* and Richard Price's *Schemes for Raising Money by Public Loans*. Later, he read the three-volume memoirs of French finance minister Jacques Necker, which provided him, in McDonald's words, with a "veritable encyclopedia of practical information on fiscal management."[3]

The new secretary of the treasury would need all of his considerable financial acumen to address the country's fiscal challenges. As historian Darren Staloff

---

[1] Quoted in Forrest McDonald, *Alexander Hamilton: A Biography* (New York: W.W. Norton and Company, 1979), 128.
[2] McDonald, *Alexander Hamilton*, 128.
[3] McDonald, *Alexander Hamilton*, 35 and 84.

observes, the government Hamilton was to serve "had inherited a staggering burden of debt" as the cost of the Revolution.[4] The United States owed about $13 million to foreign lenders and about $40 million to domestic creditors. On top of this, the state governments had on their own account borrowed a total of $25 million to pay for their contributions to the war effort. The annual interest on these debts far outstripped the government's expected annual revenues.[5] Indeed, in terms of the debt-to-revenue ratio, American indebtedness was huge by the standards of the day. Numerically, Britain's debt was much larger than America's, but then Britain also commanded a much larger revenue. In terms of its ability to pay, then, America's debt was twice as big as Britain's.[6] America was, Thomas Jefferson worried, not only "the youngest nation in the world" but also "the most indebted."[7] Shortly after Hamilton took office, the House of Representatives passed a resolution placing on his shoulders the task of finding a way to provide for the nation's debts and restore the public credit.[8]

Statesmanship, Finance, and Fame

Hamilton submitted his response to the House's resolution on January 9, 1790. He understood his *Report on Public Credit* as an act of high statesmanship, one that he hoped would win him renown as a great public servant. He thought the policies he proposed were not only necessary to setting the nation's financial house in order but were also essential to completing the work of the American founding. In contrast, Thomas Jefferson came to believe that the policies adopted pursuant to the *Report* had corrupted Congress and were the first step in a Hamiltonian plan to betray the founding and overturn America's republican Constitution. Accordingly, a full account of the clashes between Hamilton and Jefferson in the Washington administration must start from an examination of Hamilton's *Report on Public Credit*.

The contemporary reader might well recoil from such a prospect. A state paper on public credit sounds dull. Moreover, Hamilton's *Report* admittedly occupies an unenviable position in the history of the American founding: after

---

[4] Darren Staloff, *Hamilton, Adams, Jefferson: The Politics of Enlightenment and the American Founding* (New York: Hill and Wang, 2005), 91.

[5] Staloff, *Hamilton, Adams, Jefferson*, 92.

[6] Max M. Edling, "'So Immense a Power in the Affairs of War': Alexander Hamilton and the Restoration of Public Credit," *William and Mary Quarterly* 64 (2007): 308.

[7] Quoted in Edling, "'So Immense a Power in the Affairs of War,'" 308.

[8] Hamilton's subsequent *Report* was submitted in "obedience" to the House's resolution. Alexander Hamilton, *Writings*, ed. Joanne B. Freeman (New York: Library of America, 2001), 531. As Forrest McDonald notes, out of fear of the potential power of the treasury, "most members of the House of Representatives were anxious to retain a general managerial control over" its "operations." Accordingly, the secretary of the treasury "was required by law to report directly to the House as well as to the president." *The American Presidency: An Intellectual History* (Lawrence: University Press of Kansas, 1994), 225–26.

the high drama of the Revolution and the writing and ratification of the Constitution, and yet before the more spectacular battles later in Washington's administration.

Nevertheless, to ignore the *Report*, or to give it only a cursory glance, would be to alienate ourselves at the outset from Hamilton's understanding of the task he faced. He regarded the *Report* not as a mere exercise in bookkeeping but as an act of lofty statesmanship calling for the exercise of the highest political virtues – especially prudence, long regarded in the history of western political thought as the master virtue of the statesman. For Hamilton, the "interesting question" at the core of his inquiry – whether the United States could make a sufficient provision for its debts while also paying for the ongoing functions of the government – involved not just technical financial principles but also "prudential considerations," which could not properly be "overlooked."[9]

Successfully addressing the problem of the public credit required such lofty virtue, Hamilton suggested, because of the high stakes involved, both for himself and for the country. He admitted that in devising his plan he had been "influenced" in part by the "reflection" that "measures which will not bear the test of future unbiased examination" could not "be productive of individual reputation."[10] Hamilton, then, was well aware that his reputation as a statesman would depend on the adequacy of his plan for restoring America's credit. He saw in the problem of America's war debt an opportunity to win for himself a reputation for political excellence. This, for Hamilton, was no small consideration. From his youth, he had been moved by a thirst for fame. The earliest writing of his that has come down to us is a letter to a friend in which a teenaged Hamilton acknowledged that "ambition" was "prevalent" in his nature and that he longed to "exalt" his "station." Whereas the young Hamilton spoke of this ambition as a "weakness," his mature view seems to have rated it much more highly, at least as long as it was properly directed.[11] Thus in the *Federalist* he spoke of the "love of fame" not as a moral infirmity but instead as "the ruling passion of the noblest minds."[12] The desire for fame that Hamilton here attributed to the best men was not a merely selfish hunger for notoriety or for a counterfeit reputation for virtue. For Hamilton, the noblest minds seek fame through worthy acts of public service. Thus, in the *Federalist*, he spoke of this ambition as, under the proper conditions, prompting "a man to plan and undertake extensive and arduous enterprises for the public benefit."[13] Similarly, in the *Report on Public Credit*, even while noting

[9] Hamilton, *Writings*, 550–51.

[10] Hamilton, *Writings*, 573.

[11] Alexander Hamilton, *The Papers of Alexander Hamilton*, ed. Harold C. Syrett, Volume 1 (New York: Columbia University Press, 1961), 4. Subsequent references to Hamilton's papers will be abbreviated as *PAH*, followed by the volume number and page number.

[12] Alexander Hamilton, James Madison, and John Jay, *The Federalist*, ed. Jacob E. Cook (Middletown, CT: Wesleyan University Press, 1961), 488.

[13] Hamilton, Madison, and Jay, *The Federalist*, 488.

the consequences of his plan for his own future reputation, Hamilton conceded that its contribution to "public honor" and "advantage" was "of much greater consequence."[14] Hamilton saw in the problem of America's credit the opportunity to unite his own and his country's interests by winning the highest thing to which he thought men can aspire: the fame that accompanies benevolent public service.[15]

To win such a substantial fame, however, the service one renders must be of substantial importance. Hamilton thus noted that the stakes involved in the problem of the public credit were high not only for him but also for the country. According to Hamilton, to "justify and preserve" the confidence of America's "most enlightened friends of good government"; to

promote the increasing respectability of the American name; to answer the calls of justice; to restore landed property to its due value; to furnish new resources both to agriculture and to commerce; to cement more closely the union of the states; to add to their security against foreign attack; to establish public order on the basis of an upright and liberal policy. These are the great and invaluable ends to be secured, by a proper and adequate provision, at the present period, for the support of public credit.[16]

On Hamilton's view, the man who found a solution to the problem of the public debt would have truly earned a reputation for noble statesmanship. Such a statesman would have succeeded not only in easing the nation's financial situation but also in securing a wide array of economic, political, and moral goods for the country. Indeed, such a statesman would have made a decisive contribution to the completion of America's founding. After all, failure to secure several of the goods Hamilton here had in view – preserving the confidence of the most enlightened citizens, strengthening the bonds of union, enhancing national security – would have rendered the survival of the infant republic questionable.[17]

---

[14] Hamilton, *Writings*, 573.

[15] As Mackubin Thomas Owens, Jr., notes, Hamilton's ambition was evident to many of his fellow founders, with some praising it as a virtue and others denouncing it as a vice. "Alexander Hamilton on Natural Rights and Prudence," *Interpretation: A Journal of Political Philosophy* 14 (1986): 332. For a further examination of Hamilton's understanding of the relationship between fame and statesmanship, see Peter McNamara's "Alexander Hamilton, the Love of Fame, and Modern Democratic Statesmanship," in *The Noblest Minds: Fame, Honor, and the American Founding*, ed. Peter McNamara (Lanham, MD: Rowman and Littlefield, 1999), 141–62; and chapter 5 of Gerald Stourzh's *Alexander Hamilton and the Idea of Republican Government* (Stanford, CA: Stanford University Press, 1970). For a general discussion of the founders' understanding of fame, see Douglass Adair's classic essay, "Fame and the Founding Fathers," in *Fame and the Founding Fathers: Essays by Douglass Adair*, ed. Trevor Colbourn (Indianapolis, IN: Liberty Fund, 1974), 3–36.

[16] Hamilton, *Writings*, 534.

[17] It is well said by historian Jack Rakove that "Hamilton's peculiar destiny" was "to have his own quest for fame" or reputation "intimately bound up with the overriding objective of securing the national character and reputation of the United States – that is, its public credit."

The *Report on Public Credit* contains the additional suggestion that Hamilton thought of his first major policy initiative as making an important contribution to completing the work of the founding. As the *Report* drew to its close, Hamilton stated his conviction that a proper provision for the public credit was "the true desideratum towards relief from individual and national embarrassments" and that "without it, these embarrassments" would "be likely to press still more severely upon the community."[18] This language of "embarrassment" recalls the terminology used during the public debate over ratification of the Constitution to describe the various public evils that arose from the weakness of the government under the Articles of Confederation. Ratification of the Constitution was intended to end those embarrassments, but Hamilton here reminded his audience that government is more than the Constitution, that relief would require not only a constitutional framework providing adequate powers but also a government that actually used those powers energetically. Absent such an energetic application of national power, specifically with a view to securing the public credit, the embarrassments the Constitution was intended to correct would not be relieved but would instead tend to grow worse.

Finally, the *Report on Public Credit* is worthy of careful attention because in it Hamilton acted as a kind of statesman-educator, seeking to enlighten the views of both the Congress and, presumably, the public at large. As we will see, the *Report* offers not merely a plan for restoring the nation's credit but also an extended argument on the importance of sound public credit to the nation's well-being, as well as on the principles that are essential to maintaining the public credit. Hamilton thus sought to instruct the public on the relationship between the public credit and fundamental principles of effective and just government.

For Hamilton, then, the *Report on Public Credit* was an act of high statesmanship, a contribution to the completion of the American founding, and an opportunity to educate the public in the principles of good government. Accordingly, the arguments in the *Report* go well beyond the realms of public finance and economics and shed considerable light on Hamilton's understanding of human nature, justice, and the character of the American republic. Moreover, the *Report* reveals Hamilton' sense of the nature and purposes of statesmanship in a liberal, rights-based regime. Here we encounter Hamilton as a statesman attending not only to the self-interest of the parties concerned in the problem of the public debt but also to moral principle and to the common good, striving by prudence to find some acceptable harmony among these things. And by bringing to light Hamilton's approach to these great questions, the *Report* also reveals the seeds of his later clashes with Thomas Jefferson.

Revolutionaries: A New History of the Invention of America (Boston: Houghton Mifflin Harcourt, 2010), 400.
[18] Hamilton, *Writings*, 573. See also 534.

Hamilton divided his *Report* into a number of successive "enquiries." These, however, may be conveniently grouped into three major lines of argument. First, Hamilton contended that effective government depends on a sound state of public credit, which in turn depends on the government's scrupulous observance of good faith. Second, he examined three "preliminary" issues that had to be resolved before a specific plan for restoring the public credit could be put forward – although these "preliminaries," as we will see, in fact constituted the important substantive questions of policy and justice with which Hamilton had to grapple before the details of a plan could be worked out. Finally, he laid out his proposal for adjusting the nation's debts while securing the revenues necessary to provide for them and for the operations of the government. We begin, then, by examining Hamilton's account of the importance of maintaining the public credit by upholding the public faith.

Hamilton's Defense of Public Faith

Public Credit and Energetic Government

The maintenance of sound public credit is of the first political importance, Hamilton contended, because an effective government must be able to incur debt. It is a "plain and undeniable" truth, he held, that "exigencies are to be expected" in "the affairs of nations, in which there will be a necessity for borrowing." Even the "wealthiest" countries find that "loans in times of public danger, especially from foreign war," are an "indispensable resource."[19] On this view, borrowing is a recurring necessity in the lives of governments. It properly arises not from ordinary public obligations but from "exigencies" or "emergencies." While particular exigencies cannot be specifically foreseen, the fact that they will occur in some form should be well understood by anyone who attends to the nature of political life as it is revealed in the experience of nations. Accordingly, the prudent statesman will anticipate that, over time, public debt will be a predictable part of the community's life and will prepare for it responsibly.

If borrowing is a public "necessity," Hamilton continued, then it is "essential" that the nation's "credit be well established" so that the government can "borrow upon *good terms*." "For when the credit of a country is in any degree questionable, it never fails to give an extravagant premium, in one shape or another, upon all the loans it has occasion to make." Hamilton recognized that governments cannot always simply command the resources they need. In some

---

[19] For an extended discussion of Hamilton's understanding of sound public credit as essential to the nation's ability to wage war, see Edling, "'So Immense a Power in the Affairs of War,'" 287–326. It is indeed significant that Hamilton's mind would turn to the question of war when considering the proper organization of the nation's finances. As Robert W. Tucker and David C. Hendrickson observe: "For Hamilton, war was an inescapable fact of political life. It was something for which every nation must prepare." *Empire of Liberty: The Statecraft of Thomas Jefferson* (New York: Oxford University Press, 1990), 43.

cases they will have to seek those resources on voluntary terms from those who can withhold them if they wish. Those who possess the needed money can be induced to lend it if they can be assured that they will get it back with interest. If, however, they reasonably fear that the government might fail to pay back the loan according to the terms specified, they will demand an even higher rate of interest to compensate them for these risks. And this in turn drives up the cost of government. "From this constant necessity of *borrowing . . . dear*," Hamilton noted, "it is easy to conceive how immensely the expenses of a nation, in a course of time, will be augmented by an unsound state of the public credit."[20]

Hamilton next brought forth his claim that establishing sound public credit was necessary to providing the people of the United States "relief from the embarrassments they now experience."[21] As was noted before, such a claim suggests that Hamilton viewed the *Report on Public Credit* as an effort to complete the Founding, or to complete the establishment of the government formed by the Constitution. The *Federalist* had suggested that the Constitution would remedy the embarrassments the nation experienced under the Articles of Confederation, that is, the evils and inconveniences that arose from a weak and ineffective government incapable of adequately securing the common good.[22] Now, Hamilton warned that those embarrassments would continue, despite ratification of the Constitution, if the country did not finish the job by establishing the public credit on a solid basis. Although Hamilton did not here spell out how unsound credit would feed the embarrassments that had been burdening the nation, we are now in a position to understand the thinking behind his claim. As Hamilton's argument implies, a government that cannot borrow cannot meet the "exigencies" and "emergencies" that it will encounter in the course of time. To put this in the language of the *Federalist*, a government that cannot borrow cannot be energetic, at least not in response to unexpected crises. Exigencies and emergencies would seem to require energetic government action, but borrowing is the only practicable way to raise the necessary funds with the speed required. New taxes, after all, may not actually realize the revenue they are designed to raise for months or longer. Recognizing these difficulties, the Constitution establishes the legal basis for energetic government by empowering Congress to "borrow money on the credit of the United States."[23] Nevertheless, the evils that follow from a complete inability to borrow will be experienced to a lesser but still undesirable degree by a government that is constitutionally authorized to borrow but is practically hampered in doing so by unsound credit. In such a government, the high costs of borrowing will cause hesitation among government officials, and possibly among the public itself, even in cases where there is a real necessity. At the

---

[20] Hamilton, *Writings*, 532 (Hamilton's emphases).
[21] Hamilton, *Writings*, 532.
[22] See, for example, Hamilton, Madison, and Jay, *The Federalist*, 22.
[23] Article I, Section 8.

same time, if the nation's credit is bad enough, the government may have difficulty quickly finding lenders willing to take the risk even if public officials are willing to countenance the costs. In either case, the common good will be endangered by a halting or inadequate response to a pressing crisis. Moreover, in view of the fact that war is one of the exigencies that requires borrowing, hesitation or half-measures might result not only in "embarrassments" but in public calamity.

Good Faith, Self-Interest, and Moral Principle: Hamilton, Machiavelli, and Hobbes

Having established the importance of sound public credit, Hamilton proceeded to ask by what means this end could be achieved. He found a "ready answer" at hand: public credit could be maintained "by good faith, by a punctual performance of contracts." "States," he noted, are like "individuals" in this respect: those "who observe their engagements are respected and trusted," while "the reverse is the fate of those who pursue an opposite conduct." If fear of the risk of lending to the government drives up the cost of borrowing, prudence calls upon government to conduct itself such that creditors will believe that the risk is small or nonexistent. This will be the case if the government consistently repays what it owes precisely according to the terms on which it borrowed. To be sure, Hamilton recognized that this aspiration could not be fulfilled perfectly: "necessity" might sometimes require a "breach of the public engagements." This admission is consistent with the beginning point of his argument: if exigencies will arise that require public debt, then it is possible that exigencies may arise that interfere with the repayment of debt. Nevertheless, Hamilton insisted that where such a necessity does arise, it must be "palliated by a scrupulous attention, on the part of the government, to carry the violation no farther than the necessity absolutely requires, and to manifest, if the nature of the case admits of it, a sincere disposition to make reparation, whenever circumstances shall permit."[24]

Hamilton's earnestness about the public faith can be illuminated by comparing his thinking to that of some of the early modern political philosophers who initiated an intellectual tradition to which Hamilton was in some ways an heir but from which he also in some ways departed. Thus far, his treatment of the issues in the *Report* relies on the belief – very common among the founders and very important for the philosophic pioneers of modernity – that human behavior, at least insofar as it is relevant to statesmen, is powerfully influenced by economic self-interest. Consider, for example, the possible resource that Hamilton did *not* mention in discussing government's need of public credit to respond to exigencies and emergencies: the selfless service of a patriotic citizenry. On Hamilton's account, even during war – the supreme emergency that can threaten the very life of the community, and that accordingly calls forth the

[24] Hamilton, *Writings*, 532–33.

most genuine and fervent patriotism – men still act on self-interested motives. They still expect to be paid, which in turn requires that the government borrow in order to pay them.

In addition, knowledge of the power of self-interest informs Hamilton's discussion of maintaining public credit through keeping faith. As he observed, every "breach of the public engagements, whether from choice or necessity, is in different degrees hurtful to the public credit."[25] In other words, a government may fail to make payments on its debts either through the free choice of the responsible officials or through necessity, because of a lack of sufficient funds. In the former case, the government is guilty of voluntary injustice, but in the latter case the blame is mitigated or removed. Nevertheless, Hamilton warns, the public credit will be harmed in either situation. When men are creditors, it seems, they are concerned not only with the moral question of whether a breach of contract is an act of injustice or an excusable submission to necessity but also with the simpler factual question: Can I expect to get my money back or not? When they have doubts on this question, they will demand a higher rate of interest to compensate their risk in lending, whether the debtor's spotty record is due to dishonesty or incapacity.

Hamilton's implicit emphasis on man's self-interested nature, then, calls to mind the tradition of modern political thought by which he was influenced. That emphasis, coupled with Hamilton's concern with the question of "public faith," more specifically calls to mind the founder of modern political thought, Niccolo Machiavelli, who gave an entire chapter of his work *The Prince* to the question of the mode in which "faith should be kept by princes."[26] Machiavelli's spirit is perhaps also summoned up by Hamilton's suggestion that necessity might excuse a government from keeping faith or performing its obligations. We are led, then, to wonder whether Hamilton's statesmanship – as it is revealed in the *Report on Public Credit* – was informed exclusively by modern political thought's understanding of human nature as dominated by self-interest, or, more specifically, whether Hamilton could be properly understood as a Machiavellian statesman.

Further reflection, however, indicates the limits of Hamilton's intellectual kinship with Machiavelli. Although Machiavelli and Hamilton both contended that necessity could require the breaking of faith, they seem to have had different things in mind. Machiavelli suggested a rather lax understanding of necessity as whatever advances the power interests of the prince. We see "by experience," he noted, "that the princes who have done great things are those who have taken little account of faith and have known how to get around men's brains with their astuteness."[27] Elsewhere in *The Prince*, Machiavelli

[25] Hamilton, *Writings*, 532–33.
[26] Niccolo Machiavelli, *The Prince*, trans. Harvey C. Mansfield (Chicago: University of Chicago Press, 1998), 68.
[27] Machiavelli, *The Prince*, 69.

treated Cesare Borgia's deceptions, which had no end other than to increase his own power, as manifestations of virtue.

In contrast, Hamilton's understanding of necessity suggests not a government's interest in breaking faith so much as an actual inability to meet its obligations. Thus he conceded that "it cannot safely be affirmed, that occasions have never existed, or may not exist, in which violations of the public faith... are *inevitable*."[28] Such language indicates that for him the breaking of faith is not an option to be embraced when advantageous but rather a constraint to be borne when unavoidable.

The gap between Hamilton and Machiavelli is further suggested by the different ways in which they discuss the relationship between appearance and the keeping of faith. Machiavelli emphasized the virtuous prince's ability to manipulate appearances in order to create spurious justifications for breaking faith. A ruler, he observed, never lacks "legitimate causes to color his failure to observe faith."[29] In contrast, Hamilton emphasized the spurious appearance of justification that the prudent statesman must penetrate. When "an appearance of necessity seems to press upon the public councils," the part of the statesman is not to seize this opportunity to free the state from its obligations but instead to "examine well" the "reality" of this supposed necessity, to "be perfectly assured, that there is no method of escaping it" without violating faith, for while circumstances may arise that truly require violations of public faith, "there is great reason to believe," Hamilton contended, "that they exist far less frequently than precedents indicate; and are oftenest pretended through levity, or want of firmness, or supposed through want of knowledge."[30] This is the best course because, again, the nation's credit will be harmed by *any* breach of faith, whether it is truly compelled by necessity or merely chosen through dishonesty. And this unavoidable fact of public finance is, in turn, rooted in the predictable self-interest of the nation's creditors, who will decide whether to lend based on their perceptions of the risks, regardless of the causes of the risks.

Here one might wonder why Machiavelli and Hamilton, reasoning from the same assumption that human actions are powerfully influenced by self-interest, come to such different conclusions about the importance of keeping faith. The difference may be attributed, at least partly, to the following consideration: Hamilton, like Hobbes, was more impressed with the fact of a certain basic human equality and its implications for prudent conduct. Machiavelli advised deception and faith breaking because he believed it is possible to get away with it reliably, at least for the sufficiently "virtuous" prince. A clever enough leader can always find a way to deceive the ordinary run of men: "Men are so simple and so obedient to present necessities that he who deceives will always find someone who will let himself be deceived."[31]

---

[28] Hamilton, *Writings*, 533 (emphasis added).
[29] Machiavelli, *The Prince*, 69.
[30] Hamilton, *Writings*, 533.
[31] Machiavelli, *The Prince*, 70.

Hobbes, while accepting Machiavelli's assumption that men are fundamentally self-interested, nevertheless rejected Machiavelli's advocacy of injustice. His rejection rested on no high-minded moral grounds but instead on purely practical considerations. Most men, he suggested, cannot reliably be deceived in what pertains directly to their own interests. They may occasionally err in such matters, but "a man cannot reasonably reckon upon" such errors as "a means of his security."[32] Similarly, Hamilton suggested that those "who are most commonly creditors of a nation are, generally speaking, enlightened men" with a solid understanding of "their true interest."[33] To be sure, Hamilton was here suggesting that their very enlightenment makes most public creditors open to a modification of their claims if a genuine necessity presses on the public. They are wise enough to accept partial payment, for example, if they see that the alternative is total default. But this enlightened self-interest also informs Hamilton's warning that any tampering with public faith will harm public credit and raise the cost of borrowing because the public creditors are also too astute to be first denied full repayment and then duped into lending again without demanding more interest to compensate the now evidently greater risks accompanying such lending.

Hamilton, then, seems to occupy a position between Machiavelli and Hobbes. Hobbes emphasizes that all human beings are sufficiently reasonable about their own interests that one cannot reckon upon an ability to deceive them in relation to those matters. Hamilton does not here go so far but leaves it at the observation that those who are the public creditors usually cannot be deceived about their own interests. Hamilton then, unlike Hobbes, emphasizes the practical impossibility of manipulating a certain class of men who might be a cut above the ordinary in their astuteness. To that extent, his thinking might indicate a belief in a certain hierarchy of human beings that Hobbes does not make central to his own teaching. Nevertheless, Hamilton certainly does not follow Machiavelli in suggesting the kind of inequality among men that permits the virtuous prince to make deception an ordinary tool of statecraft.

Be that as it may, Hamilton proceeded in his *Report* to pivot decisively away from both Machiavelli and Hobbes by introducing moral considerations into his argument and by presenting them as even more important than calculations based on self-interest. While the observance of "that good faith" on which public credit depends is "recommended by the strongest inducements of political expediency," Hamilton claimed, it is also "enforced by considerations of still greater authority": specifically, arguments that "rest on the immutable principles of moral obligation." Moreover, he observed, these general moral obligations were strengthened by the particular "nature" of the American debt: "It was the price of liberty," and "the faith of America has been repeatedly pledged for it, and with solemnities that give peculiar force to the obligation."[34]

---

[32] Thomas Hobbes, *Leviathan* (New York: Cambridge University Press, 1991), 102.

[33] Hamilton, *Writings*, 533.

[34] Hamilton, *Writings*, 533.

To speak of governments as bound by "immutable principles of moral obligation" is to enter a realm far removed from that of Machiavelli's prince, who must learn to be good or not good as the circumstances require. It is equally removed from the thought of Hobbes, who held that the positive law made by the sovereign is the sole source of men's rights, and that accordingly the sovereign is the final judge of who owns what. On Hobbes's view, there would be no moral difficulty whatever in a government decreeing that it no longer owes what it cannot repay, or even what it no longer wishes to repay. In contrast, Hamilton's *Report* never speaks of the rights of America's creditors as if they could simply be redefined, or defined out of existence, by the authority of the government.[35] It would seem, then, that while Hamilton shares the Machiavellian and Hobbesian realism according to which a considerable part of politically relevant human action is driven by, and intelligible in terms of, self-interest, he nevertheless does not go all the way with them in holding that this realism alone is the basis of all genuine political knowledge. Equally worthy of the statesman's attention are certain fundamental and unchanging moral principles that restrain self-interest and the obligation of which apparently cannot be reduced to self-interest.[36]

Good Faith and the Public Debt as a National Currency
Hamilton concluded the first major section of the *Report*'s argument by reflecting on some "more particular" considerations that offered further support to his defense of public faith. While it is generally true that good faith is politically expedient and morally right, the specific nature of the American situation rendered the case for good faith even more compelling. It would, Hamilton contended, "procure to every class of the community some important advantages, and remove some no less important disadvantages." Here Hamilton once again acted the part of the statesman-educator, illuminating for his audience important but overlooked principles of political economy.[37]

The "advantage to the public creditors" of a proper provision for the nation's debt required "no explanation." They had an obvious interest in being repaid; and a reliable program for repayment would increase the value of the debt they held, which would in turn be advantageous should they wish to sell it to others. Hamilton, however, also sought to show that *all* Americans would

---

[35] On the question of Hamilton's deviations from Hobbes, see Michael D. Chan, "Alexander Hamilton on Slavery," *Review of Politics* 66 (2004): 213–14. Also helpful in differentiating Hamilton from Machiavelli is Chan's *Aristotle and Hamilton on Commerce and Statesmanship* (Columbia, MO: University of Missouri Press, 2006), 90–91.

[36] For further reflections on how Hamilton's thought reflects some of Machiavelli's concerns, but without finally being Machiavellian, see Michael J. Rosano, "Liberty, Nobility, Philanthropy, and Power in Alexander Hamilton's Conception of Human Nature," *American Journal of Political Science* 47 (2003): 61–74, and Karl Walling, "Was Alexander Hamilton a Machiavellian Statesman?" *Review of Politics* 57 (1995): 419–47.

[37] Hamilton, *Writings*, 534, 535–36.

benefit materially from adopting a sound plan to fulfill the nation's obligations. The key to this widespread benefit was the possibility of using the public debt as a form of currency. Hamilton believed that America's economy suffered from an inadequate money supply. While he viewed a national bank with an ability to issue a paper currency as the ultimate solution to this problem, he nevertheless thought an important step toward its amelioration could be taken through the establishment of a proper provision for the public debt. "It is," he contended, "a well known fact, that in countries in which the national debt is properly funded, and an object of established confidence, it answers most of the purposes of money." In such countries, exchanges of "stock or public debt" are "equivalent to payments in specie."[38] The same effect, Hamilton hoped, could be achieved in America.

The benefits of this increase in the money supply would be felt, moreover, by all Americans. It would create a larger capital by which to carry on trade, manufacturing, and agriculture, all of which could be expected to prosper accordingly. It would also lower the rate of interest, which is always "in a ratio" to the "quantity of money" and its "quickness of circulation," thus allowing "both the public and individuals to borrow" on better terms. Finally, it would correct the extremely depressed value of land, the price of which had fallen so far in some places that it could "command no price, which may not be deemed an almost total sacrifice" to the seller. In Hamilton's view, the cause of this deflation was the scarcity of money, and, accordingly, an increase in the money supply to be effected by a provision for the public debt would tend to raise the price of land back to its natural level, which would in turn ease the situation of landowners.[39]

The debt would only be accepted as a kind of money, however, if people had confidence that it would retain its value, which in turn depended on a solid government provision for its repayment. In the absence of such a provision, the public debt would not only fail to augment; it would actively diminish the money supply, thus doing positive harm to the economy. Without being properly funded, the public debt would become a mere commodity like any other, except that it would be more "precarious" because of the "fluctuation and insecurity incident to it." Under such conditions, any money invested in public debt would be "so much diverted from the more useful channels of circulation," for which the public debt itself would provide "no substitute." The proper funding of the public debt, then, involved a question that was "immediately interesting" not only to the public creditors but "to every part of the community": "Whether the public debt, by a provision for it on true principles, shall be rendered a substitute for money; or whether, being left as it is, or provided for in such a manner as will wound those principles, and

[38] Hamilton, *Writings*, 534–35.
[39] Hamilton, *Writings*, 535–36.

destroy confidence, shall be suffered to continue, as it is, a pernicious drain of our cash from the channels of productive industry."[40]

This step in Hamilton's argument seems to reflect his awareness of the tension between the prominence of self-interest that so much of his account presupposes, on the one hand, and his insistence on respect for immutable principles of moral obligation, on the other. Hamilton constructs his case as if he knows that self-interest can weaken men's sense of moral obligation. Up to this point, he had insisted on the immutability of such obligations and had tried to harmonize them with self-interest by showing how the good of the whole community is served, in the long run, by a scrupulous fulfillment of contracts. Yet this alone appears to be insufficient, hence his effort here to show that the consequences of a proper provision for the public credit are advantageous not only for the creditors themselves but also for "every other citizen," and that these advantages will be felt, if not immediately, then at least soon.[41] In other words, Hamilton, recognizing the influence of self-interest on human conduct, and the very real danger that it will draw men away from fulfilling their moral obligations, sought in the *Report on Public Credit* to harmonize those obligations not only with the long term interests of the whole community, but also with the near term interests of all members of the community.

Discrimination, Assumption, and Interest

Having explained "the inducements" – both moral and practical – "to a proper provision for the public debt," Hamilton turned to the next inquiry: "the nature of such a provision." This inquiry demanded some "preliminary discussions," however, which involved serious questions of policy and justice: Who would be paid, who would pay, and what would be paid? That is, before presenting a plan for funding the public debt, Hamilton had to address the questions of *discrimination* – whether anything was owed to original holders of the public debt who had sold it to others – *assumption* – whether the government of the Union should take responsibility for paying the revolutionary debt of the States – and *interest* – whether the principal of the debt should be treated as more obligatory than the interest it had accumulated. His account of these issues sheds light on the understanding of justice that guided Hamilton's statesmanship, an understanding that included but also reached beyond the simple respect for contracts that his defense of public faith had emphasized up to this point.

The Case Against Discrimination

While all Americans agreed that the foreign debt should be paid strictly according to its terms, Hamilton observed, a difference of opinion arose about how to provide for the domestic debt, the money that had been borrowed by the

---

[40] Hamilton, *Writings*, 535–36.
[41] Hamilton, *Writings*, 535.

government from Americans.[42] Some favored a plan that would discriminate between the claims of the original holders of government securities – those who purchased them when they were first issued – and those who were "present possessors, by purchase" from such original holders. On this view, a "full provision" should have been made to pay the nominal value of securities to their original purchasers, while subsequent purchasers should have gotten no more back than what they paid in the market for the securities, plus interest.[43]

The case for such discrimination depended on an appeal beyond the letter of the contracts to deeper principles of equity or fairness, which were to be brought to bear to correct an unjust inequality that would have otherwise resulted from simply honoring the contracts without regard to the circumstances under which the securities had changed hands. Many of the current holders of public securities had been able to buy them for far less than what they cost the original holders. This possibility arose because the government was delinquent in paying its debts, which depressed the market value of the securities and which induced some of the original holders to sell them, getting at least something in return from the purchasers when it seemed that they might never get anything back from the government. Now the government's new ability to provide for its debts held out the possibility of a windfall for the subsequent purchasers while doing nothing to repair the loss to the original holders. Moreover, simply honoring the contracts not only did nothing to correct the loss of the original holders; it also operated to "aggravate" their "misfortune" by making them "contribute to the profit" of those who had "speculated" on their "distresses." After all, the public debt would be paid by levying taxes on all Americans, including those who once held government securities but sold them out of necessity or out of fear that they might never be repaid.[44]

In rejecting the case for discrimination, Hamilton again organized his argument around considerations of both expediency and morality. Here, however, he began with the moral considerations, contending that discrimination would be unjust. Discrimination was "inconsistent with justice" because it involved a "breach of contract" and hence a "violation of the rights of a fair purchaser." The securities by which the debt was incurred, Hamilton pointed out, were

---

[42] As we will see later in this chapter, Hamilton held that a strict respect for faith was compatible with offering an alternative arrangement to creditors, which they would be free to accept or reject. For this reason, his acknowledgment of the strict obligation to repay foreign creditors did not preclude him from instituting inquiries as secretary of the treasury about whether the French would voluntarily agree to a temporary suspension of American payments on the principal of its debt. See the *PAH*, 5: 426 and 429.

[43] Hamilton, *Writings*, 537. One of the most vigorous proponents of discrimination was Hamilton's *Federalist Papers* collaborator James Madison. In the end, the House rejected Madison's plan, and no system of discrimination was adopted. See Mike O'Connor, *A Commercial Republic: America's Enduring Debate Over Democratic Capitalism* (Lawrence: University Press of Kansas, 2014), 15.

[44] Hamilton, *Writings*, 537–38.

explicitly designed from the very beginning to be transferrable. "The nature of the contract in its origin" was that "the public" would "pay the sum expressed in the security" to "the first holder or his *assignee*." The "intent" of this provision was to allow the owner of the security to use it as property "by selling it for as much as it *may be worth in the market*, and that the buyer may be *safe* in the purchase." Accordingly, every subsequent purchaser of a government security was to be understood as standing "exactly in the place of the seller" and as having "the same right" to "the identical sum expressed in the security." Such a buyer had acquired his right to be paid the value of the security by "fair purchase" and "in conformity to the original agreement and intention of the government," and therefore his claim could not "be disputed without manifest injustice."[45]

Moreover, although Hamilton acknowledged the "hard" lot of those who sold their securities under economic duress, he denied that it would unjustly "aggravate" their "misfortune" to have them pay taxes now to compensate those who bought the securities from them. Whatever misfortune this might involve, it was insufficient to overcome to the sellers' "implied" obligation to "contribute" to this cause. Such sellers knew, after all, that the government would be contractually bound to pay those to whom they had sold the securities, and that they, as citizens, would "bear their proportion of the contribution for that purpose." They "tacitly" agreed to do this by the act of selling, and they could not now "with integrity or good faith" try to get out of the obligation "without the consent of those to whom they sold."[46]

Despite the impression that these arguments might at first convey, Hamilton was not a strict rigorist in these matters, inflexibly demanding that the letter of contracts must always be observed without reference to any equitable considerations. He did not hold that equity is irrelevant to the justice of honoring contracts, only that the established principles of equity did not support any modifications of the contractual rights in the case at hand. This is evident in his insistence that those who bought government securities from the original holders were to be considered "fair purchasers." While the sellers might have been under a kind of "necessity" that seemed to compel them to sell their securities on unfavorable terms, that necessity was the fault of the government, which had failed to make a "proper provision for its debts." The buyers, in contrast, "had no agency" in creating the necessity and accordingly "ought not to suffer." Such buyers, Hamilton continued, could not even be charged with "having taken an undue advantage" of the sellers. These buyers had given "a fair equivalent" for the securities: they had "paid" what they were "worth in the market" at the time, taking upon themselves the risk that the government might not fulfill its obligations.[47] Although these arguments

[45] Hamilton, *Writings*, 538 (Hamilton's emphases).
[46] Hamilton, *Writings*, 538–39.
[47] Hamilton, *Writings*, 538.

offered no hope of relief for the original holders in the present case, they show that Hamilton implicitly conceded that certain circumstances could justify an equitable modification of the terms of contracts. Contracts must be honored for "fair purchasers," but Hamilton's argument implies that they might be considered "unfair purchasers" who themselves deliberately created an unfortunate necessity for sellers in order to compel them to part with their property on unfavorable terms. Similarly, his argument implies that a buyer could be charged with taking undue advantage, and that his contract might not be inviolable if he somehow finagled or duped a seller into taking less than the current market value for his property.

Hamilton, then, did not hold that the moral obligations between seller and buyer arise only from their agreement. Rather, some substantive duties preexist contracts and can help determine whether they are valid, hence his implicit suggestion that a buyer may not himself create the distress that induces a seller to sell or take undue advantage of a distressed seller by paying him less than the current market value for his property. Both of these considerations indicate that fellow citizens are under legally cognizable obligations to refrain from the more aggressive forms of economic exploitation.

Indeed, Hamilton's respect for such pre-contractual principles of equity is shown by the fact that he not only acknowledged such principles implicitly but even relied on them in his own argument against discrimination. Such discrimination, he contended, not only would be unjust as a breach of contract but would also itself be inequitable in many cases. The supporters of discrimination favored it as a departure from the formal justice of contract in favor of the substantive fairness of equity. Yet, as Hamilton tried to show, policymakers could not have the knowledge necessary to ensure that a policy of discrimination would in fact operate equitably on all concerned.

Those who favored discrimination conjured up a rather simple moral drama: economically distressed sellers of originally held government securities were victims of necessity unfairly exploited by speculating buyers seeking an easy profit. The reality, however, was probably far more complicated. Hamilton conceded that "many" of the original holders of government securities sold out of necessity. But it did not follow, he immediately added, "that this was the case with all of them." Some may have sold because they simply lacked confidence that the government would in the end honor the terms, or because some other "profitable speculation" appeared for which they needed immediate funds. Moreover, Hamilton continued, just as we lack real knowledge of the circumstances that spurred such transactions, we equally lack real knowledge of the consequences that arose from them. How can we know whether the seller might not have benefitted himself more by his use of the money he collected at the time of sale than he would have had he kept the securities until now? Or how can we know whether the purchaser of the securities – who supposedly has profited unjustly – might not have reaped an even bigger gain from some other use of his money? Further, the proponents of discrimination overlooked the fact that the same persons could be both original holders of the public debt as well as subsequent purchasers of it. Some people might have sold securities because of a pressing need for money, and then, after the need had passed, purchased new securities secondhand, at the low market rate, as a way of making up for their original loss. Would it be equitable, Hamilton asked, to deprive them "of the indemnity which they" had "endeavored to secure by so provident an arrangement?" Finally, Hamilton observed that discrimination would create an inequity between secondhand purchasers of securities who had kept them until now, on the one hand, and, on the other, those who had sold them only a short while ago at a profit. Discrimination here would reward those who had less confidence in the government and punish those who had more. On a "close inspection," problems of this kind "multipl[ied] themselves without end, and demonstrate[d] the injustice of a discrimination, even on the most subtle calculations of equity, abstracted from the obligation of contract." The complexities of circumstance were so extensive, Hamilton concluded, that the "difficulties" of devising a plan with "even the semblance of equity" would be "immense," and it was possible they would turn out to be "insurmountable," rendering any scheme of discrimination "capricious" in its operation, so "replete" with both "absurd" and "inequitable consequences" as to "disgust even the proposers of the measure."[48]

Hamilton then turned to his claim that discrimination would also be inexpedient. Here his argument is more straightforward and can be stated more briefly. The "impolicy" of discrimination, he held, arose "from two considerations." First, such a policy would deny the nation the benefits, discussed earlier, of using the public debt as a kind of money. Its use for this purpose depended on its "transferable quality," and this in turn rested "on the idea of complete security to the transferee, and a firm persuasion, that no distinction can be made between him and the original proprietor." Why, after all, would anyone accept government securities as a means of payment if the government adopted an open policy of tampering with and diminishing their value for subsequent holders? Second, discrimination would harm the public credit and thus increase rates of interest for the government. By depriving subsequent holders of their contractual rights, discrimination involved a "breach of faith" which could only undermine investors' confidence in the government. Accordingly, those who lend to the public would demand a higher rate of interest, which would cause "an absolute loss to the government."[49]

---

[48] Hamilton, *Writings*, 539–40.
[49] Hamilton, *Writings*, 540–41. John Witherspoon agreed with and may have reinforced Hamilton's thinking on these questions. While preparing the *Report*, Hamilton had written to Witherspoon for his advice. In his response Witherspoon had identified "the want of a just sense of the sacredness of public credit" as the "evil" that had "pervaded" American "affairs," adding that, in his view, "discrimination is totally subversive of public credit." See *PAH*, 5: 465.

Hamilton concluded his case against discrimination by considering a third and, he suggested, perhaps even more powerful argument. Discrimination "would be repugnant to an express provision of the Constitution" – Article VI – which provides that "all debts contracted and engagements entered into" prior to the adoption of the Constitution "shall be as valid against the United States under it, as under the Confederation." Hamilton argued that this was equivalent "to a constitutional ratification of the contracts respecting the debt, in the state in which they existed under the confederation," and that by this standard there could be "no doubt" that "the rights of assignees and original holders" were to be "considered as equal." Discrimination necessarily involved tampering with engagements entered into under the Confederation, rendering them not "as valid" but instead *less* valid than they had been before, in violation of the express promise of the Constitution to the contrary.[50]

Hamilton's Case for Assumption

Having thus "explod[ed]" – to his own satisfaction, at least – the "principle of discrimination," Hamilton turned to his own argument *for* assumption – for the government of the United States taking responsibility for paying not only its own war debt but also that of the several states. Here again Hamilton organized his argument around considerations of both expediency and morality, contending that "an assumption of the debts of the particular states by the union, and a like provision for them as for those of the union, will be a measure of sound policy and substantial justice."[51]

Hamilton began by considering the expediency of assumption. It would, he contended, contribute "in an eminent degree" to an "orderly, stable and satisfactory arrangement of the national finances." In the first, place, it would cost no more for this debt to be paid by the federal government than by the states individually. In either case the same amount of debt had to be serviced. The question then became whether a proper provision for the whole debt might be made more "conveniently" and "effectually" by "one general plan issuing from one authority" instead of "different plans originating in different authorities." Not surprisingly, Hamilton believed that the former was the more efficient mode. The latter carried with it the danger of "competition" between the federal and state governments for the "resources" necessary to provide for their separate debts. This in turn created the risk of "interfering regulations" between the two levels of government, and hence of "collision and confusion." The end result, Hamilton feared, would be a situation in which either the states or the federal government, or both, would be impeded in raising a sufficient revenue through their efforts to avoid such collisions, or, alternatively, certain "branches of industry" would be overburdened by a combination of state

---

[50] Hamilton, *Writings*, 541–42.
[51] Hamilton, *Writings*, 542.

and national taxation.[52] In contrast, a plan administered solely by the federal government would avoid these inconveniences.[53]

In the second place, multiple plans would cause damaging conflict not only between the state and federal *governments* but also between the state and federal *creditors*. "If all the public creditors" were to "receive their dues from one source, distributed with an equal hand, their interest" would "be the same." Accordingly, they would "unite in the support of the fiscal arrangements of the government."[54] Separate provisions, however, would create "distinct interests," inducing each set of creditors to undermine the provisions for the repayment of the other. A "union and concert of views" among the public creditors was thus "of great importance" to their own "security" and to that of the "public credit." Hamilton had already contended that an enlightened concern for the public good over the long term should lead wise governments to maintain good credit. Here, however, he conceded implicitly that such considerations might not always be a sufficient inducement. Another vital support for public credit is the political influence of the creditors themselves, who will, out of their own immediate self-interest, press the government faithfully to observe its engagements. And a prudent statesman will therefore seek whatever arrangement fosters the unity of interests on which this influence rests, which exerts a salutary restraint upon the government.

Such considerations were particularly important to the federal creditors, Hamilton continued. In the absence of a national assumption of the state debts, it was likely that the federal creditors would find themselves in a better position than the state creditors, for the federal government would be better able to raise an adequate revenue. Yet if "the state creditors" were to be left thus to "stand upon a less eligible footing than the others," it would be "unnatural to expect they would see with pleasure a provision for them." And the "influence" of their "dissatisfaction" would "operate injuriously" both on the "creditors, and the credit, of the United States." Therefore, Hamilton concluded, it was even in the interests of the federal creditors that the state creditors "should be comprehended in a general provision."[55]

Hamilton's arguments on this score provide further insight into his understanding of the role of self-interest in politics. In the first place, and most obviously, Hamilton's argument assumes that the political activity of men will be guided in predictable ways by their economic self-interest: those creditors

---

[52] Hamilton, *Writings*, 542–43.

[53] Max M. Edling and Mark D. Kaplanoff contend that an additional benefit of Hamilton's plan of assumption was that it permitted a considerable reduction in state taxes while introducing a federal system of taxation that was not particularly onerous. Complaints that Hamilton's fiscal policies were intended to benefit the wealthy few, they observe, tend to overlook this widely enjoyed benefit of his system. "Hamilton's Fiscal Reform: Transforming the Structure of Taxation in the Early Republic," *William and Mary Quarterly* 61 (2004): 713–44.

[54] Hamilton, *Writings*, 544.

[55] Hamilton, *Writings*, 544–45.

whose contractual rights are vindicated by a public policy will be political supporters of that policy. These passages also point, however, to the subtle ways in which men's economic self-interest interacts with their self-love and their sense of justice, their sense of what *they* are due as opposed to what others are due. Not only will those who gain from a policy support it; those who do not gain but who suppose that they should have will work to undermine it, even if their efforts lead to no direct gain for themselves. It is, Hamilton warns, "unnatural" for state creditors to take "pleasure" in a plan to provide for the federal creditors alone. One might expect that upright and enlightened citizens would take *some* pleasure in seeing justice at least partially vindicated and the public good partially protected. But the human mind apparently does not work that way, or at least not often enough that the statesman could rely on such reactions. Rather, those who are excluded from a benefit to which they think they are entitled will, out of a kind of dissatisfaction related to their sense of justice, labor against the policy that provides that benefit to others.

But could the state creditors have reasonably believed that they had a just claim on the support of the Union, as opposed to that of the particular states with which they had actually contracted to lend their money? Hamilton thought so, and his reflections on this question bring us to his second argument in favor of assumption, an argument that emphasized not the utility but the morality of such an arrangement. Assumption, Hamilton held, would be a measure not only of "sound policy" but also of "substantial justice."[56] Here the secretary of the treasury chose his words with care. One might assume at first glance that this appeal to *substantial* justice is a mere rhetorical flourish, as if he were only contending that assumption would secure justice in relation to large and important public questions. In fact, however, he used the word *substantial* with a precision that is important to the integrity of his argument.

Only a few pages earlier in the *Report*, Hamilton argued strenuously against discrimination, basing his argument primarily on the importance of respecting the *formal* justice of honoring contracts. Now, in relation to the question of assumption, he treated such considerations as dispensable: states that had contracted to borrow and repay certain monies would by Hamilton's plan be released from their obligations, which would then be taken over by another party, the federal government. What, we may wonder, has become of the solemn obligations of contract? Has not Hamilton here strayed from the principles informing his earlier argument against discrimination? The secretary of the treasury, however, was careful not to fall into such inconsistency. As we noted before, Hamilton, even while arguing against discrimination, implicitly conceded that observance of contracts is not the whole of justice, that there are extra-contractual circumstances that can justify the modification of contractual obligations. Here, when he came to his argument for assumption of state debts, he employed that principle which he had earlier acknowledged,

---

[56] Hamilton, *Writings*, 542.

hence his claim that, while assumption would surely involve some departure from formal justice, it would nevertheless be a "measure" of "substantial" – or substantive – justice.

What, then, were the substantial considerations that justified treating state and federal creditors alike, providing for them from a common source, even though they had contracted with different governments? According to Hamilton, while discrimination involved complexities that made an equitable settlement impossible, here the path of equity was more clearly marked out. It would not be "just" to favor "one class of the public creditors" over the "other," it would instead be "most equitable" that they should both receive the "same measure of retribution," because all of the debts, state and federal, were "in the main" contracted for the same purpose: to secure American liberty in the War of Independence. National assumption of the state debts would involve an equitable proportionality, Hamilton suggested, because "a great part of the particular debts of the States" had "arisen from *assumptions by them* on account of the union."[57] That is, many of the expenses incurred by the states during the Revolution were directed toward winning the war, which was a matter of vital importance to the whole nation and not only to some parts of it.

Hamilton expanded on this argument later in the *Report* while discussing the principles by which the debts between the states and the Union should be settled. There he remarked that "it appears difficult to conceive a good reason why the expenses for the particular defense of a part in a common war should not be a common charge, as well as those incurred professedly for the general defense." After all, the "defense of each part is that of the whole," and unless all these expenditures were considered as part of the same effort, the inequitable result would be to add "an increase of burdens" to the calamities already suffered by those states that were "most exposed to the ravages of war."[58] In pursuing a scheme of assumption, therefore, the government of the Union would not be shouldering the burden of paying debts that had been contracted for the mere private interests of certain states but instead for the good of the whole. Viewed in this light, one could view assumption as being consistent with the spirit of the *Declaration of Independence*, in which the "united" states pledged their "lives, fortunes, and sacred honor" to each other in pursuit of the common goal of independence from Great Britain.

Hamilton's Defense of the Obligation to Pay the Interest on the Debt
Hamilton then came to the third and final "preliminary" consideration, the question of whether the country could make a legitimate distinction between the claims of the principal and the interest on its debt. It was "well known," he pointed out," that the "arrears" of interest bore "a large proportion" to the amount of the principal, and that "immediate payment of these arrears" was

57 Hamilton, *Writings*, 545.
58 Hamilton, *Writings*, 547.

"evidently impracticable" for the public. From these circumstances had arisen the suggestion that it might be permissible for the government to release itself, at least partially, from its obligation to pay the interest, while still respecting its obligation to pay the principal.[59]

In light of the *Report*'s earlier dismissal of discrimination between different kinds of holders of public debt, it is not surprising that Hamilton announced here that the desire to discriminate between principal and interest was "not . . . well founded."[60] Indeed, his reasoning in both cases was informed by the same principle: the need to honor contracts. The government's creditors possessed contracts entitling them to be paid interest, and that interest must be paid. The arrears, Hamilton contended, "are now due, and those to whom they are due have a right to claim immediate payment." It might be impracticable to pay them, he added, but this fact did "not vary the nature of the right" at issue.[61]

The strength of Hamilton's claim here is striking and, it might seem, inconsistent with his larger argument. After all, as we observed at the outset of this chapter, Hamilton contended that solving the problem of America's public debt would require the exercise of prudence, the practical virtue by which statesmen determine how to achieve the maximum good that the circumstances permit. Prudence, thus understood, inevitably sanctions departures from what is perfectly just or good. Where, then, is there room for prudence if debts must be paid regardless of practicability, even when the debts are those of the public – that is, when payment hinders other aspects of the common good for which the government is responsible and which prudence itself is supposed to secure?

Hamilton's account, however, does in the end leave some room for the operation of prudence. While impracticability of payment cannot alter a man's right to the payment of interest that he is due by a legitimate contract, it may, Hamilton immediately added, properly alter the way in which that right would be satisfied: "Nor can this idea of impracticability be honorably carried further, than to justify the proposition of a new contract upon the basis of a commutation of that right for an equivalent." Moreover, Hamilton insisted, the equivalent offered must be "a real and fair one." And, he asked, "what other fair equivalent can be imagined for the detention of money, but a reasonable interest? Or what can be the standard of that interest, but the market rate, or the rate which the government pays in ordinary cases?"[62] Again, then, Hamilton was not doctrinaire in his insistence on the observance of contracts. They could be modified in light of pre-contractual moral principles governing the relationships of individuals, as he suggested in his discussion of discrimination, or in light of the common good, as he suggests here: the impracticability

---

[59] Hamilton, *Writings*, 547.
[60] Hamilton, *Writings*, 547–48.
[61] Hamilton, *Writings*, 548–49.
[62] Hamilton, *Writings*, 549.

of demanding immediate payment from the public must be acknowledged. Moreover, we should observe that impracticability is not the same thing as absolute impossibility. Hamilton was thus suggesting that contracts with the public could be modified not only when, say, the public simply had no revenue with which to pay, but even when payment was possible but would impede the government in fulfilling its other obligations.

While Hamiltonian prudence affords government a certain flexibility, it does not leave it free to impose whatever solution seems most consistent with the public's financial needs. Rather, there are moral limits to the means that the government may employ even in pursuit of the national interest. Prudential considerations do not, for example, authorize the public simply to absolve itself of its obligations. Hamilton thus insisted that public financial difficulties must be handled "honorably," and that honor should restrain the government from exploiting the situation to escape from its debts. Moreover, even when prudence demands a modification of terms, the modifications must be governed by respect for both formal and substantive justice. Out of respect for the formal justice of observing contracts, the impracticability of payment can justify the government only in "the proposition of a new contract." Evidently, the government cannot force a change on the creditors but only offer them some new arrangement that, it is hoped, will win their free consent. And, out of respect for substantive justice or equity, the government must offer a "fair equivalent" in return for the contractual rights that the creditors are asked to surrender. These principles were important to Hamilton's approach to the central issue, to which we now turn.

Hamilton's Plan to Service the Debt

Prudence and Public Faith

After presenting the total amount of the nation's debts and the prevailing rates of interest, Hamilton came at last to the "interesting problem" that the nation confronted: "Is it in the power of the United States, consistently with those prudential considerations which ought not to be overlooked, to make a provision equal to the whole debt at the rate of interest which it now bears, in addition to the sum which will be necessary for the current service of the government?"[63] According to Hamilton, the practical (or prudential), if not the literal, answer to this question was "no": the country did not have the power to pay the debt according to the terms of the contracts by which it was incurred and, at the same time, to provide for the ongoing operations of the government. This was the practical answer because Hamilton in fact contended that prudence counseled a modification of the terms of the debt. It was not the literal answer to the question, however, because Hamilton, in all due candor, would "not say" that a provision in strict compliance with contract "would exceed the abilities

[63] Hamilton, Writings, 550–51.

of the country." The nation, it seemed, could pay its debts and support the government, but doing so would have demanded the "extension of taxation to a degree and to objects" that would have been contrary to the community's interests. Thus, for Hamilton, a government may rightly seek a modification of its debt contracts not only because compliance is impossible but even because it is impracticable, or perhaps even inconvenient, for the public. Governments must pay their debts, but they must try to do so in a way that is not harmful to the common good. Every "discerning mind," Hamilton noted, will see that only a plan that is "satisfactory to the community" will be "entitled to confidence."[64]

Furthermore, Hamilton suggested, the prudent statesman must consider not only the present needs of government but also its possible future needs. He must weigh not only what the common good requires now but also what it might require in the future, when new circumstances may call for additional resources to be applied to presently unforeseen objects. "It will not be forgotten," he noted, "that exigencies may, ere long, arise, which would call for resources greatly beyond what is now deemed sufficient for the current service."[65] On this view, it would have been an act of imprudent moralism to demand that the government simply commit what was presently available and convenient to the payment of its debts, since it was obligated, if it was to govern responsibly, to protect its ability to navigate the dangers of an unknown future.

Moreover, Hamilton contended, prudence counseled a modification of the terms of the debt not only for the sake of the common good but also to protect the interests of the creditors themselves. While not strictly impossible, a perfect provision for them would have required "an extension of taxation to a degree and to objects" inconsistent with the "true interests of the public creditors."[66] Hamilton did not here explain why the creditors' own interests forbade such an extension of taxation. Nevertheless, we can offer two reasonable speculations on the meaning behind this remark. In the first place, these public creditors were Americans. Again, early in the *Report*, Hamilton had conceded that foreign creditors must be paid strictly according to the terms of their contracts. But the creditors at issue here were themselves members of the community that would be harmed by excessive taxation. If such taxation, say, hampered the progress of prosperity by burdening the young economy, the creditors would be harmed along with everyone else. If it undermined the government's ability to protect the nation from future threats to its security, the creditors would be endangered with everyone else. As we have seen, much of Hamilton's argument in the *Report on Public Credit* presupposes a certain individualism, or concern with individual self-interest, as an important force in the lives of the people whose affairs the statesman must manage. This understanding of human

---

[64] Hamilton, *Writings*, 551.
[65] Hamilton, *Writings*, 551.
[66] Hamilton, *Writings*, 551.

nature is qualified, however, in other passages in which Hamilton recognizes important moral obligations that even self-interested individuals cannot avoid. The present line of thinking about the "true interests" of the public creditors adds a further qualification to the importance of individual self-interest. The self-interested individual must of necessity live in a community with others, and he cannot fully disentangle his own well being from that of the whole. Public creditors – who will tend to be among the most prosperous members of a community, and thus those with the greatest interest in its stability and security – cannot simply gain by successfully winning their contractual rights if doing so damages the society in which they must live.

There was also a second reason that the interests of the creditors themselves would be harmed by their insisting on a strict compliance with contract. Hamilton was more explicit about this second reason, which was also rooted more directly in the self-interested nature of human beings. Speaking of the aforementioned possibility that future exigencies might arise requiring additional government revenues, Hamilton warned the public creditors that "should the faculties of the country be exhausted or even *strained* to provide for the public debt, there could be less reliance on the sacredness of the provision."[67] In other words, as a practical matter, the "sacredness" of the obligation to repay the public debts would depend in part on the ease with which they could be repaid. Those to whom the repayment was a direct cost – those who were not themselves public creditors – would concur most readily in repayment if the burden to themselves was not excessive. If the terms of repayment made it impossible to deal with certain exigencies that threatened the nation, the public might decide to violate faith in order to address those exigencies. Moreover, even if the repayment merely made it difficult to address such exigencies by straining the public resources, there would still be some temptation to abrogate the public's older obligations.

This warning to the public creditors further clarifies Hamilton's understanding of the interplay of self-interest and moral principle in politics. On the one hand, as we have seen, for Hamilton, moral obligations were binding irrespective of self-interest. Group self-interest certainly would not justify the public in violating faith and declaring itself absolved of its contractual obligations. To this extent, as we have observed, Hamilton cannot be understood as a Machiavellian or a Hobbesian. On the other hand, however, he was keenly aware not only of self-interest's power over men's actions, but also, as we discover here, of how men *understand* their moral obligations. Men's perception of the sacredness of their obligations can be undermined by making those obligations too burdensome to their interests. This is something that a prudent statesman will seek to avoid.

For Hamilton, then, prudence indicated that the terms of the public debt should be modified. Again, however, Hamilton also acknowledged that there

---

[67] Hamilton, *Writings*, 551.

are moral limits, arising from the contractual rights of the creditors, to what prudence may do even in pursuit of the common good. Accordingly, he insisted that any change in the terms of the public's obligations be done only with the genuine consent of the creditors. He "yield[ed]" to the prudential considerations in favor of modification, yet at the same time refused to "lose sight" of the "fundamental principles of good faith." Those principles, he averred, required that the government make "every practicable exertion" to fulfill its "engagements," that "no change in the rights of its creditors" be "attempted without their voluntary consent," and that "this consent" be "voluntary in fact, as well as in name." Accordingly, every proposed change needed to take the form of "an appeal to their reason and their interest," and not "to their necessities." This in turn required that the creditors be offered "a fair equivalent" for what they are asked to give up, and "unquestionable security for the remainder." "Without this," Hamilton concluded, "an alteration, consistent with the credit and honor of the nation, would be impracticable."[68]

Hamilton's insistence that the terms of the public debt be changed only with the consent of the creditors relates to his earlier arguments and makes his plan consistent with them. As we have seen, Hamilton objected to a plan of discrimination – between original holders of the debt and subsequent purchasers – on the grounds that it would be not only unjust and impracticable but also unconstitutional. Such a scheme would, he contended, violate Article VI's provision that "all debts contracted and engagements entered into" before the ratification of the Constitution "shall be as valid against the United States under it, as under the Confederation." Recalling this argument now, one might accuse Hamilton of inconsistency: after all, his own plan to provide for the public credit turns out to involve a modification of the terms just as would a plan of discrimination. Hamilton maintained his consistency, however, precisely by requiring that any change in the terms of the debt be effected only with the consent of the creditors. An agreement to new terms, freely entered into, would not constitute a violation of contract.

Moreover, Hamilton demanded not only that consent be obtained but that the consent be genuine, that it be won through an appeal to the reason and interests of the creditors, rather than to their necessities. This requirement, too, arose from principles he had first acknowledged in his discussion of discrimination. There he had conceded that the validity of a contract may be questioned if the buyer could be considered an "unfair purchaser," understood as someone who not only took advantage of the seller's necessities but also created them himself precisely in order to take advantage of them. Hamilton apparently recognized, and sought to avoid, the danger that the government itself could be considered something like an "unfair purchaser" if it won the formal consent

---

[68] Hamilton, *Writings*, 551. Hamilton later emphasized this point in his September 1790 *Address to the Public Creditors*: "whether you will accept the terms offered to you is certainly left to your own choice. There is not a syllable in the law that obliges you to do it." *PAH*, 7: 3.

of the creditors to a modification of terms because the public's own failure to pay its debts had made the creditors fear a total loss of their investment. Such circumstances, his argument implies, would render his plan for the public credit suspect according to the principles of equity, hence his insistence that the government ensure that it win the truly voluntary consent of the creditors by offering them a fair equivalent for their sacrifice of contractual rights.

Hamilton concluded this portion of his argument by proposing six alternative modifications of terms that he thought should be offered to the public creditors. The details of these plans need not detain us. It is sufficient to note that, consistent with the principles Hamilton had expressed, each of the plans offered something of value – for example, a certain amount of public lands – in exchange for a reduction in the rate of interest that the government had to pay. Moreover, Hamilton offered a variety of plans precisely in order to maximize the possibility that the government would be able to win the free consent of the creditors. He recognized that different "tempers" among the creditors would take a different view of their interests, and accordingly that the availability of an "option" between "a number of plans" would increase the likelihood that all would find something that they could freely accept as advantageous for themselves. Hamilton concluded his presentation of the plans by insisting again that it would not be "proper to aim at procuring the concurrence of the creditors by operating on their necessities." Thus, to ensure that none would be pressured into surrendering contractual rights, he held that any surplus revenue should be "divided among those creditors, if any, who may not think fit to subscribe to" any of the proposed new contracts.[69]

Conclusion

As the preceding discussion indicates, Hamilton's *Report on Public Credit* was not a mere exercise in competent public finance. In Hamilton's understanding, it was instead an act of founding statesmanship, one that accordingly drew on and brought to light his understanding of fundamental political principles. Moreover, Hamilton's approach to some of those principles set the stage for his later cabinet clashes with Thomas Jefferson.

Hamilton's insistence on a strict observance of public faith was based on his belief that sound public credit was essential to energetic government, particularly to a government's ability to meet the unforeseen but inevitable "exigencies" that it would encounter in the course of its life. This concern with such exigencies, as we will see, also informed Hamilton's preference for a broad understanding of the federal government's constitutional powers. It therefore led Hamilton to put forward interpretations of the Constitution that Jefferson came to believe would destroy that document as a charter of limited government.

[69] Hamilton, *Writings*, 560.

The *Report* also reveals Hamilton's earnestness about public faith under-stood as a strict respect for the obligations of public contracts – an earnestness that equaled Jefferson's own seriousness about observing strict limits on federal power. Hamilton's strictness about the public faith contributed later to his own suspicions that Jefferson was in fact an enemy of the public faith and therefore of the principles necessary to just government. Where Jefferson believed Hamilton was too flexible in his interpretation of the federal government's authority, Hamilton believed that Jefferson was too flexible in his respect for the public's contractual obligations.

Finally, the *Report* displayed a certain Hamiltonian nationalism that would soon come into conflict with what might be termed Jefferson's confederalism. Hamilton tended to view independence as the achievement of America as nation rather than as a league of allied states. This view, which Jefferson did not fully share, informed Hamilton's defense of the policy of assuming state debts. We turn to Jefferson's critique of that policy, and of the principles informing it, in Chapter 3.

3

First Signs of Division

Assumption and the Back Pay Bill

In the fall of 1789, George Washington asked Thomas Jefferson to join his cabinet as secretary of state. Jefferson's first inclination was to resist such an appointment. He wrote back to Washington that he preferred to remain in his present position, minister to France. He anticipated that the post into which Washington was trying to shift him would embrace "the principal mass of domestic administration, together with the foreign," which gave him a certain foreboding about the immensity of the task. He also feared that such an appointment "may end disagreeably for one, who, having no motive to public service but the public satisfaction, would certainly retire the moment that satisfaction should appear to languish." Despite these reservations, however, Jefferson did not rule out accepting the post, if the president really thought the appointment would be for the public good.[1]

Washington continued to press his suit but in a restrained manner that mirrored Jefferson's initial response: just as Jefferson would not flat out refuse, though he preferred not to accept, so Washington would not insist, though he really did want Jefferson for the job. The president reassured Jefferson on the amount of work the office would entail and emphasized that the appointment had in fact already given satisfaction to the public. He appealed to Jefferson's love of his fellow countrymen. "I consider the successful administration of the general government," he wrote, "as an object of almost infinite consequence to the present and future happiness of the citizens of the United States." Washington added that he did not think that anybody else could fill the position of secretary of state better than Jefferson.[2] Sufficiently reassured, it would seem,

---

[1] Thomas Jefferson, *The Papers of Thomas Jefferson*, ed. Julian P. Boyd, Volume 16 (Princeton, NJ: Princeton University Press, 1961), 34–35. In subsequent citations, Jefferson's papers will be abbreviated as *PTJ*, followed by the volume and page number.

[2] *PTJ*, 16: 117–18.

Jefferson accepted the appointment and began making his preparations to join Washington in Philadelphia.

This decision led to momentous conflicts within Washington's administration. The constitutional and political clashes that ensued could not have riven the cabinet, or at least could not have been so intense, without the addition of Jefferson's presence to Hamilton's at the highest levels of the executive branch – although these conflicts probably would have arisen, even without Jefferson in the cabinet, between the administration and its critics in Congress and in the country. The arguments made in Washington's exchange with Jefferson, moreover, already point to the possibility of such conflict between Washington's chief ministers. They suggest, in the first place, that Hamilton and Jefferson were ambitious in different ways, and that this difference might lead them into opposition with each other. Both men were ambitious: both desired to serve the public in order to win public approval. Nevertheless, they seem to have understood this desire for public approval differently.

Hamilton saw the position of secretary of the treasury as an opportunity to do big things of lasting consequence for the nation, things that would in the end win him a longstanding fame with the public his labors had benefitted. Jefferson, however, suggested in his letter to Washington that he saw the office of secretary of state as a chance to win public satisfaction and that he would certainly retire the moment that satisfaction seemed to wane. We might say that Hamilton took a longer view of fame, that he was willing to endure a temporary unpopularity in order to achieve a more permanent celebrity,[3] while Jefferson took a shorter view and was unwilling to serve the people in the face of their present dissatisfaction. If that formulation seems unfavorable to Jefferson, it would be fair to add that his posture bespeaks a greater detachment from political office and a greater willingness to lay it down.

Whatever the merits of their respective positions, however, we can certainly see how they might lead to conflict between the two men. A commonplace view presents Hamilton as the aristocrat or elitist and Jefferson as the democrat or populist. This understanding is reflected in their different views of fame. What Hamilton might view as a justifiable resistance to public opinion for the country's ultimate good, Jefferson might view as an anti-republican effort to force policies on the people that they have a right to reject. And what Jefferson might view as proper deference to a people who have a right to rule themselves – such as resigning at the first signs of their dissatisfaction – Hamilton might view as a dereliction of public duty.

In the second place, the possibility of future conflict is also suggested by Jefferson's view of the office he was about to take up. He anticipated that the post of secretary of state would involve the "principal mass" of both the foreign and the domestic administration of the government. He expected, in other

---

[3] Consider Hamilton's praise for those who have "courage and magnanimity enough to serve" the people "at the peril of their displeasure." Hamilton, Madison, and Jay, *The Federalist*, 483.

words, to be the leading official in the executive branch after the president. This expectation was certainly not realized. Hamilton instead became the driving force in domestic policy and, in addition, wielded considerable influence over the administration's foreign policy. One could well wonder whether a certain bitterness accompanied these defeated expectations and added force to Jefferson's impulse to oppose Hamilton in the coming years. Certainly Hamilton thought so: two years later, at the height of their conflict over domestic policy, he attributed some of Jefferson's opposition to personal rivalry and disappointment.[4]

Nevertheless, it would be unjust to Jefferson to leave it at the suggestion that he fought Hamilton's domestic program simply on the basis of personal resentment. After all, one could well have reservations about the thrust of Hamilton's program without having any personal stake in who was ascendant within the administration, and Jefferson's later opposition was founded on principles that he asserted so consistently that it would be unreasonable to doubt his sincerity. Indeed, the potential for such principled disagreements is already evident in Hamilton's *Report on Public Credit*, both in the presuppositions informing it and in the specific policies to which it would give rise. One of those presuppositions, as we have seen, is found in Hamilton's concern with "exigencies," his sense that there is no telling in advance what kind of crises government may have to confront.[5] Hence his later resistance to Jeffersonian arguments that would impose strict, distinct, legalistic limits on the scope of the government's power, and Jefferson's reciprocal opposition to Hamiltonian theories that seemed to leave the government free to roam about unchecked by any clear principles of restraint.

Jefferson and Assumption

If the presuppositions informing the *Report on Public Credit* set the stage for Hamilton and Jefferson's later clashes, what about the *Report*'s own core policy proposal: assumption of the state debts? Where did Jefferson stand on this question, which was coming before Congress just as he was taking office? Jefferson's position on assumption cannot be summed up as simply as his later positions on, say, the bank or Hamilton's proposals in the *Report on Manufactures*. Jefferson opposed assumption, but not as openly or as ardently as he opposed the later steps in Hamilton's program. He opposed it, but his

---

[4] Although Jefferson perhaps did not wield as much influence as he had expected, his understanding of the scope of the office of secretary of state does not seem to have been a mere projection of his own hopes. According to him, the president presented a similar view of the office in 1792. Discussing the possibility of cabinet retirements, Washington reportedly told Jefferson that the Treasury was a more limited department, since it went "only to the single object of revenue," while "that of the secretary of state embrac[ed] nearly all the objects of administration and was much more important." *PTJ*, 23: 184.

[5] Hamilton, *Writings*, 530–31.

opposition was obscured or mitigated by the following factors. First, he did not express his opposition openly in the cabinet, but only in letters to his friends – and even there he was somewhat guarded, not revealing his thoughts to everyone indiscriminately. Second, his opposition to assumption was not such as to prevent his generally satisfied acquiescence in it, and even his participation in brokering the compromise that would permit it to occur.

Before proceeding to Jefferson's reservations about assumption, however, it is worth pausing to note one point on which Jefferson agreed with Hamilton's *Report*: the absolute inviolability of the foreign debt, as opposed to the domestic debt. Jefferson wrote to William Short, his successor as minister to France, observing that the delays in providing for the foreign debt arose entirely from disagreements about how to provide for the domestic debt, since both were to be handled in a single package of legislation. He noted that the foreign debt was not even taken as a subject for debate because it was "not susceptible of any abridgment or modification."[6] Shortly thereafter, in a similar letter to C. W. F. Dumas, Jefferson went a step further than Hamilton, expressing the reasons for the inviolability that Hamilton had only postulated in the *Report*. With respect to the domestic debt, Jefferson said, "it is thought that Congress, being the representative of both parties, may shape their contracts so as to render them practicable, only seeing that substantial justice be done." The foreign debt, however, was a different matter, one in relation to which Congress could not presume to exercise such a discretion. Here, Jefferson wrote, "Congress is considered as the representative of one party only, and I think I can say with truth that there is not a single individual in the United States, either in or out of office, who supposes they can ever do anything which might impair their foreign contracts."[7]

On the plan of assumption itself, Jefferson tended at first to be ambiguous, perhaps in part because he had not fully made up his mind, and perhaps in part because he did not want to reveal his mind fully to certain correspondents. Although he later laid his objections before his son-in-law, Jefferson at first told Thomas Mann Randolph that assumption appeared to him to be "one of those questions which present great inconveniencies whichever way it is decided," that it "offers only a choice of evils."[8] Similarly, Jefferson told another

---

[6] *PTJ*, 16: 316.

[7] *PTJ*, 16: 551–53. Even here, however, Jefferson's account hints at differences between himself and Hamilton with regard to the domestic debt. Jefferson speaks without evident unease about Congress's right to reform the contracts, so long as substantive justice is done, while Hamilton's arguments in the *Report on Public Credit* treat the contractual obligations with much more deference. Hamilton in fact denied that Congress had any right to shape the contracts without securing the voluntary consent of the creditors. As we will see, this issue would continue to be a point of contention between them: Jefferson surely understood himself to be a friend of the public faith, but it is doubtful that Hamilton would have regarded him as a sufficiently strict friend of the public faith.

[8] *PTJ*, 16: 351.

correspondent that he was "apt to suppose difficulties pretty nearly balanced on both sides" when he saw "honest and able men so equally divided in senti-ment on a question." Accordingly, he concluded that "the decision either way in preference to the other will not be attended with either signal advantage or disadvantage."[9]

As 1790 wore on, however, and as Jefferson discussed the question with men he was perhaps more willing to take into his confidence, it became clear that he found serious fault with Hamilton's plan of assumption. Jefferson's objection was twofold, and it mirrored Hamilton's argument in its favor. Just as the secretary of the treasury thought assumption would be both fair and expedient, the secretary of state found it both unjust and impolitic. Both of these concerns, moreover, illustrate the gap between Jefferson and Hamilton's different ways of thinking about the United States, their different visions of what kind of community it was and how it might best be governed.

For Jefferson, the assumption as Hamilton had proposed it would have worked a serious injustice. The problem, Jefferson observed to James Monroe, was that it would leave "the states who have redeemed much of their debts on no better footing than those who have redeemed none."[10] Assumption would, in effect, provide a boon for delinquent states while offering nothing to the others. Rather, it was worse than that, for the boon in question would be paid for by federal taxation, so that the citizens of states who had paid more of their debts would be paying for the relief of states who had paid little or none. The remedy for this, Jefferson suggested, was a form of proportional assumption. This would involve the federal government in assuming a fixed sum, then allotting "a portion of it to every state in proportion to its census," and accordingly in proportion to its "contributions" in taxes to the plan. On such a scheme each "state" would "on the whole neither gain nor lose."[11] Instead each would be "exonerated towards its creditors just as much as it" would "have to contribute to the assumption, and consequently no injustice done."[12]

Even if assumption could be thus purged of its injustice, however, Jefferson still believed that it was subject to a serious policy objection: that the taxes to pay for it would be levied by the federal government and not the states. This objection primarily concerned the kind of taxation to which the federal government would have to resort, which Jefferson feared would be more bur-densome than the kind on which the states would have relied had they been left to pay their own debts. "I have no doubt," he observed, "that the states should be left to do whatever acts they can do as well as the general government."[13]

[9] *PTJ*, 16: 553–54.
[10] *PTJ*, 16: 537.
[11] *PTJ*, 16: 537, 540.
[12] *PTJ*, 16: 598.
[13] *PTJ*, 17: 270–71.

The states, however, could have taxed as effectively, or rather more effectively, than the federal government for these purposes. Had it been left to them, the states would have raised the money by taxes on "land and other property."[14] Such objects were effectively "cut off from the general government," however, because of "the prejudices existing against direct taxation in their hands."[15] As a result, the assumption would be funded by federal taxation on imports, which would "thus be overburdened."[16]

This early controversy already brings to light Jefferson's tendency to think more confederally, in contrast to Hamilton's tendency to think more nationally. Consider Jefferson's complaint about the injustice of assumption. Both Hamilton and Jefferson saw that the question of how to pay the nation's war debt was a question of justice, not merely a technical or economic issue. Nevertheless, their thinking about the question diverged insofar as each thought about America as a different kind of community. Hamilton saw America more as a single national community: the claims of justice that concerned him in his *Report on Public Credit* were primarily claims among the classes within that community, creditors and debtors. To the extent that he considered the question that concerned Jefferson, the matter of justice among the states, he did not think it reasonable or helpful to go into it. The revolution was a national effort that had benefitted the whole country, so it was reasonable that the whole country should pay for it. And if some states had retired their debts more quickly than others, it was also true that some had borne the ravages of the actual fighting more than others. Better to leave all these questions aside and handle the entire public debt, even the state debts, as a national question.

Their thinking similarly diverges on the policy issue raised by assumption. As a factual matter, Hamilton would simply have disagreed with Jefferson that the *Report*'s scheme of taxes on imports was excessively burdensome. Hamilton would also have disagreed with Jefferson's basic principle that "the states should be left to do whatever acts they can do as well as the general government." Jefferson's dictum treats the question of federal versus state responsibilities solely as one of efficiency, but Hamilton was concerned as well with political considerations: he thought the federal government should do important things so as to win the people's affections, and in particular he was aware that federal assumption of the state debts would have the salutary (to him) political effect of making the nation's creditor class more interested in the success of the new federal government.

If Jefferson's thinking was less national than Hamilton's, however, he was still a friend to the union. In fact, it was precisely for the sake of union that Jefferson was willing to accept assumption, despite his objections to it. The

[14] *PTJ*, 17: 269–70.
[15] *PTJ*, 17: 270–71.
[16] *PTJ*, 17: 269–70. On these concerns, see also Jefferson's letters to George Gilmer (*PTJ*, 17: 574–75) and Francis Eppes (*PTJ*, 16: 598).

argument over Hamilton's proposal troubled Jefferson precisely because it seemed to weaken the bonds of union among the states, or at least reveal the weakness of them. Jefferson wrote to Edward Rutledge that assumption and the question of the residency of the new seat of government had "agitated the minds of Congress more than the friends of union on catholic principles would have wished," expressing his own hope that these matters could be resolved and that then "nothing else may be able to call up local principles."[17] Over the course of the controversy Jefferson became convinced that intransigent adherence to such "local principles" on the matter of the debt might result in the "dissolution of the government" even as it was being born.[18] If assumption was not accepted, he feared, it would prove impossible to secure the votes for *any* plan to fund the nation's debt. Such a failure would lead first to a collapse of the nation's credit in Europe and then to the collapse of the government itself. As Jefferson wrote to James Monroe, if the different views in Congress could not be "reconciled by some plan of compromise, there will be no funding bill agreed to, our credit (raised by late prospects to be first on the exchange at Amsterdam, where our paper is above par) will burst and vanish, and then the states separate to take care everyone of himself."[19] Alternatively, without compromise the fear of these grave consequences might lead Congress to enact an "unqualified assumption" – that is, one without the proportionality Jefferson thought necessary to rid assumption of its injustice.[20] In view of these dangers to the "peace and continuance of the union," Jefferson concluded that "a mutual sacrifice of opinion is the duty of every one," and said that for his part he would see the assumption "pass with acquiescence.[21]

Indeed, Jefferson was not merely willing to see assumption pass Congress; he even played a key part in arranging the compromise by which it could be enacted. According to Jefferson's own account – probably written two years after the events – he was on his way to visit the president when he encountered Hamilton at the door, looking "somber, haggard, and dejected beyond description" and "even his dress uncouth and neglected." Hamilton brought up the question of assumption, indicated its importance in the "general fiscal arrangement," and further raised the possibility that its failure would lead to a collapse of the government. The New England states, he observed, "had made great expenditures during the war, on expeditions which though of their own undertaking were for the common cause," and accordingly they considered assumption of their debts "by the Union so just, and its denial so palpably injurious, that they would make it the sine qua non of a continuance of the Union." The treasury secretary added that for his own part, if he lacked the "credit" to "carry such a measure, he could be of no use and was determined to

---

[17] *PTJ*, 16: 600.
[18] *PTJ*, 16: 574–75.
[19] *PTJ*, 16: 537.
[20] *PTJ*, 16: 537. See also Jefferson's letter to Thomas Mann Randolph (*PTJ*, 16: 540).
[21] *PTJ*, 16: 537 and 17: 270–71.

resign." Having broached these grave possibilities, Hamilton sought Jefferson's help, asking whether he could "interest" his "friends from the south, who were those most opposed" to assumption. Jefferson made no commitment but indicated that he would weigh in his mind what Hamilton had "urged." As we have seen, Jefferson was just as concerned as Hamilton about the prospect of disunion, and he was therefore inclined to help. The famous expedient he devised was to invite Hamilton and James Madison to dinner to discuss the subject, as a "first step toward some conciliation of views." This meeting laid the groundwork for the legislative compromise that tied assumption to the residency of the capital. Madison relented in his opposition to assumption to the extent that he would not oppose its being brought before the House again, and though he would not vote for it himself would not be "strenuous" in his opposition. At this point, as Jefferson related the meeting, either Hamilton or Madison noted that as the "pill" of assumption would be a "bitter one to the Southern states, something should be done to soothe them." The "removal of the seat of government to the Potomac was a just measure," they agreed, "and would probably be a popular one" in the South. Accordingly, this step would be "proper to follow the assumption." On this basis, it seems, Madison was able to deliver the Virginia votes necessary to pass assumption, and Hamilton was able to deliver the Pennsylvania votes necessary to establish the new capital on the Potomac.[22]

Although the conciliation arranged by these three great figures presents an edifying spectacle, we should not lose sight of the fact that the controversy over Hamilton's first policy proposals also brought to light deep political divisions that would show themselves more clearly later in the decade. Public criticism was sufficiently troubling to Hamilton that he took to the public prints anonymously in defense of his policies – an expedient to which he would return with vigor two years later, as his breach with Jefferson became open and irreparable. Writing as "A Friend," Hamilton published his *Address to the Public Creditors* in September of 1790. He noted that there were "too many publications" that tended to "destroy" the creditors' "confidence in future" by claiming that Congress had, by enacting Hamilton's plan for the public debt, "violated" its "earlier engagements" and that therefore the holders of the debt could "place no greater reliance upon" these new provisions than on the earlier agreements they were intended to supersede. Hamilton assured his audience that this was not the case: the new arrangements were *offered* to the creditors, but no one was *compelled* to participate in them. As we have seen in the *Report on Public Credit*,

---

[22] *PTJ*, 17: 205–07. In view of the preceding discussion, it seems that Bernard Bailyn, perhaps taking Jefferson's later recollections of these events too much at face value, exaggerates when he says that the "evils of Hamilton's program and the devastating threat it posed to the nation's freedom were clear to Jefferson from the moment he returned from France." "Jefferson and the Ambiguities of Freedom," *Proceedings of the American Philosophical Society* 137 (1993): 508. Although he clearly opposed the assumption, Jefferson's contemporaneous commentary on it does not suggest that he had at that point come to the conclusion that Hamiltonianism represented the grave threat that he later came to discern.

such a procedure was essential to Hamilton, since the government had no right unilaterally to escape its obligations. In the course of thus correcting the record, Hamilton also paused to raise the question of whether such misrepresentations came from "a sincere opinion in persons who have not accurately considered the matter, or from those who wish to depreciate the government, or from those who wish to buy securities cheap, or from all these descriptions of persons."[23] Hamilton's suggestion that opposition to his plan might stem from no more than a desire to weaken the government foreshadows his more forceful polemics of 1792, in which this charge was not merely raised but positively asserted by him.

The controversy also called forth from the Assembly of Virginia two resolutions that anticipated later arguments that divided Hamilton and Jefferson, as well as Federalists and Republicans. The first of these resolutions held that the assumption of state debts was "repugnant to the Constitution of the United States, as it goes to the exercise of a power not expressly granted to the general government." The second complained that Hamilton's plan limited the rate at which the debt could be redeemed, holding that this was "dangerous" to the "rights" and "subversive" of the "interest of the people."[24] The second complaint was taken up later by Jefferson, who suspected Hamilton of wanting to create a permanent debt, the financing of which would provide a permanent method by which to corrupt the legislature. The first resolution advocated a narrow interpretation of federal power such as Jefferson would use in his denial of the constitutionality of the bank, an interpretation, moreover, that Hamilton viewed as incompatible with effective government. Even more ominously, by presuming to pronounce on the constitutionality of a federal law, the resolution presaged Jefferson's Kentucky resolutions condemning the Alien and Sedition Acts as unconstitutional. Discerning these (to him) troubling possibilities, Hamilton wrote to John Jay that the 1790 resolutions were "the first symptom of a spirit which must either be killed or will kill the Constitution of the United States." Characteristically, Hamilton's first instinct was for action: he suggested tentatively to Jay that "the collective weight of the different parts of the government" should be "employed in exploding the principles" contained in the resolutions. Perhaps equally characteristically, Jay's first instinct was for restraint: he wrote back to Hamilton that it was best to ignore the resolutions.[25]

First Clash: The Back Pay Resolutions

1790 brought forward another controversy involving Hamilton and Jefferson. Although it involved a much smaller issue than assumption, this episode is worthy of attention for two reasons. It for the first time placed Hamilton and

[23] *PAH*, 7: 1–3.
[24] *PTJ*, 18: 130–31.
[25] *PAH*, 7: 149–50 and 166–67.

Jefferson in direct opposition to each other: each wrote to Washington arguing for the opposite course of action. Moreover, although the issue itself was of limited scope, the arguments it generated shed light on Hamilton and Jefferson's thinking about principles of great public importance.

The dispute arose from Congress's efforts to protect soldiers and officers of the Virginia and North Carolina lines from abuse by speculators who were buying from them the right to the back pay owed them by the government.[26] These veterans might have despaired of ever being paid by a government so far in arrears, might have been ignorant that the effective government now established by the Constitution was going to make good its obligations, might have been pressed by some present necessity for money, and might have been ignorant of the exact amounts they were owed. Any of these factors could lead them to sell for a comparative pittance the right to the pay to which they were entitled. Speculators were apparently acting on this opportunity, so Congress moved to protect the soldiers from those who sought a windfall at their expense.

Hamilton, however, objected to the way in which Congress had tried to forestall this problem, and his concerns led him to write to Washington on May 28 urging a veto. He admitted a certain reluctance to speak out on the matter, observing that the task was made "unwelcome" by his "respect for the decisions of the two houses of Congress," for "the movements of humanity" toward the soldiers who might have been victimized, and for the "indignation against those who are presumed to have taken an undue advantage." Nevertheless, Hamilton found the principles "invaded" by Congress's action to be "of such fundamental consequence to the stability, character, and success of the government," as well as so directly of interest to the Treasury Department, that he felt "irresistibly impelled by a sense of duty" to both the president and the country to make his views known.[27]

Congress had enacted three resolutions, the first two of which Hamilton found unobjectionable. These merely directed the president to communicate to the soldiers how much they were owed and to bring about a quick payment. The problem lay with the third resolution, which required that where payment had not been made to the original claimant or his representative, it could only be made to such claimant or to "such person or persons" who could produce a power of attorney, attested to by two justices of the peace of the county in which such person or persons resided, "authorizing him or them to receive a certain specified sum."[28]

For Hamilton, such a resolution, however well intentioned it might have been, amounted to government interference with already established contracts. The law in most of the states, he contended, made claims such as those of

---

[26] For an extensive discussion of the background to the resolutions, see the editorial note provided by the editors of Jefferson's papers. *PTJ*, 16: 455–62.

[27] *PAH*, 6: 438.

[28] *PAH*, 6: 433.

the soldiers at issue here "assignable for valuable consideration."[29] In other words, under then-existing law, a soldier's right to his back pay could be sold to another person. Such an assignment or sale would amount to a contract, "express or implied, on the part of the assignor that the assignee shall receive the sum assigned to his use." These transactions, Hamilton continued, required no document of "precise form" but could be effected by any "instrument competent to conveying with clearness and precision the sense of the parties." Such was the law in most of the states, and, Hamilton added, the federal government had already been acting according to it "in the adjustment and satisfaction of claims upon the United States."[30] The resolution in question, therefore, had the effect of tampering with individual property rights that had already been acquired under existing law. It had a "retrospective operation" and laid down "with regard to past transactions, new and unknown requisites, by which the admission of claims" was "to be guided." A man might have paid money for something valuable – in this case, the right to another man's back pay – on the understanding that his right to the thing purchased was secured by the instrument ordinarily required by the law. Now, Hamilton complained, Congress had intervened and told the purchaser that his claim to the thing for which he had already paid could only be made good by some other kind of instrument, a power of attorney, that was not required at the time of the original purchase or contract. The resolution impaired, and might end up voiding, an existing contract and endangered, and might end up extinguishing, an already existing right. It suddenly made the validity of a contract contingent on legal considerations that were not in place when the contract was formed. Accordingly, Hamilton condemned it as a "contravention of the public faith, pledged by the course of public proceedings" with tendency hostile to both "public credit" and "the security of property."[31]

One might doubt whether the resolution would really go so far in infringing on the rights of the assignees. Hamilton, however, insisted on the dangers. The "assignee," he observed, would have "no method of compelling the assignor to perfect the transfer by a new instrument in conformity with the rule prescribed." Having already paid money for something he thought he had lawfully purchased, he was now to be told he must have a power of attorney to take possession of it, but without any ability to make the seller give him the power of attorney. Indeed, it was not even clear whether he could sue in order to recover his money. And even if he could, such redress was not the same thing as, nor as valuable as, the right he had already acquired. Congress had acted on the assumption that the purchasers were abusing the weakness of the soldier-sellers, but, Hamilton reminded Washington, this would not necessarily be the case. The right to the back pay might have been transferred as "security for

[29] *PAH*, 6: 434.
[30] *PAH*, 6: 434.
[31] *PAH*, 6: 434.

a precarious or desperate debt" or as an effort at a "composition between an insolvent debtor and his creditor." Congress was seeking to prevent soldiers from being victimized by speculators, but its resolution could equally victimize fair purchasers who now could not enjoy their rights without the "perplexity, trouble and expense of a suit at law." "To vary the risks of parties," Hamilton concluded, "to supersede the contracts between them," to "turn over a creditor, without his consent, from one debtor to another," to "take away a right to a specific thing, leaving only the chance of a remedy for retribution are not less positive violations of property than a direct confiscation."[32]

Hamilton also raised a kind of separation of powers objection to the resolution. Congress had apparently acted in order to prevent fraud. Members feared that speculators with knowledge that the back pay was soon to be delivered would buy – at a substantial discount – the right to it from soldiers who had no such knowledge. Hamilton agreed that fraud, when "properly ascertained," invalidated a contract. "The power of ascertaining it," however, "is the peculiar province" not of the Congress but of "the judiciary department." The allocation of this power to the courts, moreover, is not merely a requirement of the Constitution but is founded on the "principles of good government" and "justice." For it is only in the courts that "an investigation of the fact can be had as ought to precede a decision." Only there can "the parties be heard and evidence on both sides produced." And without such judicial procedures "*surmise* must be substituted to *proof*, and *conjecture* to *fact*." Legislative "interference" such as Congress was attempting in this case should be avoided, Hamilton suggested, because it creates an insoluble "dilemma." In order to avoid the danger of tampering with good contracts as well as fraudulent ones, or of letting conjecture replace fact, Congress would have to "erect itself into a court of justice and determine each case on its own merits, after a full hearing of the allegations and proofs of the parties." Yet this would be "usurpation of the judicial authority." To avoid this danger, it would have to – as it had done in this case – try to prevent the fraud by a general act of legislation, which is in effect to proceed "at best upon partial and problematical testimony to condemn in the gross and in the dark" both fair claims and fraudulent ones. Yet this would be "at variance with the rules of property, the dictates of equity, and the maxims of good government."[33]

Although Hamilton's primary aim in this letter was to enforce a limit on congressional authority, his argument also acknowledged that this limit might be transcended in the right set of circumstances. This possibility comes into view in Hamilton's response to the objection that extraordinary cases sometimes call for the extraordinary action of the legislature. This response sheds further light on Hamilton's understanding of both the limits on the legislative power and the

---

[32] *PAH*, 6: 434.
[33] *PAH*, 6: 435–36 (Hamilton's emphases).

limits of those limits, so to speak. Although Hamilton was generally a proponent of a broad legislative power, he nevertheless acknowledged that that power
was constrained not only by the positive law of the Constitution but also by the
principles of justice. Accordingly, in his letter on the resolution he emphasized
to Washington that such intervention as Congress was here attempting was an
"overleaping of the ordinary and regular bounds of legislative discretion" insofar as it departed "from the usual course of law and justice" and infringed "the
established rules of property, which ought as far as possible to be held sacred
and inviolable." Nevertheless, to hold that the established rules of property
ought to be sacred and inviolable *as far as possible* is as much as to admit that
in some cases this might not be possible and that necessity might require some
modification of those rules. Accordingly, Hamilton admitted the "doctrine"
that "there are certain extraordinary cases in which the public good demands
and justifies an extraordinary interposition of the legislature." Nevertheless,
he also tried to confine the operation of such exceptions, insisting that those
who would use them to justify Congress's back-pay resolution were being altogether too free with the doctrine. It is "highly important," he noted, that the
"nature" of the truly extraordinary cases "should be carefully distinguished."
When Congress varies the ordinary rules of property, and therefore intrudes on
the rights of property, the action "is in the nature of a resort to first principles."
But nothing other than "some urgent public necessity, some impending national
calamity, something that threatens direct and general mischief to the society,
for which there is no adequate redress in the established course of things can"
justify "the employment of so extraordinary a remedy." Hamilton could see
no such calamity threatened in the present instance. The men Congress was
trying to protect were "highly meritorious indeed, but inconsiderable in point
of numbers." The property in question amounted to "less than fifty thousand
dollars," which when distributed among those concerned came to less than
"twenty-five dollars per man." Thus Hamilton concluded that the "relief of
the individuals who may have been subjects of imposition in so limited a case"
could not justify a "measure which breaks in upon those great principles that
constitute the foundations of property." This conclusion is certainly consistent
with Hamilton's earlier reasoning in the *Report on Public Credit*. He did not
believe that the government's inability to pay its debts justified its tampering
unilaterally with contracts, so he would hardly think such tampering could be
justified by the possibility that some soldiers might be defrauded of their back
pay.[34]

Hamilton reinforced his argument by contending that the resolution would
not just be an infraction of bloodless principles but that it would also tend
materially to weaken and undermine the new government. "If partial inconveniencies and hardships occasion legislative interferences in private contracts,

[34] *PAH*, 6: 436–37.

the intercourses of business become uncertain, the security of property is lessened," and finally "the confidence in government" is "destroyed or weakened," Hamilton warned.[35] He seems to have had in mind particularly the confidence, essential to any stable government, of the best and most influential elements in the society. Hamilton made this point in relation to the Contracts Clause of the Constitution, which, though limited in scope, embodied for him a key principle of government that ought ordinarily to be obeyed even where the words of the Constitution do not require it.

The Constitution, Hamilton observed, "interdicts" only the states from enacting any laws "impairing the obligations of contracts. This provision, he added, was thought "not one of the least recommendations of the Constitution" among "the more enlightened part of the community." The states' "too frequent intermeddlings" in private contracts "were extensively felt and seriously lamented" by such citizens. Thus it was reasonable to fear that a similar intermeddling by the federal legislature would "be pernicious" because it would stir up the same dissatisfaction that had just been quieted by the ratification of the Constitution. The effect would be both direct and indirect. Such legislation in itself would immediately "alarm the same class of persons," but it would also tend to undermine the state governments' respect for the Contracts Clause. "The *example* of the national government," Hamilton suggested, would here "have a far more powerful influence than the *precepts* of its constitution."[36] Hamilton surely expected that the federal courts would enforce the Contracts Clause, but at this early date there was no telling how effectively they would do so, how strictly they would interpret it, or how cleverly the states might find ways to observe its terms but evade its substance. And such developments, encouraged by the general government's tampering with contracts in such an insubstantial case, would tend to inflame once more the very problems Hamilton and Madison had warned about in *Federalists* 9 and 10 – the kind of faction that oppresses and makes desperate the propertied classes – and that the Constitution had been intended to prevent.

Such dangers were not to be risked, especially when, as Hamilton noted in concluding his argument, any abuses could already be redressed through existing avenues. The "courts of justice" he pointed out, could provide relief where any "fact of fraud, or imposition, or undue advantage" could "be substantiated." And if some abused soldiers could not seek such relief "from their own resources," then Hamilton allowed that "the aid of the government" might be "afforded" them in a way that would be "consistent with the established order of things."[37] For example, he noted, the attorney general might be charged with defending the claims of original claimants in appropriate cases – an expedient that occurred to him, Hamilton added, after hearing reports that convinced him

[35] *PAH*, 6: 436.
[36] *PAH*, 6: 436.
[37] *PAH*, 6: 437.

that undue advantage probably had been taken in some instances. It is worth noting that here, as in the *Report on Public Credit*, Hamilton treated contracts as important but also as conditioned by other important, extra-contractual considerations. Put another way, there is a kind of justice that arises from contracts, which must be respected, but there is also a kind of justice that precedes contracts and in light of which they might be judged null. Despite arguing against the remedy chosen in this case by Congress, Hamilton acknowledged that "fraud," "imposition," and "undue advantage" are genuine moral and legal categories that can render a contract void.

Hamilton ended his letter with a plea for faithfully observing the ordinary rules in all ordinary cases, despite the problems that might arise and the humane temptation of Congress to intervene to rectify them. He acknowledged that "an inflexible adherence to the principles" for which he had contended "must often have an air of rigor" and that it would "sometimes be productive of particular inconveniencies." Nevertheless, such particular harms should be accepted as an inevitable, if unfortunate, by-product of a strict fidelity to rules, which tended to the public good. "The general rules of property, and all those general rules which form the links of society, frequently involve in their ordinary operation particular hardships and injuries; yet the public order and the general happiness require a steady conformity to them." Whatever relaxations might be justified in a case of genuine national necessity, it is, Hamilton concluded, "perhaps always better that partial evils should be submitted to than that principles should be violated."[38]

Hamilton's letter apparently raised a sufficient doubt about the resolution in Washington's mind that he chose to seek further advice from the secretary of state. There is no evidence of a written request from Washington for either Hamilton's or Jefferson's advice, yet the rhetoric of the documents implies that Hamilton wrote at his own initiative while Jefferson wrote at Washington's request.[39] Hamilton began his letter as follows: "The secretary of the treasury conceives it to be his duty most respectfully to represent" to the president his opinions on the resolution – language Hamilton would hardly have bothered to use had he been responding to his chief's request for an opinion.[40] In contrast, Jefferson's opinion was not addressed directly to the president and opened not with a justification for writing but a simple statement of the facts at issue. Moreover, he took as the point of departure for his argument a summary of the concerns Hamilton had raised in his own letter. Evidently Jefferson had read Hamilton's arguments, and it is hard to see how he could have done so unless the letter was shown to him by Washington with a request for his thoughts on the matter.[41]

---

[38] *PAH*, 6: 438.
[39] *PTJ*, 16: 459.
[40] *PTJ*, 16: 462.
[41] The editors of Jefferson's papers also draw this conclusion. See *PTJ*, 16: 459.

Jefferson began by summing up Hamilton's concerns: the resolution was "not worthy of the president's approbation" because it would "annul transfers of property which were good by the laws under which they were made," would take "from the assignees their lawful property," and was "contrary to the principles of the Constitution, which condemn retrospective laws."[42] This is not an entirely precise rendering of Hamilton's position. Hamilton had indeed, as Jefferson suggested, appealed to the principle embodied in the Contracts Clause, although without going so far as to say that the resolution was unconstitutional. He had not, however, framed the principle as broadly as Jefferson did here, as prohibiting "retrospective laws" in general. Jefferson's imprecision proves useful, however. It broadens the discussion of laws impairing the obligations of contracts to embrace retrospective laws more generally, including laws that might impose retroactive punishments. It therefore provides a window into Jefferson's thinking on the issues presented by such laws.

Jefferson suggested that he and Hamilton were united at the level of principle and differed only as regards the facts of the case. "I agree," he averred, "in an almost unlimited condemnation of retrospective laws." He admitted that such laws may serve to "redress" a "few instances of wrong." Nevertheless he also contended that these instances are "so overweighed by the insecurity they draw over all property, and even over life itself, and by the atrocious violations of both to which they lead, that it is better to live under the evil than the remedy."[43]

Jefferson's position is in fact very similar to Hamilton's, although it does differ in some noteworthy respects. Jefferson asserted an "*almost* unlimited condemnation" of such laws, thus indicating a broad agreement with Hamilton that while they are ordinarily improper and very dangerous, they cannot be categorically condemned.[44] Hence his admission that they could serve to right some wrongs in some few instances. Strikingly, Jefferson took this view not only of laws impairing the obligations of contracts but even of punitive retrospective laws that might deprive a man of his life. Hamilton did not go so far, but perhaps only because the question of punitive retrospective laws was not raised by Congress's resolution. In any case, it is not unlikely that Hamilton would have agreed with Jefferson that even a retrospective punishment could in some cases redress a wrong and thus not be unjust.

The implications of Hamilton and Jefferson's arguments on this question are somewhat startling at first, but they appear more reasonable on closer examination. They are startling because they suggest that retrospective deprivations of property and life are *not* intrinsically unjust, that they might be justifiable in certain, admittedly rare, situations. Hamilton thinks that government might abrogate existing contracts in some grave circumstances, and Jefferson speaks

---

[42] *PTJ*, 16: 468.
[43] *PTJ*, 16: 468.
[44] *PTJ*, 16: 468 (my emphasis).

of retrospective laws as bad not in themselves but because of the dangers they create and the evils to which they lead. Both men, in other words, think about the question prudentially, weighing the costs and benefits, and not in terms of moral absolutes. This position might appear to be in tension with the founding commitment to natural rights. Nevertheless, further reflection suggests that Hamilton's and Jefferson's treatment of the question is defensible. After all, it is not hard to imagine a state of society – say, when law is in an imperfect or incomplete state – in which someone might do an act that is wrong, very damaging to society, and that he ought to have known not to do, even though there was no legal prohibition on doing it. And such circumstances seem to present a situation in which an ex post facto deprivation of rights would redress a wrong, and perhaps even forestall worse consequences, such as public vengeance not governed by law at all. Such possibilities seem remote indeed to people living in a society with a long-established and highly developed code of law, but they are not inconceivable, or even without precedent, and Hamilton and Jefferson were properly careful not to condemn retrospective laws absolutely.[45]

Moving from theory to practice, however, a small but significant disagreement emerges between Hamilton and Jefferson. They agreed that the question of retrospective laws is ultimately a prudential one, yet they drew different prudential conclusions about what should be our proper disposition toward such laws. Moreover, their differing conclusions reflect their differing dispositions toward government power. Jefferson admitted that retrospective laws might in some cases serve the cause of justice, but he nevertheless adopted as his rule a complete opposition to them. He thought government should swear them off absolutely, not because they are always wrong, but because they are always so dangerous as to be not worth the risks they entail. Jefferson would have the government adhere to a clear and consistent rule against ever adopting retrospective laws. In contrast, Hamilton contended that such laws – or at least laws impairing the obligations of contracts – should never be countenanced in the ordinary operations of government, should never be resorted to as a remedy for partial evils. At the same time, he left the door open to the possibility that such laws might be necessary and defensible in the case of a real threat to the society itself. Always mindful that one cannot say with certainty what challenges the society may face in the future, Hamilton opted for a statement of principle that admits of rare exceptions and thus leaves the government with a greater reservoir of power.

In view of their considerable agreement at the level of general principles, why did Jefferson depart from Hamilton's practical advice and tell Washington that

---

[45] The imposition of retrospective punishments might also be appropriate even in a society with a highly developed code of law, if a government is guilty of enormities done under the color of law. One thinks here, for example, of the punishments imposed by the Nuremberg tribunals, which Hamilton and Jefferson might well have thought justifiable in the circumstances, despite being retrospective in their operation.

it would be proper to sign the resolution at issue here? The difference, Jefferson suggested, was not one of principle but of the proper interpretation of the facts. Unlike Hamilton, he denied that the resolution would "annul acts which were valid when they were done." Recall that Hamilton's whole concern about the resolution depended in the first place on his assumption that any previous assignments of the soldiers' debts would be valid under existing state law. This is precisely what Jefferson denied, at least in relation to Virginia, one of the two states relevant to the case. (Jefferson declined to speak about the case of North Carolina, not being familiar with its laws.) According to him, the common law of England, which had been adopted in Virginia, held that the "conveyance of a right to a debt" of which the party was not "in possession" was not only "void" but also punishable. There were certain exceptions to this general rule, when debts were put into the form of a "bill of exchange," a "promissory note," or a "bond." But since the "debts from the U.S. to the soldiers of Virginia" had not been put into any of these forms, "the assignments of them were void in law."[46] Accordingly, and contrary to Hamilton's fears, the resolution of Congress did not alter existing property rights.

A creditor, Jefferson conceded, could lawfully "give an order on his debtor in favor of another." Applying that principle to the present case, some soldier might have written up some order to that effect in favor of some speculator who had sought to acquire his back pay. Nevertheless, Jefferson continued, if the debtor refused to honor that order, he would have to be sued in the name of the original creditor, which demonstrates that such an order "does not transfer the property of the debt." In addition, the original creditor could at any time before payment revoke such an order. In that case, he continued, "the person in whose favor" such an order was given would have recourse to a court of equity. "When there, asking equity, the judge examines whether he has done equity. If he finds his transaction has been a fair one, he gives him aid: if he finds it has been otherwise, not permitting his court to be a handmaid to fraud, he leaves him without remedy in equity, as he was in law." Therefore, Jefferson concluded, "the assignments in the present case" were, "if unfairly obtained, as seems to be admitted," just as "void in equity" as they were "in law," and their "nullity" would be derived from already existing law and not "from the new resolutions of Congress," which were therefore "not retrospective" in their operation.[47] One might note that Jefferson's argument at this point assumes that all such assignees were guilty of fraud, thus ignoring Hamilton's concern that the resolution would, in seeking to address the fraudulent transactions, also impair the rights of those who had been parties to a fair agreement. Nevertheless, in their case, Jefferson's previous argument – based on law, not equity – would control. Such an assignee, though not a party to fraud, would still have been party to a transaction forbidden by the law and thus in no

[46] *PTJ*, 16: 468–69.
[47] *PTJ*, 16: 469.

position to complain of having had his property rights altered retrospectively, since those rights had not even existed legally in the first place.

In this first skirmish, Jefferson's views prevailed. Washington signed the resolutions, apparently dismissing Hamilton's concerns.

Conclusion

The issues of 1790 illustrate the different tendencies of Hamilton's and Jefferson's thinking and point to the ways in which those tendencies might lead them into outright opposition.[48] These issues, however, were insufficient to create anything like a break between the two men. In a July conversation with George Beckwith, Britain's unofficial representative to the United States, Hamilton – apparently trying to smooth any difficulties before they might appear – hinted that Jefferson's opinions might tend to impede cooperation with Britain. According to Beckwith's record of the discussion, Hamilton spoke of "some opinions" Jefferson had "given respecting your government," which were evidently unfavorable, and his "possible predilections elsewhere," which was probably a reference to Jefferson's partiality toward France. Nevertheless, Hamilton coupled these remarks with the claim that Jefferson was "a man of honor, and zealously desirous of promoting those objects which the nature of his duty calls for, and the interest of his country may require."[49] There is no reason to suppose that Jefferson thought any differently of Hamilton in 1790. The break was to come as a result of the later stages of Hamilton's domestic program, especially the Bank of the United States, to which we now turn.

[48] During 1790, Hamilton and Jefferson also submitted written opinions to Washington on American policy in relation to the Nootka Sound crisis, which threatened war between England and Spain. See *PAH*, 7: 37–57 and *PTJ*, 17: 129–30. I have omitted discussion of these opinions here because Hamilton and Jefferson's advice did not differ as deeply as it did in other cases, and because their differences on this issue were more prudential than matters of principle. Hamilton did use his opinion to raise an important matter of principle which he hoped would guide American policy in the future: namely, the role of gratitude in foreign policy. His *Pacificus* essays of 1793 developed further his thoughts on this question, and they are treated in Chapter 14.

[49] *PAH*, 7: 497.

4

Establishing Energetic Government

Hamilton's Report on a National Bank

The seeds of controversy sown by the *Report on Public Credit* began to grow and bear fruit as a result of Hamilton's second major state paper, the *Report on a National Bank*, which he submitted to the House of Representatives on December 13, 1790.[1] The controversy with which this report was connected – Hamilton and Jefferson's celebrated clash over the constitutionality of the bank – was admittedly more a consequence of its plan than a subject of its argument. Like the *Report on Public Credit*, the *Report on a National Bank* reveals that Hamilton understood that his proposal would generate controversy, but he did not anticipate the full extent or the precise nature of the objections that would come. Thus the *Report on a National Bank* actually says nothing about the question that would be so hotly contested: the constitutional legitimacy of the measure. Instead, mindful of American suspicions about banks, and especially public banks, Hamilton dedicated much of the *Report* to a defense of such institutions on policy grounds. To a considerable extent, then, the *Report on a National Bank* is a compact treatise on the fundamentals of banking, and our inquiry need not dwell on its technical arguments on such issues.

Nevertheless, much in the *Report* merits careful attention because of the light it sheds on Hamilton's understanding of important principles of government and political life. As we will see, Hamilton did not regard the national bank merely as a technical question or a matter of ordinary policy but instead, like his initial plan to restore the public credit, as an essential step in fully establishing the energetic government promised by the Constitution. For Hamilton, a national bank, no less than a proper provision for the public credit, was an essential step in completing the founding.

---

[1] Hamilton's *Report* was written in response to an order of the House issued in August 1790, but, as Ron Chernow points out, he had believed in the necessity of a national bank since as early as 1780. See his *Alexander Hamilton* (New York: Penguin Press, 2004), 347.

Accordingly, in the *Report on a National Bank* Hamilton once again presented himself as a statesman-educator, elucidating for the public principles that he believed were essential to good government. Before laying out his plan for the bank, he "entreat[ed] the indulgence of the House" in permitting him some "preliminary reflections naturally arising out of the subject." To justify his account of such preliminaries he observed that because public opinion is the "ultimate arbiter of every measure of government, it can scarcely appear improper, in deference to that, to accompany the origination of any new proposition with explanations which the superior information of those to whom it is immediately addressed would render superfluous."[2] Hamilton, then, sought not only to convince the members of Congress to enact such a bank as he proposed but also to educate the American public in the importance of a national bank to the establishment of energetic government, and in the principles by which such an institution would have to be governed for it to make that contribution successfully.

The National Bank and Energetic Government

We turn first to Hamilton's argument for the utility of a national bank. That argument contains two primary threads. The first identifies the general advantages of public banks for modern political societies. The second contends that their disadvantages are either illusory or self-correcting.

Hamilton began his general defense of public banks with an appeal to experience:

It is a fact well understood that public Banks have found admission and patronage among the principal and most enlightened commercial nations. They have successively obtained in Italy, Germany, Holland, England and France, as well as in the United States. And it is a circumstance which cannot but have considerable weight, in a candid estimate of their tendency, that after an experience of centuries there exists not a question about their utility in the countries in which they have been so long established. Theorists and men of business unite in the acknowledgment of it.

"Trade and industry," he noted, "have been indebted" to public banks "wherever they have been tried." Moreover, "government has been repeatedly under the greatest obligations to them in dangerous and distressing emergencies." Indeed, this last lesson could be drawn not only from European history but even from America's own recent experience. The government of the United States, Hamilton observed, had "received" essential "assistance" from the public banks "established among us," both in the "most critical junctures of the late war" as well as "since the peace."[3]

---

[2] Hamilton, *Writings*, 575.
[3] Hamilton, *Writings*, 575.

In view of these lessons of experience, one might expect to find in the founding generation a "perfect union of opinions" in favor of public banks. Nevertheless, Hamilton noted, among some Americans "doubts" were still "entertained," "jealousies and prejudices" still "circulated," against these beneficent institutions. Accordingly, he turned next to a more detailed defense of them, one that compared their "principal advantages" – of which Hamilton identified three – with their "disadvantages, real or supposed."[4]

The first of these advantages is the "augmentation of the active or productive capital of a country." Metal currencies, Hamilton explained, have been "not improperly" called "dead stock" when they are used only as a medium of exchange. Locked in a merchant's chest, they are inert and unproductive until he encounters some opportunity to use them. If, however, they are instead made part of the capital of a bank – either by being deposited in it or used to buy stock in it – they "acquire life, or, in other words, an active and productive quality" arising from the "paper circulation" that the bank can issue on the basis of its capital. Experience shows, Hamilton contended, that prudently administered banks can circulate a paper currency perhaps two or three times the value of their actual holdings in gold and silver. Thus, on the one hand, their capital is available to its owners whenever some advantageous use of it should appear. If they are depositors they may withdraw it, and if they are stockholders they can sell their shares for cash or obtain a loan from the bank equivalent in value to their holdings. And, on the other hand, this money, in the form of the circulating paper currency, is simultaneously available for myriad others to use as well. For them it can be had by obtaining loans from the bank, which, again, amount to a total fund of money "much larger" than the actual metal capital deposited.[5] Banks, then, increase a nation's money supply. Their circulation of paper money is "to all the purposes of trade and industry an absolute increase of capital" because "purchases and undertakings in general can be carried on by any given sum of bank paper or credit as effectually as by an equal sum of gold and silver." Whereas an insufficient money supply impedes exchanges that people would otherwise undertake – as Hamilton had noted in the *Report on Public Credit*'s treatment of the depressed value of American land – a bountiful money supply encourages such exchanges, which are in turn necessary to most productive activity. Accordingly, banks tend to "enlarge the mass of industrious and commercial enterprise," and thereby become "nurseries of national wealth."[6] Here, Hamilton later noted, the general tendency of banks corresponded to a specifically American need of the moment: the national economy, as he had held in the *Report on Public Credit* and as he reiterated here, suffered from an insufficient circulation of currency.[7]

4 Hamilton, *Writings*, 576.
5 Hamilton, *Writings*, 576–77.
6 Hamilton, *Writings*, 578.
7 Hamilton, *Writings*, 590.

The second principal advantage of public banks, Hamilton contended, is that they ease the government's efforts to obtain "pecuniary aids, especially in sudden emergencies." Through such a bank, "the capitals of a great number of individuals" are "collected to a point, and placed under one direction." This "mass" of capital, moreover, is "magnified by the credit attached to it" and is "always ready, and can at once be put in motion, in aid of the government." Finally, Hamilton observed, one can be assured that such a bank will be not only able but also inclined to assist the government in this way: "the interest of the bank to afford" such "aid, independent of regard to the public safety and welfare, is a sure pledge for its disposition to go as far in its compliances as can in prudence be desired."[8] Although Hamilton did not make explicit the "interest" of the bank in making such loans, it is not difficult to discern his intention. Properly administered, a government – which cannot die, and which can raise a revenue from taxation – must appear to a bank as among the safest possible borrowers.[9]

As we will see, when Jefferson challenged the constitutionality of the national bank, Hamilton responded at great length with all the (considerable) energy and intelligence he could muster. This account of the second advantage of public banks illuminates some of the reasons for the vehemence of that response. For Hamilton, a public bank was not a luxury but a political necessity. It not only was a necessary element of his financial plan for the infant republic but would in fact be necessary to any properly constituted modern political system. As we noted in the previous chapter, Hamilton viewed his plan for the public credit as a crucial step in completing the founding. The promise of the Constitution was to establish energetic government, government equal to the needs of the nation. Energetic government requires a power to borrow money, to incur public debt. Without this power, there is little hope that a government will be able to meet the dangerous "exigencies" that will inevitably arise. For Hamilton, however, the inclusion of such an authority in the Constitution was a necessary but not a sufficient condition for the practical exercise of this power. In addition, it must be possible for the government to borrow on reasonable terms, and this in turn required it to make a responsible provision for its existing debts. He evidently viewed a national bank as similarly essential, and for similar reasons. Emergencies may call for large sums to be raised in a hurry, an operation for which borrowing is far more suitable than taxation. At the same time, however, borrowing from a large number of small lenders is apt to be fraught with delay and the danger of falling short of the required amount, possibilities that could prove disastrous in an emergency, especially the sudden outbreak

---

[8] Hamilton, *Writings*, 579.
[9] In view of Hamilton's arguments on this point, I think that Donald F. Swanson and Andrew P. Trout understate his belief in the importance of a national bank to the public credit. See their "Alexander Hamilton, 'the Celebrated Mr. Neckar,' and Public Credit," *William and Mary Quarterly* 47 (1990): 422–23.

of war. Accordingly, for Hamilton, a public bank, which creates a large pool of credit under a single direction, is necessary to the energetic exercise of the borrowing power, and hence to the cause of effective government.

The third and final of the principal advantages of public banks is their "facilitating of the payment of taxes." This advantage, Hamilton argued, "is produced in two ways," the first of which applies only to some members of the community and the second of which is "universal." In the first place, those "in a situation to have access to the Bank can have the assistance of loans," which can enable them to pay their taxes promptly. In the second place, a bank would assist everyone, even those in no position to borrow, in paying taxes by "increasing the quantity of circulating medium" and by "quickening" the "circulation." Having already explained the first of these effects earlier in the *Report*, Hamilton offered here a brief account of the second. Banks increase the pace of circulation because paper money can be moved about more quickly than metal, the transportation of which "is attended with trouble, delay, expense and risk." By thus enhancing the "quantity of circulating money," he concluded, banks contribute to the "ease with which every industrious member of the community" can obtain the currency needed to "pay his taxes, as well as to supply his other wants."[10]

Before tracing the next steps of Hamilton's case for public banks, we may observe that his argument thus far already reveals to some extent the roots of his coming clashes with Jefferson. Hamilton's defense of public banks reveals him as a kind of conservative. Just as he opened his *Report on Public Credit* by declaring that all political experience teaches that nations need to be able to borrow, so his first point in defense of public banks was that they have been tried and found useful by other nations.[11] Such an argument reveals something important not only about Hamilton's disposition to trust the lessons of experience but also about his understanding of the new nation that he sought to guide on the basis of such experience. Hamilton viewed the political experience of the old world as more applicable to America than did Jefferson perhaps because Hamilton saw the Revolution as having effected a less thoroughgoing change in society. For the former, unlike the latter, the Revolution instituted a new mode of government but did not necessarily lay the groundwork for far-reaching changes in economic and social relationships. Thus the American republic could freely borrow institutions, like public banks, from non-republican nations, even

---

[10] Hamilton, *Writings*, 579–80.

[11] On the basis of such elements in Hamilton's thinking, Clement Fatovic presents him as a kind of Humean. Between Hume and Hamilton, Fatovic notes, there was "a fundamental philosophical agreement on the epistemic authority of experience and the limitations of unaided reason and speculative theory in politics." "Reason and Experience in Alexander Hamilton's Science of Politics," *American Political Thought* 2 (2013): 2. Hamilton's concern to establish his program on the basis of the lessons of tried experience ought to qualify Joyce Appleby's presentation of him as a "bold innovator." *Thomas Jefferson* (New York: Henry Holt and Company, 2003), 19.

monarchies like England and France. For Hamilton, such institutions were to be understood neither as republican nor non-republican but simply as part of the governing apparatus of any advanced society.[12]

Moreover, the second advantage of banks – their ability to facilitate emergency borrowing – points once again to Hamilton's concern with "exigencies." In his mind, governments will continually confront threats to the common good the exact character of which cannot be predicted but the appearance of which is a virtual certainty. This expectation informed not only his desire for a particular institution such as the national bank, but more generally his insistence on a relatively generous interpretation of the federal power, which needs to be free and flexible enough to meet such eventualities. For Hamilton, government should not be rigidly and legalistically limited, because the problems it will confront cannot be precisely foreseen. Such inclinations led Hamilton into conflict with Jefferson, who preferred a much more strictly limited government, as we will see.

"Experience Guided by Interest": Hamilton's Refutation of the Supposed Disadvantages of Banks

Having explained the advantages of public banks, Hamilton turned next to a refutation of their supposed disadvantages. A "close and candid survey," he contended, would reveal that the drawbacks are either "destitute of foundation" or at least far less important than had been suggested. To the extent that the evils really exist, they proceed from "other, or partial, or temporary causes" and are "not inherent in the nature and permanent tendency" of banks. And where such disadvantages are ongoing and inseparable from the practice of banking, they are "more than counterbalanced by opposite advantages."[13]

Hamilton first took up the charge that banks "serve to increase usury." Here the concern is not that bank lending is itself usurious but that it fosters such abusive lending by others agents. Hamilton conceded that this is sometimes the case. Banks demand prompt payment from borrowers, and sometimes imprudent borrowers turn to usurers in order to meet their obligations to the bank. Nevertheless, Hamilton argued, "experience and practice gradually bring a cure to this evil." The bank's insistence on punctuality of payment fosters a habit of punctuality among men of trade. Once this habit is established, it makes them more certain of the amount and timing of their revenues and outlays and accordingly diminishes their need to turn to usurers. Moreover,

---

[12] On this point, see also James H. Read, who observes that Hamilton "never believed that republicanism fundamentally changes the nature of politics or the extent of powers inhering in government. Any government – republican or otherwise – must have certain powers." *Power versus Liberty: Madison, Hamilton, Wilson, and Jefferson* (Charlottesville, Virginia: University Press of Virginia, 2000), 56.

[13] Hamilton, *Writings*, 581.

usurious borrowing is so disadvantageous to the borrower that some experience of it will teach most men to avoid it in the future. At the same time, bank policy will tend to discourage usury. Resort to usurious loans is evidently a sign of disorderly finances, so it damages one's credit with the bank. Hamilton also contended that the increase of experience on the part of bankers would gradually lessen resort to usury. When a bank is new it may extend loans to those who should have been refused; and these overcommitted borrowers may end up turning to usurers in order to make their bank payments. With time and experience, however, banks become more careful in their lending, better able to determine which lenders are wise risks. "In a word," Hamilton concluded, "in the course of practice" and "from the very nature of things" institutional economic "interest will make it the policy of a Bank to succor the wary and industrious, to discredit the rash and unthrifty, to discountenance both usurious lenders and usurious borrowers." In addition, Hamilton noted, the general increase in the money supply resulting from banks would tend to "counteract the progress of usury."[14]

Hamilton then examined a second and related objection: that banks tend to crowd out other forms of lending, thus confining the ability to borrow to a narrow class of citizens, with the ultimate effect that the rest are "more exposed to the extortions of usurers."[15] According to this objection, where banks exist, potential lenders will be more attracted to bank stock than other kinds of investments, so that other forms of lending will tend to disappear. According to Hamilton, the "effect" here "supposed, as far as it has existence, is temporary," and the "reverse of it takes place in the general and permanent tendency of the thing." In the long run and by their nature, banks in fact tend to *encourage* other forms of lending. There is only so much stock in a bank, and once it is sold the lending class will have no choice but to invest elsewhere, offering other kinds of loans. Moreover, by providing an "extraordinary supply for borrowers within its immediate sphere," a bank opens up a "larger supply" for "borrowers elsewhere." Finally, the aforementioned general tendency of banks to increase the "aggregate mass of money" for "the aggregate mass of demand" ensures a "greater facility in obtaining it for every purpose."[16] The more money there is, the more overall borrowing there can be.

A third complaint held that banks create "temptations to overtrading," or that the availability of bank credit sometimes induces merchants to "adventure beyond the prudent or salutary point." This very statement of the problem, Hamilton contended, shows that it is merely "an occasional ill incident to a general good." All forms of credit, as well as gold and silver money, could to varying extents be charged with creating the same temptation. Yet it would certainly not be "wise" to "decry the precious metals, to root out credit," or

---

[14] Hamilton, *Writings*, 581–82.
[15] Hamilton, *Writings*, 582.
[16] Hamilton, *Writings*, 583.

to "proscribe the means of that enterprise, which is the main spring of trade and a principal source of national wealth" because they occasionally engender "excesses, of which overtrading is one" example. "If the abuses of a beneficial thing are to determine its condemnation," Hamilton argued, "there is scarcely a source of public prosperity, which will not speedily be closed." The prudent course in relation to such difficulties is to compare the "evil" with the "good." In this case, such a comparison would show that "the new and increased energies derived from commercial enterprise" made possible by banks "are a source of general profit and advantage" which "greatly outweigh the partial ills of the overtrading" of a few imprudent men of business.[17]

Hamilton gave a similar answer to the similar objection that banks sometimes aid "unskillful adventurers and fraudulent traders." Again, this is merely a "partial ill" arising from the availability of bank credit, a bad consequence flowing accidentally from a good thing. Here again the bad has to be weighed against the good. If banks sometimes err in extending credit to such persons, "they more frequently enable honest and industrious men, of small or perhaps no capital," to carry out enterprises advantageous both to "themselves and to the community," as well as "assist merchants" possessing both "capital and credit" to overcome unfortunate economic reversals that might otherwise prove fatal to their business. Hamilton's confidence that the good effects would outweigh the bad rested on his observation that it would be in a bank's interest to do all that it could to avoid error in extending credit to unworthy borrowers. "The practice of giving fictitious credit to improper persons is," he noted, "one of those evils" that "experience guided by interest speedily corrects." The bank itself would be in considerable danger of suffering from such practices. It might be "injured immediately" by the delinquency of the persons to whom credit had been imprudently extended. Moreover, it could also suffer from the "incapacities" of other members of the community ruined by the malpractice of these original unworthy borrowers. The bank therefore would have the "strongest of all inducements to be on its guard."[18]

Finally, Hamilton turned to what he regarded as the "heaviest charge" against banks, namely, that they "tend to banish the gold and silver of the Country." The paper credit issued by banks, this complaint held, acts a substitute for metals and thus encourages their exportation. The "most common answer" given to this complaint, he noted, is that the deportation of metals is not a genuine harm to the country. According to this response it is "immaterial what serves the purpose of money, whether paper or gold or silver." Hamilton conceded some – but only some – merit to this argument. It is true, he contended, that a "vivification of industry" arising from a "full circulation" of currency aided by a "proper and well regulated paper credit" may "more than compensate" the loss of part of the nation's gold and silver. Nevertheless, he suggested, a responsible statesman – at least in Hamilton's own time – could

[17] Hamilton, *Writings*, 584.
[18] Hamilton, *Writings*, 585.

not treat the permanent "increase or decrease" of "precious metals" in the country as a "matter of indifference." As the commodity taken in lieu of every other, precious metals constituted "a species of the most effective wealth." They were the "money of the world," and the state had to be concerned that they be present in the nation in sufficient amounts to "face any demands" created by the "protection of its external interests." Hamilton's more "conclusive" answer to this concern, then, did not deny the importance of a loss of metals but denied instead that such loss is really the long-term tendency of the use of the paper circulation created by banks. Because a country with no mines will have to get precious metals through commerce with other nations, the amount it possesses will "in the ordinary course of things" correspond to its balance of trade. If the balance is favorable, if the nation sells more than it buys, then it will accumulate metals. If the reverse is the case, it will be depleted of metals. Thus, the amount of metal in the country will depend primarily on its economic productivity. On this view, however, the establishment of banks favors, in the long term, the accumulation of precious metals because, as Hamilton had already argued, banks spur economic activity by increasing the "active capital of the country."[19]

Hamilton's defense of banks against these criticisms reveals an important tendency in his thought: his expectation that rational self-interest will generally direct people's economic behavior in directions that are fruitful for themselves and for the community – at least under normal conditions and under laws that protect private property. This expectation becomes especially clear in the concluding portions of his reply to the critics of banks. Consider his response to the concern that a paper currency is harmful because it undermines the salutary frugality that would otherwise be imposed by a bad balance of trade. On this view, when the balance of trade is unfavorable, metals are exported, and the resulting lack of currency forces citizens to retrench, which in turn tends naturally to correct the balance of trade. In response, Hamilton insisted that this objection is based on an "extreme case." A condition in which the people must be forced by "distress or necessity" to live within their means "perhaps rarely results" except from "extraordinary and adventitious causes," such as a "national revolution, which unsettles all the established habits of a people, and inflames the appetite for extravagance, by the illusions of an ideal wealth" arising from "the continual multiplication of a depreciating currency," or from some "similar cause." In contrast, when "the laws are wise and well executed, and the inviolability of property and contracts" is "maintained," there "is good reason to believe" that the "economy of a people will, in the general course of things, correspond with its means."[20]

Hamilton's confidence in the generally beneficial course of economic self-interest under the rule of law and property rights is similarly suggested by his argument that many of the American evils attributed to banks in fact resulted

---

[19] Hamilton, *Writings*, 586–87.
[20] Hamilton, *Writings*, 587–88.

from the upheavals caused by the Revolution. He mentioned here, among other things, some "injudicious laws, which grew out of the public distresses" and which "aggravated the evil" by "impairing confidence and causing a part of the" country's already "inadequate" wealth to be "locked up."[21] Hamilton seems here to have had in view state laws relieving debtors of their obligations, laws that seemed humane on the surface but that further damaged the economy by discouraging lending and investment by businessmen who feared that their property rights would not be respected by the governing authorities, hence his later observation that the "extinction" of such evils could be expected "from that additional security to property, which the Constitution of the United States happily gives." Hamilton perhaps had in mind here the Contracts Clause, as well as the general security for property that would result from separation of powers as well as the multiplicity of interests of the extended republic.[22] In any case, he presented this increased security of property afforded by the Constitution as "a circumstance of prodigious moment in the scale both of public and private prosperity."[23]

The Proper Structuring of a National Bank

Having made his case for the usefulness of a national bank, Hamilton asked whether there was already in existence an institution that could act in such a capacity, and, if not, on what principles such a bank should be established. Although they are distinct, it is useful to consider these two parts of his argument together because each tends to inform the other. Hamilton found serious defects in the only existing institution that might have been able to act as a bank for the United States, and his explanation of these defects prepared the ground for his account of the correct principles on which such a bank should be organized. Those principles, as we will see, reveal the complexity of Hamilton's understanding of the requirements of energetic government because, while the cause of energetic government called for the government to exercise its power in creating a bank, that cause equally required the government to limit its control of the bank, allowing it to operate as a privately owned and managed institution, although one with a constitution devised by the government with a view to public purposes.

Of the banks then existing, only Philadelphia's Bank of North America had a plausible claim to be the national bank Hamilton sought. Incorporated by Congress in 1781, this bank alone had ever had a direct relationship with the government of the United States. Moreover, Hamilton freely admitted the "aid" this institution had "afforded to the United States" during the Revolutionary

---

[21] Hamilton, *Writings*, 589–90.
[22] At the time Hamilton prepared this report, the Fifth Amendment had not yet been ratified, so the Takings Clause was not yet a part of the Constitution.
[23] Hamilton, *Writings*, 590.

War, as well as its good conduct since the establishment of peace. Nevertheless, he identified numerous "circumstances" that undermined any "pretension" it might have to continue to act as a bank for the nation. These circumstances in turn pointed to the "propriety" of a new "establishment" erected "on different principles."[24]

Hamilton first observed that the Bank's directors had "accepted and acted under a new charter from the State of Pennsylvania, materially different from their original one."[25] The federal charter had required that the Bank should have a stock of $10 million, while the new state charter limited it to $2 million. On this basis, Hamilton noted, one could well question whether the two charters were not so different as to be contradictory, and therefore whether the acceptance of the latter did not constitute "a virtual surrender" of the former. Perhaps, then, the Bank of North America was no longer really a bank chartered by the national authority. Hamilton did not insist on this point, however, but merely observed that the bank had certainly put itself in an "at least ambiguous" position by accepting the state charter, by which move it had created a sense in public opinion that "the Bank of North America" was now only a Pennsylvania bank. Such a status, however, was not suitable to an institution that was to act as a bank for the whole United States. If it had in fact accepted the status of a "mere Bank of a particular State, liable, as the state charter stipulated, to dissolution at the expiration of fourteen years," then "it would be neither fit nor expedient to accept it as an equivalent for a Bank of the United States."[26]

Hamilton found that more decisive objections arose in relation to the substantive provisions of the charter itself. A capital of a mere $2 million, he held, "promise[d] neither the requisite aid to the government, nor the requisite security to the community" that was to be sought in a national bank. While such a capital might be sufficient for local purposes, it was "an inadequate foundation for a circulation coextensive with the United States, embracing the whole of their revenues, and affecting every individual, into whose hands the paper may come." Moreover, the state charter was apt to render the capital even less adequate in practice: it permitted a maximum capital of $2 million but left the directors or the stockholders of the bank free to keep it at an even lower level than that. Such a discretion was, Hamilton believed, inconsistent with the bank's public mission. The capital of a national bank should be fixed at a level compatible with the public needs and not left to the discretion of the institution's directors or stockholders.[27]

This question about the extent of the discretion to be accorded to the bank's directors opens a view on Hamilton's complex understanding of the proper

---

[24] Hamilton, *Writings*, 593.
[25] Hamilton, *Writings*, 593.
[26] Hamilton, *Writings*, 594–95.
[27] Hamilton, *Writings*, 595.

relationship of a national bank to the government that establishes it. Truly energetic government requires the existence of such a bank. At the same time, the effectiveness of the bank – and hence its ability to contribute to energetic government – requires that it not simply be under the control of the government, which must leave it some freedom to manage its own affairs. On the one hand, a national bank cannot be simply a private institution operated solely for the private benefit of its owners. On the other hand, neither should it be owned, nor too closely controlled, by the government. Paradoxically, the cause of energetic government requires the government to create institutions distinct from itself, over which it has limited control. And there are some powers so prone to abuse, and the abuse of which is so certain to sap the government's strength, that the cause of energetic government actually requires government to utterly disavow such powers.

As we have seen, Hamilton contended that America needed a national bank in part to increase its money supply by circulating a paper currency. Here one might wonder why it would be necessary for the government to establish a bank in order to achieve such an aim. Rather than creating a bank that can emit a paper currency based on its metal holdings, would it not be simpler to have the federal government itself issue a paper currency? Such a course is, Hamilton implied, constitutionally open to the federal government. "The emitting of paper money by the authority of government is wisely prohibited to the individual states by the national constitution," he observed, but the prohibition does not apply to the government of the Union. Nevertheless, he continued, "the spirit of that prohibition ought not to be disregarded by the Government of the United States." A paper currency issued by the general government might have some advantages over a multiplicity of paper currencies issued by the several states. Still, paper emissions are "so certain of being abused" that "the wisdom of government will be shown in never trusting itself with the use of so seducing and dangerous an expedient." While it might be harmless, and perhaps even useful, in ordinary times, "there is almost a moral certainty of its becoming mischievous" in "great and trying emergencies." "The stamping of paper," Hamilton explained, is "so much easier than the laying of taxes, that a government in the practice of paper emissions would rarely fail in any such emergency to indulge itself too far" in the use of the former expedient, in order to "avoid as much as possible" the unpopularity of using the latter. Such measures would lead to distortions of the national economy inconsistent with its permanent health: in the worst case, a "bubble," but "at least" an "inflated and artificial state of things incompatible with the regular and prosperous course of the political economy."[28] This danger of inflation is not present in the case of a bank, Hamilton argued, since its emission of paper currency will always be limited by the demand for it as well as by the extent to which its capital can support the paper issued. A bank that emits more than

[28] Hamilton, *Writings*, 590–91.

it can actually sustain invites its own ruin. Accordingly, Hamilton found a salutary "limitation in the nature of the thing" in the case of bank emissions." In contrast, "the discretion of the government is the only measure of the extent of the emissions by its own authority."[29]

Hamilton's argument here recalls and is consistent with his oft-expressed concern about the various exigencies that the government would have to confront in the course of time. As we have already noted, Hamilton would later argue that such exigencies call for a generous interpretation of the federal power. Here, however, we see that his concern about such exigencies also led him to deny the government certain powers with which he thought it could not be safely trusted. Precisely because emergencies will predictably arise in which government will need a sudden infusion of money, it is "never" to be entrusted with the power to issue its own paper currency, even though this power might be exercised safely in ordinary times. Tranquility may prevail most of the time, but emergencies will come often enough to induce a government that can issue paper to pursue a reckless policy of simply printing money. In other words, a power to print money combined with the inevitable appearance of public crises of one kind or another will lead to regularly recurring periods of government-induced inflation, a phenomenon Hamilton rejected as inconsistent with the steady health of the economy. For Hamilton, government must be energetic but not unlimited: the prudent and effective conduct of public affairs actually requires the government to disclaim some powers. This principle in turn is based on Hamilton's expectations for the kind of people who will ordinarily administer the government: people of such a quality that they are "never" to be entrusted with the "discretion" to issue a paper currency. The ultimate consequences of resorting to the printing of money in order to supply the needs of the community in an emergency can be discerned fairly easily by a reasonably informed person: Hamilton was able to sketch them in a few sentences. Nevertheless, he anticipated that the people at the head of public affairs would ignore larger considerations – the common good over the course of time – in favor of smaller ones – their own personal popularity at the present moment.

Moreover, the kinds of considerations that prevented a prudent government from itself issuing a paper currency also forbade it from owning the bank that it established for this purpose. Many who contemplated a national bank thought that the "public advantage" would be advanced if it could be established such that its "profits" would "redound to the immediate benefit of the State." Such a notion, Hamilton contended, was open to "insuperable objections." For the bank to enjoy "full confidence," it was "an essential ingredient in its structure" that it be "under a *private*" and "not a *public* Direction," that it should be "under the guidance of *individual interest*" and not "of *public policy*." A bank controlled by the government "would be supposed to be," and in some cases actually would be, influenced in its decisions too much by

[29] Hamilton, *Writings*, 592.

"public necessity." That is, such a bank would be suspected of making, and might in fact make, its decisions based upon the needs of the government for money rather than upon the need to keep the bank itself a sound and profitable operation. Such suspicions, Hamilton argued, would become a "canker" that would "continually erode the credit of the Bank" and would likely "prove fatal" precisely in those situations "in which the public good" demanded that its financial standing and reputation "should be most sound and vigorous." Indeed, Hamilton went so far as to say that it would be "little less than a miracle should the credit of the Bank be at the disposal of the Government" without there being at some point a "calamitous abuse of it."[30]

The problem here is due once again, Hamilton contended, to the short sighted self-interest of government officials, who would probably prefer the easy and popular course to the more rigorous and financially sound one. Hamilton observed that it is obviously in "the real interest of the government not to abuse" the credit of the bank but instead to "husband and cherish it with the most guarded circumspection as an inestimable treasure." Nevertheless, public officials could not be relied upon to manage a bank as prudence would dictate. What government, Hamilton asked, "ever uniformly consulted its true interest, in opposition to the temptation of momentary exigencies? What nation was ever blessed with a constant succession of upright and wise administrators?"[31] Confronted with a sudden need for money, a government that owns a bank can be expected – in order to avoid the odious expedient of taxation – to vote itself a line of credit from the bank, regardless of whether the terms of the loan are consistent with the long-term solvency of the bank itself. A national bank owned by the government is in a certain sense self-defeating, since the government can be expected sooner or later to bankrupt the bank in the pursuit of the public's immediate needs, for when the "public" owns the bank, it is actually under the control of politicians whose own money is not in fact at stake in the bank's transactions, and who therefore cannot be relied on to protect its interests.

Similar considerations about the need to link self-interest with institutional duty led Hamilton to reject an arrangement under which the bank would be owned by the public, so that the public might enjoy all of the profits, yet governed by private individuals, so as to avoid the dangers of public direction discussed above. Such an arrangement would "commit the interests of the State to persons not interested, or not enough interested, in their proper management." Instead, Hamilton argued, the bank should be privately owned and privately directed so that the private interests of its proprietors would lead them to safeguard its financial solidity. The "only security that can always be relied upon for a careful and prudent administration" of a bank is the directors'

---

[30] Hamilton, *Writings*, 601 (Hamilton's emphases).
[31] Hamilton, *Writings*, 601–02.

"keen, steady, and, as it were, magnetic sense of their own interest as proprietors, pointing invariably to its true pole, the prosperity of the institution." The private interest of private owners, therefore, is "the only basis on which an enlightened, unqualified and permanent confidence can be expected to be erected and maintained."[32]

While the self-interest of the owners was to be a key means by which the bank's proper administration would be ensured, the satisfaction of that private interest was not itself the end for which the bank was to be established. According to Hamilton, unless the interest of a bank's investors is "consulted, there can be no bank" – at least not in the sense of an institution that would be "worthy of confidence." But it "does not follow" from this fact that the interest of the investors "alone is to be consulted, or that it even ought to be paramount." "Public utility," Hamilton insisted, "is more truly the object of public Banks, than private profit." Accordingly, "it is the business of government" to establish the bank "on such principles" that private profit will "afford competent motives" for the owners to carry on the bank's business properly, but without making public utility "subservient to it." This reasoning, again, revealed the inadequacy of the existing Bank of North America. Its current state charter not only limited its capital to the insufficient sum of $2 million, it also improperly permitted the directors to keep the capital at an even lower level if they wished. This was understandably attractive to the owners themselves, Hamilton argued: a smaller capital means fewer investors, which in turn means a higher price of the stock as well as a larger share of the profits among the existing investors. Thus, that bank's charter improperly subordinated the public good to the private interests of the bank's proprietors. A properly established bank, Hamilton concluded, would be governed by rules that will not permit this but that will fix the bounds of the capital within limits "deemed safe and convenient" for the bank and the public, leaving the directors "no discretion either to stop short" or "overpass them."[33]

Finally, a proper plan would permit the government to audit the bank. While disclaiming "all pretension to control," the government "owes itself" and "the community" the reservation of a "right of ascertaining, as often as may be necessary, the state of the bank." This authority befits the bank's status as an institution that, though privately owned and directed, is nevertheless established primarily for public purposes. "If the paper of a bank is to be permitted to insinuate itself into all the revenues and receipts of a country; if it is even to be tolerated as the substitute for gold and silver, in all transactions of business, it becomes in either view a national concern of the first magnitude." As a result, "the ordinary rules of prudence require that the Government should possess the means of ascertaining, whenever it thinks fit, that so delicate a trust is executed with fidelity and care." Indeed, Hamilton added that this right

---

[32] Hamilton, *Writings*, 602–03.
[33] Hamilton, *Writings*, 595–96.

is useful not only in relation to the interests of the public but ought to be cherished as well by the proprietors of the bank. The institution's openness to a government audit at any time is "an additional title to public and private confidence" and "a thing that can only be formidable to practices that imply mismanagement."[34]

For Hamilton, the bank's role as a public institution pointed to another set of considerations that further disqualified the Bank of North America. Although the bank must be privately held and governed, its mode of governance should not be left to the discretion of its shareholders. It should instead be established by the government, through the legislation creating the bank, with a view to safeguarding the bank's public role and public confidence in its ability to fulfill it. In this context, Hamilton noted a serious defect in the constitution of the board of the Bank of North America: its charter did not provide for rotation among the directors, yet a properly established public bank would not allow the exact same people to be in control of it all the time. Rotation among the directors, Hamilton reasoned, was necessary to protect public confidence in the institution by making it less likely to render itself subservient to the views of a particular party or to the interests of any specific set of citizens. The directors, Hamilton observed, would not be elected by the "great body of the community, in which a diversity of views will naturally prevail" but by "a small and select class of men, among whom it is far more easy to cultivate a steady adherence to the same persons and objects." Moreover, the directors would "have it in their power" to "conciliate" by "obliging" the "most influential" among those who would elect them. As a result, the natural tendency would be for "changes" in the body of the directors to happen only "rarely." Such stability in a public bank's board of directors, however, is contrary to the common good. The continual administration of a bank by the same people, combined with the necessary secrecy of its "transactions," would inevitably invite popular "distrust and discontent." Since it is impracticable to make the bank's financial decisions public, the proper remedy is to provide for a periodic change among the directors, which will help to prevent both the reality and the appearance of a partial or biased administration. Such is the "delicacy" of a public bank's reputation that "everything, which can fortify confidence and repel suspicion, without injuring its operations, ought carefully to be sought after in its formation," said Hamilton.[35]

One might object to a plan of rotation on the grounds that it would in fact "injure" the bank's "operations" by depriving it of experienced leadership. Hamilton was not insensitive to this concern and was himself a critic of demands for rotation in the offices of government precisely on the grounds that such offices are better exercised by experienced and informed men. Nevertheless, he here contended that the reasons for rotation among the directors of a

[34] Hamilton, *Writings*, 603–04.
[35] Hamilton, *Writings*, 597–98.

bank do not apply so much to a government. Hamilton recommended rotation for the bank as a way of quieting fears about biased administration, fears that would arise from the secrecy of its transactions. Government's transactions, however, are ordinarily not secret but in fact announced to the public. The character of government as an institution, then, is not such that it requires rotation as a remedy for such suspicions. Moreover, the reasons that counsel against rotation in government do not apply so much to banks. The value of the "knowledge" gained from "experience" is the "only circumstance common to both" government and banking that appears to argue against rotation in both. Nevertheless, Hamilton contended that "the objects of the government of a nation," as opposed to "the government of a bank," differ so much as to undermine significantly the force of the comparison on this point. Experience is not as essential to banking as to government service. "Almost every important case of legislation," Hamilton argued, "requires, towards a right decision, a general and accurate acquaintance with the affairs of the state," as well as "habits of thinking seldom acquired" except though "a familiarity with public concerns." In contrast, a bank can be administered according to "a few simple fixed maxims, the application of which is not difficult to any man of judgment, especially if instructed in the principles of trade. It is in general a constant succession of the same details." In any case, Hamilton added, to the extent that experience is important to the government of a bank, it can be sufficiently obtained by exempting the chairman of the directors from the rotation, through the advice the directors will get from him and from the bank's inferior officers, and by the fact that the rotation will not reach the whole body of the directors at the same time.[36]

The bank's importance as a public institution also required that the public lay down a proper rule for the election of its directors and not leave this question to the directors themselves. Here we encounter an interesting problem of representation: who should have a say, and how much of a say, in the election of the directors of the bank? Hamilton took it for granted that the electors would themselves be shareholders in the bank, that the owners of the institution would choose its directors. Beyond that assumption, however, he approached the question in a rather non-dogmatic spirit. From a certain perspective it might seem obvious that each owner should get one vote for each share that he owns, such that whatever combination of men controls a majority of shares will control the bank. This would amount to governing a moneymaking institution according to the oligarchic principle and would no doubt appear the obviously just course to the man of business. Nevertheless, the bank was not to be, as Hamilton had noted, simply a moneymaking institution. It was to be a public institution serving a democratic government. Perhaps, then, each shareholder should get one vote in the selection of the directors, regardless of the number of shares held. This would amount to ruling a public institution

[36] Hamilton, *Writings*, 596–97.

according to the democratic principle and would no doubt be attractive at least to the more thoroughgoing egalitarians among a democracy's citizens. Hamilton, however, suggested that neither principle was appropriate to the case and that the question should be decided pragmatically with a view to the well working of the bank, rather than the ideological purity of its constitution. One vote "for each share," Hamilton observed, would make it "too easy" for a "combination" among a "few principal stockholders" to "monopolize the power and benefits of the bank." At the same time, permitting "an equal vote to each stockholder, however great or small his interest in the institution," would be inconsistent with the "degree of weight to large stockholders, which it is reasonable that they should have, and which perhaps their security and that of the bank require." Therefore, "a prudent mean" should be sought, one according to which large shareholders enjoy greater control over the institution but not to the extent of one vote per share.[37] Moreover, because of the importance of the bank as a public institution, the electoral formula for directors should be written into its constitution and not be changeable by any passing majority of directors.

Finally, Hamilton concluded his critique of the Bank of North America by decrying its lack "of precautions to guard against a foreign influence insinuating itself" into its "direction." "It seems scarcely reconcilable with a due caution," he contended, to allow that anyone "but citizens should be eligible as directors of a national bank, or that non-resident foreigners should be able to influence the appointment of directors by the votes of their proxies." A properly designed constitution for a national bank, then, would carefully limit foreign influence on its government. Hamilton justified this policy by referring once again to the principle that ruled his entire discussion of the question of how the bank is to be governed: "such a bank," although privately owned, "is not a mere matter of private property, but a political machine of the greatest importance to the state."[38]

Conclusion

The *Report on a National Bank* reveals much in Hamilton's political thinking that would contribute to Jefferson's opposition to the Hamiltonian program. As a policy matter, Jefferson did not, as we will see, view the creation of a paper currency as the great public benefit that Hamilton held it to be. Furthermore, Hamilton's open argument that the bank would have to be guided by its own financial interests may have contributed to Jefferson's sense that it was somehow an engine of corruption, dedicated only to the private interests of its stockholders. Most generally, and perhaps most seriously, Hamilton's willingness to be guided by Europe's political experience – and thus freely to borrow

[37] Hamilton, *Writings*, 598.
[38] Hamilton, *Writings*, 599.

institutions, like a national bank, that had been essential to the greatness and power of some monarchical nations – may have encouraged Jefferson's fears that Hamilton harbored anti-republican thoughts and aspirations.

Such political objections, however, did not become a prominent part of Jefferson's critique of Hamiltonianism until 1792, when the secretary of state presented a comprehensive list of complaints about Hamilton's treasury program to President Washington. His more immediate criticism – voiced in 1791, when the bank bill had been passed and was awaiting Washington's signature – took a constitutional form that Hamilton, for all his efforts to respond to commonplace American concerns about banks, had failed to anticipate. Jefferson contended that Congress had no power to create such a bank as Hamilton had proposed. This claim was at the center of Hamilton and Jefferson's cabinet debate over the scope of the federal authority, which is taken up in the next chapter.

5

Defending Limited Government

Jefferson's Critique of the Constitutionality of the National Bank

Compared to his program for restoring the public credit, Hamilton's plan for a national bank won quick and comparatively easy legislative approval. While Congress had deliberated for months on the assumption plan, first defeating it and only then enacting it in a modified form, the bank bill was passed by both houses within a few weeks of the submission of Hamilton's *Report*.[1] Despite the relative speed and ease of its initial success, however, the bank ultimately provoked the greater controversy by raising even more troubling questions, questions of constitutional legitimacy. The arguments against assumption had been primarily political in character, Hamilton's plan having drawn, in the words of Clinton Rossiter, "only desultory fire on the issue of its conformity with the Constitution."[2] Constitutional concerns had been raised about the assumption but had not been pressed with anything like the vehemence of the claim that the bank was not authorized by the Constitution and that it therefore represented a dangerous step toward unlimited government.

These arguments, which emerged from the unsuccessful legislative opposition to the bank bill, ended up threatening it when it came before the executive. In the House of Representatives, James Madison spoke out against the constitutionality of the bank, and his views carried sufficient weight with George Washington that the president, weighing the possibility of a veto, sought advice from his cabinet.[3] Jefferson replied with his *Opinion on the Constitutionality*

[1] See Ron Chernow, *Alexander Hamilton* (New York: The Penguin Press, 2004), 344, 349–50.
[2] Clinton Rossiter, *Alexander Hamilton and the Constitution* (New York: Harcourt, Brace, and World, 1964), 76.
[3] Gordon Wood, *Empire of Liberty* (New York: Oxford University Press, 2009), 144. Later, during his own presidency, Madison changed his mind about the nation's need for a national bank. See Lance Banning, *Conceived in Liberty: The Struggle to Define the New Republic, 1789–1793* (Lanham, MD: Rowman and Littlefield, 2004), 25.

of a National Bank, his contribution to one of the great constitutional debates of the early republic.

Protecting States' Rights

Although Jefferson's case was primarily constitutional, it also opened onto even larger issues. Just as Hamilton's reports involved more than mere policy reasoning, so Jefferson's *Opinion* was more than just an exercise in legal scholarship or constitutional interpretation. Hamilton's understanding of the fundamental principles of government and politics pervaded his treasury reports. Similarly, Jefferson's vision of just and free government informed his *Opinion*. We might begin to grasp that vision, and to understand how it differed from Hamilton's competing vision, by means of the following simple and commonplace observation: while Hamilton was primarily concerned that the federal government would be too weak, Jefferson was primarily concerned that it would be too strong. Jefferson's interest was not purely negative, however. Such strict limits as he sought to impose on the federal power he sought not only for their own sake but in defense of something else that he deemed worthy of protection: the powers of the state governments.

This concern is evident in the introductory paragraphs of the *Opinion*. Jefferson opened his case by listing the ways in which the national bank would intrude upon state powers or violate existing state laws. The bank bill, he observed, organized "the subscribers into a corporation," thus exercising a power that, as he explained later, belongs properly to the states. Moreover, by empowering this corporation to hold land, and by regulating the terms or conditions of such ownership, as well as the mode by which it could be transmitted from one owner to another, the bill went "against" the state laws of mortmain, alienage, descents, forfeiture, escheat, and distribution. The bill further gave the bank "the sole and exclusive right of banking under the national authority" and so, according to Jefferson, was also "against the laws of monopoly." Finally, Jefferson held that the bill implicitly authorized the bank to make bylaws for itself that would be "paramount to the laws of the states: for so they must be construed, to protect the institution from the control of the state legislatures."[4]

Jefferson drew no explicit conclusions about the bill's constitutionality from these observations. Nevertheless, his list of complaints clearly intended to impute an air of illegality to the bill, hence his refrain that the bill was "against" certain existing state laws. This complaint seems to imply that the federal government should, in the exercise of its own powers, be guided by what is permitted according to state law. And this idea seems further to imply that states may legislate with the purpose of restraining the federal government in the exercise

[4] Thomas Jefferson, *Writings*, ed. Merrill D. Peterson (New York: Library of America, 1984), 416.

of its own powers. This in turn suggests that the states ought to be considered as equal or even superior to the federal government – a view that is suggested by Jefferson's concluding complaint that the bill implicitly authorized the bank to make bylaws "paramount to the laws of the states."

Jefferson appeared to back away somewhat from these consequences later in the *Opinion*. After developing his interpretation of the Necessary and Proper Clause, which we will consider shortly, he returned to the issue of these state laws that he believed were violated by the bank bill. Here he presented them not merely as existing state law but as "the most ancient and fundamental laws of the several states," the "pillars of our whole system of jurisprudence," and "the foundation-laws of the state governments." He then suggested that only a "necessity invincible by any other means" could justify the federal government's "prostration" of such laws, while it would be improper for it to do so merely for the sake of its own convenience.[5] This language tends on its face to limit the extent to which Jefferson sought a subordination of the federal government to the states. He explicitly admitted here that a genuine necessity would justify the federal government in exercising its power in ways that run counter to fundamental state laws. Moreover, his emphasis on the fundamental character of the laws in question perhaps implies that the federal government might, even in the absence of real necessity and thus only for convenience, legislate counter to ordinary or non-foundational state laws. Nevertheless, Jefferson's complaints still imply a considerable power of the states to hem in the federal government in the exercise of its own powers because if the federal government must not transgress the fundamental laws of the states, then the states could limit the authority of the federal government by amending their own constitutions – that is, by making their ordinary laws into fundamental laws.

Jefferson's concern to limit the power of the federal government in order to protect the authority of the states is rendered more explicit by a second preliminary remark he made prior to moving to his argument against the constitutionality of the bank. "I consider," he observed, "the foundation of the Constitution as laid on this ground: That 'all powers not delegated to the United States, by the Constitution, nor prohibited by it to the States, are reserved to the States or to the people.'" Here Jefferson paraphrased what would become the Tenth Amendment, which, at the time he wrote his *Opinion*, had been passed by Congress and was awaiting ratification by a sufficient number of states. Immediately after positing this basic ground of the Constitution, Jefferson warned that to "take a single step beyond the boundaries thus specially drawn around the powers of Congress is to take possession of a boundless field of power, no longer susceptible of any definition."[6]

These remarks bring into view important differences between Hamilton and Jefferson, differences regarding the proper understanding of the Constitution

---

5 Jefferson, *Writings*, 420.
6 Jefferson, *Writings*, 416.

and the nature of government in general. Given his concern with energetic government, and his understanding of the Constitution as aiming to establish such government, Hamilton would surely not consent to the notion that the very "foundation of the Constitution" is grounded on a provision the primary purpose of which is to impose a limit on the government's powers. This is not to say that Hamilton would reject such limitations or prefer to ignore the Tenth Amendment. Such limits may be appropriate, and if placed in the Constitution they must be respected. Nevertheless, to elevate them to the status of the Constitution's foundation would make no sense in Hamilton's understanding. Presumably the foundation of a thing is to be discovered in its end or purpose, yet people do not create a government primarily in order to limit its power but in order to perform functions for which it must have adequate power.

For similar reasons, Hamilton would dissent from Jefferson's claim that a "boundless field of power" is seized any time the government takes a "single step" beyond the "boundaries" established on Congress's authority. In a certain sense, Jefferson's claim is undoubtedly true. To exercise a power that has not in fact been delegated is to treat the Constitution as irrelevant and thus in principle to claim a power to do anything. Nevertheless, the tenor of Jefferson's remarks here seems to imply something that Hamilton would deny: namely, that the delegation of federal powers establishes limits on government that are so specific and evident that one can discern even "a single step" beyond them.

The Bank and the Enumerated Powers

Having identified the fundamental principles that would guide his inquiry, Jefferson then turned to his argument against the constitutionality of the bank. "The incorporation of a bank, and the powers assumed by this bill," he announced, "have not, in my opinion, been delegated to the United States, by the Constitution."[7] The bank, he contended, could not be justified under any of the enumerated powers of Congress, or under more general phrases in the Constitution, such as the General Welfare Clause and the Necessary and Proper Clause.

Among the list of enumerated powers in Article I, Section 8 of the Constitution, Jefferson found that only the first three might be relevant to the case of the bank. Upon examination, however, none of them justified such an institution. The Constitution first empowers Congress to "lay taxes for the purpose of paying the debts of the United States," but, Jefferson observed, "no debt is paid" by the bank bill, "nor any tax laid." Indeed, if it were "a bill to raise money, its origination in the Senate would condemn it by the Constitution," which requires that all bills for raising revenue shall originate in the House of Representatives.[8]

[7] Jefferson, *Writings*, 416.
[8] Jefferson, *Writings*, 417.

Section 8 next authorizes Congress to "borrow Money on the credit of the United States." The bank bill, however, "neither borrow[ed] money nor ensure[d] the borrowing [of] it." As we have seen, Hamilton devised the bank as a privately held company (although one in which the government would hold a minority share of stock) and thought that private ownership was essential to its effective operation. Yet this arrangement made it impossible to regard the bank as *ensuring* the borrowing of money, as Jefferson thought would be necessary to its constitutionality. "The proprietors of the bank," he noted, would "be just as free as any other money holders, to lend or not to lend their money to the public." Hamilton's bill did require an initial loan of $2 million to the government and to that extent might appear to meet Jefferson's objection. Jefferson, however, seemed to regard this as nothing more than a legalistic ruse. The bill provided that the government would invest $2 million in the bank and immediately take a $2 million loan. Jefferson, however, held that the former transaction was in reality a *loan to the bank* by the government, and hence that the latter was properly understood as a *repayment* and "not a loan, call it by what name you please."[9]

Finally, Jefferson contended that the authority of Congress to "regulate commerce with foreign nations, and among the states, and with the Indian tribes" offers no justification for a national bank. Here he relied on two distinct lines of argument. The first considered what it means to regulate commerce, and the second what kind of commerce may properly be regulated by Congress. In the first place, Jefferson denied that the creation of the bank could reasonably be understood as a regulation of commerce. "He who erects a bank," he argued, "creates a *subject* of commerce" in the "bills" that such a bank may issue, just as does "he who makes a bushel of wheat" or "digs a dollar out of the mines." None of these persons, however, "regulates commerce" by such actions. "To make a thing which may be bought and sold" is not the same thing as "to prescribe regulations for buying and selling." In the second place, Jefferson contended that even if the creation of the bank could be viewed as a regulation of commerce, it would still be "void" because it extends "as much to the internal commerce of every state as to its external." The Constitution does

---

[9] Jefferson, *Writings*, 417. Hamilton regarded this point as "not very material to the main argument" and appears not to have remembered to respond to it until the very last paragraph of his own *Opinion*, where he mentions it as something that had been "omitted" and had "just occur[red]" to him. Jefferson, he held, was "certainly mistaken" in his presentation of the government's initial loan from the bank. Even though the sums involved in the government's purchase of stock and the bank's loan to the government were equal, this did not turn the loan into a repayment. By taking the loan from the bank, the government did not "therefore cease to be a proprietor of the stock, which would be the case if the money received back were in the nature of a repayment." Even with its loan, the government remained a partial owner of the bank and would "share in the profit or loss of the institution, according as the dividend is more or less than the interest" it would "pay on the sum borrowed. Hence that sum is manifestly and in the strictest sense a loan." Hamilton, *Writings*, 646.

not authorize Congress to regulate the internal commerce of the states, that is, the "commerce between citizen and citizen," which "remains exclusively with" the "legislature of each state." It rather authorizes Congress to regulate only a state's "external commerce," or its commerce with other states, foreign nations, or Indian tribes.[10]

Here Jefferson pressed for a narrow interpretation of the key terms in the Commerce Clause, aiming, again, to keep the federal power within strict limits. He held that to "regulate" is to "prescribe regulations" and observed that the bank bill did not directly do so for commerce among the states. His definition is a reasonable one, but a broader, and still reasonable, definition is also possible. To regulate might involve not only prescribing rules but more generally rendering a phenomenon more orderly. In this view, the bank bill might well have been regarded as a regulation of commerce, to the extent that it provided a convenient currency for the conduct of commerce – a conclusion that Jefferson also avoided by presenting the bank's bills merely as subjects of commerce, like any other commodity, and not as also, and perhaps primarily, as a medium of exchange, which Hamilton had intended.

In relation to the other terms of the Commerce Clause, Jefferson's interpretations more clearly anticipated constructions that were used by the later defenders of state power against the federal government. He defined commerce as "buying and selling," while it could be understood more broadly as covering economic activity in general. He thus narrowed the scope of activity that might fall under Congress's authority. Finally, he suggested that the commerce "among" the states must be understood strictly as each state's external commerce and not as extending to its internal commerce, or the commerce between citizen and citizen, which is instead "exclusively" reserved to the state legislatures. Here he pushed even further his introductory suggestion that state powers can restrain the federal power. There he had implied that existing state laws should regulate the federal government's exercise of its own authority. Here he held that a mere realm of activity entrusted to the states should be understood to check the federal government, even in the absence of any actually existing state laws that conflict with federal laws. Jefferson claimed that, even if the bank bill did regulate commerce, it would be "void" because it extended "as much" to the internal commerce of the states as to the external. That is, is a federal law – without violating a state law, without regulating internal commerce under the mere pretext of regulating external commerce, and without even extending *primarily* to internal commerce – must be considered void if it touches internal commerce "as much" as external commerce. It would probably be impossible completely to disentangle external and internal commerce: in many cases Congress would inevitably reach the latter while intending only to control the former. Yet Jefferson's principle here would require Congress to deny itself certain means, even when they are in themselves appropriate to the

[10] Jefferson, *Writings*, 417 (emphasis added).

task at hand, simply because they also equally impact the internal commerce of the states.

The Bank and the General Welfare Clause

Jefferson then turned from the specifically enumerated powers to the two "general phrases" that might provide a justification for the bank: the General Welfare Clause and the Necessary and Proper Clause. The former appears at the beginning of Article I, Section 8 and provides that the "Congress shall have Power to lay and collect Taxes . . . to pay the Debts and provide for the common Defense and general Welfare of the United States." Jefferson was here particularly concerned to show that this provision does not confer upon Congress a general power to legislate in pursuit of the general welfare, but that the expression "general welfare" is instead intended to qualify the single power given, the power of taxation. Properly understood, he contended, the provision authorizes Congress "to lay taxes for *the purpose* of providing for the general welfare." The "laying of taxes is the *power*, and the general welfare is the *purpose* for which the power is to be exercised." The Constitution here does not authorize Congress to lay taxes "*ad libitum for any purpose they please*; but only to *pay the debts or provide for the welfare of the Union.*" Similarly, "they are not to do anything they please to provide for the general welfare, but only to lay taxes for that purpose."[11] As Jefferson had already observed, however, the bank bill laid no taxes and so could not be authorized by this clause, however much its author might believe that it would contribute to the general welfare of the nation.

Any attempt to read the "general welfare" wording as conferring a legislative power beyond the power to tax, Jefferson contended, is to be rejected because of its unacceptable consequences. In the first place, such a reading would effectively establish unlimited government. To consider the phrase as giving "a distinct and independent power" of Congress to "do any act they please, which might be for the good of the Union," would "reduce" the whole Constitution "to a single phrase, that of instituting a Congress with power to do whatever would be for the good of the United States." But since the members of such a Congress would be "the sole judges of the good or evil, it would also be a power to do whatever evil they please." Such unlimited government was, beyond all serious dispute, not the intention informing the Constitution. "Certainly," Jefferson says, "no such universal power was meant to be given" to Congress by the Constitution, which was instead "intended to lace them up straitly within the enumerated powers, and those without which, as a means, these powers could not be carried into effect."[12]

In the second place, Jefferson contended, such a reading would render the Constitution incoherent, since the granting of such a comprehensive power

---

[11] Jefferson, *Writings*, 417–18 (Jefferson's emphasis).
[12] Jefferson, *Writings*, 418.

would render the specification of further powers unnecessary. It would make no sense, he suggested, for the Constitution to list specific powers if it had already given Congress such comprehensive authority over the good of the nation. If Congress were already authorized, by the first few words of Article 1, Section 8, to care for the "general welfare" of the nation, why, for example, would it be necessary to lengthen the section by listing particular powers relevant to the general welfare, such as the powers to regulate commerce, to provide a uniform rule of naturalization, or to punish counterfeiting? Jefferson observed that in cases "where a phrase will bear either of two meanings" it is "an established rule of construction" to select that interpretation that will "allow some meaning to the other parts of the instrument, and not that which would render all the others useless"[13] This rule requires that we understand the "general welfare" to be the purpose for which the taxing power is to be used and not as an independent source of power itself.

Before turning to the Necessary and Proper Clause, Jefferson interjected an argument based not on the Constitution's words but instead on the history of its drafting. "It is known," he contended, "that the very power now proposed *as a means* was rejected as *an end* by the Convention which formed the Constitution." The Convention considered a proposal that would have authorized "Congress to open canals, and an amendatory one to empower them to incorporate." These proposals, however, were rejected. Moreover, Jefferson added, "one of the reasons for rejection urged in debate was" that if Congress were granted a power to incorporate, it would then "have a power to erect a bank," which would "render the great cities" in the nation "adverse to the reception of the Constitution," since many of the voters of such cities held "prejudices and jealousies" on the subject of banks"[14]

Jefferson's argument implies that our interpretation of the Constitution must be guided not only by its words but also by our knowledge of its drafting and that we may not rightly claim as an implied power one that we know was rejected as an enumerated power. The existence of implied powers creates a problem of interpretation, and a danger to limited government, because in some cases it will be unclear whether the specific power in question really is implied by the Constitution or not. Although the legislative record of the Constitution could not resolve this difficulty in all cases, Jefferson apparently believed it should be used in those cases in which it can provide guidance: when, for example, a power was proposed and rejected. As was suggested by Jefferson's earlier admonition that we not take a "single step" beyond the powers delegated to Congress, he craved not only limited government but strictly or legalistically limited government. He wanted government to be limited as much as possible by clear, indisputable principles, hence his willingness to go beyond the text and general reasoning upon it to the record of the Convention, which at least in

---

[13] Jefferson, *Writings*, 418.
[14] Jefferson, *Writings*, 418 (Jefferson's emphases).

some instances can provide a more detailed understanding of precisely where constitutional lines are to be drawn, or exactly what powers are excluded.

Moreover, Jefferson's argument here touches on a principle even more fundamental, perhaps, than respect for the Constitution as a rule of law with clearly knowable boundaries. He implied that to incorporate a bank was not only to abuse the Constitution but also to abuse the people's right to give consent to the form of government under which they are to live. An enumerated power of incorporation was omitted from the Constitution, he suggested, precisely because the framers feared that a government with such a power might not win the consent of the people. Would it not be dishonest, as well as inconsistent with the people's right to choose their own institutions, to claim now as implied a power that they would have rejected had it been made explicit? Jefferson thus glanced at here what would later become a major part of his critique of Hamilton's approach to constitutional interpretation: that it amounted to a breach of constitutional faith, a deliberate effort to interpret the Constitution into what Hamilton had wanted it to be, but what the people would never have agreed to.[15]

The Bank and the Necessary and Proper Clause

Jefferson turned next to the Necessary and Proper Clause, the second of the Constitution's "general phrases" under which one might seek authority for Hamilton's bank. According to Jefferson, this clause authorizes Congress to "'make all laws necessary and proper for carrying into execution the enumerated powers.'"[16] These powers, however, "can all be carried into execution without a bank." Accordingly, a bank "is not *necessary*" within the meaning of this provision and "consequently" is "not authorized by this phrase."[17] As is well known, Jefferson's argument here turns upon a restrictive – or, as he might say, a properly precise – interpretation of the word "necessary" as it is used in the clause. Hamilton, he suggested, had "urged that a bank will give great facility or convenience in the collection of taxes." Even if this were true, it would not, for Jefferson, authorize the bank, because "the Constitution allows only the means which are 'necessary,' not those which are merely 'convenient' for effecting the enumerated powers."[18] Again, Jefferson feared that a more expansive interpretation would effectively result in unlimited government, for

---

[15] As Peter Onuf observes, in Jefferson's clashes with Hamilton, the former's concern was focused on "the principles of the new regime as they were understood by the 'people' who, through the process of ratification and amendment, had given it life." *Jefferson's Empire: The Language of American Nationhood* (Charlottesville: University Press of Virginia, 2000), 87.

[16] Jefferson's *Opinion* actually misquotes the Necessary and Proper Clause, which authorizes Congress to make "all Laws which shall be necessary and proper for carrying into Execution the foregoing Powers, and all other Powers vested by this Constitution in the Government of the United States, or in any Department or Officer thereof."

[17] Jefferson, *Writings*, 418 (Jefferson's emphases).

[18] Jefferson, *Writings*, 419.

there is no power "which ingenuity may not torture into a *convenience* in some instance *or other,* to *some one* of so long a list of enumerated powers." The result of such lax interpretation would be, again, to "swallow up all the delegated powers, and reduce the whole to one power, as before observed" – that is, to give the federal government a general power to do whatever it thinks is for the good of the Union. Precisely to foreclose such a possibility the Constitution limits Congress to "the necessary means," or "those means without which the grant of power would be nugatory."[19] On Jefferson's view, then, the Necessary and Proper Clause only authorizes implied powers without which the enumerated powers would fail of execution.[20]

Jefferson then proceeded to a more particular examination of Hamilton's account of the usefulness of a national bank, with a view to showing that such usefulness did not amount to the necessity that alone could justify the creation of such an institution. Hamilton had advocated the bank on the grounds that its paper circulation would prevent the "transportation and retransportation of money between the states and the treasury."[21] The bank might therefore afford a certain convenience to the government, Jefferson conceded, but that convenience could not be considered the same thing as the necessary expedient that the Necessary Proper Clause seems to envisage. After all, Jefferson noted, "treasury orders" and "bills of exchange" could be used to the same purpose, and they would not require the creation of a bank. Bank bills might be more convenient, but "a little *difference* in the degree of *convenience,* cannot constitute the necessity which the constitution makes the ground for assuming any non-enumerated power." Besides, Jefferson added, even if bank bills could be considered necessary to these operations, a national bank would not thereby be necessary because there were already banks in existence that could provide the service. This fact was sufficient "to prevent the existence of that necessity which may justify the assumption of a non-enumerated power as a means for carrying into execution an enumerated one. The thing may be done, and has been done, and well done, without this assumption; therefore it does not stand on that degree of *necessity* which can honestly justify it."[22]

Jefferson's Constitutional Assumptions in the Bank Opinion

Jefferson concluded his opinion by calling upon Washington to veto the bank bill. "The negative of the president," he contended, "is the shield provided by the constitution to protect" the executive, the judiciary, and the states against the "invasions" of the Congress. The "present" case involved a "right" – that

---

[19] Jefferson, *Writings,* 419.
[20] Although Jefferson's approach to the implied powers is undeniably very strict, Michael Federici goes too far in speaking of "Jefferson's rejection of implied powers." *The Political Philosophy of Alexander Hamilton* (Baltimore: The Johns Hopkins University Press, 2012), 217.
[21] Jefferson, *Writings,* 419.
[22] Jefferson, *Writings,* 419–20 (Jefferson's emphases).

of incorporating a bank – "remaining exclusively with the States" and accordingly was "one of those intended by the Constitution" to be placed under the protection of the president's power to veto legislation. Nevertheless, Jefferson also added that the president should only veto the bill if his mind was "tolerably clear" that it was unconstitutional. If instead "the pro and the con" seemed even, then "a just respect for the wisdom of the legislature would naturally decide the balance in favor of their opinion." Jefferson based this rule on the view that the Constitution vested the veto in the president's hands "chiefly for cases" in which the legislature is "clearly misled by error, ambition, or interest."[23]

Jefferson's presentation of the veto power highlights his tendency to bring assumptions to constitutional interpretation that are not required by the text of the Constitution itself. This tendency had first shown itself in the *Opinion* in his assertion that "the foundation of the Constitution" is "laid on this ground: That 'all powers not delegated to the United States, by the Constitution, nor prohibited by it to the States, are reserved to the States or to the people.'"[24] Here Jefferson quoted the language of what would become the Tenth Amendment to the Constitution. It is a little striking that he presented as the "ground" of the Constitution a provision that had not yet been ratified and was therefore not yet part of the Constitution. Nevertheless, Jefferson probably assumed – correctly, as we know in hindsight – that the amendment would end up being ratified. Apart from the timeline, we might wonder why the "foundation" of the Constitution would be located in an amendment rather than in its original body. However, it is possible that the deepest principle informing a document could be omitted in the original draft and only added later.

It is harder to justify, however, Jefferson's mere assertion that the ground or foundation of the Constitution is found in the Tenth Amendment as opposed to some other provision. Jefferson offered no argument in support of this claim, and there seems something unjustifiably arbitrary in it. For his part, Hamilton might have been tempted to posit that the "ground" of the Constitution is laid in the Supremacy Clause, which provides that the "Constitution, and the Laws of the United States which shall be made in Pursuance thereof . . . shall be the supreme Law of the Land," and to allow this assumption to color his interpretation of every provision. But such an assumption would be no more justifiable than the Jeffersonian one to which it would be opposed. Again, Jefferson adopted this assumption because it supported his concern with a strictly limited federal government. While Jefferson was entitled to this view as a policy preference, there is nothing in the Constitution on which to peg the claim that it considers limitations on power as more fundamental than the powers themselves or their purposes. Nor could Jefferson have plausibly sustained such an assumption by appealing to the history of the debate over ratification, for that debate was equally characterized by both a concern with

---

[23] Jefferson, *Writings*, 420–21.
[24] Jefferson, *Writings*, 416.

securing the power of the federal government and a concern with limiting that power.

Jefferson's account of the veto power also shows an inclination to impose a theory on the Constitution that is not derivable from its actual text. Where his treatment of the Tenth Amendment seems informed by a desire to limit the power of the federal government in relation to the states, his treatment of the veto power seems to be animated by a desire to limit the power of the president in relation to Congress. In any case, Jefferson suggested limits on the use of the veto power that are not required by the Constitution itself.

In the first place, Jefferson posited a limit on the *reasons* for which the veto power could properly be exercised by the president. Jefferson would limit the just use of the veto to acts involving violations of the Constitution, and in fact to a particular subset of constitutional infractions, ones involving congressional intrusion on the powers of other parts of the government. He held that the constitutional purpose of the veto is to protect against the federal legislature's "invasions" of the rights of the executive, of the judiciary, or of the states and state legislatures – thus omitting the idea that the veto might be exercised to prevent other kinds of constitutional violations, such as intrusions on guaranteed individual rights. He also narrowed the scope of the veto power by insisting that its use be limited to constitutional questions, without, apparently, extending to questions of policy, prudence, and justice. In other words, a president might desire to veto a law not because it violates the Constitution but simply because he regards it as bad or ill advised. Jefferson's remarks here, however, suggest that such uses would somehow be contrary to the purpose for which the veto exists. Again, however, these limits are not required by the text of the Constitution – which simply vests the power in the president with no reference to the suitable reasons for which it could be exercised – but are read into the Constitution by Jefferson.

Jefferson's understanding of the veto power clashed with Hamilton's, and perhaps in a way that made Jefferson vulnerable to a charge he leveled against Hamilton. Hamilton's account of the veto in *Federalist* 73 suggested a wider application of the power than Jefferson had admitted in his *Opinion*. Hamilton had begun by noting what Jefferson would later note: the importance of the veto in stopping the legislature from intruding on the powers of other parts of the government. Hamilton had particularly emphasized the veto's usefulness in protecting the power of the presidency from legislative usurpation. He then added, however, that the veto

has a further use. It not only serves as a shield to the executive, but it furnishes an additional security against the enaction of improper laws. It establishes a salutary check upon the legislative body calculated to guard the community against the effects of faction, precipitancy, or of any impulse unfriendly to the public good, which may happen to influence a majority of that body.[25]

---

[25] Hamilton, Madison, and Jay, *The Federalist*, 494–95.

In sum, Jefferson held that the veto was to be used only to protect against violations of the Constitution, and perhaps even only some subset of constitutional violations, while Hamilton held that the president could also wield it against legislation that he judged to be constitutional but otherwise ill advised. *The Federalist*, however, had made one of the most prominent contributions to the public's understanding of the Constitution while its ratification was being debated. Jefferson's narrowing interpretation of the veto power, therefore, tended to contradict the understanding on which the public had ratified the Constitution. It therefore skirted the kind of constitutional bad faith that he had implicitly attributed to Hamilton in his *Opinion* and that he and Madison would so vehemently attribute to Hamilton in subsequent constitutional disputes.

In the second place, Jefferson sought to impose a particular understanding of the *standards* by which the president should decide whether to exercise the veto, an understanding that is deferential to Congress. The president, Jefferson contended, should not veto a law unless he is "tolerably" sure that it intrudes on the powers of the other parts of the government. If the matter seems questionable, he should defer to Congress's judgment, because the veto primarily exists for cases in which Congress is "clearly misled by error, ambition, or interest."[26] Once more, Jefferson imposed a view of how the power is to be used that is not required by the text of the Constitution itself. One could argue that legislation even of questionable constitutionality should be vetoed on the grounds that it is best not to even risk transcending the constitutional limits on government power. Or, a certain kind of president might want to veto any law that is not clearly necessary on the assumption that government should not act unless there is a compelling case to do so. Nothing in the Constitution in fact forbids such an approach to the veto power, Jefferson's strictures to the contrary notwithstanding.

Conclusion

Jefferson's *Opinion on the Constitutionality of a National Bank* raised the controversy between Washington's two great cabinet ministers to a new plane. Jefferson found Hamilton's assumption and funding plan to be politically objectionable, but he had not challenged its constitutionality. Jefferson's opinion on the bank, however, not only denounced the bank as unconstitutional but suggested that the arguments in defense of its constitutionality tended to undermine constitutional government by effectively erasing the limits the Constitution imposed on the powers of the national government.

Faced with Jefferson's arguments, President Washington seems to have seriously considered vetoing the bank bill. He prepared for such an action by

---

[26] Jefferson, *Writings*, 421.

asking Madison to draft a veto message for him.[27] Washington also resolved, however, not to take this step without first consulting the bank's architect, the secretary of the treasury, about the constitutional questions that had been raised. The result was the exhaustive argument of Hamilton's massive *Opinion on the Constitutionality of a National Bank*, which he completed in one week, working through the last night in order to deliver the paper to the president in time for him to cast the veto if he chose to do so.[28]

This reply tended rather to heighten than to quell the controversy. Hamilton's argument was not only a defense but also a counter-attack: he tried not only to show the constitutionality of the bill incorporating the bank but also to demonstrate that the arguments that had been deployed against it were both erroneous and dangerous. Where Jefferson saw Hamilton's constitutional principles as a threat to limited government, Hamilton saw Jefferson's as a threat to energetic government. Where Jefferson thought that Hamilton's principles rendered the limits on federal power practically meaningless, Hamilton thought that Jefferson's principles rendered the powers themselves ineffective. They viewed their clash over the bank not merely as a dispute about policy but as a crucial debate over regime principles. We turn now to Hamilton's side of the argument.

[27] Wood, *Empire of Liberty*, 144.
[28] Chernow, *Alexander Hamilton*, 353.

6

Defending Energetic Government

Hamilton on the Constitutionality of the National Bank

For Hamilton, as for Jefferson, great matters were at stake in the dispute over the national bank. At issue for both men was not only the bank itself but the very nature of American constitutionalism and the possibility of good government. As we have seen, Jefferson feared that the arguments by which the bank could be justified would open the door to unlimited federal power. Hamilton saw an equally grave, if opposite, danger in Jefferson's arguments. As he began his *Opinion on the Constitutionality of a National Bank*, Hamilton noted that the "solicitude" he felt in defending the bank arose not only from his role as the originator of the measure, or from his conviction that the bank was essential to the "successful administration of the Treasury," but also and chiefly from his "firm persuasion" that "principles of construction like those espoused" by its opponents "would be fatal to the just and indispensable authority of the United States."[1] Accordingly, Hamilton devoted the majority of his argument not to a direct defense of the bank's constitutionality, to which he turned only near the end of the *Opinion*, but to an extended critique of Jefferson's principles of constitutional interpretation.

Hamilton's Appeal to General Principles

Jefferson's objections to the bank, Hamilton observed, rested on a "general denial of the authority of the United States to erect corporations."[2] Hamilton began his response with an appeal to what he regarded as a "great and fundamental rule" of politics.[3] It is, he said, a *"general principle"* that is *"inherent* in the very *definition of Government"* that

[1] Hamilton, *Writings*, 613.
[2] Hamilton, *Writings*, 613.
[3] Hamilton, *Writings*, 615.

every power vested in a government is in its nature *sovereign*, and includes by the *force* of the *term*, a right to employ all the *means* requisite, and fairly *applicable* to the *ends* of such power; and which are not precluded by restrictions and exceptions specified in the constitution; or not immoral, or not contrary to the essential ends of political society.[4]

This principle, Hamilton contended, is necessary to sound political theory and practice. In the realm of theory, it is an "axiom" that "would be admitted" in its "application to government in general." In the realm of practice, it is "in the general system of things . . . essential to the preservation of social order."[5]

Accordingly, Hamilton continued, the burden of proof must fall upon those who would deny that these fundamental precepts are applicable to the government of the United States. It is "incumbent" upon *them* to "prove" some "distinction" whereby what is true of and good for political societies in general is not so for America. In light of Jefferson's emphasis on the authority of the state governments, we might expect him to seek such a distinction in the principle of federalism, or in the division of power between the states and the federal government. Hamilton anticipated such an argument, insisting by way of response that federalism in no way mitigates the sovereignty of the federal government, properly understood. It is true that "the powers of sovereignty are in this country divided between national and state governments." From this, however, it only follows that that each "has sovereign power as to *certain things*, and not to *other things*." It does not deny the sovereignty of the "portions of powers" delegated to each of the levels of government in relation to the "*proper objects*" of those powers. Indeed, Hamilton continued, unacceptable and ultimately absurd consequences would follow from holding that sovereignty cannot be present where power is divided or limited. "To deny that the Government of the United States has sovereign power as to its declared

---

[4] Hamilton, *Writings*, 613 (Hamilton's emphases). This passage also further illustrates Hamilton's departures from Hobbes. As Karl-Friedrich Walling notes, while "many scholars have suggested that Hamilton accepted a Hobbesian understanding of sovereignty as simply unlimited, this passage reminds us of the important Lockean distinction between arbitrary and absolute power." *Republican Empire: Alexander Hamilton on War and Free Government* (Lawrence: University Press of Kansas, 1999), 163.

[5] Hamilton, *Writings*, 614. On the basis of this passage, Michael W. McConnell suggests that Hamilton argued for the bank "from general propositions about the nature of a federal union, rather than from specific powers enumerated in Section 8 of Article I." As we will see, however, while Hamilton opens with such general arguments, he does move later in the *Opinion* to a defense of the bank on the basis of specifically enumerated powers in Article I, Section 8. Indeed, the need to move on to such an argument is already implicit in his opening appeal to general principles. Hamilton indicates that every power vested in a government is sovereign. Although this principle establishes that any government will have a power to incorporate in relation to the powers with which it is vested, it does not establish a power to incorporate *a bank*, which depends on what powers specifically have been vested. And the answer to that question depends in turn on an examination of the Constitutional enumeration of powers. For this reason, I think McConnell goes too far in characterizing Hamilton's "approach to constitutional interpretation" as "loose and nontextual." It may be loose, but it is not nontextual. See "What Would Hamilton Do?" *Harvard Journal of Law and Public Policy* 35 (2012): 266–68.

purposes and trusts, because its power does not extend to all cases, would be equally to deny, that the state governments have sovereign power in any case; because their power does not extend to every case." After all, the Constitution imposes limits not only on the federal government but also on the states; for Article I, Section 10 "exhibits a long list of very important things" that the states "may not do." If opponents of the bank were inclined to deny the sovereignty of the federal government, they would also have to deny the sovereignty of the states. Such a denial, however, resulted in an unacceptable absurdity. If division of power excludes sovereignty, then the United States would exhibit "the singular spectacle of a political society without sovereignty, or of a people governed without government."[6]

From these general principles, Hamilton drew the conclusion that the federal government, contrary to Jefferson's claims, must have the power to incorporate – to "give a legal or artificial capacity to one or more persons, distinct from the natural." If all government powers are by definition sovereign, then the powers of the government of the United States must be sovereign. But if sovereignty necessarily entails the authority to employ all the means related to the ends of power, then it must also entail a power to create corporations, which are one of those means. It is, Hamilton claimed, "unquestionably incident to *sovereign power* to erect corporations." He could with confidence posit such a claim as unquestionable because, again, to deny it would be contrary to the aim of his opponents, which was not only to restrain the powers of the federal government but also to defend the powers of the states. Neither Jefferson nor the other critics of the bank would have ventured to deny that states possess a sovereign power to erect corporations.

Hamilton's opening appeal to basic principles – to the definitions of terms like "government" and "sovereignty" – might seem to open him to the criticism that he, like Jefferson in his own *Opinion*, conditioned his interpretation of the Constitution on ideas that are external to the Constitution, that he was imposing a theory of his own on the Constitution. The Constitution, after all, does not use the terms "sovereign" or "sovereignty." Hamilton perhaps sought to avoid such criticism, however, by appealing to the Supremacy Clause, which holds that the "constitution and laws of the United States made in pursuance of it" shall be "the supreme law of the land."[7] Such supremacy, Hamilton believed, implies sovereignty. If the power of the federal government can "create a Supreme law of the land" then it is "doubtless sovereign" in such a case.[8]

Although Hamilton insisted on the sovereignty of the federal government, he did not – despite the fears raised by Jefferson in his own *Opinion* – understand this sovereignty as unlimited political power. His argument, on the contrary, indicated that the power of the government is limited by both constitutional

[6] Hamilton, *Writings*, 614.
[7] See Article VI of the Constitution.
[8] Hamilton, *Writings*, 614.

and moral or philosophic principles. In the first place, his very argument that the federal government is sovereign with respect to the objects entrusted to it indicates an important limit on the federal government: its power is limited by the delegation of authority to it through the Constitution. As Hamilton said more than once, the federal government is sovereign *only in relation to its proper objects*. This does not mean that the federal government is limited only to those powers explicitly mentioned in the Constitution, as Hamilton implied here and makes clear later. It also has a right to exercise other powers that are to be understood as means to the ends of the major powers granted. Nevertheless, even here he conceded a principle of limitation: the means chosen must be both "requisite" and "fairly applicable" to the ends of the powers delegated.[9] In the second place, Hamilton also noted that the sovereignty of the federal government is limited by the "restrictions and exceptions" that are "specified in the constitution."[10] Expedients can be devised that are in truth fairly applicable to the ends of the delegated powers but that are nevertheless forbidden because expressly prohibited by the Constitution – say, in the list of denied powers of Article I, Section 9, or in the Bill of Rights, which was soon to be ratified. Third, Hamilton held that government is limited not only by the positive law of the Constitution but also by moral and philosophic principles that are apparently antecedent to the existence of government itself, hence his remark that sovereignty entails the right to all means to the ends of powers, except for those that are "immoral" or "contrary to the essential ends of political society."[11] Jefferson may have sincerely feared that Hamilton's principles led to a federal government of unlimited powers, but Hamilton clearly did not intend such an outcome, if he is to be taken at his word.

In light of the general principles he laid down, Hamilton claimed rather peremptorily to have won the debate. The "constitutionality" of the bank bill, he suggested, "might be permitted to rest" on the argument that it is indisputably incident to sovereignty to erect corporations, and that the United States is sovereign with regard to certain objects of government. This "principle," after all, had "been untouched" by the bank's critics. Nevertheless, seeking a "more complete elucidation of the point," Hamilton proceeded to a detailed examination of the specific arguments by which Jefferson had denied the power of the federal government to create corporations.[12]

Hamilton on Implied Powers

Hamilton's discussion of these more "particular" arguments began with Jefferson's claim that the "foundation" of the Constitution is laid on the Tenth

---

[9] Hamilton, *Writings*, 613.
[10] Hamilton, *Writings*, 613.
[11] Hamilton, *Writings*, 613.
[12] Hamilton, *Writings*, 614–15.

Amendment principle that "all powers not delegated to the United States by the Constitution, nor prohibited by it to the States, are reserved to the States or to the people." Jefferson, he said, implied by this claim that Congress "can in no case exercise any power not included in those enumerated in the constitution," which would certainly rule out the creation of corporations, since no such power is expressly listed. Hamilton conceded the validity of Jefferson's general principle, if not the conclusion Jefferson hoped would be inferred from it. The principle, Hamilton admitted, follows from the "republican maxim" that "all government is a delegation of power," and to that extent it "is not to be questioned." Nevertheless, it must be understood in its "true signification." Hamilton did not deny that all government power must be understood as delegated from the people, and he therefore would not contend for the existence of an undelegated power to create corporations. The real question, he held, is the *extent* of the delegation. How much power "is delegated in each case" cannot be determined by a simple appeal to the principle of delegation but is instead "a question of fact to be made out by fair reasoning and construction upon the particular provisions of the constitution – taking as guides the general principles and general ends of government."[13]

The mode of inquiry here embraced by Hamilton necessarily presupposes the validity of implied constitutional powers. No amount of "fair reasoning and construction upon the particular provisions of the constitution" could demonstrate the legitimacy of a federal corporation if all genuine powers must be found explicitly in the constitutional enumeration. Accordingly, the next step in Hamilton's argument asserted that the Constitution is properly understood to include both implied and express powers. He presented this proposition as uncontroversial, suggesting that even Jefferson's *Opinion* conceded "that implied powers are to be considered as delegated equally with express ones." If this is the case, then the absence of an authority to incorporate among the enumerated powers is not fatal to the constitutional pretensions of a federally chartered corporation, which might reasonably be presented as the work of an implied power. Thus, Hamilton argued that "a power of erecting a corporation may as well be *implied* as any other thing," that it "may as well be employed as an instrument or mean of carrying into execution any of the specified powers, as any other instrument or mean whatever."[14]

As Hamilton's language here suggests, for him implied constitutional powers are to be understood as means to other ends, ends established by the enumerated powers. The error of Jefferson and other opponents of the bank was to miss the merely incidental and subordinate character of the power to incorporate. Their overactive "imagination" had given rise to the "strange fallacy" that an incorporation is "some great, independent, substantive thing," that it is a "political end of peculiar magnitude and moment," whereas "it is truly to be

[13] Hamilton, *Writings*, 615.
[14] Hamilton, *Writings*, 616 (Hamilton's emphasis).

considered" as a tool or instrument used with a view to some genuine end. Governments do not erect corporations for their own sake but for the sake of executing some activity that the government supposes is within its authority, in relation to which the corporation is a mere means to an end.[15]

This line of argument offers some response to Jefferson's fear that acknowledging a power to incorporate would, in principle at least, open the door to unlimited government power because, in Hamilton's view, if a corporation is really only a means to some other end, then the real constitutional question is whether the end in view is actually authorized by the Constitution. His understanding that implied powers are means to the execution of ends entrusted to the government provides a principle of limitation of implied powers: they are to be judged by whether they are in truth related to the ends for which they are invoked. "The only question must be, in this as in every other case, whether the mean to be employed, or in this instance the corporation to be erected, has a natural relation to any of the acknowledged objects or lawful ends of government." Accordingly, Hamilton argued, Congress could not erect a corporation to administer the government of the city of Philadelphia, because Congress is not authorized to regulate that city's government. It could, however, erect a corporation "in relation to the collection of taxes, or to the trade with foreign countries, or to the trade between the states, or with the Indian tribes, because it is the province of the federal government to regulate those objects," and because "it is incident to a general sovereign or legislative power to regulate a thing, to employ all the means which relate to its regulation to the best and greatest advantage."[16]

Although these considerations might have been intended to allay Jefferson's concerns about unlimited government, Hamilton also at this point put forward other reflections that might tend to inflame such concerns. First, seeking to demonstrate further that the "power of incorporation has been exaggerated," Hamilton traced it to its origins. While the idea was ultimately rooted in Roman law, the American understanding was "borrowed" more "immediately" from England, where the power of incorporation "form[ed] part of the executive authority," which had often been delegated to others. In view of these apparently familiar and innocent origins, Hamilton asked where anyone could find the ground to suppose that the power of incorporation "lies beyond the reach of all those very important portions of sovereign power, legislative as well as executive, which belong to the government of the United States."[17] Whatever Hamilton's intentions, this reasoning was perhaps not the sort that would in fact tend to reassure Jefferson. It instead points to an important difference between their understandings of government. As we have seen and will see again, Hamilton believed that the ordinary powers of long-established

[15] Hamilton, *Writings*, 616–17.
[16] Hamilton, *Writings*, 616.
[17] Hamilton, *Writings*, 617.

governments should as a matter of course be understood to belong also to the government of the United States and was particularly inclined to borrow ideas from the British system. These inclinations, however, may have increased Jefferson's suspicions that Hamilton was a closet monarchist, suspicions that became almost certainties in Jefferson's mind as he observed the progress of the Hamiltonian program.

Second, Hamilton also referred in passing to yet another reservoir of federal power that he thought was not necessary to justify the bank but the existence of which he nonetheless wanted to establish "for the sake of accuracy." In addition to the enumerated and implied powers, he contended, "there is another class of powers" which can be called "resulting powers." Such powers are, like the implied powers, unwritten. They do not, however, arise as implied means to ends that are enumerated. Instead, they "result" from the entirety of the government's authority and from the country's status as a political community. Hamilton sought to clarify his meaning with an example. "It will not be doubted that if the United States should make a conquest of any of the territories of its neighbors, they would possess sovereign jurisdiction over the conquered territory." This power, he continued, would result *not* as a "consequence of the powers specially enumerated" but instead "from the whole mass of powers of the government and from the nature of political society." Moreover, such resulting powers would undoubtedly include the authority to erect corporations. The "jurisdiction" the United States would acquire over new territories "would certainly be competent to every species of legislation," and accordingly the government could, if it chose, erect a corporation to govern its newly added possessions.[18]

Hamilton on the Necessary and Proper Clause

Hamilton turned next to Jefferson's interpretation of the Necessary and Proper Clause. On its face, this portion of the Constitution was favorable to Hamilton's cause. After all, as he noted, it "gives explicit sanction to the doctrine of implied powers." Indeed, Hamilton went so far as to contend that the Necessary and Proper Clause, no less than the aforementioned Supremacy Clause, affirms the "sovereign and plenary authority" of the United States "as to its specified powers and objects," and that this authority is "in some cases paramount to that of the states" and in other cases "coordinate with it." Such sovereignty, he held, is the "plain import" of the "declaration" that Congress "may pass all laws necessary and proper to carry into execution" its specified powers.[19] Nevertheless, as Hamilton conceded, Jefferson himself did not deny the existence of implied powers. The issue between them then concerned the scope of the implied powers, or the proper interpretation of the Necessary and Proper

---

[18] Hamilton, *Writings*, 616.
[19] Hamilton, *Writings*, 620.

Clause. Jefferson, as we have seen and as Hamilton reiterated here, insisted on a narrow reading of the clause. For Jefferson, it authorized only those implied powers "without which" the enumerated grant of power to which it is related "would be nugatory," or without which the enumerated power would fail of execution or come to nothing.[20]

Hamilton put forward a number of arguments against Jefferson's account of the Necessary and Proper Clause. He objected not only to Jefferson's conclusions but even to his mode of interpretation, which, Hamilton believed, tended to confuse questions of expediency with questions of constitutionality. The unacceptable consequence of this approach would be to make the constitutionality of the measures of the government – and thus the meaning of the Constitution itself – depend on particular and variable circumstances. Hamilton first raised this concern in relation to Jefferson's argument based on the existence of state banks. Jefferson had pointed to the presence of such institutions as evidence that, even if banks were necessary to the aims Hamilton had set out, a national bank would not be, since the government could use the services of the established state banks. Not being strictly necessary, the national bank would therefore be unconstitutional. Hamilton called this argument "fallacious" and in fact "demonstrative" that there "is a radical source of error" in the secretary of state's "reasoning." The fallacy, he suggested, is to make necessity, and therefore the constitutionality of the measures of the government, to "depend on casual and temporary circumstances" – in the present instance, on the "accidental existence of certain state banks" which "happen to exist today" and, for all that the government of the United States can know, "may disappear tomorrow." Such variable circumstances reasonably influence our judgments about the "expediency of exercising a particular power at a particular time." They should not, however, influence our judgments of what is constitutional. The "constitutional right of exercising" a power "must be uniform and invariable – the same today as tomorrow."[21]

Hamilton also observed that Jefferson interpreted the term "necessary" as if "the word *absolutely* or *indispensably* had been prefixed to it."[22] That understanding leads to a problem similar to the one just noted. Hamilton, as we will see, understood "necessary" more loosely, as meaning only a means that is reasonably adapted to the end in view, or something that makes possible the realization of that end. In Hamilton's understanding, whether a measure is within the Constitution's meaning of "necessary" depends only on a relatively simple inquiry into whether it genuinely serves the enumerated power in relation to which it is being employed. "The relation between the measure and the end, between the nature of the mean employed toward the execution of a power and the object of that power, must be the criterion of constitutionality."

[20] Hamilton, *Writings*, 617.
[21] Hamilton, *Writings*, 617.
[22] Hamilton, *Writings*, 618 (Hamilton's emphases).

In contrast, Jefferson's definition would have us inquire into *just how necessary* the expedient is. Is it merely useful, in which case it is unconstitutional; or is it genuinely such that the enumerated power would be "nugatory" without it? Hamilton found such an inquiry unacceptable. "The degree in which a measure is necessary," he contended, "can never be a test of the legal right to adopt it"; for the question of degree, or of the "more or less of necessity or utility," is unavoidably a "matter of opinion" and therefore "can only be a test of expediency."[23]

Hamilton argued next that Jefferson's restrictive interpretation of the clause depends on a forced and unpersuasive reading of a key term. "Necessary" does not in fact mean absolutely or indispensably necessary, as Jefferson contended. Neither the "grammatical" nor the "popular" meaning of that term requires the strict necessity on which Jefferson insisted. According to Hamilton, in both ordinary speech and in proper usage, when we say that "it is necessary for a government or a person" to do something, we mean no more than that "the interests of the government or person require, or will be promoted," by doing the thing in question. In preferring to be guided by the ordinary meaning of the term at issue, Hamilton does not appear to have devised a principle of interpretation only for the case at hand, or even only for the purposes of constitutional interpretation. He was instead applying a principle that he had already acknowledged and acted upon in the realm of statutory interpretation. Shortly after assuming office as secretary of the treasury in late 1789, Hamilton, replying to a query about the meaning of a provision in the customs laws, instructed the collectors of customs that the "most obvious or popular sense of the words of a law" is "always of great force in their construction," admonishing them against an interpretation that would "have the aspect of too much refinement."[24]

This popular and broad sense, Hamilton continued, is the "true one" in which the term "necessary" is "used in the Constitution." The "whole turn" of the Necessary and Proper Clause "indicates" that the Convention intended it to "give a liberal latitude to the exercise of the specified powers." The clause authorizes Congress to make "*all laws*" that are "necessary and proper for *carrying into execution* the foregoing powers" as well as "*all other powers* vested by the constitution in the *government* of the United States, or in any *department* or *officer* thereof." For Hamilton, the "peculiar comprehensiveness" of these "expressions" clearly indicates that the intention of the clause is expansive rather than restrictive, and accordingly that in its context "necessary" should be understood in the "obvious and popular" broad sense rather than the narrow sense that Jefferson tried to impose.[25]

---

[23] Hamilton, *Writings*, 619.
[24] *PAH*, 5: 578.
[25] Hamilton, *Writings*, 618 (Hamilton's emphases).

The unsoundness of Jefferson's restrictive interpretation was further indicated, Hamilton argued, by its novelty. Such a conception had "never before"
been "entertained" and was in fact inconsistent with the previously established
practice of the government. As an example he pointed to the "act concerning light houses, beacons, buoys and public piers." That act could only be
"referred" to Congress's enumerated power of "regulating trade," according
to Hamilton, and was in fact "fairly relative to it." It was therefore constitutional according to Hamilton's standards. Yet the act was certainly not "strictly
necessary," as Jefferson's interpretation demanded. No one could contend that
the Commerce power would be "nugatory" without the Congressional provision of such facilities.[26] Hamilton suggested by this example that Jefferson's
was not the theory on which the government had in fact operated up to the
time the bank became controversial and its opponents sought a constitutional
argument against it.

Finally, Hamilton contended that unacceptable consequences would follow
from Jefferson's interpretation. He revealed these consequences first in relation to the very powers that Jefferson sought to preserve: those of the states.
Although the various state constitutions may or may not have had a "necessary and proper" clause, Hamilton nevertheless contended that the principle
enunciated in that federal provision in fact applies to all governments. "It may
truly be said" not only of the government of the "United States" but of "every
government" that "it only has a right to pass such laws as are necessary and
proper to accomplish the objects entrusted to it." After all, "no government
has a right to do merely what it pleases." The question in relation to every
government, then, is how broadly or narrowly to interpret this power to do
what is necessary and proper. Hamilton observed that by Jefferson's interpretation of this principle one might show that none of the *state* governments has
the authority to "incorporate a bank." Just as Jefferson had tried to show that
the business of the federal government might be carried on without a national
bank, so one could equally contend that "all the public business of" a state
"could be performed without a bank" and thus infer that state banks would
be unnecessary and hence illegitimate. Similarly, one could contend, using Jefferson's principles, that no state has "power to incorporate the inhabitants of
a town" with a view to more effective administration, since such an incorporation is not strictly necessary, "though it is better" to have it. Hamilton observed
in this context that "there is no *express* power in any state constitution to erect
corporations."[27]

We might observe here that Hamilton's concluding observation also supports his earlier argument that the power to create corporations is in its nature
not a primary, substantial power but rather a means to other ends. Jefferson
had referred to the power of incorporation as remaining "exclusively with the

[26] Hamilton, *Writings*, 619.
[27] Hamilton, *Writings*, 618.

states."[28] Nevertheless, the power was not mentioned explicitly in their fundamental law. It would seem to follow that such a power is merely an incidental one. But if it is so for the states, then why, Hamilton would surely ask, can it not be so for the federal government as well? Of course the federal government may not pursue the same ends as the states, but why would we conclude that it may not use the same means as the states in pursuing the ends entrusted to it?

According to Hamilton, Jefferson's interpretation of the Necessary and Proper Clause also carried unacceptable consequences for the authority of the federal government. Jefferson's restrictive "construction," Hamilton contended, "would beget endless uncertainty and embarrassment" for the government of the Union. Only in a small number of "palpable and extreme" cases, Hamilton suggested, could one affirm, as Jefferson demanded, that "a measure was absolutely necessary, or one without which the exercise of a given power would be nugatory. There are few measures of any government which would stand so severe a test." To "insist upon" such a standard, he concluded, "would be to make" a "case of extreme necessity" the "criterion of the exercise of any implied power." Yet the need to meet extreme necessities is not to be understood as a rule for the "ordinary exercise" of "constitutional authority" but as a rule for "overleaping" the "bounds" of such authority.[29]

The concerns expressed here are consistent with those that, as we have seen, guided Hamilton's thinking about his treasury program in the *Report on Public Credit* and the *Report on a National Bank*. Again, on Hamilton's view, the Constitution was intended to remedy the embarrassments and incapacity of the federal government under the Articles of Confederation. Energetic government requires not merely a Constitution with adequate powers but also an adequate exercise of those powers, hence the need for a sufficient provision for the public credit and a national bank, both of which facilitate the government's ability to secure the resources it needs to govern effectively. This also, as we see here, presents the need to refute the Jeffersonian theory of implied powers, which is incompatible with energetic government. A government that must justify its exercise of implied powers on the basis of absolute necessity cannot be expected to act with energy, and it can therefore be expected to encounter all manner of "embarrassments" – which the Constitution was ratified in order to avoid. Indeed, Hamilton evidently doubted that a government subjected to such restrictions could be said to govern at all, or to be secure in its existence. Thus he went so far as to claim that it is "essential to the *being* of the national government" that "so erroneous a conception of the meaning of the necessary should be exploded."[30]

Hamilton concluded this portion of his argument by explaining the "sound maxim of construction" that he would oppose to Jefferson's "restrictive

---

[28] Jefferson, *Writings*, 420–21.
[29] Hamilton, *Writings*, 618.
[30] Hamilton, *Writings*, 618 (my emphasis).

interpretation of the word *necessary*."[31] This maxim requires "that the powers contained in a government, especially those which concern the general administration of the affairs of a country" – such as its "finances, trade," and "defense" – should be "construed liberally, in advancement of the public good." This, Hamilton suggested, is a general rule of good government. It does "not depend on the particular form of a government or on the particular demarcation of the boundaries of its powers" but instead simply "on the nature and objects of government itself." The rule rests on the common experience of governments in meeting their obligations: "The means by which national exigencies are to be provided for, national inconveniences obviated, national prosperity promoted, are of such infinite variety, extent, and complexity, that there must, of necessity, be great latitude of discretion in the selection and application of those means."[32] Government's task is to meet these challenges most effectively. Since an effective response depends on constantly changing circumstances, we cannot know in advance which means will be most effective and accordingly should not insist on strict limits to government power.

Liberal Construction and Limited Government

As we have seen, Jefferson rejected Hamilton's permissive approach to the Necessary and Proper Clause because he feared it would open up a boundless field of power for the federal government and thus allow it to intrude itself into the realm properly reserved to the states. Hamilton offered a twofold response to this concern. In the first place, he denied that such a concern, even if true, would demonstrate the impropriety of his interpretation of the Necessary and Proper Clause. "It is," he contended, "no valid objection" to a liberal construction of federal power "to say that it is calculated to extend the powers of the general government throughout the entire sphere of state legislation." The same thing could be said about any recurrence to implied powers because the "moment the literal meaning" of the Constitution "is departed from, there is a chance of error and abuse." Nevertheless, "an adherence" only to the "letter" of the powers granted "would at once arrest the motions of the government." Thus it was "agreed on all hands that the exercise of constructive powers is indispensable," and, in fact, Hamilton added, everything the government had done so far had been "more or less an exemplification of" the exercise of

---

[31] Hamilton, *Writings*, 619 (Hamilton's emphasis).

[32] Hamilton, *Writings*, 619–21. Contrasting the relative flexibility of Hamilton's interpretation of the powers of government with Jefferson's preference for a more legalistic approach, Clement Fatovic rightly observes that "more than any other Founder – and perhaps more than any political thinker other than Machiavelli – Hamilton was preoccupied with the problem of emergencies. References to extremities, crises, necessities, and exigencies abound in his writings, conveying the impression that emergencies are frequent if irregular and unpredictable occurrences." "Constitutionalism and Presidential Prerogative: Jeffersonian and Hamiltonian Perspectives," *American Journal of Political Science* 48 (2004): 436.

constructive or implied powers. Here he noted again actions taken in the exercise of the power to regulate commerce – such as the establishment of lighthouses – and also the act "which declares the power of the president to remove officers at pleasure."[33] Jefferson desired a doctrine that could establish strict and distinctly discernible limits on the federal power. For Hamilton, however, such limits had to be rejected, and the consequent uncertainty about the full scope of federal power and the accompanying fear that it might intrude upon the states were simply the price that had to be paid for effective government.

Indeed, we could say that in Hamilton's view Jefferson's desire for distinct limits on the federal power was inconsistent with the nature of the government the Constitution established and hence had a tendency to turn that government into something other than it was intended to be. This is implied by Hamilton's next observation, that "difficulties on this point" – that is, the possibility of the federal government intruding on the powers of the states – are "inherent in the nature of a federal constitution. They result inevitably from a division of the legislative power," the "consequence" of which is "that there will be cases clearly within the power of the national government; others clearly without its power; and a third class, which will leave room for controversy and difference of opinion, and concerning which a reasonable latitude of judgment must be allowed."[34] The kind of strict and certain limits that Jefferson craved could only be had in a mere confederation, and his insistence on a mode of interpretation that could provide such limits threatened – if it were accepted as the standard – to turn the government of the Union back into a confederation, that form of government whose ineffectiveness for the country had already been proven.

In any case, Hamilton's argument continued, his interpretation of the Constitution did not in fact open the door to an unlimited federal power. He had just conceded, after all, that some cases would fall "clearly" outside the boundaries of the powers of the Union. Hamilton's defense of federal power did "not affirm that the national government is sovereign in all respects" but only sovereign to a "certain" limited extent – specifically, "to the extent of the objects of its specified powers." Accordingly, Hamilton's approach, contrary to Jefferson's concerns, does include "a criterion of what is constitutional and of what is not so," namely, "the *end* to which the measure" in question "relates as a *mean*." "If the end be clearly comprehended within any of the specified powers, and if the measure have an obvious relation to that end, and is not forbidden by any particular provision of the constitution," then "it may safely be deemed to come within the compass of the national authority."[35] Such a principle might not have provided the kind of limited government that Jefferson sought, but neither, in Hamilton's mind, could it reasonably be said to open up vistas of unlimited government by providing no intelligible standard

[33] Hamilton, *Writings*, 620.
[34] Hamilton, *Writings*, 621.
[35] Hamilton, *Writings*, 621 (Hamilton's emphases).

of limitation. Moreover, for Hamilton, such a principle could embrace the cause of both effective government and limited government, unlike Jefferson's approach, which sacrificed the former to the latter.

"More Particular" Objections: State Law and Constitutional Faith

Expressing the hope that he had, by the preceding arguments, "satisfactorily answered" the "general objections" to his "doctrine," Hamilton turned next to an examination of some "more particular" concerns that had been expressed. He began this section of his argument with a consideration of Jefferson's complaint that "the proposed incorporation undertakes to create certain capacities, properties, or attributes" in the bank "which are *against* the laws of *alienage, descents, escheat* and *forfeiture, distribution* and *monopoly,* and to confer a power to make laws paramount to those of the states." According to Jefferson, nothing but a *"necessity invincible by other means"* could "justify such a prostration of laws which constitute the pillars of our whole system of jurisprudence, and are the foundations laws of the state governments."[36]

In response, Hamilton first suggested that Jefferson had exaggerated the importance of such state laws. If they were "truly the foundation laws of the several states," he observed, most of the states had already "subverted their own foundations" because most had, since establishing their own constitutions, made "material alterations" in some of these areas of jurisprudence, "especially the law of descents." In any case, he added, it was hard to see "how anything can be called a fundamental law of a state government which is not established in its constitution, unalterable by the ordinary legislature."[37]

Hamilton further contended that, properly understood, the bill incorporating the bank was not "against" the state laws Jefferson had invoked. "To do a thing which is against a law is to do something which it forbids or which is a violation of it," Hamilton observed. The bank would not violate state laws, however, but was merely a kind of entity to which such laws would not properly apply. "To erect a corporation," he explained, is to create a legal or artificial person. The laws of the state should be understood as "annex[ing]" the "incidents and attributes" of such an artificial person, and not as being violated by them. In this view, it is "certainly not accurate to say that the erection of a corporation is *against*" the various state laws cited by Jefferson. It is rather the case that the incorporation creates a kind of person to which such laws are "inapplicable" and to which such laws "assign a different regimen." Accordingly, the "laws of alienage cannot apply to an artificial person because it can have no country." Similarly, the laws of descent and escheat cannot apply to it, because "it can have no heirs." Laws of forfeiture can have no operation on a corporation because "it cannot commit a crime," and laws of distribution

---

[36] Hamilton, *Writings*, 621–22 (Hamilton's emphases).
[37] Hamilton, *Writings*, 622.

do not apply to it because "it cannot die."[38] Nor is it the case, Hamilton continued, that the bank bill is "against the laws of monopoly because it stipulates an exclusive right of banking under the national authority." A monopoly "implies a legal impediment to the carrying on of the trade by others than those to whom it is granted," but the bank bill "neither prohibits any state from erecting as many banks as they please, nor any number of individuals from associating to carry on the business."[39] Finally, Jefferson also erred in suggesting that the bill grants the power to the bank "to make laws paramount to those of the states." The bylaws of the bank, he observed, would operate only on its own members, but in any case the bill "expressly" required that they "not be contrary to law," with "law" here meaning "the law of a state as well as of the United States." Therefore any law of the corporation contrary to a state law would be "overruled and void" by virtue of its inconsistency with the federal law chartering the bank. Hamilton immediately added a qualification to this point, however: A bylaw of the corporation contrary to state law is void unless that state law is itself contrary to federal law, in which case we are confronted not with a clash between the law of the corporation and the law of the state but one between the "law of the state and that of the United States."[40] Hamilton implied here, and he made explicit in the immediate sequel, that in such a case the federal law would overrule the state law. This qualification, then, might tend to reawaken the Jeffersonian fears that Hamilton had, by this line of argument, initially sought to quiet: Hamilton's full position, after all, turns out to be that the bank will not be able to make bylaws paramount to the laws of the state because the federal act of incorporation prevents this but that it could have if the act had provided otherwise.

In the last place, Hamilton contended that Jefferson's complaint about the impact of the bank bill on state laws is irrelevant to the question of the bill's constitutionality. Even if one "admitted that the erection of a corporation is a direct alteration of the state laws" Jefferson had listed, this fact "would do nothing toward proving that the measure was unconstitutional." Here Hamilton returned to the larger concern with which he had begun his *Opinion*, that Jefferson's principles, if accepted, would arrest the essential operations of the federal government. If, as Jefferson implied, the "government of the United States can do no act, which amounts to an alteration of a state law," then "all its powers are nugatory." After all, Hamilton reasoned, "almost every new law" will effect some "alteration" in the existing statute or common law of the states. Indeed, the examples that Hamilton brought forward suggested that Jefferson's principle, if earnestly followed, would incapacitate the federal government even in the exercise of undoubted enumerated powers. The federal government could not exercise its power to regulate the value of foreign coins

[38] Hamilton, *Writings*, 622.
[39] Hamilton, *Writings*, 623–24.
[40] Hamilton, *Writings*, 624.

or prescribe a rule of bankruptcy without changing existing state laws on those topics, nor could it forbid the exportation of some goods – an exercise of its authority to regulate foreign commerce – without modifying the traditional common law right of individuals to export their property. These unacceptable consequences lay bare the infirmity of Jefferson's principles. Accordingly, Hamilton concluded that it "can therefore never be good reasoning to say" that an act is unconstitutional "because it alters this or that law of a state."[41]

In his discussion of the "more particular" objections to the bank bill, Hamilton also considered Jefferson's suggestion that the arguments in defense of the bank amounted to an act of bad constitutional faith. Jefferson had argued that the bank bill should be considered unconstitutional because the Constitutional Convention had considered and rejected a proposal to "empower Congress to make corporations." In response, Hamilton both contested the facts on which Jefferson rested his argument but also denied the relevance of the consideration that Jefferson had raised. Regarding the facts, Hamilton observed that the "precise nature or extent" of the proposal in question and the "reasons for refusing it" cannot be fully ascertained from any written record of the Convention or any recollection of its members. Various "accounts" had been "given of the import of the proposition and of the motives for rejecting it." Some held that the provision concerned only canals and rivers, others that it extended to banks, and still others that it concerned a general power to erect corporations. Some said it was defeated "because it was thought improper to vest in Congress a power of erecting corporations," while others said it was "because it was thought unnecessary to specify the power, and inexpedient to furnish an additional topic of objection to the Constitution." In view of the incomplete and contradictory nature of the record, Hamilton concluded, "no inference whatever can be drawn from it."[42]

Nevertheless, Hamilton continued, even if we could know the exact nature of the failed proposal and the reasons for its rejection, this knowledge would say "nothing in respect to the real merits of the question" of the power of Congress to erect corporations. The intention of any provision of the Constitution, like that of any law, is to be sought, he contended, "in the instrument itself, according to the usual and established rules of construction," and not in the personal intentions of its framers as they might have been expressed when the provision was under consideration. "Nothing is more common," he noted, "than for laws to *express* and *effect* more or less than was intended" by their authors. Accordingly, if the "power to erect a corporation" is "deducible by fair inference from the whole or any part" of the Constitution, then we must reject any arguments to the contrary "drawn from extrinsic circumstances regarding the intention of the Convention."[43]

---

[41] Hamilton, *Writings*, 623.
[42] Hamilton, *Writings*, 624.
[43] Hamilton, *Writings*, 625 (Hamilton's emphases).

The Bank and the Enumerated Powers

As the *Opinion* drew to its close, Hamilton turned at last to his immediate practical purpose. Having shown that the implied powers of the government are to be construed broadly so as to give Congress ample latitude in its choice of means for executing the ends entrusted to it, and having shown that a corporation is properly understood as such a means, Hamilton concluded by trying to show that the incorporated bank he had proposed could fairly be regarded as a means to ends explicitly vested in the federal government. This could be accomplished, he promised, by "tracing a natural and obvious relation between the institution of a bank" and "the objects of several of the enumerated powers of the government."[44]

The bank, Hamilton began, was both "indirectly" and "directly" relevant to the constitutional power to collect taxes. Here reiterating arguments made at greater length in his *Report on a National Bank*, Hamilton observed that such an institution indirectly facilitates the collection of taxes by increasing the money supply and by "quickening" the "circulation" of the medium of exchange. Nevertheless, the bank also had a much more direct relationship to the power to collect taxes insofar as it would create "a convenient species of medium in which they are to be paid." To specify the kind of money in which taxes are to be paid, Hamilton reasoned, is necessarily a part of the power to lay and collect them. Indeed, he observed, this power had already been exercised by the federal government, which had by law provided that "duties on imports and tonnage . . . shall be payable in gold and silver." The medium of payment, then, is a matter of discretion for the government. It might call for payment in metal currencies, in the "paper money of the several states," in the bills of any or all of the major banks already in existence, or "in bills issued under the authority of the United States." But if, as seems indisputable, the federal government may issue the currency in which taxes are to be paid, then surely the "manner of issuing these bills is again a matter of discretion."[45] The government might directly issue the bills itself, or it might erect a corporation to do so. The latter, however, was precisely what was to be done under Hamilton's plan for a national bank.

A bank would also have a direct relationship to the constitutional power of borrowing money. Here again Hamilton's arguments echoed points already made in his initial *Report on a National Bank*. A national bank, he contended, is a "usual" source of loans for a government, and is in fact an "essential" source of loans in "sudden emergencies." If, for example, a nation is threatened with war, it will require "large sums" in order to "make the requisite preparations." Taxes might be imposed to raise the needed monies, but it is predictable that these revenues could not be collected in time to meet the crisis. Money might be raised by seeking loans from individuals, but the progress of this method

[44] Hamilton, *Writings*, 632.
[45] Hamilton, *Writings*, 633.

is commonly "too slow for the exigency."[46] Accordingly, if a government is effectively to exercise the constitutional power to borrow, it is necessary for it to ensure in advance that there is a large concentration of capital under the direction of a single will to which it can turn for loans. Certainly this necessity is not absolute in the sense demanded by Jefferson. Hamilton admitted as much by noting that the power to borrow could conceivably be exercised without a national bank by seeking to borrow from individuals, or from smaller banks already in existence. Nevertheless, a bank is necessary in the sense defended by Hamilton: requisite to a properly energetic use of the government's power to achieve the ends entrusted to it. Moreover, as Hamilton noted briefly a few pages later, this argument based on the power to borrow also shows that a bank is a proper instrument in relation to the "execution" of the constitutional "powers that concern the common defense" – that is, the powers to raise and maintain armies and navies.[47]

Hamilton next contended that a national bank also has a "natural relation" to Congress's power to "regulate trade among the states." The bank, after all, is "conducive to the creation of a convenient medium of exchange" among the states, and money "is the very hinge on which commerce turns." Here, however, Hamilton acknowledged, and attempted to rebut, Jefferson's argument, noted earlier, that the bank cannot properly be understood as a regulation of commerce within the meaning of the Constitution. Jefferson had held that whoever creates a bank creates a subject of commerce, just like someone who "makes a bushel of wheat" or "digs a dollar out of the mines," but does not thereby regulate commerce. Making something that may be bought or sold is not the same thing, Jefferson held, as "prescribing rules for buying and selling."[48] Jefferson thus, as we noted earlier, interpreted the commerce power narrowly by interpreting commerce narrowly – as trade, or buying and selling, rather than as economic activity more generally. Hamilton admitted that "prescribing rules for buying and selling" is "indeed a species of regulation of trade." It is not, however, the whole of it. In fact, Hamilton contended, prescribing rules for buying and selling is a part of the regulation of trade that "falls more aptly within the province of the local jurisdictions" of the country. He perhaps sought here to turn Jefferson's own deepest concerns against his argument. Jefferson favored a narrow interpretation of the federal power that would protect the sphere that belongs to the states, but Hamilton averred that, contrary to Jefferson's intention, a narrow interpretation of the commerce power as a power to regulate buying and selling invites the federal government to intrude into local "details" that are better left to the states. The federal government, Hamilton believed, has more important concerns. Its regulations of trade ought to be "directed to those general political arrangements concerning trade on which" the nation's "aggregate interests depend." Its commercial

[46] Hamilton, *Writings*, 635.
[47] Hamilton, *Writings*, 638.
[48] Hamilton, *Writings*, 637.

legislation should aim to "give encouragement to the enterprise of our own merchants, and to advance our navigation and manufactures." And, he concluded, the bank – "an establishment which furnishes facilities to circulation and a convenient medium of exchange" – may certainly "be regarded as a regulation of trade" in relation to such "general relations of commerce."[49]

Hamilton at this point also responded to Jefferson's other objection to any effort to justify the bank on the basis of the commerce power. Jefferson had observed that if the bank were a regulation of commerce it would be unconstitutional because it would extend as much to the internal commerce of the states as to their external commerce. The Commerce Clause authorizes the federal government to regulate commerce "among" the states. On Jefferson's view, this formulation implicitly excludes a power to regulate commerce within the states. In response, Hamilton suggested that Jefferson's argument, if accepted, would effectively negate the federal government's commerce power because, Hamilton contended, any federal regulation of commerce among the states – and of commerce with foreign nations, for that matter – is bound to touch the internal commerce of the states as well. Indeed, he argued, this was the case with the commercial regulations already established by the federal government. He asked, rhetorically:

What are all the duties upon imported articles amounting to prohibitions, but so many bounties upon domestic manufactures affecting the interests of different classes of citizens in different ways? What are all the provisions of the coasting act, which relate to the trade between district and district of the same state? In short what regulation of trade between the states, but must affect the internal trade of each state? What can operate upon the whole but must extend to every part?[50]

Hamilton, then, found Jefferson's account of the Commerce Clause, no less than his account of the Necessary and Proper Clause, not only mistaken but dangerously hostile to the cause of good government.

Finally, Hamilton added that the bank could be justified in relation to the federal government's Article IV power to make "all needful rules and regulations" concerning the "property belonging to the United States." Money raised through taxation, he argued, is the property of the government as much as any land or buildings it might hold. Accordingly, the government could choose to incorporate a bank as a tool by which to manage such property.[51]

Conclusion

Hamilton found Jefferson's line of thinking about the bank and the Constitution incompatible with the country's well being. The secretary of the treasury

49 Hamilton, *Writings*, 638.
50 Hamilton, *Writings*, 638.
51 Hamilton, *Writings*, 638–40.

had begun his *Report on a National Bank* by claiming that such an institution was "of primary importance to the prosperous administration" of the nation's "finances" and "would be of the greatest utility" in relation to the government's policies in "support of the public credit." Accordingly, he could only deplore an argument that would, if successful, deprive the United States of such a useful establishment. Looking beyond the debate over the present proposal, however, he also feared that Jefferson's principles of constitutional interpretation would, if they prevailed, destroy the possibility of the energetic government that the Constitution had been written and ratified to secure. Jefferson wanted to limit the powers of the federal government as much as possible, up to the point beyond which further limitation would render them nugatory. Hamilton, however, thought Jefferson's mode of interpretation actually went so far as to render those powers practically nugatory. He accordingly concluded that Jefferson's approach to the Constitution was incompatible with the welfare of the Union.

Hamilton's argument paid off in relation to the immediate issue: President Washington signed the bank bill into law.[52] Hamilton failed, however, to quiet Jefferson's concerns. The secretary of state continued to regard the bank as an unconstitutional exercise of federal authority. More importantly, Jefferson continued to believe – and would soon argue strenuously to Washington himself – that Hamilton's approach to the Constitution was destructive of limited government.

Indeed, Hamilton's *Opinion* revealed tendencies in his thought pointing to his next major policy proposal, which in turn would deepen the rift with Jefferson, confirming in the latter's mind the anti-constitutional character of Hamilton's program. As he brought his defense of the bank to a close, Hamilton made a final, general appeal to the "practice of mankind" – that is, to the practice of the established European powers – which he held "ought to have great weight against the theories of individuals." Why, Hamilton asked, could not the United States constitutionally use the proven tools of statecraft that had been employed – often with great success – in other nations? Other countries had, for example, incorporated trading companies as tools of their commerce with foreign nations; and while Hamilton did not advocate such a course for America, he thought that the practice showed that the creation of such companies was "an incident to the regulation" of foreign commerce and therefore within the constitutional power of the federal government. Similarly, banks were a "usual engine in the administration of national finances, and an ordinary and most effectual instrument of loans." These facts argued "strongly against the supposition that a government" – like that of the United States – "clothed with most of the most important prerogatives of sovereignty in relation to" revenue, debt, credit, defense, and trade was "forbidden to make use

[52] Richard Brookhiser, *Alexander Hamilton: American* (New York: The Free Press, 1999), 92.

of" a bank "as an appendage to its own authority."[53] This desire to imitate the European powers in some respects – or perhaps we should say this belief that energetic government and American security and prosperity *required* such imitation – informed Hamilton's call, in his *Report on Manufactures*, for policies designed to build up America's industrial power. Hamilton justified these policies constitutionally on the basis of an interpretation of the General Welfare Clause that Jefferson deemed even more dangerous than the construction of the Necessary and Proper Clause that Hamilton had ventured in defense of the bank. We consider next the political and constitutional arguments of Hamilton's *Report on Manufactures*, which set the stage for the comprehensive critique of Hamiltonianism that Jefferson advanced to Washington in 1792.

[53] Hamilton, *Writings*, 644.

PART II

A CLASH OF RIVAL PARTY LEADERS

7

Securing American Independence

Hamilton's Report on Manufactures

Although he submitted it in December of 1791, Hamilton's *Report on Manufactures* had its origins much earlier in the administration. Like his two previous reports, it was written in response to an order of the House of Representatives. On January 15, 1790 the House had sought the secretary of the treasury's advice on "the subject of manufactures," and "particularly" the "means of promoting such as" would "tend to render" America "independent on foreign nations for military and other essential supplies."[1] The House's order in turn followed upon Washington's January 8 speech to Congress, in which the president had observed that one of the best ways to preserve peace was to prepare for war, and that a free people should promote such "manufactories as would tend to "render them independent on others for essential" and "particularly for military supplies."[2] Hamilton took immediate steps to comply with the wishes of the House. As early as January 25 he prepared a letter seeking information on the current condition of manufacturing in the various states.[3] Nevertheless, where the earlier reports on public credit and the bank had taken only a few months to complete, almost two years elapsed between the House's order and Hamilton's submission of the *Report on Manufactures*.

The amount of time it took Hamilton to produce the *Report on Manufactures* was perhaps due not only to his need to devise the earlier steps in his

---

[1] Hamilton, *Writings*, 647. In preparing the report, Hamilton was not merely acting on orders. As we will see, he believed that the development of American manufacturing was essential to American independence. Indeed, as Robert E. Wright and David J. Cowen observe, Hamilton's own interest in the development of American manufacturing can be traced all the way back to his revolutionary essay *The Farmer Refuted* (1775). *Financial Founding Fathers: The Men Who Made America Rich* (Chicago: University of Chicago Press, 2006), 33.

[2] *PAH* 6: 208–09, n. 3.

[3] *PAH* 6: 207–08.

program and shepherd them through Congress but also to the sheer size of the report itself: it is more than twice as long as either the *Report on Public Credit* or the *Report on a National Bank*. Much of its bulk derives from its extensive account of the existing state of manufactures – which includes discussions of American facilities for producing iron, lead, copper, wood, skins, and other articles – as well as its detailed policy recommendations. Of greater interest for the present study, however, is the *Report*'s general argument for special government support for manufacturing. Unlike the earlier reports, the policy proposals of which could more easily be presented as generally benefitting the American economy, here Hamilton had to make the case for government's special solicitude toward a particular sector of the economy. He had to show why steps to nurture this part would in fact benefit the whole.

As with the earlier reports, Hamilton presented the *Report on Manufactures* as an act of high statesmanship, necessary to the completion of the founding and the full establishment of energetic government and American independence. It thus reveals his understanding of human nature and the kind of social, economic, and political conditions under which it could flourish, and the kind of constitutionalism necessary for the government to promote those conditions. The *Report*'s treatment of the Constitution, moreover, contributed significantly to the transformation of his dispute with Jefferson from an argument between cabinet colleagues to a clash between rival party leaders, representing sharply divergent views of constitutionalism and republican government.

In the *Report* Hamilton set out to show that government support for manufacturing was essential to American well being. In order for the government to act on that understanding, however, he also had to show that the kind of policies he recommended were consistent with the Constitution. His overall argument, therefore, can be divided into two parts: first, a policy argument in defense of government aid to manufacturing, and second, a constitutional argument that the federal government could reasonably be understood to possess the authority to undertake such a policy.

The Productivity of Manufacturing

Hamilton's policy argument can in turn be divided into two portions: a negative argument and a positive argument. Before making the positive case for why American interests called for government support of manufacturing, he first sought to refute the various common objections to such support. He began by responding to the claim that manufacturing should not be encouraged because agriculture is the more productive undertaking. This was especially the case, said the proponents of this view, in a nation like the United States, with its "immense tracts of fertile territory, uninhabited and unimproved." No other pursuit, this argument ran, could "afford so advantageous an employment for capital and labor" as the "conversion" of America's "extensive wilderness into cultivated farms," and nothing besides agriculture could "contribute" so much "to the population, strength, and real riches of the country."[4]

Contrary to what one might expect in light of his reputation as a strong proponent of manufacturing, Hamilton did not reject this view out of hand but instead conceded that it possessed considerable merit. He freely admitted that "the cultivation of the earth" has *intrinsically a strong claim to pre-eminence over every other kind of industry.*" This claim rested on agriculture's status as "the primary and most certain source of national supply," as the "immediate and chief source of subsistence to man," as "the principal source of those materials which constitute the nutriment of other kinds of labor," and as the pursuit "perhaps" more "conducive" than any other "to the multiplication of the human species." Furthermore, showing that his account was animated by political as well as economic concerns, and that his thinking on these questions was not wholly alien to Jefferson's, Hamilton even added to agriculture's list of virtues that it included "a state most favorable to the freedom and independence of the human mind."[5]

Although Hamilton thus admitted agriculture's strengths, he nevertheless denied that they could be carried so far as to support the conclusion that agriculture was entitled to "anything like an exclusive predilection in any country." On the contrary, without contending that manufacturing of itself was necessarily more productive than agriculture, Hamilton proceeded to argue that it did tend to make the whole economy more productive than it otherwise would be. This increased productivity, he contended, arose from seven "circumstances" connected with manufacturing.[6]

First, Hamilton argued, manufacturing favors a "proper division of labor" – than which "scarcely anything" is "of greater moment in the economy of a nation." This "separation of occupations" permitted "each to be carried to a much greater perfection than it could possibly acquire if they were blended." "A man occupied on a single object," after all, will be better able and more inclined to devise "methods to facilitate and abridge labor than if he were perplexed by a variety of independent and dissimilar operations." Moreover, division of labor enhances productivity by allowing for increased "use of machinery." From these considerations, Hamilton concluded that the separation of farming from manufacturing "has the effect of augmenting the productive powers" of labor and hence total revenues of the nation.[7]

Hamilton's second argument built upon the first, further emphasizing manufacturing's ability to extend the use of machines. Machinery constitutes an artificial force added to the natural force of the human worker. For all

---

[4] Hamilton, *Writings*, 647–48.
[5] Hamilton, *Writings*, 649 (Hamilton's emphasis).
[6] Hamilton, *Writings*, 649, 658.
[7] Hamilton, *Writings*, 659–60.

practical purposes, it amounts to an increase in labor, but without the expense of maintaining the laborer. Hamilton accordingly suggested that "those occupations which give greatest scope to the use of" machinery "contribute most to the general stock of industrious effort" and therefore "to the general product of industry." Here manufacturing held an advantage over agriculture, insofar as the former was more adaptable to the use of machinery than the latter.[8]

Hamilton contended in the third place that manufacturing would further increase the productivity of the nation by increasing the raw quantity of human work that could be performed. Manufacturing could be pursued part time by people primarily engaged in other pursuits, and it opened the workforce to people who might be incapable of contributing to a purely agricultural economy. Some, Hamilton noted, tended to be "idle" and even a "burden on the community" because they were excluded from the "toils of the country" by some "bias of temper, habit," or "infirmity of body." Moreover, the kind of work involved in manufacturing was more open to women and children. In sum, the addition of manufacturing to agriculture could draw more work out of the same population and hence make that population more productive than it otherwise would have been.[9]

Hamilton's favorable view of child labor was not based exclusively on economic considerations. Later in the *Report*, he remarked that in some districts of America a large portion of the clothing used by the local inhabitants was "made by themselves." This in turn resulted from the "progress" that had been made in "family manufactures," a development Hamilton regarded as important in both "a moral and political view."[10] Hamilton did not here spell out his meaning, but it is perhaps suggested by a later discussion of "family manufacture" in which he observed that "the great proportion" of persons occupied in making American nails and spikes were "boys, whose early habits of industry are of importance to the community, to the present support of their own families, and to their own future comfort."[11] For Hamilton, it seems, the availability of manufacturing work in America was beneficial not only because it added to the nation's wealth but also because it fostered the dispositions by which the young were enabled to take care of themselves, help their families, and benefit their communities.

Fourth, Hamilton contended that an American manufacturing sector would stimulate "emigration from foreign countries," which would increase America's population and hence its productivity. America already possessed many advantages that would tempt foreign manufacturers to leave their homelands. Some of these advantages were economic. In America, Hamilton suggested, the

---

[8] Hamilton, *Writings*, 660.
[9] Hamilton, *Writings*, 661.
[10] Hamilton, *Writings*, 687.
[11] Hamilton, *Writings*, 712.

prices of manufactured goods and the wages of workers were higher than in Europe, while the cost of "provisions and raw materials" was lower. An additional economic advantage arose from the character of public policy: in general, the American system of taxation and regulation was less burdensome than that found "in the old world." Some of the existing inducements to immigration were more political in character. America had a "more equal government" than any in the old world, and it could boast a "perfect equality of religious privileges" that was "far more precious" than the mere "religious toleration" found in Europe. As a result, those who came to America could expect a "greater personal independence and consequence" than they could possibly enjoy in the countries of their birth. Nevertheless, Hamilton continued, these inducements to immigration could not be fully effective without a substantial American manufacturing economy. Men were reluctant, after all, to quit the occupation to which they were accustomed in the hope of "doing better in some other way." Old world manufacturers could only "with difficulty" be induced to move to America in order to become farmers, but they "would probably flock from Europe to the United States" if they knew that they could continue to "pursue their own trades or professions" and "were inspired with assurance of encouragement and employment." Moreover, such immigration would constitute a clean gain in productivity, since it would increase the nation's manufacturing capacity without diverting anyone from agriculture.[12]

This argument opens a window on Hamilton's political psychology, on his understanding of the springs of human action. For Hamilton, self-interest is powerful enough to overcome the ties of patriotism: it can induce men to leave the lands of their birth and education. This self-interest, however, is not purely economic or materialistic. Hamilton also acknowledged the importance of what Plato called the spirited part of the soul because, in his telling, men might be moved to immigrate not only to make more money in the same profession but also by the prospect of a higher social status, by the possibility of having greater "independence" and "consequence" than they could have at home. European levels of taxation and regulation were an impediment to human acquisitiveness in comparison to which America's freer economy looked attractive, and the European system of political and religious privilege was an irritant to human spiritedness in comparison to which American political and religious equality looked attractive. For Hamilton, both acquisitiveness and spiritedness were powerful enough to be relevant to the statesman's calculations.

This was not the only part of the *Report*'s argument informed by this Hamiltonian political psychology, which understood the importance of honor in addition to economic self-interest. As we will see, Hamilton favored "bounties" – or direct subsidies – as one of the most effective means of promoting manufacturing. One can easily see how such a policy would appeal to the desire

---

[12] Hamilton, *Writings*, 662–63.

for gain. Nevertheless, he also admired the effects of "premiums," an expedient similar to bounties but "distinguishable from them in some important features." Where bounties are simply paid to all manufacturers of a certain article, premiums "serve to reward some particular excellence or superiority, some extraordinary exertion or skill, and are dispensed only in a small number of cases." Premiums, therefore, are "both honorary and lucrative" and accordingly "address themselves to different passions, touching the chords as well of emulation as of interest." Hamilton's belief in the real effectiveness of this appeal – in the real power of the love of honor, even, we may observe, in men dedicated primarily to commerce – is shown in his confidence in the capacity of premiums to "stimulate general effort" even though they are only awarded to a few. "They are," he averred, "a very economical mean of exciting the enterprise of a whole community."[13]

Hamilton's fifth and sixth arguments shed further light on the political psychology informing his statesmanship. Here he contended that manufacturing would diversify the economy, which would in turn call forth greater productive energies from the people. "It is a just observation," he said, "that minds of the strongest and most active powers for their proper objects" tend to "fall below mediocrity and labor without effect" when they are "confined to uncongenial pursuits." We may therefore expect "that the results of human exertion" would be "immensely increased by diversifying its objects," since such diversity would give workers greater freedom to choose the occupation most suitable to their tempers. "When all the different kinds of industry obtain in a community," Hamilton argued, "each individual can find his proper element, and can call into activity the whole vigor of his nature," with the result that the whole "community is benefitted by the services of its members, in the manner in which each can serve it with most effect." Moreover, he continued, diversity generally tended to stimulate the mind more than uniformity, and accordingly the multiplication of "the objects of enterprise" was an important means "by which the wealth of a nation may be promoted." Each "new scene" that was "opened to the busy nature of man to rouse and exert itself" would constitute an "addition of a new energy to the general stock of effort." The "spirit of enterprise" would "necessarily be contracted or expanded in proportion to the simplicity or variety of occupations and productions" present "in a society," and it would therefore increase for a nation that added manufacturing to agriculture.[14]

---

[13] Hamilton, *Writings*, 703. In view of this evidence of Hamilton's understanding of the role of spiritedness in economics, Bruce Miroff offers a too-simple dichotomy when he suggests that for Hamilton "men of business were satisfied with the acquisition of wealth," while "statesmen yearned for the higher rewards of political glory." "Alexander Hamilton: The Aristocrat as Visionary," *International Political Science Review* 9 (1988): 51.

[14] Hamilton, *Writings*, 663–64. In contrast, as Joyce Appleby observes, Jefferson emphasized agriculture's potential to "nurture the unfolding of a human potential long blocked by poverty and ignorance." "What is Still American in the Political Philosophy of Thomas Jefferson?"

Finally, Hamilton contended that American manufacturing would increase the productivity and prosperity of American agriculture by creating a better market for the latter's products. The "exertions of the husbandman," he held, depend on the quality of the market for his surplus production.[15] A domestic market, however, was more reliable than a foreign one. The causes of this foreign unreliability were both natural and artificial. The leading natural cause was, of course, the agricultural productivity of foreign nations, which could vary from year to year and thus cause fluctuations in the demand for the products of American soil. The policies of foreign governments created the leading artificial cause of the unreliability of foreign markets. Nations in general, Hamilton argued, made it a "primary object" of their "policy" to "be able to supply themselves with subsistence from their own soils," and "manufacturing nations" in particular similarly sought as much as possible to derive the "raw materials" for their products from the same domestic source. Such aspirations, unobjectionable in themselves, were sometimes, however, "urged by a spirit of monopoly" and thus "carried to an injudicious extreme."[16] Seeking to maintain a complete agricultural independence, the governments of manufacturing countries sometimes tried to exclude the merchandise of foreign nations. Such governments were forgetting, Hamilton observed, that nations with no manufacturing or mining could only purchase the fruits of those enterprises by selling their own agricultural goods. By cutting off or impeding the sale of foreign agricultural products, such nations in effect encouraged the farming nations from which these products came to develop their own manufacturing facilities. By refusing to buy from others, they also made it harder to sell to others. Such protectionism was, Hamilton held, ultimately counterproductive for all involved. The manufacturing nations that practiced it reduced the "natural advantages" of their own "situation" by preventing "agricultural countries" from using their own. By artificially propping up their own less efficient agricultural economies, they induced more efficient agricultural nations artificially to prop up their own inefficient manufacturing sectors. Thus, such nations sacrificed "the interests of a mutually beneficial intercourse to the vain project of *selling everything* and *buying nothing.*"[17] While Hamilton may have disapproved of such policies, he also viewed them as a reality that the prudent statesman had to face. Considering them in conjunction with the aforementioned natural causes, he concluded that foreign markets for American agriculture were too uncertain. As a

---

William and Mary Quarterly 39 (1982): 297. Also of interest here is Appleby's account of Jefferson's understanding of political economy in "Economics: The Agrarian Republic," in *Thomas Jefferson and the Politics of Nature,* ed. Thomas S. Engeman (Notre Dame, IN: University of Notre Dame Press, 2000), 143–63; and Richard K. Matthews's comparison of Hamiltonian and Jeffersonian economics in chapter 6 of his *The Radical Politics of Thomas Jefferson* (Lawrence: University Press of Kansas, 1984).

[15] Hamilton, *Writings,* 664.
[16] Hamilton, *Writings,* 664.
[17] Hamilton, *Writings,* 664–65 (Hamilton's emphasis).

result, he advised substituting an "extensive domestic market" for American agriculture, which could be done by promoting domestic manufacturing, since manufacturers were the main consumers of surplus agricultural products.[18]

Hamilton thus concluded that, contrary to the claims of the critics, the pursuit of manufacturing promised to enhance America's total output and wealth.

The Limits of Laissez-Faire

The second objection to which Hamilton responded built on an argument he had already acknowledged. As we have just seen, Hamilton contended that the efforts of some nations to keep out foreign agricultural products amounted to an "artificial" interference with the natural course of trade, one that was counter-productive for all involved. Might not a similar line of reasoning actually undercut his policy recommendations in the *Report on Manufactures*? After all, Hamilton sought active government support for manufacturing. Would not such a policy artificially interfere with the domestic economy and in the end decrease its vitality by working against its natural inclinations?

Before responding, Hamilton stated this laissez-faire position with considerable force. According to this view, the "quick-sighted guidance of private interest" would, "if left to itself, infallibly find its own way to the most profitable employment," which would also turn out to be the employment most conducive to the "public prosperity." Accordingly, it was almost always "the soundest as well as the simplest policy" to "leave industry to itself." In contrast, to use government to "accelerate the growth of manufactures" was to try "by force and art" to shift "industry" from its "natural current." And since, on this view, the natural current was necessarily the best, such governmental interference was "unwise."[19] Surely, then, American "manufacturing" would "grow up as soon and as fast as the natural state of things and the community may require" without any special support from the government.[20]

Admitting the "solidity of this hypothesis," Hamilton nevertheless found four reasons why it ought not to control the question at issue, four reasons why private interest alone could not reliably advance the state of manufacturing to the level required by America's national interest.[21] First, Hamilton

---

[18] Hamilton, *Writings*, 666.

[19] Hamilton, *Writings*, 648.

[20] Hamilton, *Writings*, 670.

[21] For a further discussion of this issue, see Christine Margerum Harlen's presentation of Hamilton's *Report on Manufactures* as advancing a position that combined economic liberalism and economic nationalism. "A Reappraisal of Economic Nationalism and Economic Liberalism," *International Studies Quarterly* 43 (1999): 733–44. Given the pragmatic and non-ideological terms in which Hamilton discusses these questions, Harlen's assessment is surely more accurate than Louis M. Hacker's suggestion that the *Report on Manufactures* reveals Hamilton as, at bottom, a "libertarian" whose pro-industrial policies were merely a temporary response to the existing pro-industrial policies of rival nations. *Alexander Hamilton in the American Tradition*

contended that private interest alone would not necessarily lead by the shortest route to national prosperity because men are creatures of habit as well as self-interest. The laissez-faire argument presupposed that human acquisitiveness is ever restless and ambitious, always on the lookout for some new and more effective means of gain. In fact, Hamilton countered, most human beings, while certainly motivated by self-interest, are somewhat more inert. They are often content to accept what they consider to be an adequate satisfaction of their self-interest won by the means they have long known and hesitant to seek even greater gains from means that are untried. "Experience teaches," he claimed, "that men are often so governed by what they are accustomed to see and practice" that they will only with "reluctance" adopt "the simplest and most obvious improvements" in their "most ordinary occupations." Therefore, the "spontaneous transition" to entirely "new pursuits, in a community long habituated to different ones," would be even slower and more uncertain.[22] No doubt self-interest would begin to move men out of a particular line once it ceased to be profitable enough to sustain them. In the meantime, however, many would stick with it as long as a "bare support" could be wrung from the work to which they were accustomed, even though "resort to a more profitable employment might be practicable." In the words of Hamilton scholar Peter McNamara, "Hamilton did not believe that the desire to better our condition was a natural and spontaneous growth."[23] It required some encouragement from government policy. Experience suggested that the mere operations of private interest often brought economic changes more slowly than was consistent with the well-being of either "individuals or of the society," and that "the incitement and patronage of government" might be needed in order to "produce the desired changes as early as may be expedient."[24]

Second, Hamilton observed that fear of failure in a new activity also tended to limit the spontaneous development of manufacturing. He conceded that natural desire might overcome this fear of failure in some cases, but he also noted that this process alone might not lead reliably to an adequate development of the new business. After all, the "dispositions apt to be attracted by the mere novelty of an undertaking" are "not always those best calculated to give it success." The perfection of a new branch of industry required not so much the energy of the impulsive but the experience and sobriety of "cautious" and "sagacious capitalists." Here, in Hamilton's account, the undirected economy encountered a paradox: those who had the virtues necessary to develop a new

---

(New York: McGraw-Hill, 1957), 166. Also, contrast Russell Kirk's judgment that Hamilton's approach to political economy amounts to "mercantilism." *The Conservative Mind: From Burke to Eliot*, seventh revised edition (Chicago: Regnery Books, 1986), 78.

[22] Similarly, Hamilton had observed in his bank report that men "often prefer the certainties they enjoy to probabilities depending on untried experiments, especially when these promise rather that they will not be injured than that they will be benefitted." Hamilton, *Writings*, 596.

[23] Peter McNamara, *Political Economy and Statesmanship: Smith, Hamilton, and the Foundation of the Commercial Republic* (DeKalb: Northern Illinois University Press, 1998), 10.

[24] Hamilton, *Writings*, 670.

sector of the economy would be deterred by their very virtues from entering it. Therefore, it fell to the government to "inspire" them with "confidence" that the "new" and "precarious" undertaking would receive public "countenance and support" sufficient to overcome "the obstacles inseparable from first experiments."[25]

Hamilton pointed in the third place to the "superiority" enjoyed by nations that had already "perfected" their manufacturing establishments. This, he contended, posed another and an even "more formidable obstacle" to "the introduction of the same branch" of industry in America. Ordinarily, long established foreign manufacturers would be able to provide higher quality goods at better prices than those that could be offered by a domestic infant industry. And this "disparity" would usually be so "considerable" as to exclude the development of the domestic industry, unless the "government" interposed with some "extraordinary aid and protection."[26]

Finally, Hamilton turned to "the greatest obstacle of all" to the spontaneous development of American manufacturing: the "bounties, premiums, and other aids" granted by other nations to their own established industries. Some governments, Hamilton explained, "grant bounties on the exportation of certain commodities" precisely with a view to allowing "their own workmen to undersell and supplant all competitors in the countries to which those commodities are sent." Thus, those seeking to develop such manufactures in a new country would have to contend not only with "natural disadvantages of a new undertaking" but also with the "gratuities and remunerations which other governments bestow" on their own manufacturers. Such newcomers needed the "interference and aid of their own government" if they were to compete successfully.[27]

On the basis of these last two considerations especially, Hamilton concluded that the laissez-faire argument was truer in theory than in practice. It might have merit in itself, but it did not fit the real circumstances that Hamilton as a statesman had to confront. We might reasonably expect that "the industry of a people" under the direction of nothing but "private interest" will "upon equal terms" find its way to the "most beneficial employment for itself." There was no reason to think, however, that such forces could "struggle" successfully "against the force of unequal terms," that they could on their own "surmount all the adventitious barriers" created either by the natural advantage of more experienced foreign manufacturers or by the "positive regulations" and "artificial policy" of foreign governments.[28]

---

[25] Hamilton, *Writings*, 671.
[26] Hamilton, *Writings*, 671.
[27] Hamilton, *Writings*, 671–72.
[28] Hamilton, *Writings*, 672. Hamilton's belief in the need for some government supervision of American trade was not one that he developed only once he became secretary of the treasury. As John Koritansky observes, Hamilton's *Continentalist* essays, written in 1781, had already argued against the notion that trade was self-regulating and required no government direction.

Manufacturing and America's "Particular Situation"

Hamilton then addressed the claim that, over and above the general considerations already examined, America's "particular situation" argued against any attempt by the government to promote manufacturing. Of special interest here are his additional responses to the case for a purely free market policy of governmental non-interference in the economy. According to the objection made here, while it might be reasonable for the government to spur manufacturing when the country is isolated from foreign commerce, this was not the situation of the United States, which in fact enjoyed the ability to buy manufactured items from Europe. Indeed, the objection ran, specialization – the efficiency of which Hamilton had made part of his earlier argument – seemed to counsel America to focus on its natural advantages in agriculture and rely on Europe's natural advantages in manufacturing. Leaving each nation to its own most effective activities would secure "the great advantage of a division of labor, leaving" the American "farmer free to pursue exclusively the culture of his land" and "enabling him to procure with its products the manufactured supplies" he needed or desired.[29] Free trade would thus be most beneficial to all nations concerned.

As before, Hamilton responded that this objection, while fine in theory, was not based on a realistic assessment of how other nations were actually behaving. Just as they artificially supported their own manufacturers at the expense of America's ability to develop a similar industry, so they artificially protected their own farmers from competition from American agriculture. While not isolated from European commerce, neither was America exactly free to submit its agricultural products to that commerce on equal terms. "If the system of perfect liberty to industry and commerce were the prevailing system of nations," Hamilton argued, America might well choose to leave its economy free of government interference. In such a state of freedom, "each country would" indeed "have the full benefit of its peculiar advantages to compensate for its deficiencies," and a "free exchange, mutually beneficial, of the commodities which each was able to supply, on the best terms, might be carried on between them, supporting in full vigor the industry of each." Under these conditions, the purely agricultural nation, lacking the aforementioned advantages of manufacturing, might not achieve the "degree of opulence" it would if it added manufacturing to its economy. Nevertheless, increased wealth through the improvement of its agriculture might well compensate for the absence of domestic manufacturing, and in light of these possibilities, Hamilton conceded that it could be better for the government to "leave industry to its own direction."[30]

"Alexander Hamilton's Philosophy of Government and Administration," *Publius* 9 (1979): 108.

[29] Hamilton, *Writings*, 667.

[30] Hamilton, *Writings*, 667–68.

The "system" of "perfect liberty to industry and trade," however, was "far from" being "the general policy of nations" – a policy that was in fact for the most part "regulated by an opposite spirit." As a result, Hamilton contended, America was "to a certain extent in the situation of a country precluded from foreign commerce." America could indeed buy what it needed from Europe, but it was not genuinely free to sell what it made to Europe, since several European nations had put up "numerous and very injurious impediments to the emission and vent" of American "commodities." The United States, then, was in no position to "exchange with Europe on equal terms," and the obvious remedy to this problem was reciprocity of American policy: government intervention in support of American manufacturing. Without such a policy, Hamilton warned, Europe's system would confine America to agriculture. As a result, America's steady and rising appetite for European manufactured goods, combined with the merely "partial and occasional" European market for the products of American agriculture, would "expose" the country to a comparative "impoverishment" – a state unequal to the "opulence" to which its "political and natural advantages" should lead it to aspire.[31]

While Hamilton characterized the European system as depriving Americans of trade on "equal terms," he did not – unlike some contemporary Americans – speak of such policies as imposing "unfair" trade. He seemed rather to take it for granted that governments would try to use policy to promote their own nations' interests and development at the expense of foreigners. The extent to which this was carried was not so much a matter of fairness as of prudent calculation. Thus he noted that his account of European policy was not offered "in the spirit of complaint" and that it was for the nations he had referenced to "judge for themselves whether, by aiming at too much, they do not lose more than they gain." By the same token, it was "for the United States to consider by what means" it could make itself "least dependent on the combinations, right or wrong, of foreign policy."[32]

This is not to say that Hamilton thought that the question of justice did not arise at all in relation to a nation's commercial policy. The relevant considerations of justice, however, were not international but domestic: they involved not the duties of one nation to another but of a nation's government to its own people. Apparently, a government did nothing unfair or unjust in seeking to impose unequal terms of trade on foreigners who sought access to its domestic market. But in the face of such a policy, another government might well have an obligation to pursue a reciprocal policy in order to promote the interests of its own citizens. Thus, Hamilton suggested that since "a monopoly of the domestic market to its own manufacturers" was the "reigning policy of manufacturing nations, a similar policy on the part of the United States in every proper instance is dictated, it might almost be said, by the principles

[31] Hamilton, *Writings*, 668–69.
[32] Hamilton, *Writings*, 669.

of distributive justice," but "certainly by the duty of endeavoring to secure" American citizens "a reciprocity of advantages."[33]

A Partial Policy?

Finally, Hamilton responded to the objection that government support for manufacturing would benefit some Americans at the expense of others. This objection took two forms, the first of which focused on class and the second of which focused on region. According to the first argument, the encouragement of manufactures would tend to "give a monopoly of advantages to particular classes at the expense of the rest of the community." Hamilton had indeed admitted that his plan aimed to protect American manufacturers from their European rivals precisely because the former could not effectively compete with the latter either in terms of the quality or the price of the goods produced. It would seem, then, that under the prevailing conditions Americans could "procure the requisite supplies of manufactured articles on better terms from foreigners than from our own citizens."[34] Hamilton's policies would eliminate this situation, so advantageous to domestic *consumers* of manufactured goods, and replace it with one in which the American *makers* of manufactured goods would enjoy a "virtual monopoly," the "inevitable" outcome of which would be increased prices, which would be "defrayed at the expense of the other parts of the society."[35]

Hamilton conceded that "measures" that "abridge the free competition of foreign articles" would tend to raise prices. Nevertheless, he argued that in this case the result would be temporary. Indeed, he contended on the contrary that a decline in price would be the "ultimate effect" of his policy. The purpose of the protective measures he proposed was to give some space for the development of domestic manufacturing. When such manufactures had attained to their "perfection," however, their products "invariably" became "cheaper." A domestic product, after all, was "free from the heavy charges" required to "import foreign commodities," and so usually ended up being, "in the process of time," less expensive "than was the foreign article for which it is a substitute." Nor was there any real danger of monopoly. The aim was not to develop a single American manufacturer for any given good but to develop the American manufacturing sector. Accordingly, there would in the end be "internal competition" among American manufacturers, which would eliminate "everything like monopoly" and would "by degrees" lower prices "to the *minimum* of a reasonable profit on the capital employed."[36] Accordingly, Hamilton concluded, "to encourage the growth of manufactures" was not a

---

33 Hamilton, *Writings*, 698.
34 Hamilton, *Writings*, 687.
35 Hamilton, *Writings*, 649.
36 Hamilton, *Writings*, 688 (Hamilton's emphasis).

policy of partiality but instead in the "interest" of the whole "community with a view to eventual and permanent economy." Taking a "national view," any "temporary enhancement of price must always be well compensated by a permanent reduction of it." And if anyone might object that this benefit, even if truly general, was nevertheless won at the expense of one portion of the community, namely the farmers, Hamilton hastened to deny the truth of even this more limited complaint. The "eventual diminution of the prices of manufactured articles" resulting from fostering "internal manufacturing establishments" would also "benefit agriculture." By allowing "the farmer" to buy the "manufactured articles" he needed with a "smaller quantity of his labor," it raised "the value of his income and property."[37]

This final observation also tended to refute the second version of the objection with which Hamilton was here concerned: that support for manufacturing would benefit the region of the country in which manufacturing was practiced – the North – at the expense of the region in which agriculture predominated – the South. After all, if the eventual effect of support for a domestic manufacturing sector was a decrease in prices for manufactured goods, then Hamilton's policy could not fail in the end to benefit the southern states along with the northern ones. Nevertheless, Hamilton gave this objection fuller consideration. As before, he responded by conceding that the complaint might be true in a limited sense, but that it was not true in the larger scheme of things. "Particular encouragements of particular manufactures may" operate at the expense of "the interests of landholders," Hamilton admitted. However, he continued, "experience" has established the "maxim" that "the *aggregate* prosperity of manufactures and the *aggregate* prosperity of agriculture are intimately connected."[38] In support of this maxim, he referred to his earlier argument that the creation of a domestic manufacturing economy would create a more steady and reliable domestic market for America's own farmers. Moreover, Hamilton observed, encouraging manufacturing would create a domestic market for the South not only because northern manufacturers would need to be fed but also because their manufacturing itself would require raw materials, many of which – such as timber, hemp, cotton, iron, lead, and coal – would come from the South.[39]

In taking up this objection, Hamilton also expressed a concern similar to one raised by Jefferson in his discussion of the earlier debate over assumption: that arguments about regional costs and benefits manifested a spirit that tended to undermine the Union. Thus Hamilton condemned complaints that support for manufacturing would help the north at the expense of the south not only as erroneous but also as "mischievous": it was "unfriendly to the steady pursuit of one great common cause, and to the perfect harmony of all the parts." He

37 Hamilton, *Writings*, 688.
38 Hamilton, *Writings*, 694 (Hamilton's emphasis).
39 Hamilton, *Writings*, 695.

therefore urged his readers not to think in terms of "solicitudes and apprehensions which originate in local discriminations" but instead to fix their minds upon "the intimate connection of interest which subsists between all the parts of a society united under the same government" and on "the infinite variety of channels which serve to circulate the prosperity of each to and through the rest." "It is a truth as important as it is agreeable," he admonished his audience, "that everything tending to establish substantial and permanent order in the affairs of a country, to increase the total mass of industry and opulence, is ultimately beneficial to every part of it."[40]

The Positive Case for Support of Manufacturing

Having responded to the various objections that could be made to encouraging manufacturing, Hamilton then turned to the more positive case for his policy. This positive statement turned out to be much shorter than the negative argument that had preceded it. The reason for this comparative brevity was that Hamilton's rejoinders had already identified many of the positive benefits a pro-manufacturing policy would bring. Thus Hamilton proposed in this section of his argument to content himself with a "few" observations that would fortify the "considerations" in favor of support for manufacturing that had already "appeared in the course of the discussion."[41]

This positive case for supporting manufactures was advanced under two distinct heads: economic and political. Hamilton's economic argument contended that the "trade of a country which is both manufacturing and agricultural will be more lucrative and prosperous than that of a country which is merely agricultural."[42] He advanced several arguments in support of this conclusion. In the first place, he observed once again that, because nations generally try to supply their needs with the products of their own soil, foreign demand for American agricultural goods would tend to be unsteady. At the same time, however, American demand for foreign manufactured goods would be relatively "constant and regular." This inequality, he concluded, this "uniformity of demand on one side and unsteadiness of it on the other" would necessarily make the course of trade "turn to the disadvantage" of a "merely agricultural" nation like the United States.[43] It would, all other things being equal, tend to impoverish itself by its constant need to buy and its fluctuating ability to sell. This problem could be avoided, however, if the nation took steps to develop its manufacturing economy.

Second, Hamilton contended that the diversity of an economy including both manufacturing and agriculture would enhance America's commerce with

[40] Hamilton, *Writings*, 694–95.
[41] Hamilton, *Writings*, 689.
[42] Hamilton, *Writings*, 689.
[43] Hamilton, *Writings*, 689.

other nations. Foreign customers, he observed, would be more inclined to frequent a market in which "commodities, while equally abundant, are most various." From this it followed, too, that such diversification would operate to the advantage of American merchants. The "field of enterprise" open to them must be "enlarged" by their access to a greater "variety" of "commodities" that they could export to "foreign markets."[44] Foreign merchants were more likely to come to America to buy if they could find there more than one sort of product, and American merchants were more likely to find customers abroad if they could deliver more than one kind of product.

Third, Hamilton held that the productive diversity provided by manufacturing would tend to protect America's economy from the commonly experienced "stagnations of demand for certain commodities which at some time or other interfere more or less with the sale of all." When such stagnations struck, a nation that offered only a few products would be more likely to find itself with an excess of those products on hand, and hence would be pushed to "make injurious sacrifices" in order to procure needed foreign articles. In contrast, a nation producing a "great variety of commodities" would ordinarily find "itself indemnified" against the low prices of some of its products by the high prices of others. Such a nation could avoid the "injurious sacrifices" confronting the less diversified economy, because by relying for the time being on the "prompt and advantageous sale of those articles which are in demand" its merchants could more easily "wait for a favorable change in respect to those which are not."[45]

Finally, from these three "circumstances" Hamilton drew two additional "important inferences." First, a manufacturing and agricultural nation was more likely to have a favorable balance of trade than a purely agricultural nation. Second, and as a consequence of the first, the former nations were likely to be wealthier than the latter.

Turning from the economic to the political, Hamilton argued that not only the "wealth" but also the "independence and security" of the country would be enhanced by "the prosperity of manufactures."[46] Here Hamilton suggested that support for manufacturing touched on the most important national aspirations. Independence and security, he admonished, were "great objects," the attainment of which required every country to strive to "possess within itself all the essentials of national supply," which included "the means of *subsistence, habitation, clothing,* and *defense.*"[47] "The possession of these goods," he continued, "is necessary to the perfection of the body politic, to the safety as well as to the welfare of the society." To lack any of them is to lack "an important organ of political life and motion," and "in the various crises which await a

---

[44] Hamilton, *Writings*, 689–90.
[45] Hamilton, *Writings*, 690.
[46] Hamilton, *Writings*, 691–92.
[47] Hamilton, *Writings*, 692 (Hamilton's emphasis).

state, it must severely feel the effects of any such deficiency." For evidence in support of these propositions, Hamilton appealed to America's own experience in the Revolution, to the "extreme embarrassments" it had faced when unable to provide itself the goods it needed. "A future war," he warned, might well bring these same "mischiefs and dangers" upon the country again, unless the nation's deficiencies in manufacturing were corrected by "timely and vigorous exertion." This correction, he concluded, "merits all the attention and zeal of our public councils" and is "the next great work to be accomplished."[48]

Here we may see that Hamilton regarded the policy put forward in the *Report on Manufactures* as an act of high statesmanship on a par with that undertaken in the *Report on Public Credit* and the *Report on a National Bank*. Here, as before, Hamilton contended that the policy in question was essential to completing the work of the founding, or to realizing in practice the Constitution's promise of energetic government. A domestic manufacturing sector, he insisted, was not just a luxury but a necessity. Without it, the "body politic" would remain imperfect or incomplete, lacking an "important organ of political life and motion," to the detriment not only of society's "welfare" but even its "safety."[49] Accordingly, the establishment of American manufacturing was the "next great work to be accomplished" – following, presumably, on the earlier necessary but insufficient steps of ratification of the Constitution, provision for the public debt, and establishment of a national bank.

As we have seen, Hamilton thought that a good society required energetic government, and that a proper energy required the government to be able to borrow. This power, however, was not fully established in practice by the mere constitutional authorization to borrow money. Rather, it required in addition a government that was considered by the creditor class to be a reliable debtor, so that it could borrow at a reasonable rate of interest, hence the need to establish a sufficient provision for the country's existing debts. In addition, to meet the "exigencies" that might emerge – especially war – the government needed to be able to borrow large sums in a short amount of time, hence the need for a national bank, a sizeable accumulation of capital to which the government could turn, without the possibly disastrous delays occasioned by borrowing from a multitude of small lenders.

A similar line of thinking informed Hamilton's insistence that a domestic manufacturing sector was necessary to an energetic government capable of defending the nation. To take the problem in its narrowest and most obvious sense, a nation that could not make its own weapons could not adequately defend itself. Once war broke out, it would have to rely on foreign nations to supply its arms, and those nations might be unable or unwilling to do so. Indeed, Hamilton's concerns on this score were sufficiently acute that he went so far as to argue that it might be best if the government actually manufactured

[48] Hamilton, *Writings*, 692.
[49] Hamilton, *Writings*, 692.

its own military supplies. He admitted that as a "general rule manufactories on the immediate account of the government are to be avoided." Nevertheless, he perceived an exception with regard to the "necessary weapons of war." Government manufacturing of such items was "agreeable to the usual practice of nations," which in turn rested on "sufficient reason." After all, Hamilton observed, there was a certain "improvidence in leaving these essential instruments of national defense to the casual speculations of individual adventure, a resource which can less be relied upon in this case than in most others," because such goods are not "objects of ordinary and indispensable private consumption or use."[50]

Hamilton's argument, however, also indicated that the need for military supplies is only one aspect of the problem. He spoke not only of military goods but more broadly of those goods that are the "essentials of national supply," not only the material for "defense" but also for "subsistence," "habitation," and "clothing." To carry on war successfully, the nation needed to be able to provide for itself not only whatever was required to put a formidable military into the field but also whatever was necessary for the rest of the society to live, even to live comfortably, or to live on the level to which it was accustomed. Perhaps here we gain insight into Hamilton's understanding of what was required not just for government to be energetic but more specifically for a *republican* government to be energetic. In another context, Hamilton had observed to Washington that a government like that of the United States could not carry on war successfully without the support of public opinion.[51] Yet public support would surely be more inclined to flag if war meant that the citizens had to endure privation. Such privation was less likely, however, if the nation could supply for itself all that it needed, both for the military and for the society at large to flourish.

The Constitution and Support for Manufactures

Having established the propriety, or even the necessity, of government support for manufacturing, Hamilton turned to the question of the means to be employed to this end. To judge properly of these means, he observed, "it will be of use to advert to those which have been employed with success in other countries."[52] Here, as when he justified the necessity of a national bank, Hamilton showed a certain conservatism, a willingness to employ any policy tools that had been approved by experience, even if this meant being guided by the experience of the non-republican governments of the old world. This tendency contributed to his breach with Jefferson because here, as in the case of the bank, his argument for the constitutionality of the means to be employed led him to

---

[50] Hamilton, *Writings*, 713–14.
[51] *PAH*, 7: 49–50.
[52] Hamilton, *Writings*, 697.

an interpretation of the Constitution that Jefferson regarded as impermissible and dangerous.

Seeking the best way to encourage manufacturing, Hamilton weighed the advantages of a variety of common expedients.[53] His favor fell most emphatically, however, on "pecuniary bounties," or direct government payments to manufacturers of favored goods. Such bounties, Hamilton believed, had proven to be "one of the most efficacious means of encouraging manufactures" and "in some views" even "the best." Bounties provided a more direct support for new manufactures than any other expedient, and, unlike protective duties, had less of a tendency to cause a temporary scarcity or increase in prices.[54] The "direct" and "powerful" encouragement provided by bounties, Hamilton concluded, was "generally speaking essential" to surmount the "obstacles which arise from the competitions of superior skill and maturity elsewhere," especially where foreign governments supported their own industry with such bounties.[55]

Here Hamilton encountered a problem. Some questioned "the constitutional right of the government of the United States to apply this species of encouragement." To show that "there is certainly no good foundation for such a question," Hamilton had to turn once again to constitutional interpretation in defense of his program.[56] And the interpretation he put forward confirmed, as we will see, all of Jefferson's worst fears about the tendencies of Hamilton's constitutional thought.

The Constitution, Hamilton began, expressly authorized Congress to "lay and collect taxes, duties, imposts and excises, to pay the debts and provide for the *common defense* and *general welfare*" of the United States. This power, moreover, was subjected only to a handful of qualifications, the most emphatic of which pertained to the mode of taxation, rather than the purposes for which the money raised could be spent. Thus the Constitution required "that 'all duties, imposts and excises shall be uniform throughout the United States,' that no capitation or other direct tax shall be laid unless in proportion to numbers ascertained by a census or enumeration taken on the principles prescribed in the Constitution and that 'no tax or duty shall be laid on articles exported from any state.'" Apart from these three limitations, the government of the United States enjoyed a very broad power of taxing and spending. On the one hand, Hamilton suggested, the power to "*raise money*" was no less than "*plenary* and *indefinite*": Congress could levy any taxes it wanted on any items it chose for any reasons it thought proper. On the other hand, the "objects to which" such money could be "appropriated" were "no less comprehensive than the payment of the public debts and the providing for the common defense

[53] Hamilton, *Writings*, 697–707.
[54] Hamilton, *Writings*, 698–99.
[55] Hamilton, *Writings*, 701.
[56] Hamilton, *Writings*, 702.

and '*general welfare.*'" According to Hamilton, this last expression – "general welfare" – was "doubtless intended to signify more than was expressed or imported in those which preceded." It thus empowered Congress to raise and spend money for purposes beyond the payment of the public debt and the common defense. An alternative reading, one treating this expression as adding nothing of substance, was unreasonable because it would have "left" many "exigencies incident to the affairs of a nation" with no "provision." Indeed, Hamilton contended that the terms chosen were "as comprehensive as any that could have been used" precisely "because it was not fit that the constitutional authority of the Union to appropriate its revenues should have been restricted within narrower limits than the 'general welfare' and because this necessarily embraces a vast variety of particulars, which are susceptible neither of specification nor of definition."[57] A narrower reading of the General Welfare Clause would be inconsistent with the kind of energetic government that Hamilton believed the Constitution aimed to establish.

Hamilton's claim that the vast and various elements of the "general welfare" could not be specified or defined suggested that the spending power was not only not limited to paying the nation's debts and providing for its defense but also that it was not limited by the subsequent enumeration of powers in the rest of Article 1, Section 8 of the Constitution. Hamilton did not say this in so many words, but it seems to be a sufficiently clear implication of what he did say. He went on to affirm that the Constitution left it to the "discretion of the national legislature" to decide what "objects" pertain to the "general welfare, and for which under that description an appropriation of money is requisite and proper" – adding that "there seems no room for a doubt that whatever concerns the general interests of *learning*, of *agriculture*, of *manufactures*, and of *commerce*" would fall "within the sphere" of Congress's power "*as far as regards an application of money.*"[58] The payment of bounties was therefore within Congress's spending power because that power extended to objects – such as manufactures, learning, and agriculture – that were not included in the Article I enumeration of powers, and that indeed were not mentioned anywhere else in the Constitution.

Perhaps anticipating the unease that such an interpretation might provoke in certain readers, Hamilton proceeded to identify two limits to the broad power he had just defined. In the first place, he contended that the General Welfare Clause contained within itself a "qualification" of its own scope. Its terms, after all, implied that "the object to which an appropriation of money is to be made" must be "*general* and not *local.*" This limit was not as strict as it might at first appear, however, as Hamilton immediately added that it meant that the spending's "operation" must not be "confined to a particular spot" but must extend "throughout the Union," either "in fact or by possibility."[59]

[57] Hamilton, *Writings*, 702 (Hamilton's emphases).
[58] Hamilton, *Writings*, 702 (Hamilton's emphases).
[59] Hamilton, *Writings*, 703 (Hamilton's emphases).

The government, then, would be free to spend money in such a way as would directly benefit some locality, so long as it could mount a plausible claim that "by possibility" it would redound to the "general welfare." This understanding is not in itself unreasonable. If Congress selected some particular site as most suited to the manufacture of some good and then subsidized the building of a factory there, it would directly benefit the local inhabitants while at the same time doing something that might benefit the whole nation. Nevertheless, such considerations were unlikely to quell Jefferson's concerns.

The second limit to which Hamilton pointed anticipated the objection that Jefferson would later raise to this portion of the *Report on Manufactures*. Here Hamilton emphasized that the power to spend money for the general welfare did not imply a power in the federal government to do just anything for the general welfare. Spending, Hamilton implied, was one mode of exercising governmental power but not the only mode. Contending that this mode could be exercised with such latitude did not mean that other modes could be exercised with a similar latitude. Congress could spend money for any purpose it thought advanced the general welfare, but from this it did not follow that it could regulate, or forbid, or punish for any purpose it thought advanced the general welfare. "A power to appropriate money" with such "latitude" did not "carry a power to do any other thing not authorized in the Constitution, either expressly or by fair implication." Therefore, no one ought to object to Hamilton's "construction" on the grounds that it "would imply a power to do whatever else should appear to Congress conducive to the general welfare."[60]

As if to emphasize his good faith in making this distinction – and in therefore insisting that his argument did not amount to a brief in favor of unlimited government – Hamilton went on in a subsequent part of the *Report* to identify a way of promoting American manufactures that he seemed to admit was outside the power of the federal government. He observed that the "encouragement of new inventions and discoveries at home, and of the introduction into the United States of such as may have been made in other countries" was "among the most useful and unexceptionable aids which can be given to manufactures." The ordinary means of such "encouragement" were twofold: in the first place, "pecuniary rewards," and in the second place, a right to "exclusive privileges" for some limited time, that is, a legal right to be the only one who may sell or make use of the discovery in question. Pecuniary rewards, of course, were constitutionally unproblematic: they were essentially the same as bounties and could be justified under Hamilton's interpretation of the spending power. Exclusive privileges, however, were another matter, since they involved the government in exercising other powers. To grant such an exclusive privilege, the government would have to make it a crime for others besides the discoverer or introducer to make use of the discovery during the stated period of time, or at least make intrusion on the discoverer's or introducer's right an injury for which one could be sued. The exercise of such powers could only be justified

[60] Hamilton, *Writings*, 703.

by some grant of power in the Constitution. Such a grant of power existed in Article I, Section 8's clause regarding copyrights and patents, but Hamilton found that this provision accomplished only part of the good that he had in view. It authorized Congress to "promote the progress of science and useful arts, by securing for limited times to authors and inventors the exclusive right to their respective writings and discoveries." While this was certainly fine as far as it went, Hamilton contended that "in regard to improvements and secrets of extraordinary value" it was also "desirable" to "extend the same benefit to introducers as well as authors and inventors." In other words, Hamilton believed that America's manufacturing progress could be stimulated not only by granting exclusive privileges to those Americans who made useful discoveries but also by granting them to whoever brought to America such discoveries as have been made in other counties. Yet the Constitution did not authorize such a benefit for "introducers," and Hamilton had to admit that here "and in some other cases there is cause to regret that the competency of the authority of the national government to the good which might be done is not without a question." He accordingly concluded that if the federal government "cannot do all the good that might be wished, it is at least desirable that all may be done which is practicable" – which presumably meant that it should use pecuniary rewards to encourage the introduction of new discoveries, since it was not permissible to grant exclusive privileges to do so.[61]

Hamilton certainly conceded for present practical purposes that the government was not authorized to grant exclusive privileges to introducers of new discoveries. Nevertheless, it is also worthy of comment that his careful choice of words did not entirely foreclose the possibility of some construction of the Constitution that would justify such a measure. After all, he did not flatly say that no such authority existed, only that such authority was "not without a question." And he made this limited concession, it would seem, only in the context of a discussion of the Patents and Copyright Clause of the Constitution. Given Hamilton's generally expansive interpretation of the national power, he might have foreseen the possibility that the granting of such privileges could be defended as an exercise of the government's authority over commerce, or perhaps as a "necessary and proper" adjunct of that power.[62]

---

[61] Hamilton, *Writings*, 705–06.

[62] Doron Ben-Atar notes that Hamilton's desire to encourage the introduction of foreign technology into American manufacturing and his desire to stimulate emigration of skilled European manufacturers to America belie the presentation of Hamilton by his enemies as an Anglophile seeking to make America subservient to Great Britain. Ben-Atar observes that British law and policy sought to prohibit the exportation of British manufacturing knowledge and the emigration of the people who possessed it. To that extent, Hamilton wished, for the sake of American power and prosperity, to encourage violations of British law. Ben-Atar more generally observes that Hamilton's desire to imitate Great Britain was aimed not at making America a "British satellite" but instead at elevating it to the position of "a strong egocentric competing power." "Alexander Hamilton's Alternative: Technology Piracy and the Report on Manufactures," *William and Mary Quarterly* 52 (1995): 389–414.

Hamilton also acknowledged a question of constitutional authority in relation to another of the means he proposed for promoting manufactures: the facilitation of "the transportation of commodities" by improving the nation's roads and waterways. Such improvements, Hamilton contended, in fact advanced *all* the "domestic interests of a community" but were also worthy of mention as a way of promoting manufactures. Perhaps nothing, he suggested, had done so much to build up the manufacturing establishments of Great Britain as "the ameliorations of the public roads of that kingdom, and the great progress which has been of late made in opening canals." Superior facilities of transportation enlarged the domestic market for manufactured goods, since they opened all localities to them – permitting transportation to places within the country where it had before been impossible, or at least making it less expensive where before the cost had been too burdensome. Hamilton therefore praised the improvements in transportation facilities that had been accomplished "in some quarters" of America and hoped that such examples would "stimulate the exertions of the government and citizens of every state."[63]

He also warned, however, that the most effective plan of improving the nation's means of transportation could be implemented only by the national government. Such "improvements," he argued, "could be prosecuted with more efficacy by the whole than by any part or parts of the Union," since efforts by state governments were likely to be impeded by the "collision of some supposed local interests." After all, local producers – who might be powerful enough to influence state and local policy – sometimes had an interest in preventing the improvement of transportation facilities, precisely because the difficulty and expense of transportation of goods gave them an effective monopoly over the local market. This "spirit" of short-sighted local interest had shown itself so "frequently to the eye of the impartial observer," Hamilton argued, that "patriotism" would "wish" that "the body in this country in whose councils a local or partial spirit is least likely to predominate" – in other words, the Congress of the United States – "were at liberty to pursue and promote the general interest" by the improvement of transportation. Here again, however, Hamilton seemed to concede the questionable character of such a power. While it might be best, from the standpoint of policy, for the federal government to play a leading role in improving the nation's facilities for transportation, it was not clear that it had the authority to do so. It "were to be wished," Hamilton wrote, that there was no doubt of the power of the national government to lend its direct aid" to such schemes of improvement "on a comprehensive plan."[64]

Once more, Hamilton's circumspect language acknowledged without actually endorsing a doubt about the scope of the federal government's power. Hamilton wished that there were no doubt about the authority of Congress to improve transportation, which could be taken as a wish that the Constitution had bestowed a more copious power upon Congress. However, it could

---

[63] Hamilton, *Writings*, 707.
[64] Hamilton, *Writings*, 707–08.

equally be understood as a wish that some contemporary figures did not entertain mistaken doubts about the genuine reach of Congress's power under the Constitution. It seems more likely that the latter is Hamilton's meaning, since interpretations he had already advanced could easily be used to find a constitutional basis for federal action in this area. After all, the broad understanding of the Necessary and Proper Clause he defended in his opinion on the bank could be invoked in defense of federal efforts to build up the nation's transportation infrastructure. Such efforts could readily be understood as necessary and proper with a view to the regulation of commerce. One might contend that such an argument would be an abuse of the commerce power, since the government would be not so much regulating as promoting commerce. Even if this argument were to prevail, however, the present report identifies another line of argument to which Hamilton could recur. As we have seen, just a few pages earlier Hamilton had, in defending the constitutionality of bounties, contended that Congress was authorized to spend money for any object that advanced the general welfare. It is hard to believe that he would not have seen that this very argument identified a way in which Congress could build up the means of transportation by directly subsidizing those who undertook to do it, whether they were state governments, private businesses, or both.[65]

Conclusion

The Report on Manufactures represented the final step in Hamilton's effort to complete the founding by bringing energetic government fully into being. Like the previous steps, it illustrated his understanding of the mutual dependence of energetic government and a flourishing private sector. His *Report on Public Credit* sought to secure the government's ability to borrow at reasonable rates

---

[65] Hamilton had sufficient doubts about the constitutionality of such measures – or at least about the public perception of their constitutionality – that he later suggested a constitutional amendment to authorize some of them. Troy E. Smith, "Divided 'Publius': Democracy, Federalism, and the Cultivation of Public Sentiment," *Review of Politics* 69 (2007): 575. Nevertheless, even in the context of such a proposal, Hamilton seemed to stop short of admitting the unconstitutionality of such measures under the then existing Constitution. He suggested that an "article ought to be added to the constitution for empowering Congress to open canals in all cases in which it may be necessary to conduct them through the territory of two or more states or through the territory of a state and that of the UStates." He placed this suggestion, however, under the following heading: "Arrangements for confirming and enlarging the legal powers of the Government." His use of the term "confirming" indicates some sense that the power might already exist on a proper construction of the Constitution but was still in need of being made manifest for prudential reasons. Moreover, earlier in the letter in which he made this proposal, he spoke of a federal policy of improving the nation's roads as if it were constitutionally unproblematic and required no amendment. See *PAH* 23: 599–604. Jefferson, not surprisingly, held that a federal policy of internal improvements would require a constitutional amendment. See Joseph H. Harrison, Jr., "'Sic et Non': Thomas Jefferson and Internal Improvement," *Journal of the Early Republic* 7 (1987): 341.

by making a sufficient provision for the public debt, thus fostering the development of a creditor class that could view the government as a worthy borrower. His *Report on a National Bank* aimed to further solidify the government's borrowing power – as well as to promote a flourishing national economy – by creating a bank that, though chartered by the government, depended for its efficacy on its being held and governed by private owners. Similarly, in his *Report on Manufactures* he hoped to use the spending power to foster a vibrant manufacturing economy, which he viewed as essential to American prosperity and to the government's ability to defend the nation. One might say that Hamilton's whole program was animated by a desire to make energetic use of the government's power with a view to creating the kind of economy and society that could in turn sustain energetic government in the long term.

Hamilton's *Report on Manufactures*, however, bore less immediate fruit as public policy than its predecessors. To be sure, in the longer run America developed into the manufacturing power that Hamilton had envisaged. Indeed, as Mike O'Connor notes, many of Hamilton's "recommendations would eventually be implemented, in a supreme irony, during the presidencies of Jefferson and Madison."[66] After the close of his political career, Jefferson conceded Hamilton's view that American manufacturing was essential to American independence: "Experience has taught me," he wrote, "that manufactures are now as necessary to our independence as to our comfort."[67] Nevertheless, the short-term policy consequences of the *Report* were more modest. Congress enacted most of Hamilton's tariff proposals in the *Report* but not the bounties that Hamilton thought so essential to promoting American manufacturing.[68]

What the *Report* lacked in immediate policy impact, however, it more than made up in immediate political explosiveness. Jefferson, in particular, regarded the *Report*'s interpretation of the General Welfare Clause not as merely more of the same kind of thing about which he had already raised the alarm but instead as a qualitative, and highly disturbing, step beyond even the dangerously loose constitutionalism that had informed the bank. The secretary of state was to highlight these and other concerns in a comprehensive critique of Hamiltonianism that he would submit to the president a few months after the appearance of Hamilton's *Report on Manufactures*.

[66] O'Connor, *A Commercial Republic*, 46.
[67] Quoted in Douglas A. Irwin, "The Aftermath of Hamilton's 'Report on Manufactures,'" *Journal of Economic History* 64 (2004): 820. See also O'Connor, *A Commercial Republic*, 46.
[68] See Irwin, "The Aftermath of Hamilton's 'Report on Manufactures,'" 800–21.

8

The Revolution, Alienation of Territory, and the Apportionment Bill

In 1792, Jefferson and Hamilton had a complete break over domestic policy. By summer, Jefferson had written to Washington with an extensive critique of Hamilton's program, which Jefferson believed to be unconstitutional and anti-republican in character. In response, Hamilton defended himself and his system and mounted his own counter-critique of Jefferson, which he made both in letters to Washington and in the public newspapers.

Before turning to this momentous debate, however, it is worthwhile to examine two relatively minor arguments of early 1792, both of which help to illustrate the divergent tendencies of Hamilton and Jefferson's political and constitutional thought.[1] The first of these took place in relation to a report on the instructions to America's ministers to Spain, which Jefferson had prepared and then showed to Hamilton, seeking the latter's advice. Hamilton submitted his thoughts to Jefferson in writing, and Jefferson in turn wrote out his own responses to Hamilton's remarks. As a result, we have a record of an exchange between the two men on the proper understanding of the American Revolution and of the scope of the powers of the federal government.

Hamilton opened with praise for Jefferson's report, the "general tenor" of which he found to be "solid and proper." His very next comment, however, called into question the way in which the report presented the American Revolution. According to Jefferson's draft, America had been "oblig[ed]" by

---

[1] During 1791–92, Hamilton and Jefferson also differed over the question of coinage, which was raised by Hamilton's recommendations in his *Report on the Establishment of a Mint*. In his famous letter to Edward Carrington (discussed in detail in Chapter 10), Hamilton identified the disagreement over the mint as one of the factors that had increased Jefferson and Madison's "spirit of opposition." Hamilton, *Writings*, 747. Nevertheless, I have omitted a discussion of that dispute here, because it does not raise the kinds of differences of political principle between the two men with which this book is concerned. For a helpful discussion of Hamilton and Jefferson's different approaches to the coinage issue, see Elkins and McKitrick, *The Age of Federalism*, 234.

"circumstances" to "discontinue" its "foreign magistrate" and in his place name new ones "within every state." This move had in turn "brought on us a war on the part of the former magistrate, supported by the nation among whom he resided."[2] Hamilton disputed whether it put "our Revolution upon the *true* or the best footing" to say that our decision to discontinue the king had brought the war. Was it not rather the case that the "war" had existed "previously" and had in fact brought on this "*discontinuance*"? Was not the war "rather the *cause* than the *effect*?"[3]

Jefferson seems on second thought to have agreed with Hamilton: he noted that the report was "amended in conformity with this observation."[4] Nevertheless, one may fairly say that this exchange illustrates two markedly different tendencies of thought regarding the Revolution. Jefferson's first impulse, it would seem, was to think that American independence had been justified by the various abuses the colonies had suffered up to 1775, prior to the existence of an actual state of war between Britain and America. In contrast, Hamilton's instincts were more conservative: independence had been chosen not because of mere discontent with British policy, however offensive it may have been, but by nothing less than the king's decision to wage war on his American subjects. It is likely that behind these different ways of interpreting the facts of America's revolution lay different principles for justifying revolution in general. Hamilton's principles were more conservative in the sense that he thought graver abuses were required to make revolution a justifiable option.

The report also brought to light the two men's disagreement about how to understand the powers of the federal government. Jefferson's draft had contended that America could not offer land in exchange for free navigation of the Mississippi: "for as to territory, we have neither the right nor the disposition to alienate an inch of what belongs to any member of our union."[5] As we have seen, Hamilton tended to favor expansive interpretations of federal power out of a concern that the government be understood to possess sufficient authority to meet whatever exigencies it might encounter in the future. Unsurprisingly, then, he balked at Jefferson's bald disclaimer of any power to alienate territory, doubting whether it was "true" or "useful." Hamilton seems to have assumed that Jefferson was reasoning from – but misunderstanding – general principles of the law of nations. Thus, in relation to the truth of Jefferson's denial of power, Hamilton noted that "the doctrine which restricts the alienation of territory to cases of extreme necessity is applicable rather to peopled territory than to waste and uninhabited districts." In relation to the usefulness of such a denial, he admonished Jefferson that "positions restraining the right" of the

[2] *PAH*, 11: 69, n. 3.
[3] *PAH*, 11: 68–69 (Hamilton's emphases).
[4] *PAH*, 11: 68.
[5] *PAH*, 11: 71, n. 10.

United States "to accommodate exigencies which may arise ought ever to be advanced with great caution."[6]

Here Jefferson did not budge, and the rejoinder he penned alongside Hamilton's remarks illustrates once again their very different understandings of both the basis and the scope of the powers of the federal government. Hamilton's remarks implied that the United States held certain powers simply by virtue of being a national government and that the scope of these powers could be determined with reference to the customary law of nations. Jefferson held instead that the powers of the government arose only from the Constitution and that those powers were to be construed strictly. The power to alienate territories, he suggested, was out of bounds because it was not one of the powers "given by the Constitution to the general government." Moreover, in a complaint that would become a familiar refrain, he contended that Hamilton's mode of thinking pointed to a government unrestrained by any clear limitations and hence empowered to do all manner of frightening things. According to Jefferson, Hamilton invited us to go "out" of the Constitution to find a power to alienate unpeopled territories, for the sake of accommodating "exigencies which may arise." If we may do that, however, then we may also "accommodate ourselves a little more by alienating that which is *peopled*, and still a little more by selling the *people* themselves. A shade or two more in the degree of exigency is all that will be requisite, and of that degree we shall ourselves be the judges." He concluded by hoping that such possibilities would be "forever laid to rest" by the new amendment to the Constitution "declaring expressly that the 'powers not delegated to the U.S. by the Constitution are reserved to the states respectively."[7]

The Apportionment Bill

A second constitutional disagreement arose over the apportionment bill that came before the president in the spring of 1792. The bill emerged after several months of wrangling between the two houses of Congress over expanding the size of the House of Representatives and how to apportion the House seats among the states. The Constitution itself determined the original apportionment but also empowered the Congress to set, within limits, the size of the House. By late 1791, the House voted to increase its size from 67 to 112 members. The plan it approved would have given each state one representative for every 30,000 inhabitants – the maximum permitted by the Constitution – and disregarded for purposes of apportionment any remaining fraction of population less than 30,000. Thus, for example, a state with a population of 60,000 would be awarded two representatives, while a state with, say, 85,000 would

[6] *PAH*, 11: 71.
[7] *PAH*, 11: 71–72 (Jefferson's emphases).

still receive only two seats. Seeking to diminish the size of such remainders, the Senate passed the bill in an amended form that would have awarded each state one representative for every 33,000 inhabitants. Dissatisfied with the size of increase in membership this plan would yield – it generated only 105 members and not the desired 112 – the House rejected this amendment and the bill was not enacted. Trying again in early 1792, the House passed a new apportionment bill identical to its first but with the addition of language requiring another census and reapportionment by 1797. The Senate once again spurned the work of the lower chamber and responded by passing a plan that would have simply apportioned 120 House members among the various states but without explaining what underlying principle it had used to determine the state-by-state allocations. According to the editors of Jefferson's papers, the Senate had apparently proceeded as follows: It "first determined the size of the House by applying the ratio of one representative per 30,000 to the aggregate U.S. population," then applied "the same ratio to each state individually, producing a total of 112 representatives," and finally "assigned the remaining seats to the eight states with the largest fractions."[8] This Senate version was passed by narrow majorities in each house of Congress. Nevertheless, opponents raised objections to its constitutionality, specifically to its lack of a stated ratio of representation and its reliance on the aggregate national population. These complaints were sufficiently troubling to President Washington that he sought the cabinet's advice on whether he should veto the measure. Jefferson and Hamilton both submitted their opinions to Washington in writing on April 4, 1792.[9]

Jefferson's opinion on the apportionment bill, like his earlier opinion on the bank, displays his inclination to understand the Constitution's grants of power as providing strict and unmistakable rules limiting Congress's discretion. He conceded that the bill's distribution of House seats among the states, "whether tried as between great and small states, or between North and South," was "tolerably just" and could not be "objected to on that ground" alone.[10] Congress's work, however, needed to pass an additional test: it also had to conform to the Constitution, which did not leave the national legislature utterly free to judge what was just and prudent in relation to the apportionment of House seats. The Constitution, Jefferson observed, "prescribed" a certain "process" of apportionment, departure from which would be "arbitrary and inadmissible." The relevant portions of Article I required that "Representatives and direct taxes shall be apportioned among the several states according to their

---

[8] These quotations are from the explanatory note provided by Jefferson's editors (*PTJ*, 23: 376–77), and my explanation of the development of the apportionment bill given in this paragraph is deeply indebted to their detailed account.

[9] *PAH* 11: 227 (introductory note by Hamilton's editors).

[10] *PTJ*, 23: 370.

respective numbers" and that "the number of representatives shall not exceed one for every 30,000 but each state shall have at least one representative."[11] According to Jefferson, the provision that apportionment be done according to the states' respective populations required that there be a "common ratio" or a "common divisor." In other words, if the bill had followed the Constitution's instructions, there should be some single number that would, when the various state populations were divided by it, yield the numbers of their House delegations. Although the bill crafted by the Senate did not proclaim the principles it had used in reaching the numbers it prescribed to each state, Jefferson showed – by performing the calculations and laying them out in a series of tables – that it had relied on no such common divisor. Thus, Jefferson concluded, "the bill reverses the Constitutional precept" because by it representatives were not apportioned among the states according to their respective numbers.[12]

Of course, there was a problem with the strict method of apportionment on which Jefferson here insisted, one that Congress had already encountered in its various efforts to frame an acceptable bill: the neat uniformity of the common divisor was achieved at the expense of fractions of population in each state that appeared to be unrepresented. Jefferson acknowledged this difficulty but held that it was a necessary cost of Constitutional fidelity. Some would object, he noted, that while in the case of taxes one could always find a divisor that would apportion them exactly according to population without any remainder, the same thing could not be accomplished in the case of representatives. Jefferson answered that "taxes must be divided *exactly*, and Representatives *as nearly* as the *nearest ratio* will admit." The population "fractions" remaining from the latter operation "must be neglected," because the Constitution wills "absolutely that there be an apportionment, or common ratio; and if any fractions result from the operation, it has left them unprovided for." Indeed, Jefferson contended that the Constitution must have envisioned that such fractions would result and had intended to "submit to them," knowing that "they would be in favor of one part of the union at one time, and of another at another, so as, in the end, to balance occasional inequalities." The present bill, however, had applied at least two divisors to reach its results, and, Jefferson warned, "if two ratios may be applied, then 15 may, and the distribution become arbitrary instead of apportioned to numbers."[13]

Jefferson then turned to the alternative constitutional interpretation that seemed to have informed the Senate's work. In defense of the bill, some had said that the phrase limiting representation to no more than one per 30,000 could refer either to the population in each state or to the aggregate population of all the states. On the latter interpretation, the rule was intended only to

[11] *PTJ*, 23: 370.
[12] *PTJ*, 23: 370–71.
[13] *PTJ*, 23: 371–72 (Jefferson's emphases).

determine the total number of representatives. The Constitution intended that the representation in the House be apportioned according to population, but it did not intend to prescribe a strict rule governing that apportionment, leaving the matter instead to Congress's discretion, so long as the total number of representatives did not exceed the limit expressed: one per 30,000. According to this interpretation, the Senate bill was constitutional and there would be no need for a presidential veto.

Jefferson marshaled a number of arguments against this interpretation of the apportionment provision. In the first place, he contended that, while the relevant passage might well bear either interpretation, his own was the one that "common sense" would apply. The common divisor interpretation, he suggested, represented the "universal understanding" the country had applied, and indeed the understanding on which the Senate and House had operated throughout most of their recent deliberations, until at the last minute some legislators had seized upon the novel alternative construction in order to legitimize their work. Moreover, he added, the disputed phrase "stands in the midst of a number of others, every one of which relates to states in their separate capacity," thus inviting "common sense" to "understand it, like the rest of its context, to relate to states in their separate capacities."[14]

Jefferson appealed not only to the words, context, and public understanding of the provision but also to the consequences that would arise from whichever construction prevailed. "Where a phrase is susceptible of two meanings," he held, "we ought certainly to adopt that which will bring upon us the fewest inconveniencies." The meaning he had defended caused a "single inconvenience": the existence of large unrepresented fractions of population in some states. Even this real inconvenience, however, was mitigated by the impartial workings of chance: "it being a mere hazard on which states this" inconvenience "will fall, hazard will equalize it in the long run." At the same time, the alternative interpretation was no better in regard to its consequences, for it gave rise to the very same inconvenience. After all, it gave Congress some latitude to ameliorate the problem of unrepresented fractions, but nothing could completely eliminate it.

Moreover, Jefferson continued, the aggregate population interpretation carried other "grievous" inconveniences. Since that interpretation permitted Congress to ameliorate but not eliminate the problem of unrepresented fractions, it led to a plan, such as the present one, that awarded additional House seats to the states with the largest unrepresented fractions, necessarily leaving some of the smaller ones in other states unrepresented. In effect, Jefferson suggested, this approach allowed "the large fraction in one state to choose a representative for one of the smaller fractions in another state," thus taking "from the latter its election, which constitutes real representation," and substituting "a virtual representation of the disfranchised fractions." Jefferson then

[14] *PTJ*, 23: 372–73.

appealed to the American Revolution as having established the unacceptability of virtual representation. The "tendency" of this principle, he claimed, "has been too well discussed and appreciated by reasoning and resistance, on a former great occasion, to need development now."[15]

The other "grievous" inconvenience that Jefferson saw arising from the Senate approach was that it invited future political conflict over apportionment by freeing Congress from any unmistakable rule, a problem that was exacerbated by the bill's failure to explain the principle by which it had fixed the apportionment. The bill, Jefferson observed, in fact distributed "residuary representatives" to the states with the largest fractions of population, although it did not state that it had done so. It thus appeared to "have avoided establishing" this method as a "rule, lest it might not suit on another occasion." "Perhaps," Jefferson warned, it will be found on some future occasion more convenient to allocate additional representatives "among the smaller states," on another "among the larger states," and "at other times according to any crotchet which ingenuity may invent and the combinations of the day give strength to carry." Alternatively, a future Congress might use the discretion given by the aggregate population interpretation to distribute residual seats "arbitrarily, by open bargain and cabal." "In short," Jefferson concluded, "this construction" would introduce into "Congress" a "scramble" for "the surplus members" and thus would cause "waste of time, hot-blood," and perhaps even go so far, at a time when "passions are high," as to cause Congress to deadlock. In contrast, all these dangerous possibilities were avoided by Jefferson's "construction," which "reduces the apportionment always to an arithmetical operation, about which no two men can ever possibly differ."[16] Jefferson thus concluded his opinion by urging Washington to veto the bill.

Just as Jefferson's opinion had once again shown his inclination to understand a constitutional grant of power as providing a strict rule limiting its use, so Hamilton's once again illustrated his opposite tendency to understand it as giving Congress a wide latitude of discretion. Like Jefferson, Hamilton understood the controversy over the bill as presenting two possible interpretations of the Apportionment Clause of the Constitution. Adopting the minimum number specified in the Constitution, Congress had used 30,000 as its ratio, but it had begun by applying it to the total population in order to determine the total size of the House. This raised the question of whether "this ratio ought to have been applied in the first instance to the aggregate numbers of the United States or to the particular numbers of each state." Unlike Jefferson, however, Hamilton argued "that either of these courses might have been constitutionally pursued – or in other words that there is no criterion by which it can be pronounced decisively that the one or the other is the true construction." Moreover, Hamilton added that this uncertainty as to meaning – and hence the absence of a clear

[15] *PTJ*, 23: 375.
[16] *PTJ*, 23: 375.

rule such as Jefferson desired, and the presence of the legislative discretion that Jefferson feared – was not so unusual: "Cases so situated often arise on constitutions and laws."[17]

The Constitution, Hamilton observed, required that "*Representatives* and *direct taxes* shall be *apportioned* among the several states according to their *respective numbers.*" It was clear, to begin with, that "the same rule is to be pursued" in allocating both taxes and representatives. In apportioning direct taxes, Hamilton contended, one would first determine the "total sum" to be raised, and would then apportion it among the states by the "following rule": "As the aggregate numbers of the United States are to the whole sum required so are the particular numbers of a particular state to the proportion of" taxes due from "such state." This was the "process" that would "naturally" be followed in the matter of taxes, but it was also "so far the exact process that has been followed by the bill, in the apportionment of representatives." This much, Hamilton suggested, amounted to "a strong argument for" the bill's "constitutionality." Indeed, if the Constitution had mentioned no specific ratio, then it was "evident" that Congress could have used no other method of apportionment than that just sketched, and "no doubt" about its "propriety" could have been raised.[18]

The constitutional question, then, depended on the passage's subsequent mention of the ratio of 30,000. Here Hamilton argued that the Constitution was sufficiently ambiguous to permit Congress to adopt either method of apportioning House members among the states. The text provided that "the number of representatives shall not exceed one for every 30,000 but each state shall have at least one representative." As we have seen, Jefferson held that this language bound Congress to apportion according to a strict rule of one representative per 30,000 people in each state. Hamilton, however, contended that it could just as "naturally be read" to mean only that the total size of the House shall not exceed more than one per 30,000 of the aggregate population of the United States. In his own words, the passage might be "understood" as follows:

The whole number of representatives of the United States shall not exceed one to every 30,000 of the aggregate numbers of the United States; but if it should happen that the proportion of the numbers of any state to the aggregate numbers of the United States should not give to such a state one representative – such a state shall nevertheless have *one*. No state shall be without a representative.

According to Hamilton, there was "nothing" in the Constitution's "form of expression to confine the application of the ratio to the several members of the states." It rather "equally permits" the ratio to be applied to either the "joint or *aggregate numbers.*" The point of the passage was "merely to determine

[17] *PAH*, 11: 228–29.
[18] *PAH*, 11: 229 (Hamilton's emphases).

a proportionate limit which the number of representatives shall not exceed," and that aim would be "as well satisfied by resorting to the collective as to the separate population of the respective states."[19] In other words, contrary to Jefferson's reading, the Constitution need not be understood here as establishing a strict rule from which Congress could not depart in apportioning representatives. Rather, it could equally be read merely as establishing a minimum size to the House member's constituency, and a maximum size of the House in relation to a given aggregate population, and beyond that leaving Congress free to apportion the seats as it thought proper, so long, of course, as the apportionment could be said to be "according to population."

Nevertheless, Hamilton acknowledged, one might contend that the bill's allocation of residual seats to the states with the largest "remainders" of population" is "unconstitutional because it renders the representation not strictly according *to the respective numbers* of the states." In reply, Hamilton contended that this outcome was simply the "necessary consequence" of apportioning House seats in the most obvious way, that is, in the same way as one would apportion direct taxes. If Congress began with a total sum to be sought and then applied a given ratio to the populations of the several states, the fact that the common divisor could never result in whole numbers meant that the total size of the House would invariably come up smaller than Congress had intended. According to Hamilton, the remaining "unapportioned residue" of representatives would "of necessity" have to be "distributed among the states according to some rule." Yet no rule "more equal or defensible can be found than that of giving a preference to the greatest remainders" of population in the states. Moreover, he noted, if this process made the "apportionment not mathematically 'according to the *respective numbers* of the several states,'" the same objection could be made to the other mode of apportionment and the constitutional interpretation that insisted on it. "Fractions more or less great" would in either case "prevent" a perfect "conformity of the proportion of representatives to numbers." Indeed, he added, this objection in fact lay more heavily on Jefferson's interpretation, since it prevented Congress from doing anything to ameliorate the problem of the unrepresented fractions.[20]

"Upon the whole," Hamilton concluded, the bill "apportions the Representatives among the several states according to their respective numbers," so that "the number of representatives does not exceed one for every 30,000 persons" and with "each state having at least one member." The bill "therefore performs every requisition of the Constitution" and does so, moreover, "in the manner most consistent with equality." On this view, then, the bill could not be said to be unconstitutional. The most that could be said was that "there may be another construction of which the Constitution is capable." The possibility of such an alternative, however, was not a sufficient reason for the president

---

[19] *PAH*, 11: 229–30 (Hamilton's emphasis).
[20] *PAH*, 11: 230 (Hamilton's emphasis).

to exercise the veto. "In cases where two constructions may reasonably be adopted, and neither can be pronounced inconsistent with the public good, it seems proper that the legislative sense should prevail."[21]

In this case, however, it was Jefferson's, and not the legislature's, sense that prevailed. At the secretary of state's urging, President Washington issued the first presidential veto. Congress then returned to the drawing board and conformed its work to the principles on which Jefferson had insisted. The new apportionment bill, which Washington signed into law, "created a House of 105 members by applying the ratio of one representative per 33,000 to the respective populations of the states," while "disregarding the left-over fractions."[22]

Conclusion

The specific issues over which Hamilton and Jefferson sparred in early 1792 generated nothing like the lasting fame of the previous year's debate over the Bank of the United States. For Hamilton and Jefferson, however, these relatively minor matters involved major principles. On Hamilton's side, they revealed his preference for a more conservative interpretation of the American Revolution – and probably a more conservative understanding of the right to revolution in general – and brought forth, once again, his preference for broad interpretations of federal power, which he thought necessary to meet the exigencies that the nation might encounter in the future. In Jefferson's case, they showed his opposite inclinations: his greater willingness to justify revolution as a response to unjust government and his insistence on strict and clear limits on federal power as a way of preventing abuse and corruption. These differences of constitutional understanding, moreover, would play a key role in the complete break between them that emerged in the summer of 1792.

[21] *PAH*, 11: 230.

[22] These quotations are from the editorial note to Jefferson's opinion, *PTJ* 23: 377. Jefferson's editors also observe that Congress continued to apportion according to Jefferson's interpretation until 1840, "when the inequities of this system became too great to be ignored." For an account of this development, they point the reader to Zechariah Chafree, Jr., "Congressional Reapportionment," *Harvard Law Review* 42: 1015–47.

9

Aiming for Monarchy

Jefferson's Critique of Hamiltonianism

The full extent of Jefferson's opposition to Hamilton's program can be gleaned from a lengthy letter he wrote to George Washington on May 23, 1792. The letter's immediate purpose was to convince Washington, contrary to his earlier resolution, to serve a second term as president. For Jefferson, however, this aim led more or less directly to his critique of the Hamiltonian system. At an earlier time, Jefferson suggested, the nation was in a "favorable state" for "making the experiment" of continuing the new government without Washington at its head, because then "the public mind" was "calm and confident." Now, however, Washington's reassuring presence was required because that serenity and confidence had eroded.[1] Yet, as Jefferson would attempt to show, Hamilton's policies, and his approach to the Constitution, had caused this dangerous public dissatisfaction.

Jefferson approached Washington on these issues somewhat coyly. He assured the president that these discontents arose "from causes in which you are no ways personally mixed" – despite the fact that they all stemmed from policies that had been adopted under Washington's administration. Moreover, Jefferson began the letter by assuming the position of a man who was merely reporting on concerns then current among the public, without taking a position on them himself. He suggested that although these worries had been "hackneyed" in the public newspapers, it would nevertheless be helpful, "in order to calculate" their possible consequences, for him to review them for Washington, "giving to each the form, real or imaginary, under which they have been presented."[2] Nevertheless, it is evident from the mode of expression to which Jefferson eventually resorted in this letter, and from what he wrote in letters to other correspondents, that the concerns he raised were in fact also his own.

[1] *PTJ*, 23: 535.
[2] *PTJ*, 23: 535.

Indeed, Jefferson had himself raised some of these concerns in conversation with Washington some months before.[3]

The Dangers of Hamilton's Debt and Revenue System

Jefferson began by citing a number of complaints about the character of Hamilton's debt and revenue system. These complaints may be arranged under three headings: a concern about the size of the debt, a concern about its consequences for tax policy, and finally a concern about how the debt was structured and the monetary consequences of that structuring. Regarding the size of the debt, Jefferson reported that some had claimed "that a public debt, greater than we can possibly pay before other causes of adding new debt to it will occur, has been artificially created, by adding together the whole amount of the debtor and creditor sides of accounts, instead of taking only their balances, which could have been paid off in a short time." As if that were not bad enough, there were proposals in Congress, and suspicions of further proposals to come, which would increase the debt even further.[4]

Turning to tax policy, Jefferson noted that this "accumulation of debt" had "forever" placed beyond the government's reach "those easy sources of revenue" that could have "habitually" paid for "the ordinary necessities and exigencies of government" and thus would have shielded the government from the "habitual murmurings against taxes and tax-gatherers, reserving extraordinary calls for those extraordinary occasions which would animate the people to meet them." Indeed, Jefferson continued, even though the demand for revenue had so far been no more than what was to be expected, the government was already "obliged to strain the *impost* till it produces clamor, and will produce evasion, and war on our own citizens to collect it," and "even to resort to an excise law, of odious character with the people, partial in its operation, unproductive unless enforced by arbitrary and vexatious means, and committing the authority of the government in parts where resistance is most probable and coercion least practicable."[5]

Finally, with regard to the structuring of the debt and its monetary consequences, Jefferson noted public complaints that the debt might be retired more quickly by refinancing it at current rates of interest, "but that from this we are precluded by" the debt's "having been made irredeemable but in small portions and long terms." This "irredeemable quality", it was contended, was given to the debt "for the avowed purpose of inviting its transfer to foreign countries." This transfer, moreover, would, when completed, "occasion an exportation of 3 millions of dollars annually" to pay the interest, a "drain of coin of which as

---

[3] See Jefferson's account of his conversations with Washington on Februrary 28 and 29, 1792. *PTJ*, 23: 184.

[4] *PTJ*, 23: 535.

[5] *PTJ*, 23: 535 (Jefferson's emphasis).

there has been no example, no calculation can be made of its consequences." It was further feared that the "banishment of our coin will be completed by the creation of 10 millions of paper money in the form of bank bills, now issuing into circulation," and that the "10 or 12 percent annual profit paid to the lenders of this paper medium are taken out of the pockets of the people, who would have had without interest the coin it is banishing."[6]

Jefferson then turned to a critique of the effect of Hamilton's policies on the nation's economy and even on its moral character. The economic complaint held that Hamilton's system drew American capital into "speculation" in "paper," an activity that was "barren and useless, producing," like money placed on a "gaming table, no accession to itself," and thus diverting that capital from "commerce and agriculture, where it would have produced addition to the common mass."[7] The moral critique that Jefferson related held that this paper speculation "nourishes in our citizens habits of vice and idleness instead of industry and morality."[8]

Jefferson's letters from this period reveal that most of these concerns that he here presented to the president as being held by the public were also concerns that Jefferson entertained himself. Just a few weeks before submitting his critique to Washington, Jefferson had written to Nicholas Lewis, observing that a "further assumption of state debts," had been "proposed by the secretary of the treasury" and that, while it had been narrowly defeated, "we all fear" that it will be enacted in one way or another, since "the chickens of the treasury have so many contrivances and are so indefatigable within doors and without." With Lewis, however, Jefferson went a step further and identified the thinking that he believed lay behind these efforts to increase the debt: "As the doctrine is that a public debt is a public blessing, so they think a perpetual one is a perpetual blessing, and therefore wish to make it so large as that we can never pay it off."[9]

The summer before he had written to Edmund Pendleton complaining that the public had to pay interest for the "paper circulation" issued by the national bank, which circulation at the same time banished from the nation the "gold and silver" currency for which the people "would have paid no interest."[10] He had also written to James Madison suggesting that "subscriptions to the bank" had capital "locked up in a strong box" in Philadelphia rather than being "employed in commerce."[11] Similarly, he had noted to Pendleton the "rapidity" with which the bank subscriptions had been filled and had questioned "whether in a country whose capital is too small to carry on its own commerce, to

---

[6] *PTJ*, 23: 535.
[7] *PTJ*, 23: 535.
[8] *PTJ*, 23: 535.
[9] *PTJ*, 23: 408.
[10] *PTJ*, 20: 669.
[11] *PTJ*, 20: 615.

establish manufactures," and "erect buildings" it was wise that "such sums should have been withdrawn from these useful pursuits to be employed in gambling."[12] Jefferson went so far with Edward Rutledge as to suggest that Hamiltonian "scripomany" had ground American commerce to a halt:

Ships are lying idle at the wharfs, buildings are stopped, capitals withdrawn from commerce, manufactures, arts and agriculture, to be employed in gambling, and the tide of public prosperity almost unparalleled in any country is arrested in its course and suppressed by the rage of getting rich in a day.[13]

The problem, Jefferson believed, was that paper speculation promised, at least in the short term, huge profits with which more productive activities could not hope to compete. Noting with alarm the prospect that bank investors might get a twenty percent return in one year, he lamented that "agriculture, commerce, and everything *useful* must be neglected, when the *useless* employment of money is so much more lucrative."[14]

Jefferson believed there was something addictive about gambling in paper speculation. Such was the weakness of the human spirit that the outsized profits that were "*sometimes*" won led men to hope for them "*always*," resulting in a "rage of gambling in the stocks."[15] "No mortal can tell where this will stop," Jefferson wrote to Rutledge. "For the spirit of gaming, when once it has seized a subject, is incurable. The tailor who has made thousands in one day, though he has lost them the next, can never again be content with the slow and moderate earnings of his needle."[16] He took a similarly ominous tone in a letter to Gouvernor Morris. Noting the "spirit of gambling in the funds," which had "laid up our ships at the wharves as too slow instruments of profit," he observed that some held that "the evil will cure itself." Said Jefferson in response: "I wish it may. But I have rarely seen a gamester cured even by the disasters of his vocation."[17]

Distortions in the Government

Jefferson next presented Washington with the concern that Hamilton's system had "furnished effectual means of corrupting such a portion of the legislature as turns the balance between the honest voters whichever way it is directed."[18] Later, when he met with Washington to discuss the letter, he reinforced this issue in particular, naming it, along with the increase in the size of the national debt, as one of the "two great complaints." The president "must know," and

[12] *PTJ*, 20: 669.
[13] *PTJ*, 22: 74.
[14] *PTJ*, 23: 27 (Jefferson's emphasis).
[15] *PTJ*, 23: 27 (Jefferson's emphases).
[16] *PTJ*, 22: 73.
[17] *PTJ*, 22: 104.
[18] *PTJ*, 23: 535.

indeed "everybody knew," Jefferson contended, "that there was a considerable squadron" in both houses of Congress "whose votes were devoted to the paper and stockjobbing interests." The "votes of these men" were "uniformly for every treasury measure," Jefferson complained, "and because "most of these measures had been carried by small majorities they were carried by these very votes." "It was," he added, "a cause of just uneasiness" when we see lawmakers "legislating for their own interests in opposition to those of the people."[19] Jefferson's concerns on this score were perhaps rooted in, and were at least encouraged by, a private conversation in 1791 among Hamilton, Jefferson, and John Adams in which Hamilton had supposedly said that the British constitution would have been an *"impractical* government" if it were purged of its "corruption," and that even with such corruption it was "the most perfect government which ever existed."[20]

While Jefferson worried that the paper interest gave the treasury a disproportionate influence over the Congress, he also feared that the treasury was growing too powerful within the executive branch. Although he did not raise this issue in his letter to Washington, Jefferson had raised it earlier in conversation with the president. In March, Jefferson had spoken with Washington about the position of the post office within the executive branch. There had been some question, Jefferson suggested, about whether the law creating the post office was "considered as a revenue law, or a law for the general accommodation of the citizens," and hence a question about whether the post office was under the secretary of the treasury or the secretary of state. Recent legislation, however, seemed to have "removed the doubt" on this score "by declaring that the whole profits of the office should be applied to extending the posts and that even the past profits should be returned to the treasury for the same purpose." This development, Jefferson contended, made clear that the postal service was not simply a source of general revenue and that it therefore belonged "in the department of the secretary of state." Jefferson raised this point, moreover, not out of petty bureaucratic politics but with a view to placing "things on a safe footing" within the executive branch. It was, he urged Washington, "advantageous" to declare the post office under the secretary of state because "the department of the treasury possessed already such an influence as to swallow up the whole executive powers." Jefferson saw this danger extending into the future and thus warned that future presidents, lacking Washington's "weight of character," would be unable "to make head against this department."[21] Jefferson had confided similar fears to James Madison. In a postscript to a

---

[19] *PTJ*, 24: 210.

[20] Quoted in Kevin J. Hayes, *The Road to Monticello: The Life and Mind of Thomas Jefferson* (Oxford: Oxford University Press, 2008), 394 (emphasis in original). Jack Rakove traces this idea to Hume's influence on Hamilton. *Revolutionaries*, 399.

[21] *PTJ*, 23: 184. In the event, Washington decided to keep the post office under the secretary of the treasury. See the editorial note provided by Jefferson's editors. *PJT*, 23, 187.

June 1792 letter to his fellow Virginian, Jefferson expressed dismay that Hamilton's office controlled the "revenue cutters." "How comes an armed force to be in existence, and under the revenue department and not the department of war," he asked.[22]

Hamilton's Undermining of Constitutional Limits

Jefferson's letter linked the corruption of the legislature to an even more serious problem: the undermining of constitutional government itself. The members of the "corrupt squadron" that held the balance of power in Congress had "manifested their dispositions to get rid of the limitations imposed by the Constitution on the legislature, limitations on the faith of which the states acceded to that instrument."[23] Although, as we have seen, Jefferson objected to the national bank as unconstitutional, by this point he was even more worried by Hamilton's proposal in the *Report on Manufactures* that the federal government use bounties to encourage new industries and by the interpretation of federal power Hamilton had advanced in support of such a policy. As his "Notes on the Constitutionality of Bounties to Encourage Manufacturing" indicate, Jefferson had begun to grapple with this problem earlier in 1792, perhaps to prepare himself for a meeting with Washington on the topic.[24] Although these somewhat fragmentary meditations suggest that Jefferson agreed, at least to some extent, with Hamilton's overarching aim of encouraging American manufacturing, he did not share Hamilton's enthusiastic endorsement of bounties as the most effective means to that end. Bounties, he conceded, had "in some instances been a successful instrument" for introducing "new and useful manufactures," but they had also "been found almost inseparable from abuse." More important, Jefferson believed that the kinds of abuse to which bounties were prone had led the Constitution to deny them to Congress as an instrument of public policy. The Constitution, he reflected, "seems to have been jealous" of authorizing such direct means of encouraging manufacturing out of a "fear of partiality" in their distribution. Accordingly, Jefferson concluded, while the government could certainly encourage domestic manufacturing through "heavy duties" on foreign goods, the "power of dispensing bounties has not been delegated" by the Constitution to the general government. Rather, this power was left with the states, "whose local information renders them competent judges of the particular arts and manufactures" to which bounties might properly be dealt out.[25] Jefferson, moreover, did not view Hamilton's proposed bounties as a

---

[22] *PTJ*, 24: 90.

[23] *PTJ*, 23: 535.

[24] According to the editors of Jefferson's papers, these "Notes" cannot be dated precisely but were "probably written about the time of this meeting with the president, and perhaps even in preparation for it." *PTJ*, 23:173.

[25] *PTJ*, 23: 172.

trivial infraction of the Constitution but rather as presenting a serious test of the new nation's constitutional fidelity. In his reflections, he emphasized that the "general authority" was obligated "by every tie to preserve" the government "adopted by our country" and thus to "render sacred" by its "respect" the "line which has been drawn between" the general and the state governments, and "not to set the example of committing infractions" of the Constitution, apart from which the general government had "neither powers nor existence."[26]

Jefferson, however, could not simply leave it at this. Presumably nobody would dispute his insistence on constitutional fidelity, but the question was precisely whether bounties would in fact violate the Constitution. Jefferson had claimed that a concern about "partiality" in distribution had led the Constitution to withhold this power from the Congress, but invoking such a concern did not on its own show that the Constitution had in fact withheld such a power. Accordingly, Jefferson completed his argument by returning to the reasoning that had informed his critique of the bank. The authority to "levy money to be given out in premiums," he observed, was not among the federal government's "enumerated" powers, nor was it "among those necessary to carry the enumerated powers into execution."[27]

Jefferson's second point here responded to an argument that Hamilton had not made but that one can certainly imagine him making. Given the capacious understanding of the Necessary and Proper Clause that Hamilton had advanced in his *Opinion on the Constitutionality of the Bank*, one can readily envision him contending that bounties were "necessary and proper" in relation to, say, the government's enumerated power to regulate commerce or to make war. Hamilton, as we have seen, understood "necessary" to mean "convenient" or "requisite." The *Report on Manufactures*, however, had presented bounties as the best, or most convenient, way to promote domestic manufacturing, which in turn could be seen as a way of promoting American commerce. And if one were to respond that a power to regulate was not a power to promote, Hamilton might have observed that a power to regulate could be understood as a power to "make regular": and the *Report on Manufactures* had explained how the absence of a domestic manufacturing sector subjected American commerce to certain damaging irregularities that arose from the fluctuations of foreign demand for American products. Similarly, since a domestic manufacturing establishment was important to the nation's ability to make war successfully, one could contend that bounties were justified under the Necessary and Proper Clause in relation to the government's war power or in relation to its power to raise and maintain a military force. Conversely, Jefferson's narrower understanding of "necessary" as "indispensable" rendered Hamilton's bounties unconstitutional, since they certainly were not absolutely essential to the regulation of commerce or the nation's ability to make war.

---

[26] *PTJ*, 23: 173.
[27] *PTJ*, 23:173.

Hamilton, however, had not in fact contended that the bounties were justified under the Necessary and Proper Clause. He had instead suggested that they were a straightforward exercise of an enumerated power. By providing the bounties, Congress would be spending public money for what it regarded as a beneficial purpose, yet the Constitution clearly authorized the national legislature to levy taxes and appropriate money for the general welfare. To Jefferson, this defense of the constitutionality of the bounties was far more scandalous and dangerous than the bounties themselves. He presented these concerns to Washington in their conversation of February 29, 1792, in which he expressed his concerns about the effects of Hamilton's *Report on Manufactures*. Congress, Jefferson warned, had already "from time to time aided in making such legislative constructions of the Constitution as made it a very different thing from what the people thought they had submitted to." Now there was a danger that Congress would go even further on this course and render the power of the federal government effectually unlimited. The federal legislature, he contended, "had now brought forward a proposition, far beyond every one yet advanced, and to which the eyes of many were turned, as the decision which was to let us know whether we live under a limited or an unlimited government." Jefferson made clear that he referred to the *Report on Manufactures*, which, he contended, proposed a system of bounties to encourage manufacturing as mere "color" or pretext for establishing "the doctrine that the power given by the Constitution to collect taxes to provide for the *general welfare* of the U.S. permitted Congress to take everything under their management which they should deem for the *public welfare*, and which is susceptible to the application of money." Thus, Hamilton's bounties, and more particularly his defense of their constitutionality, presented a "very different question from that of the bank." The bank had been defended as "an incident to an enumerated power." Jefferson had of course disagreed with that defense, but it at least as a matter of principle kept the government tethered – albeit too loosely, in Jefferson's view – to the enumeration in Article I, Section 8. Hamilton's construction of the Necessary and Proper Clause fostered a government that was not as limited as Jefferson would have liked but that was still limited in some respect. In contrast, he contended, Hamilton's construction of the General Welfare clause effectively eliminated the enumeration as a limit on federal power. As a result of the interpretation put forward in the *Report on Manufactures*, Jefferson argued, the "subsequent enumeration" of Congress's "powers was not the description to which resort must be had, and did not at all constitute the limits of their authority."[28] Jefferson put the problem still more strongly in a later letter to Washington. Hamilton's *Report on Manufactures*, he said, "expressly assumed that the general government has a right to exercise all powers which may be for the general welfare, that is to say, all the legitimate powers of government: since no government has a legitimate

---

[28] *PTJ*, 23: 186–87 (Jefferson's emphases).

right to do what is not for the general welfare of the governed."[29] Hamilton had tried in the *Report* to head off such an objection by distinguishing the spending power from other exercises of authority. A power to appropriate money for any purpose tending to the general welfare was not, he had insisted, a power to do just anything for the general welfare. On this view, the enumeration still stood as a limit on the powers of the federal government. Jefferson, however, told Washington that this argument was nothing more than a "sham-limitation of the universality" of the power Hamilton had asserted. Hamilton held that the power was limited "to cases where money is to be employed," but, Jefferson asked rhetorically, "about what is it that money cannot be employed?"[30]

We can discern in Jefferson's critique of the constitutionality of Hamilton's program two other themes on which the two men differed substantially. First, Jefferson was much more inclined to recur to the framers' and the public's understanding of the newly ratified Constitution as authoritative in its interpretation. Jefferson criticized Hamilton's interpretations as not only opening the door to unlimited government but also as amounting to violations of the public's faith. In his letter to Washington laying out his comprehensive critique of Hamiltonianism, he had contended that Hamilton's minions in Congress had shown their disposition to "get rid of the limitations imposed by the constitution on the legislature, limitations on the faith of which the states acceded to that instrument."[31] Similarly, in his conversation with Washington, he contended that Congress had indulged interpretations of its power that rendered the Constitution "a very different thing from what the people thought they had submitted to."[32] Jefferson had also laid heavy emphasis on this issue in his recommendation that Washington veto the apportionment bill, which was, Jefferson contended, based on an understanding of the Apportionment Clause different from that which had always been held by the public. In contrast,

---

[29] *PTJ*, 24: 351. Jefferson continued to hold this view much later in life, after he had served in the presidency himself. In 1815, he expressed his "hope" that "our courts will never countenance the sweeping pretensions which have been set up under the words 'general defense and public welfare.' These words only express the motives which induced the Convention to give to the ordinary legislature certain specified powers which they enumerate, . . . and not to give them the unspecified also; or why the specification? They could not be so awkward in language as to mean, as we say, 'all and some.' And should this construction prevail, all limits to the federal power are done away." Quoted in David N. Meyer, *The Constitutional Thought of Thomas Jefferson* (Charlottesville: University Press of Virginia, 1994), 199.

[30] *PTJ*, 24: 351. Considering Jefferson's famous vision of America as an agrarian republic, his objections to Hamilton's *Report on Manufactures* may have gone further than the constitutional issues discussed here. For Jefferson's concerns about economic relations that fostered a non-republican dependence of some citizens on other citizens, see Claudio J. Katz, "Thomas Jefferson's Liberal Anticapitalism," *American Journal of Political Science* 47 (2003): 1–17, and O'Connor, *A Commercial Republic*, 30–36.

[31] *PTJ*, 23: 535.

[32] *PTJ*, 23: 186–87.

Hamilton's arguments ordinarily eschewed such considerations. Like the later Hamiltonian John Marshall, Hamilton tended to think that the meaning of the Constitution "is to be collected chiefly from its words" and thus to avoid the dangers involved on relying on "extrinsic circumstances," such as suppositions about what the public or the framers had thought about it.[33]

Second, Jefferson's arguments about violations of faith revealed a certain ambiguity in his thought about precisely what authority lay behind the Constitution or what authority had created the new national government. In one formulation he spoke of "what the people thought they had submitted to" in the Constitution.[34] In another, however, he taxed the Hamiltonian Congress with jettisoning "limitations on the faith of which *the states* acceded to" the Constitution.[35] The latter expression suggests the compact theory that Jefferson would later openly espouse in the Kentucky Resolutions: the view that the Constitution was an agreement among the states, which therefore had a right to judge whether the federal government had overstepped its constitutional limits. This seems to be a variation on a view that Hamilton strongly condemned. Hamilton had, as we have seen, written to John Jay that Virginia's resolutions condemning the assumption manifested a spirit that had to be killed or would kill the government of the United States.

The Threat of Monarchy

Finally, Jefferson's letter to Washington turned to his most serious charge: that the ultimate aim of Hamilton's system was to undermine republicanism and lead the country into a monarchical form of government. It was believed, Jefferson reported, that the final "object" of all the preceding steps – increasing the size of the debt, corrupting the legislature, transcending the limits of the Constitution – was "to prepare the way for a change, from the present republican form of government, to that of a monarchy, of which the English constitution is to be the model." This form of government was "contemplated at the Convention," Jefferson reminded Washington. "To effect it then was impracticable," but its "partisans" were "still eager after their object" and were "predisposing everything for its ultimate attainment."[36]

Jefferson had been expressing this concern to others for more than a year, and in terms that had become more and more decided as time had passed. Apart from the machinations of particular individuals and sects, Jefferson believed that the general tendency of the government was in favor of monarchy. In

---

[33] The quoted words here are from Marshall's opinion in *Sturges v. Crowninshield* and are quoted in Charles F. Hobson's *The Great Chief Justice: John Marshall and the Rule of Law* (Lawrence: University Press of Kansas, 1996), 99.
[34] *PTJ*, 23: 186–87.
[35] *PTJ*, 23: 535 (emphasis added).
[36] *PTJ*, 23: 535.

December 1791, he wrote that, while the "experiment" of the new government had

> not yet had a long enough course to show us from which quarter encroachments are most to be feared, yet it is easy to foresee from the nature of things that the encroachments of the state governments will tend to an excess of liberty which will correct itself (as in the late instance) while those of the general government will tend to monarchy, which will fortify itself from day to day, instead of working its own cure, as all experience shows.

He added that he would "rather be exposed to the inconveniencies attending too much liberty than those attending too small a degree of it."[37]

In addition to his fears about these general tendencies, however, Jefferson also had a strong and growing concern precisely about the machinations of particular sects and individuals. In summer 1791, Jefferson wrote to Lafayette that while the French were "exterminating the monster aristocracy, and pulling out the teeth and fangs of its associate monarchy," a "sect" had appeared in America made up of "champions for a king, lords and commons." These men now declared that they had "espoused our new constitution, not as a good and sufficient thing in itself, but only as a step to an English constitution, the only thing good and sufficient in itself, in their eye."[38] He similarly told William Short that Fenno's *Gazette of the United States* aimed to subvert "the present form of government" in order to "make way for a king, lords and commons" – a "doctrine," he added, that was supported by some "high names" in America.[39] By the end of the year, Jefferson had adopted the term "monocrats" to refer to the Hamiltonian faction in American politics.[40]

Jefferson's concerns on this score extended to Hamilton himself. In 1791 and 1792, the secretary of state wrote memoranda to himself documenting the evidence of the secretary of the treasury's monarchical sympathies. He noted a conversation with Hamilton in which the latter had "condemned" some of John Adams's recent writings – which Jefferson believed to be monarchical – as tending to "weaken the present government." According to Jefferson, Hamilton had acknowledged that it was indeed his "own opinion," though he did "not publish it in Dan and Beersheba, that the present government is not that which will answer the ends of society by giving stability and protection to its rights, and that it will probably be found expedient to go into the British form." Hamilton had added, however, that since the nation had "undertaken the experiment," he was "for giving it a fair course, whatever" his own "expectations may be." Indeed, Hamilton told Jefferson the "success" of the American republic had been "greater" than he had "expected" and that a satisfactory outcome "seemed more probable than it had done before." Moreover, there

---

[37] *PTJ*, 22: 435.
[38] *PTJ*, 24: 85.
[39] *PTJ*, 20: 692–93.
[40] See Jefferson's letters to Thomas Mann Randolph. *PTJ*, 24: 556 and 623.

were "still" other steps for "improvement" which "ought to be tried before we give up the republican form altogether." It was necessary to give republicanism a fair chance, Hamilton intimated, because "that mind must be really depraved which would not prefer the equality of political rights which is the foundation of pure republicanism, if it can be obtained consistently with order." Therefore, although Adams's intentions were no doubt "pure," he was "really blamable" for writing in such a way as to "disturb the present order of things."[41]

It would seem that both Hamilton and Jefferson were republicans, but not in the same way. Judging from what he said to Jefferson, Hamilton viewed republican government as desirable but not essential. Since he thought it obligatory where it could safely be achieved, Hamilton could reasonably be presented as a supporter of republican government. At the same time, he clearly viewed the establishment and maintenance of a certain kind of "order" as a more compelling goal. The most important aim, he suggested, was not to be governed in a republican manner but to have a government that would "give stability and protection" to society's "rights."[42]

In contrast, Jefferson's commitment to republicanism was far more absolute, far more a matter of fundamental principle. Hamilton was inclined to be a practical monarchist but open to being a practical republican. He was a practical monarchist to the extent that, while not insisting on it as the only legitimate form of government, he thought that experience showed some form of it was more likely to secure society's rights than a republic would. But he was open to being a practical republican, because he was cautiously pleased with the results of the American experiment in republican government and indeed thought that republicanism's equality of political rights was to be preferred, where it could be achieved consistent with society's purposes. Jefferson, in contrast, was much more a republican through and through, a practical and a theoretical republican. He was much more inclined to present republican government not only as desirable but as a requirement of justice.

To be sure, Jefferson sometimes acknowledged the virtues of the British form. Even in the spring of 1792, while his concerns about the monarchism of Hamilton and his followers was growing, Jefferson still spoke of Britain as having a "free" government, in contrast to the "arbitrary" or "despotic" ones of most of the rest of Europe."[43] Whatever the advantages of the British government, however, Jefferson could not look on it with Hamilton's sense of approval. A check to the success of the French Revolution, Jefferson wrote to George Mason in early 1791, "would retard the revival of liberty in other countries" – a formulation that implicitly equated the cause of liberty with that of French revolutionary republicanism. The "establishment and success" of the new French government, he continued, was "necessary to stay up our own

---

[41] *PTJ*, 22: 38–39.
[42] *PTJ*, 22: 38–39.
[43] *PTJ*, 23: 286. See also his similar observations to Charles Pinckney. *PTJ*, 23: 360.

and prevent it from falling back to that kind of half-way-house, the English constitution." He noted the existence of American partisans of the English constitution but expressed his hope that "the great mass of our community is untainted with these heresies, as is its head." On these latter forces, he pinned his "hope that we have not labored in vain, and that our experiment will prove that men can be governed by reason" – a formulation that implied that men were not governed by reason under the English constitution, or that a return to that form of government was not something that reason could approve.[44] Similarly, in the summer of 1792 he wrote to Joel Barlow criticizing those Americans who were "disposed to move retrograde and take their stand in the rear of Europe," even as Europe, in the French nation, was "now advancing to the high ground of natural right."[45] In such communications Jefferson's mode of expression indicated that for him republican government was a requirement of "reason" or of "natural right" in a way that it was not for Hamilton.[46]

In any case, Jefferson believed that his letter to Washington had traced the train of consequences by which the government could be subverted and a non-republican alternative erected in its place, and he continued to emphasize and develop this argument in subsequent letters to and conversations with the president. Hamilton's system, he later wrote to Washington, "flowed from principles adverse to liberty, and was calculated to undermine and demolish the republic."[47] The steps of the process, as Jefferson summarized them, were as follows. First, Hamilton's system had effectively lifted the constitutional limits on congressional authority, thus drawing "all the powers of government into the hands of the general legislature." Second, Hamilton's financial system provided the "means for corrupting a sufficient corps in that legislature to divide the honest votes and preponderate, by their own, the scale which suited." Third, this corruption placed that "corps under the command of the secretary of the

---

[44] *PTJ*, 19: 241.

[45] *PTJ*, 24: 101. Jefferson's language here – which contrasts "retrograde" movement to "advancing" – suggests a philosophy of history and a conception of progress. James W. Ceaser comments on Jefferson's attraction to such a doctrine. As Ceaser observes, the belief in progress did not fit well with the common American belief in nature as providing a permanent standard for politics, a tension that some American proponents of progress "tried to elide or hide." Jefferson's letter to Barlow reflects this tension by using the language of progress but at the same time speaking of "natural right." *Nature and History in American Political Development* (Cambridge, MA: Harvard University Press, 2006), 27–28.

[46] Jefferson scholar Kevin J. Hayes gives expression to Jefferson's way of thinking when he remarks: "Given his passionate devotion to the principles of natural law and natural rights, Jefferson was shocked when he started hearing high ranking members of Washington's administration questioning the value of a republican form of government and wanting something closer to a monarchy." The men Hayes has in mind here – such as Hamilton and John Adams – were, however, just as devoted to principles of natural law and natural rights as Jefferson, but they did not think those principles required a republican form of government. Hayes, *The Road to Monticello*, 393.

[47] *PTJ*, 24: 351.

treasury."[48] Or, as Jefferson later put it in conversation with Washington, since there was a decisive group in Congress "devoted to the nod of the treasury, doing whatever he directed," the "executive had swallowed up the legislative branch."[49] Finally, he added, Hamilton, the man at the pinnacle of all this power, was a monarchist. It was "natural" to be "jealous" of Hamilton's aims, Jefferson contended, "when we reflected that he had endeavored in the Convention to make an English constitution of it, and when failing in that we saw all his measures tending to bring it to the same thing."[50]

Jefferson's argument displayed a certain unpleasant self-righteousness about which Hamilton would later complain to Washington. Jefferson routinely resorted to the language of "heresy" and "apostasy" in describing the views of Hamilton and his supporters. They had "apostatized from the true faith," he said.[51] Jefferson went even further, however. After all, even the most fervent believer might concede that a heretic or apostate had gone astray out of sincere error. Jefferson, however, did not give his political enemies even this much credit. His free use of the word "corruption" implied that they were moved not by an earnest concern for the common good but by raw self-interest, and Jefferson made this clear in a number of his remarks to Washington and to others. Those members of Congress who supported Hamilton's legislative program were "interested" and should have "withdrawn" from the votes in which their voices had been decisive. Theirs were not the "votes" of "the representatives of the people, but of deserters from the rights and interests of the people." It was, Jefferson insisted, "impossible to consider their decisions, which had nothing in view but to enrich themselves, as the measures of a fair majority, which ought always to be respected."[52]

This party, Jefferson went on, supported a move to aristocracy not out of any concern for the protection of society's rights but merely because they themselves hoped to become aristocrats. In the summer of 1792, Jefferson wrote to Thomas Paine that America had a "sect preaching up and panting after an English constitution of king, lords, and commons" because their own "heads" were "itching for crowns, coronets and mitres."[53] Around this same time he wrote to Jean Antoine Gautier that there were heads in America "itching for crowns, coronets and mitres" but also expressing his belief that "we shall sooner cut them off than gratify" such a desire.[54]

---

[48] *PTJ*, 24: 351.

[49] *PTJ*, 24: 433.

[50] *PTJ*, 24: 433.

[51] See, for example, *PTJ*, 20: 391 and 293.

[52] *PTJ*, 24: 353.

[53] *PTJ*, 20: 312 (and see also 703).

[54] *PTJ*, 24: 42. Later in life Jefferson, acknowledged Hamilton's personal integrity by making a distinction between private conduct and the use of corruption as a political tool. "Hamilton," he wrote, was "disinterested, honest, and honorable in all private transactions, amiable in society, and duly valuing virtue in private life, yet so bewitched and perverted by the British example

Conclusion: Washington as the Indispensable Man

As Jefferson's letter to Washington drew to its conclusion, his rhetoric intensified and he seemed to drop any pretense of merely reporting concerns that were held by others. Of all the "mischiefs" he had reviewed, he contended, the most "afflicting" and the most "fatal to every honest hope" was the "corruption of the legislature." This was the first step in Hamilton's system, it had then become "the instrument for producing the rest," and it would become "the instrument for producing in future a king, lords and commons, or whatever else those who direct it may choose." The Hamiltonian Congress, Hamiltonianism, Jefferson warned, would become "the most corrupt government on earth if the means of their corruption be not prevented."[55]

The Union was approaching a crisis that Jefferson feared would endanger its very life. Either the monarchical federalists or the republicans would gain the upper hand, but either outcome threatened secession and violence. Jefferson contended, however, that the success of the republicans would be less dangerous to peace and unity. "The only hope of safety," he argued, depended on the more "numerous representation" in the House of Representatives that would result from the next Congressional elections. Some of the new members would be with the existing Hamiltonian majority, but Jefferson expected that "the great mass will form an accession to the republican party." This new majority could then begin a series of reforms to allay the concerns that Jefferson had laid out in his preceding arguments. It would not, he admitted, be able to undo everything that had been done in the first two congresses, and especially in the first. "Public faith and right" would "oppose" such measures. Nevertheless, the new Congress could "rightfully" reform some parts of the system, pursue "a liberation from the rest" as quickly as "right" would allow, and foreclose the possibility of "similar commitments of the nation" in the future. Although Jefferson clearly desired this course, he also perceived the dangers of political convulsion that it involved. If the new legislature were to pursue these measures, he acknowledged, they would thereby "draw upon them the whole monarchical and paper interest." Still, he thought the nature of this coalition was such that it would be somewhat restrained in the measures it would take. The "paper interest," he suggested, would not "go all lengths" with the monarchists, since creditors would "never, of their own accord, fly off entirely from their debtors." He therefore concluded that this course of events presented the "alternative least likely to produce convulsion."[56]

Jefferson found the continued progress of Hamiltonianism far more politically dangerous. If the coming elections should return a Congress "still in the

---

as to be under the thorough conviction that corruption was essential to the government of a nation." Quoted in Jean M. Yarbrough, *American Virtues: Thomas Jefferson on the Character of a Free People* (Lawrence: University Press of Kansas, 1998), 141.

[55] *PTJ*, 23: 537.

[56] *PTJ*, 23: 538.

same principles" as the "present" one, and thus "show that we have nothing to expect but a continuance of the same practices," then, Jefferson warned, "it is not easy to conjecture what would be the result, nor what means would be resorted to for correction of the evil." He acknowledged that "true wisdom" required that any steps taken in response be "temperate and peaceable," and that he himself could "scarcely contemplate a more incalculable evil than the breaking of the union into two or more parts." Nevertheless, he proceeded to review the factors that made such a calamity a distinct possibility. The difference of "sentiment and interest" dividing the nation was "unfortunately" so "geographical" that no one could say that a "wise and temperate" course would "prevail" over one that was "more easy and obvious." This geographical division was to some extent present from the very birth of the new government, Jefferson suggested, because opposition to ratification had been primarily southern. This problem had been exacerbated, however, by the conduct of the new government since it had become operational. The legislature had "availed themselves on no occasion of allaying" southern concerns, "but on the contrary whenever northern and southern prejudices have come into conflict, the latter have been sacrificed and the former soothed." There was, moreover, a difference not only of prejudices but also of interests, since "the owners of the debt are in the southern and the holders of it in the northern division." In addition, Jefferson continued, the behavior of the Congress had tended to strengthen the position of the anti-federalists by confirming their worst fears and thus undermining the arguments of "republican federalists" in support of the Constitution. And, returning to the theme of bad faith constitutionalism, he observed that this confirmation of the anti-federalists' fears, this transformation of their "prophecy" into "true history," had been "brought about by the monarchical federalists themselves, who, having been for the government merely as a stepping stone to monarchy," had "themselves adopted the very constructions of the constitution of which" they had "declared it insusceptible" when they had been "advocating its acceptance before the tribunal of the people." No one could be sure, Jefferson concluded, that these considerations would not "proselyte the small number" needed to create a state of public opinion opposed to the continuation of the government.[57]

Amid these dangers, Jefferson argued, it was of the utmost importance that Washington agree to serve a second term as president. If events took the course for which Jefferson hoped – if the upcoming elections returned an "honest majority" and the monarchical and paper interests would "acquiesce" in the government's new direction – then Washington's "wishes for retirement" could be "gratified with less danger," as soon as these new conditions became "manifest." However, if Jefferson's worst fears were realized – if the new Congress was of a Hamiltonian stamp and resolved to continue on a Hamiltonian course – then Washington's presence would be absolutely essential to

[57] *PTJ*, 23: 538–39.

calm the political passions that would necessarily arise. According to Jefferson, a loss of majority support for the government and the Constitution provoked by continuing Hamiltonianism was "the event at which I most tremble." To prevent it, he considered Washington's "continuance at the head of affairs" as indispensable: "The confidence of the whole union is centered on you. Your being at the helm will be more than an answer to every argument which can be used to alarm and lead the people in any quarter into violence or secession."[58]

This was a strange kind of political analysis. According to Jefferson, if a majority of voters signaled their acceptance of Hamilton's program by electing a Hamiltonian majority to Congress, the resulting policies would alienate a majority from the government and the Constitution. And Washington was obliged to serve a second term in order to quell public alarm over policies that had been enacted with Washington's approval during his first term.

[58] *PTJ*, 23: 539.

10

Tending toward Anarchy

Hamilton's Critique of Jeffersonianism

Writing from Mount Vernon on July 29, 1792, Washington sent Hamilton, "in strict confidence, and with frankness and freedom," a letter on an "interesting and important subject." This subject was Jefferson's critique of Hamilton's system, which Washington provided for the secretary of the treasury almost word for word. The president did not, however, reveal Jefferson as the author, but instead presented the critique as having been discovered by him as a result of his efforts, during his trip home and since his arrival there, to learn "the sentiments which are entertained of the public measures."[1]

Washington's introduction suggested that he did not take all the points of Jefferson's critique with equal seriousness. Some of the complaints, he indicated, came from "sensible and moderate men – known friends to the government," who agreed that the nation was "prosperous and happy," but who were nevertheless "alarmed at that system of policy, and those interpretations of the Constitution, which have taken place in Congress." Other criticisms he attributed to other men, such as George Mason, "less friendly perhaps to the government, and more disposed to arraign the conduct of its officers."[2] While Washington may have regarded some aspects of the critique as more "sensible" than others, he nevertheless took the whole seriously enough that he wanted Hamilton's response. Aiming only to "obtain light and to pursue truth," and "wishing" for "explanations as well as complaints on measures" which involved the "public interest, harmony and peace" as well as his own

---

[1] *PAH*, 12: 129.
[2] For this reason, perhaps, Henry Cabot Lodge speaks of Hamilton's rejoinder as numbering and addressing "all the objections made by Mason." *Alexander Hamilton* (New Rochelle, NY: Arlington House, n.d.), 142. Nevertheless, while Washington mentioned Mason as a source of criticism that he heard while visiting Virginia, the summary Washington provided Hamilton was taken almost word for word from Jefferson's letter of May 23, 1792.

"public conduct," Washington asked for Hamilton's "ideas upon the discontents" to be "enumerated" in what followed.[3]

Hamilton's Defense of his Policies

Hamilton answered Washington on August 18 with a lengthy, point-by-point reply to the concerns that had been raised. He titled his report "Objections and Answers respecting the Administration of the Government."[4] In the accompanying letter, Hamilton admitted that the report contained at certain points "some severity" of tone. This arose, Hamilton said, because the critique Washington had forwarded included not only "imputations of error of judgment" on Hamilton's part but also "calumnies" upon his character as the "principal agent in the measures censured." He could not, he said, be "entirely patient" in the face of "charges which impeach the integrity of my public motives or conduct," feeling as he did that he deserved them *in no degree.*" He therefore relied on the president's "goodness" to make "the proper allowances" for the occasional "expressions of indignation" in his response.[5]

The Debt and the Excise
Hamilton took up the objections in Jefferson's order, turning first to the concerns regarding the size of the debt, the taxes it required, and the way it was structured. Any complaints about the size of the debt were misplaced, Hamilton suggested, since it was not something the government had gratuitously created but instead had been "produced by the late war." The government could not be faulted for its existence, "unless," he added, "it can be proved that public morality and policy do not require of a government an honest provision for its debts." Whether the debt was too big to extinguish before new causes of debt were encountered, as Jefferson had contended, could not be determined, Hamilton replied, but "by experience."[6] He also observed, however,

---

[3] *PAH,* 12: 133.

[4] *PAH,* 12: 229.

[5] *PAH,* 12: 228–29 (Hamilton's emphasis).

[6] *PAH,* 12: 229 (Hamilton's emphasis). At this point in his "Objections and Answers" Hamilton dedicated a good deal of space to Jefferson's claim that the debt had been artificially increased by adding together the debtor and creditor sides of the accounts. Hamilton claimed that he did not know what Jefferson meant by this, and then proceeded to work through and refute several possible meanings. In one of his conversations with Washington that summer, Jefferson explained that "with respect to the increase of the debt by the assumption . . . what was meant and objected was that it increased the debt of the general government and carried it beyond the possibility of payment. That if the balances had been settled and the debtor states directed to pay their deficiencies to the creditor states, they would have done it easily, and by resources of taxation in their power, and acceptable to the people, by a direct tax in the South, and an excise in the North." *PTJ,* 24: 210. Jefferson's explanation here seems to contradict an earlier explanation he had given for supporting assumption, which noted "the impossibility that certain states could ever repay the debts they had contracted." *PTJ,* 17: 270–71.

that this question depended to some extent on the "temper of the people." If they were made "dissatisfied by misrepresentations" of current policy, then the government would be "deprived of an efficient command of the resources of the community" that could be used for paying down the debt. Accordingly, he concluded, "those" – like Jefferson – "who clamor" against the government "are likely to be the principal causes of protracting the existence of the debt."[7]

As we have seen, Jefferson attributed Hamilton's efforts to increase the debt to the belief that, since a public debt was a public blessing, a perpetual debt would be a perpetual blessing. Hamilton did not address this charge in his "Objections and Answers" because Jefferson had not included it in his letter to Washington. Nevertheless, the charge was sufficiently commonplace that Hamilton was well aware of it and replied to it in the newspapers that year. Writing under the pseudonym "Fact" in the *National Gazette*, he observed that the secretary of the treasury had been "pretty plainly alluded to" as someone "advocating the pernicious doctrine that 'public debts are public blessings,'" and as accordingly supporting "a perpetuation of the public debt of the country." Hamilton claimed that he had in fact never maintained such a doctrine. He had instead contended that "that the *funding* of the existing debt of the United States would render it a national blessing." Here he recalled his arguments from the *Report on Public Credit* that America had been suffering from a shortage of currency, and that he hoped the funding of the debt could provide a partial remedy. He claimed that his policy had been successful. One had "only to travel through the United States with his eyes open, and to observe the invigoration of industry in every branch, to be convinced that the position was well founded." Nevertheless, whether he had been right or wrong in his thinking on this question, his argument for funding the debt was "quite a different thing from maintaining, as a general proposition, that a public debt is a public blessing."[8]

Indeed, Hamilton continued, not only had he not endorsed such a proposition, he had actually warned against it. Here he appealed to no less than three of his official reports, which showed that his thinking and conduct had in fact been "in uniform opposition to the doctrine charged upon him." The *Report on Public Credit*, for example, concluded that "the proper funding of the present debt will render it a national blessing" but then immediately repudiated "the position, in the latitude in which it is sometimes laid down, that 'public debts are public benefits.'" The latter view was an invitation to "*prodigality* and *liable to dangerous abuse*." Accordingly, Hamilton had said that he "ardently" wished "to see it incorporated, as a *fundamental maxim* in the *system of public credit* of the United States, that the *creation of debt should always be accompanied with the means of extinguishment*." Such a policy, he had told

---

[7] *PAH*, 12: 230.
[8] *PAH*, 12: 362 (Hamilton's emphasis).

his readers, was "the *true secret* for *rendering public credit immortal.*"[9] Hamilton had issued similar warnings in his *Report on Manufactures* and his more recent report on raising additional supplies for prosecuting the Indian war. The latter, indeed, had included an admonition against government's general tendency to take the political path of least resistance by relying on borrowing rather than taxes to pay its way. Because taxation was "never welcome to a community," governments often showed "a too strong propensity" to "anticipate and mortgage the resources of posterity rather than encounter the inconveniences of a present increase in taxes." Hamilton condemned this policy, when it was not demanded by extraordinary circumstances, as being "*of the worst kind.* Its obvious tendency is, by enhancing the permanent burdens of the people, to produce lasting distress, and its natural issue is in national bankruptcy."[10]

The "Objections and Answers" turned next to Jefferson's complaints about the extent and the character of the taxes that had been imposed to service the debt. Hamilton simply dismissed Jefferson's suggestion that the nation was overtaxed. So far, Hamilton observed, the "only sources of taxation which have been touched are imported articles and the single internal object of distilled spirits." Thus, contrary to what Jefferson had suggested, most sources of revenue were still available for any "extraordinary conjunctures" that the country might encounter. Indeed, Hamilton added, his system had made this truer than it had been before. Assumption had relieved the states of much of their war debt and had therefore permitted them to leave off the taxation necessary to make their payments. Thus, the overall result of Hamilton's system had been to lighten the tax load the people carried. It was, he concluded, "a mockery of truth to represent" the United States "as a community burdened and exhausted by taxes."[11] Similarly, Jefferson's complaints about the impost – that the government had "strained" it to the point that it would generate "clamor," "evasion," and finally "war on our own citizens to collect it" – were dismissed by Hamilton as "mere painting and exaggeration." For the most part, he contended, American imposts were "moderate, lower than in any country of whose regulations we have knowledge, except perhaps Holland." Of course merchants had complained about them, as men would complain of any tax that touched their business, but there was no reason to doubt that the collection was "essentially secure."[12]

Hamilton then took up the question of the excise tax. He began by denying Jefferson's specific complaints: that the excise was "of odious character with the people, partial in its operation, unproductive unless enforced by arbitrary and vexatious means, and committing the authority of the government in parts

---

[9] *PAH*, 12: 363 (Hamilton's emphasis).
[10] *PAH*, 12: 364–65 (Hamilton's emphases).
[11] *PAH*, 12: 233–34.
[12] *PTJ*, 23: 535; *PAH*, 12: 234.

where resistance is most probable and coercion least practicable."[13] The excise, Hamilton replied, was no more partial in its operation than "any other tax on a consumable commodity" which was adjusted on "exactly the same principles." In any such case, the "consumer in the main pays the tax." In other words, any apparent "partiality" in the tax burden arose from inequalities of consumption, a phenomenon that would occur with any such tax, unless it happened – as was not to be expected – that consumption should be absolutely uniform across the country. And if it were the case that some states consumed more "domestic spirits" and were thus more burdened by the excise than others, this inequality was ameliorated by the fact that other states consumed more foreign spirits, and so paid more in import duties.[14]

Moreover, Hamilton continued, the excise had already proven "considerably productive" of revenue, despite the "prejudices against it in some states." This productivity, he added, did not require any "arbitrary" or "vexatious" means of enforcement. At least, the means of collection could not appear vexatious and arbitrary except "to men who regard all taxes and all the means of enforcing them as arbitrary and vexatious."[15] In response to Jefferson's claim that the excise was "odious" to the American people, Hamilton observed that in fact the tax was being collected without serious problems in most of the Union, and that opposition was decreasing in most of the districts in which it had shown itself.[16]

Hamilton took much more seriously Jefferson's claim that the excise had committed the government's "authority" in places where "resistance" was "most probable" and "coercion least practicable." This concern, he said, had "more weight" than any of the others. Nevertheless, he continued, this "hazard" had been "wisely run" if there were "sufficient motives for" instituting the excise. A measure is not "bad" merely "because it is attended with a degree of danger."[17] By raising this question of the reasons for the policy, Hamilton elevated his defense of the excise to the level of high principles, which he invoked by linking the tax to the need to provide for the nation's debts.

The most straightforward part of this argument emphasized the need to provide for the country's Revolutionary War debt. High reasons of justice and policy required such a provision. Justice demanded that "the public faith and integrity" be preserved "by fulfilling as far as was practicable the public engagements." Justice similarly required that the government show a "due respect for property by satisfying the public obligations in the hands of the public creditors," which were just "as much their property as their houses or their lands, their hats or their coats." This respect for justice was also a

---

[13] *PTJ*, 23: 535.
[14] *PAH*, 12: 235.
[15] *PAH*, 12: 235.
[16] *PAH*, 12: 237.
[17] *PAH*, 12: 235.

measure of the highest public expediency. Providing for the public debt would "revive and establish public credit, the palladium of public safety." It was also necessary to "preserve the government itself by showing it worthy of the confidence which was placed in it, to procure to the community the blessings which in innumerable ways attend confidence in the government and to avoid the evils which in as many ways attend the want of confidence in it."[18]

Equally weighty reasons, Hamilton continued, had argued in favor of the assumption of the state debts. As a matter of policy it had made good sense to "consolidate" the nation's "finances and give an assurance of permanent order in them," thus "avoiding the collisions of thirteen different and independent systems of finance" and the "scramblings for revenue which would have been incident to so many different systems." Avoiding such "entanglements" had the additional policy advantage of securing to the federal government "the resources of the Union for present and future exigencies."[19]

Assumption of the state debts was also an act of justice, Hamilton contended, returning to a theme he had introduced in the *Report on Public Credit*. By taking responsibility for the debts of the states, the federal government had sought to "equalize the condition of the citizens of the several states in the important article of taxation," thus "rescuing" some of them "from being oppressed with burdens" that were "beyond their strength." Such an equalization was just, Hamilton argued, because the large debt and burdensome taxation experienced by some states had arisen from their "extraordinary exertions in the war" and their lack of "certain adventitious resources" possessed by others. Opponents of assumption – such as Jefferson himself, as we have seen – had complained of the inequalities it worked by favoring precisely those states that had so much debt remaining. Such inequalities, Hamilton contended, could "bear no comparison with the more lasting inequalities" that would have existed in the absence of assumption: a state of things in which the people of the states that "had done most or suffered most" during the war would have been left to carry "the great additional weight of burden" of high debt and high taxation.[20] Hamilton returned to this same point later in the "Objections and Answers" when responding to Jefferson's complaint that there were new plans afoot to assume even more of the state debt. Such plans, Hamilton urged, would be just because the states to be benefitted by them, Massachusetts and South Carolina, were known by everybody to have endured considerable "exertions, sufferings, sacrifices, and losses" during the Revolution, even as some other states had "failed in their federal duty."[21]

These considerations of justice and policy, Hamilton concluded, justified the excise, despite the risks that might attend it. If these "inducements" to

[18] *PAH*, 12: 235.
[19] *PAH*, 12: 236.
[20] *PAH*, 12: 236.
[21] *PAH*, 12: 238.

providing for the debt "were sufficiently cogent," then some source of revenue would be necessary. Since the "duties on imports" alone were insufficient, something else was required, and nothing besides the excise could have been found "equally productive" and at the same time "so little exceptionable to the mass of the people."[22]

Hamilton closed his defense of the excise by reviewing some additional political considerations that he believed made it a prudent step. These considerations emphasized the role the introduction of the excise played in establishing the federal government's power on a firm footing for the future. It was wise, he suggested, for the federal government to "lay hold of so valuable a resource of revenue before it was generally preoccupied by the state governments." Moreover, it was "not amiss that the authority of the national government should be visible in some branch of internal revenue, lest a total non-exercise of it should beget an impression that it was never to be exercised," which could in turn foster a conviction "that it ought not to be exercised." These steps, he concluded, could not have been taken "with a greater prospect of easy success" than at an early period, when the federal government "enjoyed the advantage of first impressions – when state factions to resist its authority were not yet matured – when so much aid was to be derived from the popularity and firmness of the actual chief magistrate."[23]

Next, Hamilton took up Jefferson's objections to the structuring of the debt. Hamilton's plan, Jefferson had said, made the debt irredeemable except in small amounts and over long terms, and this prevented its being refinanced at current lower rates of interest and thus paid off more quickly. This irredeemable quality, Jefferson had added, was given to the debt "for the avowed purpose of inviting its transfer to foreign countries," a transfer that, when completed, would drain America of money in order to pay the interest overseas.[24] Hamilton replied that the very system Jefferson "reprobated" had itself lowered interest rates by raising America's credit. It was a strange objection, he implied, to make the lower interest rates created by his system the basis for blaming the system and proposing another in its place.[25] Besides, the funding plan, by deferring payment of some of the interest, had effectively lowered the rates of interest on the debt in comparison to what they had been when it had originally been incurred.[26] More generally, Hamilton found an air of unreality in Jefferson's complaint that the debt could have been paid off more quickly on some other plan. "Some gentlemen seem to forget," said Hamilton, "that the faculties of every country are limited." Such men "talk as if the government could extend is revenue ad libitum to pay off the debt," yet on any "rational calculation" of

---

[22] *PAH*, 12: 236.
[23] *PAH*, 12: 237.
[24] *PTJ*, 23: 535.
[25] *PAH*, 12: 239.
[26] *PAH*, 12: 240–41.

the nation's wealth the debt was being paid off as quickly as realistically could be desired.[27]

Moreover, Jefferson had descended to "palpable misrepresentation" in contending that the debt had been made irredeemable "for the avowed purpose of inviting its transfer to foreign countries." In fact, it had been given that character as "an equivalent for the reduction in interest, that is, for deferring the payment of interest on 1/3 of the principal for three years and for allowing only 3% on the arrears of interest."[28] The provision for the debt, Hamilton here reminded Washington, had required that the nation's creditors give up some things to which they were legally entitled. As a practical matter, the nation could not pay all the principal and interest that it owed. As a matter of justice, it could not unilaterally free itself from its obligations or from any part of them. What was required, then, and what Hamilton had devised, was a system that restructured the debt so as to make it payable, but without violating the rights of the creditors. This then required that they be given something in return for accepting deferral of interest payments and lower rates of interest: namely, the irredeemable quality of which Jefferson complained. Proponents of Hamilton's plan had indeed argued that the debt's irredeemable character would make foreign purchasers willing to pay more for it, precisely because that character increased its real value. This, however, was not the same as saying that this structuring of the debt was intended to foster its sale to foreigners. Besides, Hamilton added, the objection presupposed that foreigners would have been less likely to purchase American debt if it had been structured in some other way. Nothing, he said, could be "more ill-founded or more contrary to experience." Even under the Confederation, when there was no effective system to pay the debt, foreign investors had still purchased it to the tune of "five or six millions." Under "any provision" that could produce "confidence" in America's credit and ability to pay foreign "purchases would have gone on just as they now do."[29]

Hamilton then considered Jefferson's worry that the transfer of the debt would result in a drain of money from the country as interest was paid out to its foreign purchasers. This objection, Hamilton responded, depended to some extent on the improbable assumption that the entire debt would be bought up by foreign purchasers. It also assumed that interest paid on the debt to foreign holders would simply be taken out of the country. Instead, Hamilton believed, a "considerable part" of that interest would be "invested" by its foreign owners in new American undertakings, such as "canals, roads, manufactures," and "commerce." A "young country" like America, after all, held out numerous opportunities for useful foreign investment. In addition, Jefferson's concerns about the "drain of coin" overlooked the most obvious point: that foreign

[27] *PAH*, 12: 242.
[28] *PAH*, 12: 242.
[29] *PAH*, 12: 243.

purchasers would not be getting American debt for "nothing." They had to give something – capital – in exchange for the interest they would be getting. If that capital were "well employed in a young country" like America, it would increase "considerably" and "yield a greater revenue than the interest" paid to the foreign holders of the debt.[30]

Finally, Hamilton turned to Jefferson's complaint that the paper money circulated by the bank would "complete the banishment" of American "coin," and that the "10 or 12 percent annual profit paid to the lenders of this paper medium" was "taken out of the pockets of the people, who could have had without interest the coin it is banishing."[31] Hamilton denied that the paper medium would necessarily banish the nation's coin. While admitting that theorists differed on the question, he indicated that he was inclined to doubt that a paper currency would drive the coin out of the country. The supposed tendency, he observed, arose from the paper's "serving as a substitute" for coin. To leave it at that, however, overlooked the beneficial economic effects of a paper currency as an aid to commerce. Since the quantity of currency circulated was in proportion to the demand for it, paper currency, by putting in motion a "greater quantity of industry," would in the end call forth demand for an even greater quantity of currency and thus "prevent the banishment of the specie." In any case, he added, "sound theorists" – here he called on the authority of Adam Smith's *Wealth of Nations* – agreed that banks more than made up for any banishment of specie "in other ways" – presumably, again, precisely by creating a paper money, which permitted a level of economic activity that had been previously impeded by an inadequate money supply, as Hamilton had argued in the *Report on a National Bank*.[32]

Jefferson was also utterly wrong in expressing a fear that the bank's profits were taken out of the people's pockets in order to pay for the use of a paper currency, when they could have used a metal one for free. The bank's profits, Hamilton contended, could "in no just sense be said to be taken out of the pockets of the people." Part of those profits came from the "interest paid by the government on that part of the public debt" that had been "incorporated into the stock of the bank." Such debt had existed before the bank was created, and payment of interest on it would have been obligatory no matter who owned it. Accordingly, this interest constituted "nothing new taken out of the pockets of the people." The other part of the bank's profits came from the interest paid by individuals who had borrowed money from the bank. Such interest could hardly be said to be taken out of the pockets of the people, any more that it could be said in any other instance of borrowing at interest. In every case, the interest was paid by the borrower, and the "rest of the community have nothing to do with it." Bank bills, Hamilton continued, could be used

[30] *PAH*, 12: 243–44.
[31] *PTJ*, 23: 535.
[32] *PAH*, 12: 244.

as a medium of exchange; but those who so used them did not pay interest on them any more than they did in using a metal currency. Interest was paid on either coin or bank paper when one was oneself the borrower, but not otherwise. Indeed, Jefferson's concern was not only groundless but even the reverse of the truth: to the extent that the government owned stock in the bank, it shared in the profits, and thus money was "*put in to the pockets of the people.*" The facts of this matter, Hamilton concluded, were "so plain and so palpable" that Jefferson's complaint betrayed "either extreme ignorance or extreme disingenuousness."[33]

The Evils of Speculation

Hamilton then turned to the concerns Jefferson had raised about the effects of the Hamiltonian system on America's economy and even on its moral character. Here Jefferson had charged that Hamilton's policies fostered a useless "speculation in paper" that diverted American capital from productive enterprises like commerce and agriculture. Moreover, Jefferson argued, such speculation, and the easy wealth that it sometimes gave, fostered a corrupt spirit of gambling and idleness in the citizenry. Hamilton conceded that money employed in paper speculation was "barren and useless" to the extent that it could not be used elsewhere. This complaint, however, overlooked the fact that – as Hamilton had argued in his *Report on Manufactures* – such "paper itself constitutes a new capital, which, being saleable and transferrable at any moment, enables the proprietor to undertake any piece of business as well as an equal sum in coin." Indeed, Hamilton continued, since a given amount of metal could sustain an even bigger circulation of paper, "the new capital put in motion" by the investment of metal in paper speculation "considerably exceeds the old one which is *suspended*." The ultimate result of such speculation, therefore, was not less but "more capital to carry on the productive labor of the society."[34]

Similar considerations answered Jefferson's worry that paper speculation corroded the nation's moral character by fostering a spirit of gambling and idleness. Once again, Hamilton conceded the reality of the phenomenon, but only in a limited and immediate sense. "Jobbing the funds," he admitted, "has some bad effects among those engaged in it. It fosters a spirit of gambling, and diverts a certain number of citizens from other pursuits." But since, as he had just observed, the paper in which the jobbers speculated acted as capital, the "effect upon the citizens at large" would be quite different. By acting as a much-needed currency of exchange, the paper encouraged "industry by furnishing a larger field of employment."[35]

Finally, Hamilton contended, even if the funding system caused the evils Jefferson had noted, those evils were inevitable, given the situation that the country

---

[33] *PAH*, 12: 245–46.
[34] *PAH*, 12: 246 (Hamilton's emphasis).
[35] *PAH*, 12: 247.

faced. The debt had to be serviced, and any provision for servicing it would have fostered speculation. Hamilton believed he had created a sound provision, and it had admittedly fostered speculation. At the same time, an "unsound or precarious provision" for the debt would also have fostered speculation "in its most odious forms," since under such an arrangement men would have speculated on the "defects and casualties of the system" just as much as on the "debt itself." In the latter case, however, unlike under the sound system Hamilton had devised, the "public stock would have been too uncertain" in its value to act "as a substitute for money," and accordingly all the money "employed in it would have been diverted from useful employment without anything to compensate for it." Any provision for the debt would have influenced its value and therefore would inevitably encourage speculation.[36] "Nothing but abolishing the debt could have obviated" this difficulty, and such an expedient was as impractical as it was immoral, since it would have destroyed the nation's credit by reneging on its obligations. In this view, it was "the fault of the Revolution" and "not of the government that speculation exists."[37]

The Corruption of the Legislature

Next, Hamilton addressed Jefferson's charge that the financial system was a tool for corrupting the legislature. This, Hamilton began, "is one of those assertions which can only be denied and pronounced to be malignant and false. No facts exist to support it, and being a mere matter of fact, no *argument* can be brought to repel it." Those who made such claims, he continued, merely begged the question. They assumed that the policies with which they disagreed were not only bad but so obviously bad that no honorable man could reasonably reach a different conclusion. Thus, they assumed "infallibility" to "themselves and to those" that thought "with them," presenting themselves as "the only honest men in the community."[38] Indeed, Hamilton might have added that Jefferson's own complaint on this score typically admitted that the supposedly "corrupt squadron" in the legislature was a minority, tipping the balance between two opposed but honest factions. Thus, even in Jefferson's telling, there was a substantial plurality in the Congress that voted for Hamilton's policies on

---

[36] Indeed, as Peter McNamara notes, Hamilton believed that speculation is "inseparable from the spirit and freedom of commerce" itself and not merely inevitably incident to debt. Quoted in McNamara, *Political Economy and Statesmanship*, 121. Nevertheless, Hamilton also believed that there were moral standards in light of which such speculation could be evaluated. In 1792, he wrote to Philip Livingston that "certain characters" were "sport[ing] with the market and with the distresses of their fellow citizens." It was, he added, "time" that "there should be a line of separation between honest men and knaves; between respectable stockholders and dealers in the funds, and mere unprincipled gamblers. Public infamy must restrain what the laws cannot." Quoted in Bruce Miroff, "Alexander Hamilton: The Aristocrat as Visionary," *International Social Science Review* 9 (1988): 52.

[37] *PAH*, 12: 247.

[38] *PAH*, 12: 248.

disinterested and honorable grounds. If this was the case, it is not clear on what basis Jefferson could presume to know that the paper holders in Congress were acting corruptly rather than doing what they thought good for the country according to their best lights.

Hamilton denied that there were any stock-jobbers or paper dealers, properly so called, in the Congress. Evidently, to him such terms signified men who tried to make money by the constant buying and selling of the nation's debt and stock in the bank. There were, admittedly, members of Congress who held some of the public debt or who were stockholders in the Bank of the United States. For Hamilton, however, neither of these conditions could be understood as a form of corruption. Only by a "strange perversion of ideas," one "as novel as it is extraordinary," he contended, could men be "deemed corrupt and criminal for becoming proprietors in the funds of their country." In fact, Hamilton continued, the funding system he had established tended to prevent a form of corruption that otherwise certainly would have accompanied paying the nation's revolutionary debts. For those who intended to make good on the nation's commitments, the alternative to a funded debt was an annual provision. Nothing, Hamilton suggested, could be "a more fruitful source of legislative corruption than" such a procedure. By such a policy, all the legislators who were so inclined "would have an annual opportunity of speculating upon their influence in the legislature to promote or retard or put off a provision. Every session the question whether the annual provision should be continued would be an occasion of pernicious caballing and corrupt bargaining." Hamilton's system had avoided such problems by settling the question of the debt "once for all" and thereby putting it "out of the way."[39]

Similarly, it was difficult for Hamilton to see how it could be corrupting for a member of Congress to be a proprietor in the bank. Any decision to purchase shares would have to be subsequent to the bank's creation and therefore could not be said to have corrupted the decision to erect the institution in the first place. Hamilton professed that he could see nothing "blamable" in a legislator's decision "to invest property in an institution which has been established for the most important national purposes." Such an investment would surely make a legislator more "friendly to the preservation of the bank," but there was no "corruption" in that, since it involved "no collision between duty and interest and could give him no improper bias in other questions."[40]

Transcending the Limits of the Constitution

Hamilton turned next to Jefferson's claim that the "corrupt squadron" in Congress had shown its willingness to transcend the limits of the Constitution. Here again, Hamilton claimed, Jefferson begged the question and assumed his own infallibility. Those who make such complaints "take it for granted that

39 *PAH*, 12: 250.
40 *PAH*, 12: 250.

their constructions of the Constitution are right and that the opposite ones are wrong, and with great good nature and candor ascribe the effect of a difference of opinion to a disposition to get rid of the limitations on the government." Such dogmatism was unwarranted. There were "some things which the general government has clearly a right to do," other things "which it has clearly no right to meddle with," and in between a "good deal of middle ground, about which honest and well-disposed men may differ." Accordingly, the most that could be said about the recent constitutional disputes was that "some of this middle ground may have been occupied by the national legislature." Going so far, however, was "surely no evidence of a disposition to get rid of the limitations in the Constitution," and no man of "candor" would view it "in that light."[41]

Hamilton viewed the young nation's constitutional disputes in a very different light. Those men that Jefferson presented as trying to do away with the limits on the Constitution Hamilton presented as trying to "do the essential business of the nation by a liberal construction of the powers of the government." Opposed to them were those who from "disaffection" or "overweening jealousy" would "fritter away those powers," as well as those who "from party and personal opposition are torturing the Constitution into objections to everything they do not like."[42] This rejoinder showed that Hamilton not only denied Jefferson's charge but in fact returned it: each man thought the other was doing violence to the Constitution, one in the service of expanding its powers, the other in the service of constricting them.

Aiming for Monarchy

At last Hamilton came to Jefferson's most explosive claim: that the treasury program's ultimate purpose was to destroy America's republican form of government and establish in its place a monarchy on the British model. Hamilton regarded this charge as utterly fantastic. Two days before submitting his "Objections and Answers" to Washington, Hamilton had written to John Adams, noting the alarm some felt "at a supposed system of policy tending to subvert the republican government of the country." "Were ever men more ingenious," Hamilton had asked, "to torment themselves with phantoms?"[43] To Washington Hamilton suggested that such a charge could only be answered by "a flat denial." He also, however, added to his denial an argument that the charge was so implausible as to be unworthy of credence. The "absurdity" of such a "project," he claimed, "refutes" the belief in it. The notion that "a monarchy or aristocracy" could be introduced in America "by employing the influence and force of a government continually changing hands," was a "visionary" undertaking "that none but madmen could mediate and that no

[41] *PAH*, 12: 251.
[42] *PAH*, 12: 251.
[43] *PAH*, 12: 209.

wise men will believe." Such an undertaking could stimulate no one's "interest or ambition" because even if it could be accomplished – which Hamilton thought "utterly incredible" – it would take so long that its completion would occur "beyond the life of any individual" then living. It was "still more chimerical" yet to think that a people "so enlightened and so diversified" as the Americans could be "cajoled into giving their sanction" to monarchical or aristocratic "institutions."[44]

Hamilton's answer also revealed that he did not share Jefferson's fears about a natural tendency in the direction of monarchy. According to Jefferson, the encroachments of the state governments would tend in the direction of anarchy but would also be self-correcting, while the encroachments of the federal government would be in the direction of monarchy, which would not be self-correcting. For Jefferson, the natural course of events would tend to empower the federal government, so that it was necessary to pull hard in the other direction. For Hamilton, this was the reverse of the truth. Thus he observed to Washington that those who were "calumniated" with desiring monarchy actually desired to keep the government in its present state, which would be "no easy task" because of the "natural tendency in the state of things to exalt the local" governments "on the ruins of the national" one.[45]

Jefferson had also resorted to "palpable misrepresentation" in claiming that some men at the Constitutional Convention – most especially Hamilton himself – had openly avowed an intention to establish in America a monarchical form of government on the British model. "No man that I know of," Hamilton averred, had "contemplated" such an effort. Jefferson's fears, it would seem, were based on a failure to appreciate the difference between political theory and actual political aims. Hamilton admitted that there were a few men at the Convention who had "manifested theoretical opinions favorable in the abstract to a constitution like that of Great Britain." Nevertheless, he continued, entertaining such a theoretical opinion did not amount to a practical intention to establish such a government in the United States. Thus, everyone at the Convention had "agreed" that the British form – "except as to the general distribution of departments and powers" – was "out of the question in reference to" America. For his own part, Hamilton had expressed himself at the Convention in much the same terms as he had in conversation with Jefferson. He had

declared in strong terms that the republican theory ought to be adhered to in this country as long as there was any chance of its success – that the idea of a perfect equality of political rights among the citizens, exclusive of all permanent or hereditary distinctions, was of a nature to engage the good wishes of every good man, whatever might be his theoretic doubts – that it merited his best efforts to give success to it in practice – that hitherto from an incompetent structure of government it had not had a fair trial,

44 *PAH*, 12: 251–52.
45 *PAH*, 12: 252.

and that the endeavor ought then to be to secure to it a better chance of success by a government more capable of energy and order.[46]

Hamilton carried this defense of himself further in the public prints. Writing for the *National Gazette* as "Amicus," Hamilton contended that he had "never made a single proposition" at the Convention that "was not conformable to the republican theory." Even his "highest-toned" proposals, he implied, did not justify a charge that he had advocated for monarchy on the British form. Indeed, these "propositions," though they failed, were deemed sufficiently reasonable to win the support of several of the state delegations, including certain "individuals who, in the estimation of those who deem themselves the only true republicans, are pre-eminent for republican character."[47] Hamilton did not provide specifics, but, as the editors of his papers observe, on July 17, 1787 an amendment changing the presidential term to "during good behavior" won the support of "the delegations from New Jersey, Pennsylvania, Delaware, and Virginia" – the last of which included men such as "James Madison, George Mason, and Edmund Randolph."[48]

Hamilton's Counter-Critique of Jefferson

Hamilton did not content himself – and probably could not have contented himself – with a mere defense of his measures. The energy of his mind and the vehemence of his nature prompted him to mount his own counter-critique of Jefferson and of the republican party of which Jefferson was now the de facto leader. The only point on which they agreed, it seems, was the gravity of the young republic's situation. The government was indeed in danger of destruction, but for Hamilton that danger arose not from his policies but from the irresponsible character of the Jeffersonian opposition. Hamilton developed

---

[46] *PAH*, 12: 253.

[47] *PAH*, 12: 355.

[48] *PAH*, 12: 357, note 4. Hamilton continued in later life to defend his proposals at the Convention as compatible with republican government. In 1803, he wrote to Timothy Pickering that "the highest toned propositions which I made in the Convention were for a president, senate, and judges during good behavior – a house of representatives for three years. . . . This plan was in my conception conformable with the strict theory of a government purely republican, the essential criteria of which are that the principal organs of the executive and legislative departments be elected by the people, and hold their offices by a *responsible* and temporary or *defeasible* tenure." Quoted in Morton J. Frisch's "Introduction" to *Selected Writings and Speeches of Alexander Hamilton* (Washington, DC: American Enterprise Institute, 1985), 6 (emphasis in original). Also, as Stephen Knott observes, at the Convention, Hamilton also advocated that the House be "elected by universal male suffrage, a proposal more democratic than that which ultimately emerged under the new government." "'Opposed in Death as in Life': Hamilton and Jefferson in American Memory," in *The Many Faces of Alexander Hamilton: The Life and Legacy of America's Most Elusive Founding Father*, ed. Douglas Ambrose and Robert W.T. Martin (New York: New York University Press, 2006), 30.

this argument in a private letter to Edward Carrington of May 26, 1792, as well as in numerous public articles he wrote that year under various pseudonyms.[49]

The Motives of Jefferson's Opposition

Hamilton, like Jefferson, did not hesitate to speculate on the motives of his rival and to present him as moved in part by something other than a pure commitment to the public good. Jefferson's opposition, Hamilton contended, sprang from the reciprocal influence of sincere belief and personal interest. Jefferson's personal history, Hamilton suggested to Carrington, had perhaps fostered in him an inclination against the kind of energetic government that Hamilton thought essential to the country's well being. Jefferson had left the country "before we had experienced the imbecilities" of the Articles of Confederation, and while in France he had seen "government only on the side of its abuses." Moreover, he had drunk "deeply of the French philosophy in religion, in science, and politics" and had left "France in a moment of fermentation which he had had a share in exciting, and in the passions and feelings of which he shared both from temperament and situation."[50] To this extent, it would seem, Jefferson's own experiences had fostered in him an excessive attachment to liberty understood in opposition to strong government, a view that Hamilton regarded as mistaken, if also understandable.

Jefferson's other motives, however, were less reputable. Personal and political disappointment, Hamilton suspected, had contributed to Jefferson's opposition. He had returned to the United States "probably with a too partial idea of his own powers, and with the expectation of a greater share in the direction of our councils than he has in reality enjoyed." Jefferson might even have desired for himself "the department of the finances." The early course of the administration – in relation, for example, to the debt and assumption – had "left Mr. Madison a very discontented and chagrined man" and had begotten "some degree of ill humor in Mr. Jefferson." Then had come the "affair of the bank," on which Jefferson and Madison had made a "mighty stand" and been beaten. Thus a "current of success on one side and defeat on the other" had developed, rendering "the opposition furious" and producing in its members "a disposition to subvert their competitors, even at the expense of the government."[51]

Moreover, Hamilton believed, Jefferson's own ambition for the presidency was at work. It was "evident beyond a question from every movement" that Jefferson aimed "with ardent desire at the presidential chair," which was at the same time "an important object of the party politics." Yet it was "supposed," on the basis of Hamilton's "personal and political connections," that he would "favor some other candidate than Mr. Jefferson." Hamilton's "influence

---

[49] *PAH*, 12: 426.
[50] *PAH*, 11: 439.
[51] *PAH*, 11: 440–41.

therefore with the community" had to be "resisted and destroyed" on "ambitious and personal grounds."[52]

Finally, just as the disappointment of sincerely held aspirations had fostered a more personal and selfish opposition, so the operation of those selfish passions had perhaps generated further beliefs which Hamilton could recognize as sincere, even if not innocent in their origins. Since "men easily heat their imaginations when their passions are heated," it was "possible" that Jefferson and Madison had "by degrees persuaded themselves of what they may have at first only sported to influence others – namely, that there is some dreadful combination against state governments and republicanism, which according to them are convertible terms." There was "much absurdity" in such a supposition, Hamilton noted, but it at least tended to "apologize" for Jefferson and Madison's "hearts," if "at the expense of their heads."[53]

Jefferson as the Disloyal Opposition

Moreover, Hamilton contended, Jefferson's opposition to the treasury program had led him to take improper steps against the very administration of which he was an officer. Jefferson, Hamilton complained to Carrington, had given his support and encouragement to Philip Freneau's *National Gazette*, a paper that Hamilton characterized as "devoted to the subversion of me and the measures in which I have had an agency" and even as having a "tendency *generally unfriendly* to the government" of the United States. Indeed, Jefferson had drawn on government resources to support a paper whose mission was to attack the government, since he employed Freneau as a foreign languages clerk in the department of state.[54] Hamilton pressed this point hard in his pseudonymous journalism of that year, contending that Jefferson had placed himself in a false position by supporting an opposition newspaper while serving in the government himself. Writing as "Metellus" in the *Gazette of the United States*, Hamilton argued that Jefferson, as an officer of the government, certainly should not have given his support to anything his conscience disapproved. However, neither was it right for him to resort to "*intriguing* and *machinating*" against the government's policies. The "true line of propriety," Hamilton contended, was to be found in a "medium" position: opposing, where duty required it, measures one could not approve by advising against them but then not interfering with their execution if the government decided to pursue them

---

[52] *PAH*, 11: 441.

[53] *PAH*, 11: 441–42. Hamilton gave a similar account of the personal and political motives of his republican rivals in *The Vindication* No. 1 and in his reflection "On James Blanchard." See *PAH*, 11: 461 and *PAH*, 13: 523. Also, for an account of Hamilton and Madison's early collaboration and subsequent political alienation, consider Mary Stockwell, "Madison and Hamilton: The End of a Friendship," in *James Madison: Philosopher, Founder, and Statesman*, ed. John. R. Vile, William D. Pederson, and Frank J. Williams (Athens: Ohio University Press, 2008), 175–92.

[54] *PAH*, 11: 430–31 (Hamilton's emphasis).

contrary to one's advice.[55] If Jefferson had judged the government's measures to be so bad that it was necessary to go further, the honorable path would be resignation, not opposition from within.

Jefferson's Constitutional Infidelity

Hamilton's counter-critique, moreover, suggested that Jefferson himself was subject to the same kinds of complaints about constitutional fidelity that he had raised in relation to Hamilton. Hamilton had argued at the Constitutional Convention for arrangements different from those that had in the end been adopted and had been known in conversation to doubt whether the Constitution would prove sufficient for the country. On the basis of these facts, Jefferson attributed to Hamilton a desire to replace the current government with another form. Yet, as Hamilton suggested, Jefferson's own history provided materials from which to fashion similar accusations. Jefferson, after all, had not entirely approved the Constitution as it was originally written. While ratification was being debated, Jefferson had said that he "disliked and *greatly* disliked" the Constitution's "abandonment of the principle of *rotation* in office," especially "in the case of the president," and had also indicated his desire to see steps taken to secure changes in the Constitution to make it more to his liking. In one place, he had suggested that the last four states decline to ratify the Constitution, so as to create pressure for it to be amended. In another, he had indicated that we might secure the "manifold good things in the constitution" while also "*getting rid of the bad*," either by ratifying it in hopes of amending it later or by not ratifying it and calling a second convention to make changes in it.[56] If Hamilton's preference for something different from what had been adopted could be invoked as evidence of a lack of commitment to the Constitution, why could the same argument not be made against Jefferson?

Hamilton also returned Jefferson's charge that not only his past opinions but also his conduct in office bespoke a lack of constitutional fidelity. Here their complaints mirrored each other. Jefferson complained that Hamilton had by construction destroyed the limits that the Constitution established on the federal government. Conversely, Hamilton complained that Jefferson had by construction tried to establish limits that did not really exist. In his unpublished *Vindication* essay, Hamilton had noted the "indiscreet clamors of those who in and out of the legislature with too much levity torture the Constitution into objections to measures which they deem inexpedient."[57] He did not name Jefferson here, but he surely had him in mind. Hamilton, after all, had complained that Jefferson's *Opinion on the Constitutionality of a National Bank* tended to confuse questions of constitutionality and expediency. In Hamilton's

---

[55] *PAH*, 11: 614–15 (Hamilton's emphasis).
[56] *PAH*, 12: 394, 581 (Hamilton's emphasis).
[57] *PAH*, 11: 463.

view, Jefferson had engaged in a kind of violence against the Constitution, perverting its principles so that he would have a ground to condemn as unconstitutional the policies with which he happened to disagree.

Jefferson and the Public Faith

Hamilton also contended that Jefferson and his followers had behaved in such a way as to undermine the country's commitment to public faith. While they had admittedly not sought a repudiation of the debt, their rhetoric and their principles implied something less than a perfect commitment to observing the country's obligations. Jefferson had, of course, decried the debt, at least as Hamilton had restructured it, as an engine of corruption, and similar complaints had been publicized through the newspaper he had encouraged. Such rhetoric, Hamilton suggested, could not but imply some desire to escape the contractual obligations by which the debt had been created. Expressions such as "vile matter" and "corrupt mass" had been used to describe the debt itself, and the "owners of it" had been "indiscriminately maligned as the harpies and vultures of the community." There was good ground, Hamilton held, to suspect that men who used such "language" had in mind "a more summary process for getting rid of debts than that of paying them," even though they would not "dare to avow" such views openly.[58]

Jefferson had not called for a repeal of the funding system, but he was certainly "an avowed enemy to a funded debt."[59] Moreover, the newspaper he supported had "labored for months" to make the funding system "an object of popular detestation" and had ended by declaring that it had "had its day," thus "very clearly, if not expressly," establishing the republican party's aim "to overthrow it."[60] Jefferson's principles, moreover, implied a right on the government's part to escape its obligations. Jefferson had held that the present generation has no authority to bind its successors. On this basis, Hamilton believed, James Madison had privately suggested that the funding system could be repealed. Madison publicly disavowed "any intention to undo what has been done," but in a private conversation he had, so Hamilton had heard, Madison supported a speech in which John Mercer had held "that a legislature had no right to *fund* the debt by mortgaging permanently the public revenues because they had no right to bind posterity." Such reasoning implied, Hamilton observed, "that what has been unlawfully done may be undone." Such ideas filled Hamilton with "*indignation* and *horror*." Whatever its "original merits," the funding system had been "solemnly adopted" by the government, which had therefore undertaken responsibility for "a great transfer of property." What, he asked Carrington, "would become of the government" and of the

[58] *PAH*, 11: 468.
[59] *PAH*, 11: 436.
[60] *PAH*, 12: 500.

"national reputation" if the funding system were "reversed"? And on "what system of morality" could "so atrocious a doctrine be maintained?"[61]

Furthermore, just as Jefferson had recalled Hamilton's part at the Convention in order to impeach his commitment to republican government, so Hamilton's 1792 journalism delved into Jefferson's past for evidence that the secretary of state held opinions inconsistent with a proper respect for public faith. In his first "American" essay, Hamilton claimed that Jefferson, while minister to France, had written to the Congress suggesting that since America was unlikely to be able to pay its French debt in a timely fashion, the government might consider seeking a transfer of that debt to private Dutch lenders. Hamilton characterized such a move as an effort to transfer the debt "from a government able to vindicate its rights" to "the breasts of individuals" who would "first be encouraged to become substitutes to the original creditor" and then could "afterwards" be "defrauded without danger."[62] Hamilton returned to this issue later that summer in "Catullus" Number 2, this time providing details that "An American" had omitted. In Jefferson's correspondence with Congress, Hamilton contended, Jefferson had mentioned a Dutch company's offer to buy America's French debt, then had used the following "extraordinary expressions": "If there is a danger of the public payments not being punctual," Jefferson had written, "I submit whether it may not be better that the discontents which would then arise should be transferred from a court of whose good will we have so much need to the breasts of a private company."[63] Hamilton's "Catullus" condemned such advice as an act that could never be "vindicated from the imputation of political *profligacy*" without throwing overboard "ancient notions of justice" and substituting "some new fashioned scheme of morality in their stead." Jefferson's conduct in this matter presented no "complicated problem which sophistry" might "entangle or obscure" but rather a "plain question of *moral feeling*." Jefferson had encouraged the government, "on the express condition of *not having a prospect*" of paying its debts promptly, "to concur in a transfer of that debt from a nation well able to bear the inconvenience of failure or delay to individuals whose total ruin might have been the consequence of it." And he had suggested this on the "*interested* consideration" of America's need for "the good will of the creditor-nation, with the dishonorable motive" being "clearly implied" of having more to fear "from the discontents of that nation than from those of disappointed and betrayed individuals."[64]

Jefferson, bitterly resenting Hamilton's imputations on his commitment to the public faith, responded strenuously in letters to President Washington. Although Hamilton had written under pseudonyms, Jefferson had no doubt

[61] *PAH*, 11: 436–37 (Hamilton's emphases).
[62] *PAH*, 12: 162.
[63] *PAH*, 12: 399.
[64] *PAH*, 12: 400 (Hamilton's emphases).

as to the identity of his public antagonist. He observed to Washington that "neither the style, matter, nor venom of the pieces" that had appeared in "Fenno's gazette" could "leave a doubt as to their author."[65]

With regard to the question of his advice on the French loan, Jefferson complained that Hamilton had quoted him selectively, omitting passages that were necessary to understand the true tenor of his remarks. Jefferson had indeed said all that Hamilton had quoted. His letter, however, had then gone on and proposed a different course of action than the one Hamilton had condemned. After noting the possible purchase by the Dutch investors, and the advantage that the United States would gain by having the loan held by private parties rather than the French government, his letter to Congress had continued as follows:

But it has occurred to me that we might find occasion to do what would be grateful to this court and establish with them a confidence in our honor. I am informed that our credit in Holland is sound. Might it not be possible then to borrow there the four and twenty millions due to this country, and thus pay them their whole debt at once? This would save them from any loss on our account; nor is it liable to the objection of impropriety in creating new debts before we have more certain means of paying them: it is only transferring a debt from one creditor to another, and removing the causes of discontent to persons with whom they would do us less injury. Thinking that this matter is worthy the attention of Congress, I will endeavor that the negotiation shall be retarded till it may be possible for me to know their decision, which therefore I will take the liberty of praying immediately.[66]

Jefferson, then, had only noted the Dutch proposition and had observed "that it might perhaps be better, if the payments should not be punctual, to have a weak enemy rather than a strong one." He saw nothing wrong in raising the question of which creditor would be more advantageous for the government of the United States. Making such a "choice between two adversaries," he contended to Washington, would surely offend "no man's morality or politics." In any case, his actual proposal to Congress was not to encourage the Dutch purchase but instead to take advantage of America's good credit in Holland to borrow the money necessary to pay off the entire French debt. This approach would have saved the French from having to take a loss by accepting a Dutch offer to buy the debt at a discount, and, at the same time, it would have "retain[ed] the same advantage of giving us a weak instead of a strong enemy in the event of a want of punctuality" in payment. The Dutch, Jefferson had believed, would require that the debt be repaid by installments over a period of ten to fifteen years. The aim of Jefferson's suggestion, then, was to foster a delay in payment by securing new loans, so that the government of the United States would have time to get "into a way of collecting money" by which to pay its debts. Hamilton's incomplete account, however, had made it sound as if Jefferson

[65] *PTJ*, 24: 351.
[66] *PTJ*, 24: 496–97 (Jefferson's emphasis).

wanted to collude in a transaction – the Dutch purchase at a discount – that would have left France "under the loss of four millions of livres" and the United States "under the pressure of *immediate payments* or dishonor."[67]

Jefferson was certainly correct that Hamilton's initial criticism of him had misrepresented the facts. In a later essay Hamilton, writing again as "Catullus," had to admit that Jefferson had indeed "mentioned an alternative" to the Dutch purchase of the French debt. Nevertheless, Hamilton also insisted that this did not diminish the fact that Jefferson had countenanced such an objectionable plan.[68] At the same time, Jefferson's response in some ways missed the point of Hamilton's criticism on the moral question involved. Indeed, Jefferson's response here tended to convict him of the very disregard for public faith of which Hamilton had accused him. Despite Jefferson's complaint to Washington, Hamilton's original criticism of his proposal had not even mentioned the problem that the discounted Dutch purchase would have imposed a loss on the French government. Hamilton did mention this in a later essay as adding to the discreditable character of the proposal, but this was more of an afterthought.[69] The gravamen of his complaint was the effort to transfer the debt, which the United States was unable to service punctually, to private Dutch creditors, something that Jefferson's proposal still sought to accomplish by having the United States itself take out new Dutch loans to pay the French. Jefferson clearly saw the difference in material advantage between the two loans: if you cannot pay, it is better to have a weak creditor than a strong one. But his argument overlooked an important moral difference between them, one that bore on the question of respect for public faith. It was one kind of breach of public faith not to pay on the nation's debt. This was the situation in which America found itself in relation to France. It was something else, and an even more serious neglect of public faith, to take out a loan while *expecting* not to be able to pay on it. Jefferson's advice suggested that America could do this in relation to the Dutch lenders. Jefferson's letter to Congress had denied that his proposal involved the impropriety of creating new debt before we had more certain means of paying it, because it only transferred an existing debt from one creditor to another. This overlooked, of course, the position of the Dutch investors: it would certainly be a new debt *to them*. And Jefferson's expectation that America would not be prompt in its payments – an expectation incompatible with Hamilton's insistence on a strict respect for public faith – was inseparably bound up with his calculations about why the private Dutch investors would be better creditors for the United States than would the Court of France, calculations that he continued to defend in his letter to Washington.

[67] *PTJ*, 24: 497 (Jefferson's emphasis).
[68] *PAH*, 12: 585.
[69] *PAH*, 12: 586.

At the time of Jefferson's proposal, Congress took the same dim view of it as did Hamilton five years later. Reviewing the whole of Jefferson's advice – and not the truncated version that Hamilton had at first put forward – the board of treasury rejected it as both "unjust" and "impolitic." It was unjust, the board explained, because by taking the course Jefferson had recommended "the nation would contract an engagement without any well-grounded expectation of discharging it with proper punctuality." It was impolitic "because a failure in the payment of interest accruing from this negotiation (which would inevitably happen) would justly blast all hopes of credit with the citizens of the United Netherlands, when the exigencies of the Union might render new loans indispensably necessary." The board acknowledged that gratitude for French assistance would of course encourage Congress to make every effort to pay back its loan but also noted its doubt "that it would tend to establish in the mind of the French Court an idea of the national honor" of the United States "to involve individuals in a heavy loan at a time when Congress were fully sensible that their resources were altogether inadequate to discharge even the interest," let alone "the installments of the principal which would from time to time become due." In relation to this point, the board noted a factor that Hamilton would also emphasize: that America's "failure in the punctual payment of interest" would surely be more "distressing" to individual lenders, whose support might depend on faithful and regular payments, than to a nation that was "powerful in resources." The "public integrity," the board observed, "is the best shield of defense against any calamities" the country might encounter. America's respect for that principle could not "be called into question" in relation to her French loans, but "the reverse would be the case should the sanction of the United States be given, *either* to the transfer of the French debt, *or* to the negotiation of a loan in Holland for the purpose of discharging it." Accordingly, the board concluded, it could not regard Jefferson's advice "either as eligible or proper," and it recommended instructing him "not to give *any* sanction to *any* negotiation which may be proposed for transferring the debt due from the United States to any state or company of individuals who may be disposed to purchase the same."[70] Despite Jefferson's complaints about Hamilton's initial inaccuracy, the board of treasury had received his advice in the same sense that Hamilton gave it, and rejected it with the same disapproval that Hamilton expressed, in 1792.

The gap between the two men's conceptions of the public faith is further illustrated by Jefferson's response to Hamilton's more general accusation that the republicans' principles and rhetoric suggested a willingness to leave the nation's debt unpaid. Writing to Washington, Jefferson observed that Hamilton had charged him "with a desire of not paying the public debt." This was "untrue," Jefferson claimed: "My whole correspondence while in France, and

---

[70] *PAH*, 12: 162–64, n. 10 (my emphasis).

every word, letter, and act on the subject since my return, prove that no man is more ardently intent to see the public debt soon and sacredly paid off than I am." Indeed, Jefferson continued, this point "exactly" marked the "difference between Colo. Hamilton's views and mine, that I would wish the debt paid tomorrow; he wishes it never to be paid, but always to be a thing wherewith to corrupt and manage the legislature."[71]

Leaving aside the charges of corruption, Hamilton's response to which we have already examined, let us consider the implications of Jefferson's wish that the debt could be paid immediately. Jefferson seems to have thought that this wish was a testimony to his earnestness about public faith. This wish, however, overlooked a point that Hamilton regarded as of the utmost importance: the debt could not be paid immediately without repealing the funding system, which in turn would mean violating the contracts that were a part of it. Jefferson, as we have seen, complained that part of the debt had been given an "irredeemable" quality: it was to be paid in installments and could not be paid off in advance of the established schedule. Yet, as Hamilton had explained in his "Objections and Answers" written for Washington, this quality had been given to the debt as a consideration for a reduction in interest from the original terms. Thus, from Hamilton's point of view, to arrange to pay the debt "tomorrow" would necessarily involve a violation of commitments the government had made and would therefore constitute a breach of the public faith.

Nor can Jefferson be defended on this score by suggesting that his letter to Washington merely expressed a wish that things had been arranged some other way, which would not necessarily indicate a lack of commitment to abide by what had in fact been established. There is evidence that Jefferson did contemplate undoing the funding system, just as Hamilton feared. Around July of 1792, Jefferson prepared for himself a "Note" outlining an "Agenda to Reduce the Government to True Principles" – probably in anticipation of the more republican House of Representatives he was hoping would result from the upcoming elections. This agenda included several points, two of them expressed as queries. One of these queries was expressed as follows: "Repeal irredeemable quality and borrow at 4 pr. Cent." While expressing the idea as a query does not establish Jefferson's determination to do it if at all possible, it does show his willingness to give it serious consideration. Moreover, the second point on the agenda – "abolish the bank" – was not expressed as a query. Yet Hamilton would surely have regarded this step, too, as a breach of public faith. Hamilton would have agreed that the government had every right to decline to renew the charter of a bank of which it no longer approved. The Bank of the United States, however, had been given a charter to operate for a specified period of time, and private money had been invested in it on that understanding. Thus, the same principles of public conduct that would be breached by a repeal of the

---

[71] *PTJ*, 24: 354–55.

funding system would be similarly breached by an abolition of the bank prior
to the lapse of its charter. In his letter to Washington laying out his critique of
Hamilton, Jefferson had indirectly affirmed his commitment to public faith. He
had expressed hope that a new republican Congress would repeal some of what
he found objectionable, but he had also admitted that not all of it could be
repealed consistent with the public faith. Nevertheless, Hamilton would have
regarded even the limited reforms that Jefferson contemplated as violations of
the public faith.

The Jeffersonian Threat to the American Regime

Finally, Hamilton threw back at Jefferson the charge that his politics would, if
unchecked, destroy the existing regime. There was a real danger that the government of the United States would be overturned, but the danger came from
Jefferson's principles and not Hamilton's. Jefferson and Madison, Hamilton
told Carrington, were "*actuated by views*" that were "*subversive of the principles of good government and dangerous to the union, peace and happiness of
the country.*"[72]

Several aspects of the Jeffersonian and republican ideology tended toward
this terrible outcome. In the first place, Hamilton believed that Jefferson's
understanding of the power of the federal government was insufficient to the
government's obligations and threatened to undermine the union of the states
in one community. Hamilton began his letter to Carrington by stating "*two
essential points*" of his "political creed": first, that the union was essential
to American "respectability and happiness"; second, that an "efficient general
government" was necessary to "maintain" the Union,[73] hence his complaint
later in the letter that Jefferson and Madison were "disposed to narrow the
federal authority."[74] Jefferson's mode of interpreting the powers of the federal
government endangered the great substantive end to which the Constitution
was merely a means: a union of the states into a single community, at least
for certain important common interests. That end, Hamilton believed, could
not be achieved and maintained without a properly energetic federal government, that is, a government with powers such as he had sought to establish
and exercise through his treasury program. Hamilton stated the problem even
more directly in his "Objections and Answers," prepared for Washington in
response to Jefferson's critique of his policies. There Hamilton had contended
that Jeffersonian "rules of construction for the authorities vested in the government of the Union would arrest all its essential movements and bring it back
in practice to the same state of imbecility which rendered the old confederation contemptible."[75] This imbecility and contemptibility, however, had been

---

[72] *PAH*, 11: 429 (Hamilton's emphasis).
[73] *PAH*, 11: 426 (Hamilton's emphasis).
[74] *PAH*, 11: 437.
[75] *PAH*, 12: 249.

thought a danger to the Union itself, since it was feared that the incapacity of the government to secure the common good would provoke the states to strike off on their own. Thus, for Hamilton, Jefferson's narrow construction of the federal power was not merely inefficient but positively dangerous even to the life of the government.

This critique of Jefferson also reveals that Hamilton simply perceived a different political reality than the one Jefferson saw. Their principles were no doubt different, but such differences were exacerbated by their divergent judgments about the empirical correlation of forces. As we have seen, Jefferson feared the institution of an American monarchy not only because he believed there were powerful men bent on such an object but also because he thought the natural tendency of the government was to run in the direction of centralized power. Hamilton thought the opposite. He raised with Carrington the Jeffersonian fear that there was a movement afoot to destroy the state governments, but he contended that, on the contrary, the genuine danger was on the other side. The "*great* and *real* anxiety," Hamilton argued, was "to be able to preserve the national" government "from the too potent and counteracting influences" of the states.[76] Hamilton had no interest in any plan to "prostrate the state governments." On the contrary, he claimed that he wished to see the present arrangement maintained, that he believed the state governments would prove "useful and salutary" if they could be "circumscribed within bounds consistent with the preservation of the national government." That remark itself, however, showed his fear that the states were potentially dangerous to the existence of the government established by the Constitution. There would be no such danger, he claimed, if the states were all of moderate size, like Maryland, Connecticut and New Jersey. Yet some of the states were bigger than these, and Hamilton admitted "the most serious apprehensions" about whether the federal government would be "able to maintain itself against their influence." Indeed, Hamilton summed up the situation in language that almost perfectly mirrored Jefferson's opposite assessment: he saw, he said, "a tendency in the nature of things towards the preponderancy of the state governments."[77]

In this context, Hamilton acknowledged to Carrington that his "disposition" in favor of a "liberal construction of the powers of the national government" was connected with his aim to "erect every fence to guard it from" the "depredations" of the states. Hamilton did not view these political concerns as absolutely dictating his constitutional interpretation, as if he could make the Constitution mean whatever was necessary to secure the common good as he

---

[76] *PAH*, 11: 443 (Hamilton's emphasis).

[77] *PAH*, 11: 443–44. Hamilton had entertained similar fears while the Constitutional Convention was meeting. See Paul A. Rahe, *Republics Ancient and Modern, Volume III: Inventions of Prudence: Constituting the American Regime* (Chapel Hill: University of North Carolina Press, 1994), 117.

understood it. Thus he emphasized that he had not embraced any "fence" to the federal authority that he could not judge to be "consistent with constitutional propriety."[78] Nevertheless, he did make clear that his interpretation was political at least in the sense that it took more into account than the language in the document itself: it was also informed by his understanding of the needs of the community. At any rate, we can here see that Hamilton and Jefferson's opposed understandings of the political situation led to equally opposed understandings of the character of Hamilton's construction of the federal power: what Jefferson saw as an aggressive grab for power, Hamilton understood as a defensive effort to protect the federal government from the states.

Indeed, one point of Jefferson's own conduct, although unknown to Hamilton, would have confirmed the latter's fear that there was a tendency afoot in the country to bring the power of the state governments to bear against the government of the Union. In October of 1792, Jefferson wrote to Madison about the "plan" of Virginia Governor Henry Lee to "oppos[e] the federal bank by setting up a state one." Jefferson told his friend that he found such a measure "not only inadequate, but objectionable highly, and unworthy of the Virginia assembly." He went on to denounce Lee's plan as a "milk and water measure" that recognized rather than prevented the "planting" of "a source of poison and corruption." The Virginia legislature "should reason thus," Jefferson continued:

The power of erecting banks and corporations was not given to the general government. It remains then with the state itself. For any person to recognize a foreign legislature in a case belonging to the state itself is an act of *treason* against the state, and whoever shall do any act under color of the authority of a foreign legislature whether by signing notes, issuing or passing them, acting as director, cashier or in any other office relating to it shall be adjudged guilty of high treason and suffer death accordingly, by the judgment of the state courts. This is the only opposition worthy of our state, and the only kind which can be effectual. If N. Carolina could be brought to a like measure, it would bring the General government to respect the counter-rights of the states. The example would probably be followed by some other states. I really wish that this or nothing should be done. A bank of opposition, while it is a recognition of the one opposed, will absolutely fail in Virginia.[79]

When the Virginia legislature had denounced the assumption plan as unconstitutional, Hamilton had told John Jay that it manifested a spirit that had to be killed or would kill the government of the United States. He would surely have found that this spirit had shown itself in an even more dangerous manner in Jefferson's advice here.

---

[78] *PAH*, 11: 443.
[79] *PTJ*, 24: 432–33 (Jefferson's emphasis). For a different side of Jefferson, the side that acknowledged the power of the Union over refractory states, see Brian Steele, "Thomas Jefferson, Coercion, and the Limits of Harmonious Union," *Journal of Southern History* 74 (2008): 823–54.

In the second place, Hamilton contended that the rhetoric employed by Jefferson and his party tended to undermine the government. He did not hold that the government should be immune from criticism or opposition. He complained, rather, that there was a spirit of intemperance and intolerance in the republican critique, which threatened to render the new government detestable to the citizens, on whose support its continuation depended. In the draft of his first *Vindication* essay, Hamilton noted that some of the opposition talked as if they were not only "the most zealous" but even "the only friends to liberty." They "continually" made "a parade of their purity and disinterestedness" while "heaping upon others charges of peculation and corruption." Other opponents, he continued, acted as "a sect of political Doctors – a kind of *Popes* in Government – standards of political orthodoxy who brand with heresy all opinions but their own." Hamilton found this strident self-righteousness not only irritating but politically dangerous.[80] The vehemence of Jefferson and Madison's efforts to subvert him, he observed to Carrington, ran the "risk" of "rendering the government itself odious." They perhaps thought that once they had brought him down they could then "easily recover the lost affections and confidence of the people" for the government. If so, they were naïve. They failed to appreciate "as they ought to do the natural resistance to government which in every community results from the human passions, the degree to which this is strengthened by the *organized rivalry* of state governments, and the infinite danger that the national government once rendered odious will be kept so by these powerful and indefatigable enemies."[81] Later, as "Catullus," he observed that "in a popular government" "to *render odious*" and "to *subvert*" are "convertible terms."[82] If a popular government could survive the people's disagreement or dissatisfaction with some lines of policy, it could not survive the popular hatred that Jefferson and his party had so recklessly sought to stir up – the dangers of which would be all the more acute for a government that was still, as Hamilton observed in a related context, "in the infancy of its existence."[83]

---

[80] Ari Helo and Peter Onuf link the "self-righteous moral tone so characteristic of" Jefferson's "political writing" with his belief that he was speaking on behalf of "progressive moral standards" that were "generated within – and inconceivable without – enlightened civic communities." "Jefferson, Morality, and the Problem of Slavery," *William and Mary Quarterly* 60 (2003): 586. Elsewhere, Onuf similarly notes Jefferson's tendency to eschew "complexity" in favor of "morally absolute judgments." "The Scholars' Jefferson," *William and Mary Quarterly* 50 (1993): 674.

[81] *PAH*, 11: 442 (Hamilton's emphasis).

[82] *PAH*, 12: 499 (Hamilton's emphasis).

[83] *PAH*, 12: 499. For a discussion of Hamilton's belief in the importance of public confidence in government officials to maintaining a stable republic, see Robert W. T. Martin, "Reforming Republicanism: Alexander Hamilton's Theory of Republican Citizenship and Press Liberty," *Journal of the Early Republic* 25 (2005): 21–46. Similarly, Jonathan O'Hara notes the "popular deference" to elected officials that Hamilton thought was necessary to a properly functioning republic. "Aristocratic and Confederate Republicanism in Hamiltonian Thought and Practice," *Publius* 38 (2008): 57.

If we are tempted to think that Hamilton was carrying these fears too far, that there was no real danger of the government's collapse, we should reflect that Jefferson had expressed the same fear in his letter to Washington criticizing Hamilton's program. There, as we have seen, he warned that a substantial portion of the community had opposed the Constitution and that a continuation of Hamilton's policies might alienate enough citizens to create a majority in opposition to the government. Jefferson feared this as the outcome of a spontaneous public reaction against the excesses of Hamiltonianism, while Hamilton feared it as the outcome of a public reaction provoked by the irresponsibly fanatical rhetoric of Jefferson's republican supporters.

In the third place, Hamilton contended that the Jeffersonian indifference to public faith struck at the roots of just government and threatened to overturn the existing political order. Here Hamilton's concerns about Jeffersonianism were even more serious than Jefferson's fears about Hamiltonianism. Jefferson thought that Hamilton aimed to subvert the existing republican constitution and replace it with something monarchical and aristocratic, modeled on the British form of government. Jefferson was vehemently opposed to such a project because he viewed it as a step backward, a departure from the high ground of natural right toward which he thought Europe was heading. Nevertheless, he also admitted that such a government was better than many insofar as it deserved to be called free. Hamilton, in contrast, thought that Jefferson and his party were undermining the principles necessary for *any* just government, particularly respect for faith and for private property.

In his letter to Carrington, Hamilton developed the radical implications of some republican arguments that he believed undermined public faith. Jefferson and some of his followers had suggested that the present generation had "no right to bind posterity." "What are we to think of those maxims of Government," Hamilton asked, which deny to the legislature the right "to bind the Nation by a *Contract* in an affair of *property* for twenty four years? For this is precisely the case of the debt." Such a doctrine threatened the property rights of those who had entered into such a contract with the government, but Hamilton believed that its pernicious influence did not end there. If the Jeffersonian doctrine were true, Hamilton asked, what would "become of all the legal rights of property, of all charters to corporations, nay, of all grants to a man, his heirs and assigns forever?" The right to property as it had always been understood included a right to dispose of it by stipulations that would be legally valid even after the death of the person who made them. Jefferson's notion that the present generation had no right to bind posterity called all this into question. Hamilton concluded that "questions might be multiplied without end to demonstrate the perniciousness and absurdity of such a doctrine."[84]

Hamilton further developed his thoughts on the fundamental importance of respect for faith in his third *Vindication* essay. Fruitful reasoning about respect for public faith, or about any subject, Hamilton began, required "as a point

[84] *PAH*, 11: 436–37 (Hamilton's emphasis).

of departure some principle in which reasonable and sound minds will agree."
For the purposes of this subject, he continued, the principle to be "assumed" is
the following: "that the established *rules of morality and justice are applicable
to nations as well as to individuals*; that the *former* as well as the *latter* are
bound *to keep their promises*, to *fulfill their engagements*, to *respect the rights
of property* which others have acquired under contracts with them."[85] This
same principle, however, was also the basis of "all distinct ideas of right or
wrong, justice or injustice in relation to society and government." Without it,
there could "be no such thing as rights," and "no such thing as property or liberty." Without it, "all the boasted advantages of a constitution of government"
would "vanish in air," and everything would "float on the variable and vague
opinions of the governing party of whomsoever composed."[86] For Hamilton,
one could not assail strict observance of public faith without also unraveling
the distinction between tyranny and just government. Jefferson insisted on a
strict observance of the Constitution, yet his party's neglect of public faith
threatened to undermine a fundamental principle even more essential than the
specific limitations in the Constitution. Indeed, if a government could break
faith in relation to contracts regarding property – if the same morality did not
rule governments and individuals – then there would be no reason to expect
that the same government should keep faith with the people as a whole by
respecting the Constitution, or that the officers of such a government should
keep faith by executing their offices according to the oaths they took to uphold
the Constitution.

This was not to say, Hamilton continued, that a government could never
justly, in any circumstances, violate the public faith. He conceded that while
the "doctrine" asserted above was "true" in "general," there were nevertheless certain "cases" that acted as "exceptions to the rule and in which the
public good may demand and justify a departure from it." Nevertheless, such
exceptions must be understood narrowly. The cases in which exceptions were
permissible were indeed real, but the "admission of them" was also "one of
the most common as well as the most fruitful sources of error and abuse." It
was accordingly "of the greatest importance" to form "just ideas" of the "true
nature, foundation, and extent" of such cases. There was a dangerous temptation, Hamilton warned, to justify such exceptions far too easily. "Depraved
or feeble" minds, he reflected, or those "under the influence of any particular passion or prejudice," would plead an exception to the rule merely when
encountering "some *extraordinary circumstances*." "*Convenience* is with them
a substitute for *necessity*, and some temporary partial advantage is an equivalent for a fundamental and permanent interest of society." Indeed, America had
already shown itself all too susceptible to "this species of levity." The nation's
"treaties," as well as "the sacred rights of private property," had been "too

[85] *PAH*, 11: 470 (Hamilton's emphases).
[86] *PAH*, 11: 470.

frequently sported with" from an excessive "facility in admitting exceptions to the maxims of public faith and the general rules of property." The Constitution and the new national government were established in part precisely to escape the "evil" of such levity in relation to faith and property, and it "behooved" the friends of that government to be "particularly cautious" not to "set an example of equal relaxation" of principle "in the practice of that very government."[87]

Hamilton then proceeded to explain the character and scope of the two justifiable exceptions to the general rule he had laid down. A valid plea of necessity constituted the first exception. Necessity, Hamilton argued, was "admitted in all moral reasonings as an exception to general rules." Therefore, necessity could absolve a government from the duty to perform its engagements. In the affairs of nations, necessity could show itself in two forms. Sometimes there would be an actual "want of ability" to execute the obligation in question. If "extraordinary circumstances" had "disabled" a nation from "performing its stipulations, or its duty in any other respect," then the non-performance was to be considered "involuntary" and "excusable." Nevertheless, Hamilton emphasized that a government must not abuse the plea of necessity in order to escape its obligations or any part of them. The "inability" invoked must be "real" and not merely "pretended," having been "experimentally ascertained" and demonstrable to "the satisfaction of all honest and discerning men." Moreover, any "deviation" from duty justified on the basis of necessity should be "as small as possible. All that is practicable ought to be done."[88] Sometimes necessity would take the form not of actual inability but of extreme danger arising from performance of the government's obligation. Thus Hamilton contended that a "nation is alike excusable in certain extraordinary cases for not observing a right or performing a duty if the one or the other would involve a *manifest* and *great* national calamity." Here again Hamilton emphasized that only a genuinely "extreme case" could justify a plea of necessity. The "calamity to be avoided," he explained, "must not only be evident and considerable" but must even be such as is likely "to prove fatal to the nation," one that "threatens its existence or at least its permanent welfare." This meant that ordinarily even so great a "calamity" as war had to be accepted to protect "even a part of the community injured or annoyed" or to perform "the condition of a defensive alliance with some other nation." Nevertheless, a duty could "excusably be forborne" if either case presented "such circumstances" that "going to war would eminently endanger the existence or permanent welfare of the nation."[89]

The second exception was constituted by a case in which "some great and permanent national good" could "be obtained" by departing from a strict

---

[87] *PAH*, 11: 470–71 (Hamilton's emphases).
[88] *PAH*, 11: 471.
[89] *PAH*, 11: 471–72 (Hamilton's emphases).

observance of rights and duties. As an example of this second kind of exception, Hamilton put forward "the case of certain feudal rights which once oppressed all Europe" and which still oppressed "too great a part of it." Such "rights," he contended, "made absolute slaves of a part of the community and rendered the condition of the greatest proportion of the remainder not much more eligible." These feudal rights, although they involved the right of "property," could nevertheless be "justifiably abolished" because they were "contrary to the social order and to the permanent welfare of society." Here again, however, Hamilton stressed that the imposition on existing rights should be minimized to the extent possible. Whenever a "right of property" was "infringed for the general good," he argued, "if the nature of the case admits of compensation, it ought to be made." Such compensation could be omitted, however, if it was "impracticable."[90]

Hamilton concluded this discussion by emphasizing once again that these exceptions were created only by "cases of extremity – where there is a palpable necessity where some great and permanent national evil is to be avoided – where some great and permanent national good is to be obtained." Governments must not, however, depart from a strict observance of right and obligation merely to evade some "temporary burden," even if it is a "considerable" one, or, alternatively, to "secure" some "partial advantage." Hamilton's discussion of true extremities had already relaxed the general rule as much as was proper. Any further "relaxation," he claimed, "would tend to dissolve all social obligations, to render all rights precarious and to introduce a general dissoluteness and corruption of morals."[91] Finally, returning to the present controversy, Hamilton contended that even a "glance" was sufficient to show that the case of America's public debt "was not one of those cases which could justify a clear infraction of the fundamental rules of good faith and a clear invasion of the rights of property." If there had been any doubt about this before, the operation of the funding system should have dispelled it. It was clear that the debt imposed no extreme national hardship, since it was serviced by "no source of internal revenue" other than "a *very moderate* duty" on "the single article of distilled spirits."[92]

For Hamilton, then, the casual way in which the republicans sported with the public faith struck at the very roots of the morality that was necessary to

---

[90] *PAH*, 11: 472. The relevant passage in the Hamilton papers actually indicates that such compensation may never be omitted, but I think this is clearly the result of a dropped word. The passage runs as follows: "Wherever indeed a right of property is infringed for the general good, if the nature of the case admits of compensation, it ought to be made; but if compensation be impracticable, that impracticability ought to be an obstacle to a clearly essential reform." The only way to make sense of this is to conclude that Hamilton dropped a "not" from the last few words, so that the concluding portion should read: "if compensation be impracticable, that impracticability ought *not* to be an obstacle to a clearly essential reform."

[91] *PAH*, 11: 472.

[92] *PAH*, 11: 472 (Hamilton's emphasis).

just government. Thus, in his "Objections and Answers," he had suggested to Washington that the "politics" of the republican faction "originate[d] in immorality, in a disregard of the maxims of good faith and the rights of property" and warned that if such a politics could "prevail" they "must end in national disgrace and confusion."[93] Later, in his third "Catullus" essay, he outlined for the public how he thought Jeffersonian principles went from moral chaos to political chaos. Jefferson's partisans had talked "familiarly of undoing the funding system as a meritorious work." This kind of politics tended toward "national disunion, insignificance, disorder, and discredit." It was obvious, Hamilton contended, that "the subversion of the funding system would produce national discredit." "Loss of credit," after all, had to befall both "nations" and "individuals" that "voluntarily and without necessity" chose to "violate their formal and positive agreements." "Insignificance and disorder," he continued, were for both individuals and communities the "natural offspring of a loss of credit, premeditatedly and voluntarily incurred." "Disunion," or the destruction of the present government, he warned, "would not long lag behind":

Sober-minded and virtuous men in every state would lose all confidence in, and all respect for, a government which had betrayed so much levity and inconsistency, so profligate a disregard to the rights of property and to the obligations of good faith. Their support would of course be so far withdrawn or relaxed as to leave it an easy prey to its enemies. These comprise the advocates for separate confederacies; the jealous partisans of unlimited sovereignty in the state governments – the never to be satiated lovers of innovation and change – the tribe of pretended philosophers, but real fabricators of chimeras and paradoxes – the Catalines and Caesars of the community (a description of men to be found in every republic) who leading the dance to the tune of liberty without law, endeavor to intoxicate the people with delicious but poisonous draughts to render them the easier victims of their rapacious ambition; the vicious and fanatical of every class who are ever found the willing or the deluded followers of those seducing and treacherous leaders.[94]

Indeed, Hamilton continued, repeal of the funding system would threaten destruction to the government not only by alienating the affections of the virtuous but also by its attack on the rights of those directly interested. Tampering with "sixty millions of property," he warned, "could not be perpetrated without violent concussions." Those states whose citizens owned "the largest portions of the debt" could not for long remain "in the trammels of a party which had so grossly violated their rights." The "consequences" of the project would "quickly awaken" in such citizens and states "a sense of injured right" and "interest." "Where," Hamilton asked, "would all this end but in disunion and anarchy, in national disgrace and humiliation?"[95]

93 *PAH*, 12: 249.
94 *PAH*, 12: 500–01.
95 *PAH*, 12: 501.

The Real Source of the Monarchial Danger

Hamilton contended that it was precisely by fostering such chaos that Jeffersonianism threatened to lay the groundwork for the very thing that it claimed most to fear: the establishment of an American monarchy. Hamilton agreed with Jefferson that there was a real danger of the country turning to monarchy. This end, however, could not be brought about, as Jefferson foolishly feared, through the ordinary operations of the existing government but instead through irresponsible opposition to the government. Under any ordinary circumstances, the American people would never approve of monarchy. Nevertheless, they might be bought to embrace it "from convulsions and disorders" brought on by the "acts of popular demagogues." Hamilton presented it as "unquestionably" true that "the only path to a subversion" of America's "republican system" was "by flattering the prejudices of the people, and exciting their jealousies and apprehensions," with the ultimate effect of throwing the nation's "affairs into confusion" and creating "civil commotion." Then, weary "at length of anarchy," the people might choose to "take shelter in the arms of monarchy for repose and security." Accordingly, the "true artificers of monarchy" were not those who, like Hamilton, sought to give the government powers adequate to securing public peace and prosperity but rather those who opposed "a confirmation of public order."[96]

This outcome was not, Hamilton admitted, *intended* by "the generality" of those who had undermined public order by raising a paranoid alarm over his program. Nevertheless, he suggested that there might be a few among them who could "justly be suspected" of actually preparing the way for monarchy by *design*.

When a man unprincipled in private life, desperate in his fortune, bold in his temper, possessed of considerable talents, having the advantage of military habits – despotic in his ordinary demeanor – when such a man is seen to mount the hobby horse of popularity – to join in the cry of danger to liberty – to take every opportunity of embarrassing the general government and bringing it under suspicion – to flatter and fall in with all the nonsense of the zealots of the day – It may justly be suspected that his object is to throw things into confusion that he may 'ride the storm and direct the whirlwind.'"[97]

This somewhat cryptic warning undoubtedly referred not to Thomas Jefferson but to Aaron Burr.[98] "As a public man," Hamilton had written elsewhere, Burr

---

[96] *PAH*, 12: 252.

[97] *PAH*, 12: 252.

[98] John Ferling mistakenly, I think, suggests that Hamilton was here referring to Jefferson. *Hamilton and Jefferson*, 232. Much of the description Hamilton offers – "bold in his temper," "having the advantage of military habits," "despotic in his ordinary demeanor" – does not seem to fit either what we know of Jefferson's character or what Hamilton thought about Jefferson's character. It is also doubtful that Hamilton would have referred to Jefferson as "unprincipled

was "of the worst sort – a friend to nothing but as it suits his own interest and ambition." Moreover, Burr's ambitions were ultimately anti-constitutional: he aimed "to climb to the highest honors of state, and as much higher as circumstances may permit," caring "nothing about the means of effecting his purpose." Burr aimed to place himself "at the head of what he calls the 'popular party'" simply because this faction provided "the best tools for an ambitious man to work with." In private, Burr ridiculed liberty, but in public he knew "as well as most men how to make use of" its name. "In a word," Hamilton concluded, "if we have an embryo-Caesar in the United States, 'tis Burr."[99]

It might seem strange that an ardent partisan of the people could in fact be animated by a desire to destroy self-government, yet such was the lesson of experience, according to Hamilton. Cato, he observed, was the Tory of his day: often opposing the people, yet ever a defender of the republic. Conversely, Caesar was the Whig of his day: "always" flattering the people's "follies" and in the end destroying the republic. "No popular government was ever without its Catalines and Caesars," Hamilton concluded, and these were "its true enemies."[100] Hamilton did not believe that Jefferson was this kind of man, but he did believe that Jefferson's political irresponsibility created an environment that this kind of man could exploit with a view to overthrowing the republic.

Conclusion

The clash between his two great ministers compelled President Washington to formulate his own position on the controversy. For the most part, he sided with Hamilton, defending the secretary of the treasury's policies and intentions in two meetings with Jefferson in the summer and fall of 1792. Washington, Jefferson discovered, really approved the funding system and the excise. And while he did not exactly defend the bank, neither did the president approve Jefferson's denunciations of it. The bank "had been an act" of "much complaint," Washington noted, but "until there were some infallible criterion of reason" by which to evaluate its effects, "a difference of opinion must be tolerated."[101] The president was positively dismissive of Jefferson's more extreme claims. In response to the charge that Hamilton had made the Congress a corrupt

---

in private life." Hamilton scholar Harvey Flaumenhaft also reads Hamilton here as referring to Burr. *The Effective Republic: Administration and Constitution in the Thought of Alexander Hamilton* (Durham, NC: Duke University Press, 1992), 173. So does James H. Read, "Alexander Hamilton's View of Thomas Jefferson's Ideology and Character," in *The Many Faces of Alexander Hamilton: The Life and Legacy of America's Most Elusive Founding Father* (New York: New York University Press, 2006), 94.

[99] *PAH*, 12: 480.
[100] *PAH*, 12: 252.
[101] *PTJ*, 24: 24, 210 and 433.

tool of the treasury, Washington reminded Jefferson that an "interested spirit in the legislature" was unavoidable "in any government, unless we were to exclude particular descriptions of men, such as the holders of the funds, from all office."[102] And "as to the idea of transforming this government into a monarchy," Washington said "he did not believe there were ten men in the U.S. whose opinions were worth attention who entertained such a thought."[103]

Washington's remarks in these conversations also suggest that Jefferson's earlier effort at coyness with the president might have backfired. Recall that in the introduction to his letter laying out his critique of the Hamiltonian system, Jefferson had assured the president that he was in no way personally involved in the troubling circumstances that endangered the country. This was a strange – indeed, a highly implausible – suggestion, since all of the policies of which Jefferson complained had been pursued by Hamilton under Washington's authority and in many cases with Washington's express approval. Washington's letter to Hamilton communicating the substance of Jefferson's critique showed that he had not been taken in by this soothing effort to divorce the president from administration policy. In that letter, Washington had sought Hamilton's reactions to Jefferson's criticisms precisely because, as Washington said, his own "public conduct was so much involved" in those criticisms.[104] In his July conversation with Jefferson, Washington raised the issue of an assessment of his administration that praised him personally while condemning all of the leading measures that had been pursued. The president intimated that he found such a combination of praise and condemnation to be insulting. He told Jefferson that he considered the *National Gazette*'s denunciation of his administration as "attacking him directly" and that the authors of such attacks "must think him a fool indeed to swallow the little sugar plums here and there thrown out to him" while disregarding the attacks on his policies. Washington continued that "in condemning the administration of the government" such critics also "condemned him, for if they thought there were measures pursued contrary to his sentiment, they must conceive him to be too careless to attend to them or too stupid to understand them."[105] Although Washington only spoke explicitly of the *National Gazette*, it is hard to avoid the suspicion that he

---

[102] *PTJ*, 24: 434.

[103] *PTJ*, 24: 433–34. Jefferson's concerns about a scheme to establish an American monarchy might seem paranoid to a modern reader, but, as Lance Banning observes, there is a sense in which such fears were understandable. "Years of revolutionary exhortations had induced in many Americans of the early 1790s a hypersensitive preoccupation with the incursions of power on liberty. Close familiarity with the maxims that had shaped the Revolution and suffused Antifederalist attacks on the new Constitution had instructed men in the subtlest signs of conspiratorial purpose, the earliest indications of constitutional decay. More than a few Americans expected constitutional degeneration, and they thought they knew the warning signals of decline." Lance Banning, *The Jeffersonian Persuasion: Evolution of a Party Ideology* (Ithaca, NY: Cornell University Press, 1978), 127.

[104] *PAH*, 12: 133.

[105] *PTJ*, 24: 210.

aimed this rebuke at Jefferson as well, since Jefferson's own letter to him had similarly tried to separate the president from his own policies.[106]

Washington, then, was largely unmoved by Jefferson's critique – unless it was to be moved to exasperation. It did not follow, however, that Washington no longer wanted Jefferson in his cabinet. On the contrary, in their October conversation he told Jefferson that he wished him to remain in the administration. He expressed this wish in such a way, moreover, as to suggest that he sympathized with Jefferson's concerns. As Jefferson put it in his record of the discussion, the president said that "he thought it important to preserve the check of my opinions in the administration in order to keep things in their proper channel and prevent them going too far."[107]

Wishing to keep both Hamilton and Jefferson, and wishing for a harmonious administration, the president tried to reconcile the two men. He wrote to them both, urging mutual forbearance for the sake of the Union itself. The country was surrounded by "avowed enemies and insidious friends," and it could not afford to have "internal dissentions . . . harrowing and tearing" at its "vitals." If Jefferson and Hamilton could judge each other's "opinions and acts" with "more charity," then things would "go on smoothly, and, if possible, more prosperously." If not – if his two ministers continued to traffic in "wounding suspicions and irritable charges" – then "everything must rub, the wheels of government will clog – our enemies will triumph – and by throwing their weight into the disaffected scale, may accomplish the ruin of the goodly fabric we have been erecting."[108]

Unfortunately, Washington failed to bring about a reconciliation. Hamilton wrote back to Washington volunteering that he would "cheerfully embrace" any "prospect" that might "open" for "healing or terminating the differences which exist," but also adding, more ominously, that he considered himself to be "the deeply injured party." Hamilton effectively admitted his part in the newspaper campaign against Jefferson and insisted, no doubt to Washington's dismay, that he was "not able to recede *for the present.*"[109] Besides attacking him personally, Hamilton contended, Jefferson's minions represented an organized party "deliberately bent on the subversion of measures which in its consequences would subvert the government." The "undoing of the funding system," he argued, had become "an avowed object" of this party, which was

---

[106] As Jefferson's biographer Joseph Ellis notes, Jefferson's belief in a conspiracy to establish monarchy in America required him "to claim that Washington himself was oblivious to the plot," which in turn required him "to suggest that Washington was unaware of much that was going on around him." *American Sphinx: The Character of Thomas Jefferson* (New York: Alfred A. Knopf, 1997), 256. Washington seems to have sensed this and understandably found it demeaning.

[107] *PTJ*, 24: 433.

[108] *PTJ*, 24: 317. Washington pleaded to Hamilton for amity in much the same terms. See *PAH*, 12: 276.

[109] *PAH*, 12: 347–48.

doing all in its power "to produce that effect by rendering it odious to the body of the people." Subversion of this policy, however, amounted to subversion of the government. Whatever one thought of its original merits, Hamilton contended, repealing the funding system "would prostrate the credit and the honor of the nation, and bring the government into contempt with that description of men who are in every society the only firm supporters of government." Therefore, Hamilton concluded, he had "considered it as a duty to endeavor to resist the torrent," and "as an essential mean to this end" he had turned to journalism to "draw aside the veil from the principal actors."[110]

Jefferson's reply to the president was no more encouraging. Much of Jefferson's letter was dedicated to his forceful rejections of the charges made against him in Hamilton's public counter attack: that he had not fully supported the Constitution when it was being debated, that he was no friend to the public credit, and that he had improperly lent his support to the *National Gazette*. And much of the rest of his letter simply renewed his own charges against Hamilton: that he favored a federal government of unlimited powers, that he sought to undermine America's republican form of government and replace it with a monarchy, and that he had used corruption as a tool by which to manage the legislature.[111]

By the end of his first term, George Washington's two most important department heads could hardly have had lower opinions of each other. In his reply to Washington's plea for peace in the cabinet, Jefferson pledged that he would not at present engage in any journalistic warfare with Hamilton, but he also noted that he might choose to reply in kind once he had left public office. "I will not," he said, "suffer my retirement to be clouded by the slanders of a man whose history, from the moment at which history can stoop to notice him, is a tissue of machinations against the liberty of the country which has not only received him and given him bread, but heaped its honors on his head."[112] Hamilton's assessment was equally severe, and in his third "Catullus" essay, he published his opinion that Jefferson, who had "hitherto been distinguished as the quiet, modest, retiring philosopher – as the plain, simple, unambitious republican," had revealed his real character instead as that of "the intriguing incendiary – the aspiring turbulent competitor."[113] More simply, Hamilton judged Jefferson to be "a man who is continually machinating against the public happiness."[114]

It is not surprising that two men whose disagreements over domestic policy had fostered such venomous mutual assessments should also be led into conflict over the proper conduct of the nation's foreign policy. Indeed, the argument

---

[110] *PAH*, 12: 348–49.
[111] *PTJ*, 24: 355.
[112] *PTJ*, 24: 357.
[113] *PAH*, 12: 504.
[114] *PAH*, 12: 196.

up to this point already hinted at the possibility of such a conflict. In his letter to Edward Carrington laying out his critique of Jefferson and Madison, Hamilton had noted in passing that he regarded their "views" on "foreign politics" as just as "unsound and dangerous" as their views on the nation's internal administration. They had, Hamilton claimed, "*a womanish attachment to France and a womanish resentment against Great Britain*" – dispositions that, if permitted to influence policy, would endanger the peace and security of the United States.[115] We turn now to Hamilton and Jefferson's famous clashes over foreign policy in Washington's second presidential term, and especially the disputes between them arising from American policy toward the war between revolutionary France and its monarchical European enemies.

[115] *PAH*, 11: 439 (Hamilton's emphasis).

PART III

FOUNDING FOREIGN POLICY

11

Two Views of the French Revolution

The momentous events of 1793 precipitated the last great debate between Hamilton and Jefferson as members of Washington's cabinet. Jefferson resigned as secretary of state by the end of the year, and Hamilton followed him into retirement a little over a year later. While these formidable antagonists continued to represent opposed approaches to the questions that dominated American politics for the rest of that decade, and indeed became the de facto heads of the political parties that had formed around those questions, their departure from the administration prevented their engaging so directly and with such clarity as they had done while they both served the same president.

The events of 1793 also shifted the field of their intellectual combat from domestic to foreign policy. In February, revolutionary France declared war on Great Britain and ended up at war with most of the monarchical nations of Europe. These developments placed America in a difficult position, insofar as it had ties to both of the leading belligerents. Great Britain was America's antagonist in the recent struggle for independence but was still the mother country, related to its former colonies by ties of history, ethnicity, and language. France had helped America against Britain, was united to America by a treaty of alliance, and, having thrown off monarchy and adopted republicanism, apparently shared America's deepest political principles. That America was a young and weak nation, with little to gain and much to lose from becoming involved in a war between such great powers, added to the perplexity and danger.

The debates of 1793 were also somewhat different in their scope. The earlier disputes had been about both policy and principle. On the international questions of 1793, however, Hamilton and Jefferson did not oppose each other on the basic question of policy. Although they engaged in considerable wrangling over details of implementation, both agreed that America should not involve itself in the war between France and Great Britain. They nevertheless found matter about which to disagree, and they argued their positions with no less vehemence than that with which they had contested the earlier issues of domestic governance. Men can agree on what to do while disagreeing about how to think about what they are doing, and their agreement about how to act may not prevent them from zealously prosecuting their disagreement about how to think about their actions, for the latter dispute involves questions of principle, which can have important consequences extending far beyond the present case.

Important questions of political principle were raised not only by the foreign policy challenges caused by the French revolutionary wars but also by the French Revolution itself. It was, as Edmund Burke famously remarked, the "most astonishing" revolution that had "hitherto happened in the history of the world."[1] As such it compelled the attention and the judgment of any serious observer of politics in any country, whether or not it had any implications for that country's security. Hamilton and Jefferson were, of course, such observers and had formed opinions on the merits of the French Revolution itself. We turn first, then, to their different evaluations of that revolution as of 1793, both because these views shaped their thinking about American policy but also because their judgments of the Revolution reveal their thinking about fundamental political principles.

Hamilton on the French Revolution

Hamilton was at first ambivalent about the French Revolution. He approved of what he thought it aimed to accomplish, but he feared things would go too far. In October of 1789, he wrote to Lafayette that he viewed the recent "events" in France "with a mixture of pleasure and apprehension." Professing himself "a friend to mankind and to liberty," he "rejoice[d]" in French "efforts" to "establish" liberty. Nevertheless, he also "fear[ed] much for the final success" of these exertions, for the "fate" of those he respected who were "engaged" in the project, and "for the danger" that would arise from the "success of innovations greater than" would "consist with the real felicity of your nation."[2] Hamilton, like Jefferson, approved of the movement to establish liberty in France. At the same time, however, he saw the effort as beset by serious dangers. It could fail, and the country might then revert to some unfree order such as it had been trying to throw off. Alternatively, the "innovations" might "succeed" too well and go further than was prudent or sensible. Moreover, the convulsions of the revolution might destroy the very people who were trying to establish the liberty of their country.

Hamilton went on to explain the grounds of his "foreboding," identifying four factors as particular objects of his "dread." He noted first the potential

---

[1] Edmund Burke, *Reflections on the Revolution in France* (Indianapolis, IN: Hackett Publishing, 1987), 9.
[2] *PAH*, 5: 425.

for "disagreements among those who are now united ... about the nature" of the new "constitution." Second, he feared "the vehement character" of the French "people," whom he thought leaders like Lafayette would "find it more easy to bring on than to keep within proper bounds after" they had been "put" into "motion."[3] Third, Hamilton dreaded "the interested refractoriness of" the French "nobles, who" could not "all be gratified and who" might prove "unwilling to submit to the requisite sacrifices." Finally, in a remark that sounded somewhat like Edmund Burke, Hamilton said that he dreaded "the reveries" of France's "philosophic politicians," who seemed "to have great influence and who being mere speculatists" might "aim at more refinement than" would suit "either with human nature" or the "composition" of the French "nation."[4]

This was, on the whole, a rather sober assessment of France's prospects. Hamilton suggested that it would be difficult under any circumstances for the French to maintain sufficient unity in their efforts. As he knew from observing the American Revolution and the movement to write and ratify the Constitution, it was easier for men to be united in opposition to a regime they reviled than to remain united while taking positive responsibility for framing a new form of government. Hamilton indicated to Lafayette that once such disagreements emerged, they would probably "be improved by the adverse party."[5] In other words, the defenders of the old regime would, for their own purposes, exploit the divisions that would inevitably emerge among those who sought to construct a new order. In addition, France simply seemed to lack the human materials necessary for a successful movement toward liberty. On the one side, the people were too "vehement": once roused it would prove difficult to restrain them. On the other side, the nobles were stubborn and selfish and therefore likely to resist the necessary reforms. As we have seen, Hamilton thought that the abolition of feudalism was one of those rare occasions that justified tampering with the rights of property, but he had no illusions that those whose traditional rights would be abridged by such a project would go along with it happily. In sum, for Hamilton, the two great forces in France were likely to come into conflict. The people were inclined to demand too much, and the nobles were inclined to give too little.

In Hamilton's account, there was another class that belonged neither to the people nor the nobles. These men had some influence and might have been able to manage the relations between the people and the nobles with a view to the good of the whole. For Hamilton, however, the influence of this

---

[3] In general, Hamilton seems to have found it dangerous to stir up the people. In contrast, Jefferson thought efforts to stir them up were essential to preserving the spirit of liberty. On Jefferson's thinking on this question, see Paul A. Rahe, "Thomas Jefferson's Machiavellian Political Science," *Review of Politics* 57 (1995): 461. On this point, see also Federici, *The Political Philosophy of Alexander Hamilton*, 220–33.

[4] *PAH*, 5: 425.

[5] *PAH*, 5: 425.

final faction was more a source of dread than hope. They were impractical men: "philosophic politicians," "mere speculatists" whose "reveries" might lead them to aim for "more refinement" than was consistent with "human nature" or the "composition" of the French nation.[6] On the whole, Hamilton's assessment pointed more to a fear that that revolution would go too far than that it would not go far enough. Of the three forces he identified, two were inclined in this direction. There was real danger that the vehemence of the people would combine with the impractical "reveries" of the leaders to take things beyond all bounds of prudence.[7]

As the Revolution passed through its early stages, Hamilton continued to express such a combination of hope and fear. A postscript to his 1789 letter to Lafayette indicated that the "latest accounts from France" had "abated some of" Hamilton's "apprehensions." He noted that the "nobles in the States General" had supported some "abdications of privileges." Such concessions were "truly noble" and showed a "patriotic and magnanimous policy" that portended "good both to them and their country."[8] Almost a year later, when advising Washington about what to do in the event of war between Britain and Spain, he again showed ambivalence about the Revolution. It was, he said, an effort to move from "slavery to liberty."[9] Nevertheless, such a movement was not entirely unproblematic. It was difficult, Hamilton suggested, to say what part France would play in any such war, and the difficulty of calculating its conduct arose precisely from all the uncertainty caused by its own internal revolution.

The great body of malcontents comprehending a large proportion of the most wealthy and formerly the most influential class; the prodigious innovations which have been made – the general and excessive fermentation which has been excited in the minds of the people, the character of the prince, or the nature of the government likely to be instituted, as far as can be judged prior to an experiment, does not prognosticate much order or vigor in the affairs of that country for a considerable period to come.[10]

However, Hamilton conceded, it was "possible indeed that the enthusiasm which the transition from slavery to liberty" might "inspire" could act as "a substitute for the energy of a good administration" and as the "spring of

---

[6] *PAH*, 5: 425.

[7] In view of the sobriety of Hamilton's early assessment, it is hard, as Conor Cruise O'Brien notes, to see why Stanley Elkins and Eric McKitrick would list Hamilton as one of the "early enthusiasts" of the French Revolution. See O'Brien, *The Long Affair: Thomas Jefferson and the French Revolution* (Chicago: University of Chicago Press, 1996), 85–86, and Elkins and McKitrick, *The Age of Federalism* (New York: Oxford University Press, 1993), 310. Tucker and Hendrickson go too far in the other direction in saying that "from its earliest beginnings, to be sure, revolutionary France was for" Hamilton "an object of horror." *Empire of Liberty*, 45.

[8] *PAH*, 5: 426.

[9] *PAH*, 7: 51.

[10] *PAH*, 5: 50–51.

great exertions." Nevertheless, he added, "the ebullitions of enthusiasm must ever be a precarious reliance," and it was in any case "quite as possible that the greatness, and perhaps immaturity, of that transition" would "prolong licentiousness and disorder" in France. "Calculations of what may happen in France," Hamilton concluded, "must be unusually fallible; not merely from the yet unsettled state of things in that kingdom but from the extreme violence of the change, which has been wrought in the situation of the people."[11]

By 1793, Hamilton's ambivalence had given way to a more decidedly negative view of the Revolution. He expressed this view in a May 1793 letter in which he discussed the reception given at Philadelphia for the French minister, Edmond Genet. He began with a warning about the possible political implications of the American public's appearing to have endorsed the French revolution. According to Hamilton, "public demonstrations of attachment to the cause of France" could do America no good. It was "certainly not wise," he argued, "to expose ourselves to the jealousy and resentment of the rest of the world" – meaning the European world that was largely at war with France – by a "display of zeal for that cause." Indeed, a promiscuous approval of France might even do America "much harm" by provoking France's powerful enemies.[12]

Hamilton, however, did not limit his argument to such prudential considerations regarding foreign policy. He also warned about the Revolution's bad reputation in Europe in such a way as to show that he shared the negative judgment on which that reputation was based. In other words, for Hamilton, the French Revolution now *deserved* to be held in low esteem. America, he argued, would necessarily incur "danger and inconvenience" to its "interests" if it were "to impress on the nations of Europe an idea that we are actuated by the *same spirit* which has for some time past fatally misguided the measures of those who conduct the affairs of France and sullied a cause once glorious and that might have been triumphant."[13]

Hamilton disapproved in the first place of the kind of means that the French revolutionaries had used.

The cause of France is compared with that of America during its late revolution. Would to heaven that the comparison were just. Would to heaven that we could discern in the mirror of French affairs the same humanity, the same decorum, the same gravity, the same order, the same dignity, the same solemnity, which distinguished the course of the American Revolution. Clouds and darkness would not then rest upon the issue as they now do.

The leaders of the Revolution, Hamilton suggested, had committed crime with impunity. He noted "the horrid and systematic massacres of the 2nd and 3rd of

[11] *PAH*, 5: 51.
[12] *PAH*, 14: 475.
[13] *PAH*, 14: 475 (Hamilton's emphasis).

September" and observed that it had proven impossible to bring those responsible "to justice." Indeed, these "assassins" were rewarded with power. Men
like "a Marat and a Robespierre, the notorious prompters of those bloody
scenes," could afterward "sit triumphantly in the Convention and take a con-
spicuous part in its measures."[14] France's "unfortunate prince" – a man who,
"though educated in the lap of despotism," had shown that "he was not the
enemy of liberty" – had been "brought precipitately and ignominiously to
the block – without any substantial proof of guilt as yet disclosed – without
even an authentic exhibition of motives, in decent regard to the opinions of
mankind."[15] "I own," said Hamilton, "I do not like the comparison" of such a
spectacle with the American Revolution.[16] For him, neither the American nor
the French cause could have justified such methods.

  Hamilton's criticism of the Revolution did not stop at the tactics it had
employed but extended as well to its ultimate aims. By 1793, he could no
longer regard the French as merely using bad means for good ends but believed
that the ends themselves had been corrupted. He observed that "the doctrines
of atheism" were "openly advanced in the Convention and heard with loud
applauses," that the "sword of fanaticism" had been "extended to force a political creed upon citizens who were invited to submit to the arms of France as the
harbingers of liberty," that the "hand of rapacity" had been "outstretched to
prostrate and ravish the monuments of religious worship erected by" the French
and their "ancestors," and that "passion, tumult, and violence" had usurped
the places of authority where "reason and cool deliberation ought to preside."
In view of these developments, he concluded, there was "no real resemblance
between what was the cause of America and what is the cause of France."
The difference between them was "no less great that that between liberty and
licentiousness." Hamilton regretted, then, whatever tended to "confound" the
two revolutions and was "anxious, as an American, that the ebullitions of
inconsiderate men among us may not tend to involve our reputation in the
issue."[17]

  Hamilton also thought that his negative judgment would be shared more and
more by his fellow Americans as the wildness of the French course became more

---

[14] For an account of these events by modern historians, see Peter McPhee, *The French Revolution:
1789–1799* (Oxford: Oxford University Press, 2002), 97–99; and William Doyle, *The Oxford
History of the French Revolution*, second edition (Oxford: Oxford University Press, 2002), 190–
93. In his biography of Robespierre, McPhee contends that, contrary to Hamilton's claims here,
there is "no evidence that Robespierre incited or connived at" these "killings." *Robespierre: A
Revolutionary Life* (New Haven, CT: Yale University Press, 2012), 129.

[15] For a modern recounting of the trial and execution of Louis XVI, see John Hardman, *Louis
XVI: The Silent King* (New York: Oxford University Press, 2000), 157–81.

[16] *PAH*, 14: 475. Hamilton's language here ("decent regard to the opinions of mankind") closely
parallels that of the first paragraph of the *Declaration of Independence* ("decent respect to
the opinions on mankind"). For Hamilton, the Americans had had the decency to give an
explanation to the world for breaking off their relationship with their king, but the French had
not had the decency to do so when they killed their king.

[17] *PAH*, 14: 475–76.

manifest. The American "zeal for the liberty of mankind" had, he observed, generated a "universal" "sympathy" for "the cause of France in the first stages of its revolution." Americans, however, were "a sober, temperate, and humane people, friends of religion, social order, and justice, enemies to tumult and massacre, to the wanton and lawless shedding of human blood." Such a people's sympathy, he suggested, would at some point give way to a "just reprobation" for the "extravagancies, excesses, and outrages which" had "sullied" and imperiled the French revolutionary "cause."[18]

Jefferson on the French Revolution

Jefferson was aware of, and troubled by, Hamilton's reservations about the French Revolution. As he had done regarding Hamilton's opinions on the merits of monarchy and republicanism, Jefferson made notes to himself recording what he could discover of his cabinet colleague's views on the French cause. In November 1793, he made the following record: "E.R. [Edmund Randolph, the Attorney General] tells me that Ham. in conversation with him yesterday said: 'Sir, if all the people in America were now assembled . . . to call on me to say whether I am a friend to the French revolution, I would declare that *I have it in abhorrence.*'"[19] Indeed, Jefferson seems to have regarded the two issues – Hamilton's doubtful commitment to republicanism and his lack of support for the French Revolution – as related: opposition to the latter was further evidence of opposition to the former. Thus, in July of that same year, Jefferson made a note to himself that he had heard from Genet, the French minister, that "Colo. Hamilton had never in a single instance addressed a letter to him as the Minister of *the republic of France*, but always as the minister of France."[20]

Jefferson was much more favorably disposed to the French Revolution – and to France itself – than was Hamilton. Writing to his French acquaintances about his decision to join Washington's cabinet as secretary of state, Jefferson expressed a warm affection for France. To Madame d'Enville he confided that the "most powerful" of the "circumstances" which reconciled him to the position of secretary of state was the "opportunities it will give me of cementing the friendship between our two nations. Be assured that to do this is the first wish of my heart." "I have but one system of ethics for men and nations," he told her. "To be grateful, to be faithful to all engagements and under all circumstances, to be open and generous, promotes in the long run the interests of both: I am sure it promotes their happiness." He remarked that France's recent change in "government" would "approximate" her and America "more to one another." Noting the "checks" and "horrors" that France had encountered since he had departed, Jefferson assured Madame d'Enville that "the way to heaven, you know, has always been said to be

---

[18] *PAH*, 14: 503.
[19] *PTJ*, 27: 545 (Jefferson's emphasis).
[20] *PTJ*, 27: 545 (Jefferson's emphasis).

strewed with thorns. Why your nation have had fewer than any other on earth, I do not know, unless it be that it is the best on earth."[21]

Whereas from the start the Revolution had filled Hamilton with a sense of foreboding, Jefferson tended to view its prospects with serenity. Throughout 1790 and 1791 his correspondence is filled with expressions of confidence that "affairs in France were going on perfectly well."[22] In March of 1791, he wrote to his daughter, Martha Jefferson Randolph, that "things are going on well in France, the revolution being past all danger. The national assembly being to separate soon, that event will seal the whole with security."[23] Where the news was less than ideal, Jefferson tended to express confidence that all would come right in the end. He noted to Lafayette that he had heard about "difficulties and dangers" encountered in the course of the Revolution, but he reassured the Marquis that "we are not to expect to be translated from despotism to liberty in a feather-bed."[24] The letter to Lafayette shows that Jefferson was aware of the grave dangers France might encounter in the progress of its revolution. Like Hamilton, he worried that those for whom he cared might be destroyed by the political convulsions. He implored Lafayette: "Take care of yourself, my dear friend," lest France were to "lose you." And Jefferson saw, too, that these political convulsions might result in the loss of more than a few friends. Thus he warned that the loss of Lafayette might in turn "cost" France "oceans of blood, and years of confusion and anarchy." Nevertheless, he differed from Hamilton in that even such ghastly prospects did not shake his belief in the goodness of the ultimate outcome. Even if France lost Lafayette and suffered oceans of blood and years of anarchy and confusion, Jefferson still thought she "would in any event work out her salvation."[25]

Jefferson's greater confidence in the outcome of the revolution seems to have rested on his greater confidence in its leadership and in the material with which it had to work. Hamilton derided France's "philosophic politicians" as "mere speculatists," unlikely to keep the Revolution in a prudent course, a course that would have been difficult to maintain in any case given the potential for conflict between the excessively vehement people and the selfishly refractory nobles. In contrast, Jefferson saw wisdom where Hamilton saw folly and unity where Hamilton saw division. Thus he wrote to John Adams that the flight and recapture of the King in 1791 did not change his "confidence in the favorable issue" of the "revolution, because it has always rested on my own ocular evidence of the unanimity of the nation and" the "wisdom of the patriotic party in the national assembly."[26]

---

[21] *PTJ*, 26: 290–91.
[22] *PTJ*, 20: 100.
[23] *PTJ*, 19: 604. See also 601–02, and Volume 22, 232–33.
[24] *PTJ*, 26: 293.
[25] *PTJ*, 26: 293.
[26] *PTJ*, 20: 310.

As the Revolution progressed, Jefferson received the same kind of news that had destroyed Hamilton's good opinion. Such news, however, left Jefferson's support for the French cause unshaken. Some reports of revolutionary lawlessness he dismissed as coming from unreliable, anti-republican sources. In a record of his consultations with the president in March and April of 1792, he observed that Washington had said that he began to "doubt very much of the affairs of France." Jefferson attributed Washington's flagging confidence to the influence of the minister to France, Hamilton's Federalist friend and ally: "The fact is that Gouverneur Morris, a high flying monarchy-man, shutting his eyes and his faith to every fact against his wishes, and believing everything he desires to be true, has kept the president's mind constantly poisoned with his forebodings."[27]

Equally disturbing reports, however, also came to Jefferson from a source that he could not so easily dismiss: William Short, his successor and Morris's predecessor as minister to France. During Jefferson's time in Paris, Short had, in the words of Jefferson biographer Dumas Malone, served as his "able and devoted secretary" and had "lived with" Jefferson "as a son."[28] Short's letter of July 24, 1791, contained material that might well have undermined Jefferson's confidence in the unanimity of the French nation and the wisdom of its new leaders.

Acts of rigor are now used against that class of people who have been long employed as the arms of the revolution and who had become too strong for the government. Their disgust will necessarily increase and it will not be surprising if in time they act against their former leaders in favor of any party who should be strong enough to offer them a change. It is the misfortune of this country to have too many of those who will always desire disorder and changes because having nothing to lose they have nothing to fear. It must be agreed also that the conduct of the assembly gives fair play to their enemies whether royalists or republicans. The acts of irregularity and despotism which they tolerate or authorize are overlooked by a great many as they consider them the only remedy to the greater evil of anarchy. But they are reproached by many also as the indirect cause of this anarchy in taking the government into their own hands instead of organizing and separating its parts. It is evident that the true principles of liberty are either not known or not attended to. They are avowedly violated every day under the long known pretext of the common good. Where such things will lead to or when they will end it is impossible to say, but it is evident that they obscure the horizon and give alarm to such as have time to reflect on their future progress.[29]

---

[27] *PTJ*, 23: 260. For an interesting extended discussion of Jefferson's and Morris's views of the French Revolution, see Philipp Ziesche's "Exporting American Revolutions: Gouverneur Morris, Thomas Jefferson, and the Struggle for Universal Rights in Revolutionary France," *Journal of the Early Republic* 26 (2006): 419–47.

[28] Dumas Malone, *Jefferson and the Rights of Man* (Boston: Little, Brown and Company, 1951), 131.

[29] *PTJ*, 20: 673–74.

A year later, Short, by then America's minister to The Hague, continued to monitor developments in France closely and to report to Jefferson. The news by then was worse than it had been the year before. Short informed Jefferson of "the arrestation, massacre or flight of all those who should be considered as the friends and supporters of the late constitution in France with a monarch at its head. The mob and demagogues of Paris had carried their fury in this line as far as it could go."[30]

A few weeks later, in the wake of the September massacres that had so shocked Hamilton, Short wrote again of "scenes" in France "too horrid and distressing to behold":

The names of the unfortunate victims who were known to you will show you that the constant practice of public and private virtues – continued sacrifices of rank and fortune and whatever men value highest to the desire of public good – constant and disinterested efforts in favor of public liberty, so far from securing respect and protection have become the motives for proscription, imprisonment and massacre in the eyes of those monsters who then directed the blind multitude – who persuaded them that deliberately massacring prisoners confined without guilt and even without suspicion – murdering unarmed and helpless individuals in the bosom of their families, was gloriously combating the enemies of their country – who excited them under the pretext of establishing freedom to overthrow their own government – and who placed all their ideas and efforts for liberty in the infamous audacity of rising against the law known to be too weak to chastise or check them.[31]

Jefferson was largely unfazed by such reports. Even after the events of 1792, he could write to his son-in-law that "news from France continues to be good and to promise continuance. The event of the revolution there is now little doubted of, even by its enemies."[32] The rise of the Jacobins, so troubling to some, could not disturb the tranquility of Jefferson's mind. In March of 1792, Short wrote to him of their latest political victory. They had, he observed, "forced the king to take the members of his council from their body, so that all the present ministers except that of the war department are the most violent, popular and leading members of the club des Jacobins, whose exaggerated and dangerous principles have been long known wherever the French Revolution has been heard of."[33] Three months later, Jefferson, writing to Madison, showed that he was mostly unmoved by Short's assessment:

This ministry, which is of the Jacobin party, cannot but be favorable to us, as that whole party must be. Indeed, notwithstanding the very general abuse of the Jacobins, I begin to consider them as representing the true revolution-spirit of the whole nation, and as carrying the nation with them. The only things wanting with them is more experience in business, and a little more conformity to the established style of communication with

30 *PTJ*, 24: 322.
31 *PTJ*, 24: 390–91.
32 *PTJ*, 25: 30.
33 *PTJ*, 23: 337.

foreign powers. The latter want will I fear bring enemies into the field, who would have remained at home; the former leads them to domineer over their executive so as [to] render it unequal to its proper objects. I sincerely wish our new minister may not spoil our chance of extracting good from the present situation of things.[34]

The final sentence here refers to Gouverneur Morris, about whose prejudices against the Revolution Jefferson had earlier complained. Examining the situation in France in the middle of 1792, Jefferson worried not so much about the power of the Jacobins but about the influence of the American minster.

By 1793, when Hamilton's negative judgment on the Revolution had solidified, Jefferson continued to support it. The trial and execution of the king, which Hamilton regarded as an act of lawlessness, Jefferson saw as a harbinger of good for all of Europe. If the "ferment in Europe" failed to "produce republics everywhere," the "decapitation of the king of France" would "at least soften the monarchical governments by rendering monarchs amenable to punishment like other criminals, and doing away with that aegis of insolence and oppression, the inviolability of the king's person."[35] Jefferson's commentary of 1793 showed that he was capable of serious criticism of the French Revolutionary government, but, again, his criticism was very limited in comparison to Hamilton's. He tended to see errors of judgment where Hamilton saw incapacity and criminality. Thus Jefferson wrote to his son-in-law in the summer of 1793 that the French had been "guilty of great errors in their conduct towards other nations, not only in insulting uselessly all crowned heads" but also in "endeavoring to force liberty on their neighbors in their own form." Still, Jefferson expressed hope that they seemed "to be correcting themselves in the latter point."[36]

Jefferson was so protective of the French Revolution, it would seem, because he believed it was ideologically akin to the American Revolution, and because he believed that the success of the French Revolution was important to the preservation of freedom in America and, indeed, to the establishment of freedom everywhere. He emphasized the ideological kinship between the American and French regimes in a 1792 letter to Gouverneur Morris upon the latter's appointment as minister to France. Knowing Morris's reservations about the French Revolution, Jefferson admonished him that, concerning the new French government, America was "under no call to express opinions which might please or offend any party" and that it would be best to avoid any expressions on that subject. Nevertheless, Jefferson continued, if "any circumstances" were to arise that would "require unavoidably such expressions, they would naturally be in conformity with the sentiments of the great mass" of Americans, "who having first, in modern times, taken the ground of government founded

---

[34] *PTJ*, 24: 134.
[35] *PTJ*, 25: 402.
[36] *PTJ*, 26: 356.

on the will of the people," could not help but "be delighted on seeing so distinguished and so esteemed a nation" as France "arrive on the same ground and plant their standard by our side."[37]

Viewing the two nations as standing side by side on the same political ground, Jefferson worried that the destruction of the French republic would tend to undermine its American counterpart. In the worst case, Jefferson feared that if the monarchical powers of Europe succeeded in restoring something like the old regime in France, they might then be emboldened to try to exert their power to make America surrender its own republican form of government. If "great successes were to attend the arms of the kings," he wrote to Harry Innes, they "might" then "choose to finish their job completely by obliging us to change the form of our government at least" – an outcome, he added, that would be "grateful to a party" in America, "not numerous, but wealthy and influential.[38] Even if America remained secure from such external coercion, however, Jefferson worried that the failure of the Revolution would undermine America's own commitment to republican government. Such a failure, he suggested, would constitute "a powerful argument with those who" wished "to introduce a king, lords, and commons" in America.[39] Even a partial reversal of the French enterprise – such as a "falling back" to the "constitution of 1791" – would, Jefferson feared, "give wonderful vigor" to the American "monocrats, and unquestionably affect the tone" with which "our government" was administered.[40] The tone of the administration, moreover, could effect a serious change in the nature of America's government. Whatever happened in France would "influence the tone and principles" of the "administration" of America's "constitution" so "as to lead it to something very different in the event from what it would be in the other."[41] Such fears were consistent with the ones Jefferson had expressed in relation to domestic policy in 1792. He already feared, as we have seen, that some leading Americans did not think that republican government was workable and that they in fact planned to move the nation in the direction of monarchy. The collapse of French republicanism could only strengthen their belief in the weakness of republican government and perhaps win some American converts to their way of thinking.

This connection between French and American republicanism, however, was not the limit of Jefferson's belief in the importance of the French cause. For him, the French Revolution was an event of world historic significance, the success of which was crucial to the future of the human race. Jefferson told Condorcet that he looked "ardently to the completion of the glorious work" in which France was engaged because he viewed "the general condition of Europe

[37] *PTJ*, 23: 55.
[38] *PTJ*, 26: 99.
[39] *PTJ*, 20: 670.
[40] *PTJ*, 26: 169.
[41] *PTJ*, 26: 99.

as hanging on the success or failure of France."[42] With other correspondents, Jefferson carried this theme to even greater lengths. Remarking on the flight and recapture of the king, he said that it "would be unfortunate were it in the power of any one man to defeat the issue of so beautiful a revolution. I hope and trust it is not, and that for the good of suffering humanity all over the earth" that the French Revolution would "be established and spread throughout the whole world."[43] Jefferson maintained this view even in the face of the bloody events of 1792 and 1793. Thus, in May of 1793, he wrote to Brissot de Warville that he was "happy in a safe occasion of assuring you that I continue eternally attached to the principles of your revolution. I hope it will end in the establishment of some firm government, friendly to liberty, and capable of maintaining it. If it does, the whole world will become inevitably free."[44]

Jefferson invested these grand hopes with a religious significance. As we have already seen, he spoke of the French Revolution as promising a kind of political "salvation" and compared its challenges to the "thorns" that were said to strew the path to "heaven." In view of the transcendent good the Revolution promised, Jefferson could not react to the bloodshed it occasioned with anything like the horror expressed by Hamilton and Short. He expressed his thinking in a letter in which he actually rebuked Short for his complaints about the violence of the French proceedings:

The tone of your letters had for some time given me pain, on account of the extreme warmth with which they censured the proceedings of the Jacobins of France. I considered that sect as the same with the Republican patriots, and the Feuillants as the Monarchical patriots, well known in the early part of the revolution, and but little distant in their views, both having in object the establishment of a free constitution, and differing only on the question whether their chief Executive should be hereditary or not. The Jacobins (as since called) yielded to the Feuillants and tried the experiment of retaining their hereditary executive. The experiment failed completely and would have brought on the reestablishment of despotism had it been pursued. The Jacobins saw this, and that the expunging that officer was of absolute necessity, and the nation was with them in opinion, for however they might have been formerly for the constitution framed by the first assembly, they were come over from their hope in it, and were now generally Jacobins. In the struggle which was necessary many guilty persons fell without the forms of trial, and with them some of the innocent. These I deplore as much as anybody, and shall deplore some of them to the day of my death. But I deplore them as I should have done had they fallen in battle. It was necessary to use the arm of the people, a machine

---

[42] *PTJ*, 20: 99.

[43] *PTJ*, 22: 77.

[44] *PTJ*, 25: 679. Although the hopes Jefferson invested in the French Revolution may seem exaggerated, they were not unique to him or even to Americans of his political persuasion. Later, even John Marshall – who was very far from being a Jeffersonian – recalled that at the time "I sincerely believed human liberty to depend in a great measure on the success of the French Revolution." Quoted in Elkins and McKitrick, *The Age of Federalism*, 310.

not quite so blind as balls and bombs, but blind to a certain degree. A few of their cordial friends met at their hands the fate of enemies. But time and truth will rescue and embalm their memories, while their posterity will be enjoying that very liberty for which they would never have hesitated to offer up their lives. The liberty of the whole earth was depending on the issue of the contest, and was ever such a prize won with so little innocent blood? My own affections have been deeply wounded by some of the martyrs to this cause, but rather than it should have failed, I would have seen half the earth desolated. Were there but an Adam and an Eve left in every country, and left free, it would be better than as it now is.[45]

Hamilton would surely have regarded this letter as shocking confirmation of Jefferson's political fanaticism. Leaving aside Jefferson's somewhat cavalier attitude toward the deaths of the innocent, Hamilton might have been even more outraged by his comments about the "guilty." According to Jefferson, the French experiment with the middle ground of constitutional democracy had failed, so that the only options left were reversion to despotism or a movement forward to pure republicanism. That movement, in his view, made "necessary" a "struggle" in which "many guilty persons fell without the forms of trial, and with them some of the innocent." This formulation implied that the opponents of the Jacobins were "guilty" of some kind of crime for which they received a deserved punishment, but without the proper formalities, and that in the absence of such formalities some of the innocent had regrettably been cut down as well. The supposedly "guilty" opponents of Jacobinism, however, had committed no offense other than seeking to maintain the constitution that the Jacobins had decided it was necessary to overthrow. As Short's letters to Jefferson had made clear, they had not really been punished as criminals, however summarily, but eliminated as politically undesirable elements.

Leaving aside the language of crime and punishment, Jefferson next analogized the revolutionary violence to warfare. The "innocent" supporters of Jacobinism, he suggested, had been killed as if in "battle," struck down, as it were, by misdirected friendly fire from their own side. Jefferson thus implied that the enemies of the Jacobins, too, had been killed in battle, but properly and legitimately. It is doubtful, however, that Hamilton would have found this formulation any more reassuring. It implied that the "guilty," the enemies of the Jacobins, had died fighting. Again, as Short's communications made clear, this was not the case. They had not died in battle but had been rounded up and massacred.

Hamilton would probably have been reluctant to concede that any cause could justify such methods. He would certainly have repudiated Jefferson's position, however, which was not only that *this* cause justified *these* methods but that this cause could justify practically *any* methods that could be conceived. For Jefferson, the holiness of the revolutionary cause legitimized anything that might be done in its service. This was surely the upshot of his remarks to Short about preferring that half the earth be desolated rather than the Revolution fail, and that Europe would be better off with just one free man and woman in each nation than continue as it had been. For Hamilton, a republican revolution could be discredited by recurrence to immoral means, and the French Revolution had in fact so discredited itself. For Jefferson, it had not so discredited itself because, in his mind, there were no means that could discredit such a revolution.

Conclusion

Hamilton and Jefferson's disagreement over the merits of the French Revolution did not require that they come into conflict over the question of American policy toward France and its enemies once war broke out. The questions involved are on some level distinct and separable. One could approve of the French Revolution and still not want America to get involved in the wars arising out of it, just as one could oppose the Revolution and think that it was necessary or advantageous for America to play a role in the fighting.

Nevertheless, without determining their foreign policy clashes, these statesmen's different assessments of the Revolution did influence their foreign policy arguments, as well as their judgments of each other's positions. As we will see, Hamilton's conviction that the Revolution had veered into a course of immorality and violence informed his belief that any association with the new regime would be disgraceful and dangerous to America. On the other side, Jefferson, not sharing Hamilton's horror at the means to which the revolutionaries resorted, could only view his cabinet colleague's hesitation to be associated with France as a sign of his hostility to republican government.

Faith among Nations I

Jefferson's Opinion on the French Treaties

Upon hearing that France had declared war on Great Britain, President Washington sought advice from his cabinet about the proper American line of policy. The question for Washington was not *whether* America should remain neutral but *how* it should go about remaining neutral.[1] The president did not regard the basic decision to remain neutral a controversial one, and neither did the other leading members of his administration. Hamilton, of course, is famous as a vigorous proponent of neutrality. "Every discreet man," he wrote, "must perceive at once that it is highly the interest of this country to remain at peace and as a mean to this to observe a strict neutrality in the present quarrel between the European powers."[2] Jefferson was no less convinced of the necessity of such a policy. Even before Washington sought the cabinet's advice, Jefferson had written to him to express his "opinion that we take every justifiable measure for preserving our neutrality" in the war.[3] Hamilton and Jefferson's differences about the merits of the French revolution did not lead them to disagree about whether America should take any active part in the war that could determine its success or failure.

This agreement as to the country's basic posture toward the warring parties, however, did not prevent disagreements between Hamilton and Jefferson regarding other questions of policy and principle that arose in relation to American neutrality.[4] These disagreements were brought into play by a set of written questions that Washington submitted to the cabinet as a basis for its

---

[1] *PTJ*, 25: 541.

[2] *PAH*, 14: 449.

[3] *PTJ*, 25: 518.

[4] For an account of Hamilton and Jefferson's wrangling over the details of neutrality policy, see chapters 8 and 9 of John Lamberton Harper's *American Machiavelli: Alexander Hamilton and the Origins of U.S. Foreign Policy* (New York: Cambridge University Press, 2004).

deliberations about neutrality policy. The first of these queries asked whether the government should actually issue some kind of "proclamation" in order to prevent "interferences of the citizens of the United States in the war between France and Great Britain" and whether, if such proclamation were issued, it should or should not "contain a declaration of neutrality." Most of the rest of the queries dealt more specifically with the question of America's relationship to France – a relationship that, involving treaties of commerce and alliance, could complicate America's effort to remain neutral. Should the government of the United States receive a French minister, and, if so, with or without qualifications? What was the status of the treaties between France and America? Was the United States "obliged by good faith to consider" the treaties "as applying to the present situation of the parties," or could the government hold them to be "suspended" until such time as the government of France was clearly established, or even go so far as to "renounce" them entirely? If there actually was an option to suspend or renounce the treaties, could a failure to do so be construed as a breach of neutrality? If the treaties were to be considered in operation, how were their provisions to be interpreted? Was the guarantee to France in the treaty of alliance intended to apply to any war in which France might be involved, or only a defensive war? Was the present war offensive, defensive, or of a mixed character on the part of France?[5]

This line of inquiry regarding France opened up the possibility that the United States might do more than just remain neutral in the present war. It suggested that America might choose not to recognize the new revolutionary government of France and that it might treat the change in government as having nullified the treaties into which America had entered with the old regime. The introduction of such possibilities into the cabinet's deliberations, Jefferson believed, was Hamilton's handiwork. In his notes on the questions Washington had proposed, Jefferson remarked that while they were in the president's "own handwriting," it was nevertheless "palpable from the style, their ingenious tissue and suite that they were not the president's, that they were raised upon a prepared chain of argument, in short that the language was Hamilton's, and the doubts his alone."[6] Attorney General Edmund Randolph seemed to confirm Jefferson's suspicions. The day before the president had submitted the written questions, Randolph told Jefferson, Hamilton had, in conversation with Randolph, gone through "the whole chain of reasoning of which" Washington's written questions were "the skeleton."[7]

The evidence of Hamilton's own papers confirms Jefferson's suspicions. On April 9, Hamilton had written to John Jay, seeking his advice and laying out a line of reasoning about America's relationship to France very similar to that implied by the questions Washington later submitted to the cabinet. Hamilton

[5] *PTJ*, 25: 569.
[6] *PTJ*, 25: 665.
[7] *PTJ*, 25: 666.

worried that America might compromise its neutrality even by receiving a minister sent by the new French republic. The war was in effect being fought to determine who would rule France. Would America really stand on neutral ground, Hamilton wondered, if it received a minister from the revolutionary government but not one that might be sent by a regent claiming to be the successor to the recently executed king? Would receiving the republic's minister confer implicit recognition on the new French government, thus placing it in a position to invoke the American treaty of alliance, which would in turn draw America into the war? Could America evade these dangers by refusing to receive the minister or by receiving him with qualifications – that is, while reserving a right to hold the treaties suspended or discontinued? Such questions, Hamilton told Jay, would require the government's "utmost wisdom."[8]

Cabinet Deliberations

The cabinet met on April 19 to consider the issues the president had raised. On two important questions it reached decisions that were acceptable, although not perfectly satisfactory, to Jefferson and Hamilton. Everyone – including Jefferson – agreed that the government should issue a proclamation "forbidding our citizens to take part in any hostilities on the seas with or against any of the belligerent powers, and warning them against carrying to any such powers any of those articles deemed contraband according to the modern usage of nations, and enjoining them from all acts and proceedings inconsistent with the duties of a friendly nation towards those at war." Everyone – including Hamilton – agreed that the minister from the Republic of France should be received.[9]

Both Jefferson and Hamilton, however, had certain reservations about the policies here adopted. Hamilton had voted to receive Genet, but he also expressed "his great regret that any incident had happened which should oblige us to recognize the government" of France.[10] Jefferson had argued that America should put off declaring its neutrality in the hope that it might extract some concessions from the warring parties in exchange for it. In response, Hamilton had argued that American neutrality was not negotiable.[11] Hamilton's view prevailed, the cabinet decided to issue an immediate proclamation, and Jefferson concurred. Here, however, Jefferson won one point. For constitutional reasons to which we will return in a later chapter, Jefferson argued that the term "neutrality" should not be used in the proclamation, and the cabinet agreed that the document should be framed accordingly.

Practical agreement broke down, however, on the question of whether the French minister should be received with or without qualifications and on

[8] *PAH*, 14: 297–98.
[9] *PAH*, 14: 328.
[10] *PTJ*, 25: 665.
[11] Chernow, *Alexander Hamilton*, 435.

the related matter of whether America should or could extricate itself from the French treaties. According to Jefferson's account of the meeting, he and Edmund Randolph took the view that Genet should be received without qualification and that the treaties were still valid. Hamilton, however, invoking the authority of Vattel, pressed hard the argument that the government could legitimately declare the treaties "void." The cabinet divided on these questions. Secretary of War Henry Knox sided with Hamilton. Attorney General Edmund Randolph sided with Jefferson, but on hearing Hamilton's argument Randolph added that he would like more time to consider the matter and that "in so great a question he should choose to give a written opinion." As a result, it was agreed that Jefferson and Hamilton should submit written opinions as well.[12]

Jefferson's *Opinion on the French Treaties*

Jefferson completed his *Opinion* first and submitted it to Washington on April 28, 1793. He ignored the question of whether Genet should be received conditionally and addressed himself instead to what he apparently took to be the more fundamental issue: "Whether the U.S. have a right to renounce their treaties with France, or to hold them suspended till the government of that country shall be established?"[13]

Jefferson began by summarizing his understanding of the Hamiltonian position he aimed to refute. At the recent cabinet meeting, he contended, the secretary of the treasury had argued as follows. France had been a monarchy when the United States had "entered into treaties with it," but it had "now declared itself a republic" and was "preparing a republican form of government." There was no telling, however, what form of government would actually result from France's efforts. The Revolution might "issue in a republic, or a military despotism, or in something else." Moreover, the form which the new government took might turn out to "render our alliance" with France "dangerous to ourselves." Accordingly, Hamilton had argued, America had a "right of election to renounce the treaty altogether, or to declare it suspended till" the government of France was "settled" in its "ultimate" form. If the United States declared the treaty temporarily suspended, Hamilton continued, it could, once the French government was solidified, then determine whether it would "call the treaties into operation again" or instead "declare them forever null." America's freedom of action, however, would be undercut by receiving the French minister without qualification. Receiving Genet absolutely, Hamilton had contended, would "amount to an act of election to continue the treaties." If the French government should then take a form that would render the treaties dangerous to the United States, the American government would no longer be

[12] *PTJ*, 25: 666.
[13] Jefferson, *Writings*, 422.

"free to renounce them." Indeed, Hamilton had gone so far as to argue that since the United States was free to renounce the treaties, the decision not to renounce them was "equivalent" to entering into a new treaty with a "clause of guarantee." But, he held, to "make a treaty with a clause of guarantee" with a nation presently at war was in fact a "departure from neutrality." In that light, Hamilton had argued, failure to renounce the treaties effectively made the Unites States "associates in the war." Therefore, he concluded, to "renounce" or at least to "suspend" the treaties was "a necessary act" of American "neutrality."[14]

The Right of Revolution and the Obligation of Treaties

Jefferson admitted the "ingenuity" of such reasoning but declined to concede its "soundness." He proceeded to "lay down the principles" that he believed ought to "govern the case."[15] He contended in the first place that the mere change in France's government could not liberate America from its treaty obligations. According to Jefferson, "the people who constitute a society or nation" are "the source of all authority in that nation." The people therefore had a right to establish whatever government they wished – were "free," in other words, "to transact their common concerns by any agents they think proper." This included a right to change the persons holding office under the government, as well as a right to change the form of government itself. The people could "change" their "agents individually," or even "the organization of them in form or function, whenever they please."[16] Here, of course, Jefferson echoed his famous argument in the *Declaration of Independence*, although he now expressed himself with less restraint. The *Declaration* clearly endorsed a popular right to revolution, but it also stressed the role of prudence in mediating the use of that right, indicating that the people should act to change their government not "whenever they please[d]" but whenever they found themselves subjected to a long train of abuses that threatened to end in despotism. Writing for the nation in 1776, Jefferson had offered a markedly more conservative presentation of the right of revolution than he gave to Washington in 1793.

Moreover, Jefferson continued, "all the acts done by" the people's "agents under the authority of the nation" were to be considered "the acts of the nation" itself and therefore "obligatory on" the nation. Such obligations could not "be annulled or affected by any change" in the "persons administering" the government, or even by a "change in the form of the government" itself. The treaties between the United States and France, therefore, "were not treaties between" the United States and "Louis Capet," who were merely agents of the American and French peoples. They were instead treaties "between the two nations of America and France." And since these two nations remained in

[14] Jefferson, *Writings*, 422.
[15] Jefferson, *Writings*, 422.
[16] Jefferson, *Writings*, 422.

existence, "the treaties" were "not annulled by" the "changes" in government both had experienced.[17]

Treaties and the Moral Law of Nature

This argument on its own, however, did not entirely settle the question of the treaties' status, for Jefferson did not contend that treaties were absolutely and irrevocably binding, irrespective of any change in circumstances. Jefferson therefore turned next to an examination of the "law of nations, by which," he claimed, the question at hand was to be determined. That law was "composed of three branches": First, the "moral law of our nature"; second, the "usages of nations," or the customary principles governing international conduct; third, the "special conventions" of nations, or the treaties they had made. Jefferson contended that the first branch alone – "the moral law to which man has been subjected by his creator, and of which his feelings, or conscience as it is sometimes called, are the evidence with which his creator has furnished him" – was relevant to the present question. Jefferson held that moral duties between men could and did exist in the state of nature, prior to their entering into society. In addition, the moral duties that existed "between individual and individual in a state of nature" remained in force after those individuals had entered "into a state of society." Accordingly, "the aggregate of the duties of all the individuals composing the society constitutes the duties of that society towards any other." It then followed that "between society and society the same moral duties exist as did between the individuals composing them while in an unassociated state, their maker not having released them from those duties on their forming themselves into a nation." Jefferson concluded that "compacts" between nations were "obligatory on them by the same moral law which obliges individuals to observe their compacts."[18]

Writing officially for Washington, however, Jefferson was more circumspect than he had been when writing as a friend to Madame d'Enville, telling her that his "system of ethics" for both "men and nations" required both "to be faithful to all engagements and under all circumstances."[19] In his *Opinion*, Jefferson conceded that there were two "circumstances" that could "sometimes excuse the non-performance of contracts between man and man," as well as between "nation and nation." First, if performance were to become impossible, then "non-performance" could not be judged "immoral." Second, if performance were to become "*self-destructive* to the party" called upon, then "the law of self-preservation overrules the laws of obligation to others." "For the reality of these principles" Jefferson appealed "to the true fountains of evidence, the head and heart of every rational and honest man," where, he contended, "nature had written her moral laws, and where every man" could "read them for himself."

[17] Jefferson, *Writings*, 422.
[18] Jefferson, *Writings*, 423.
[19] *PTJ*, 26: 290–91.

Thus consulting his head and heart, no rational or honest man could ever "read there permission to annul his obligations for a time, or forever, whenever they become 'dangerous, useless, or disagreeable.'" It was therefore beyond question that, whatever Hamilton thought he had found in Vattel, mere uselessness or disagreeableness could not liberate a nation from its engagements. Danger could procure such liberation, but even here, Jefferson insisted, the "danger must be imminent and the degree great." It was true that the degree and imminence of the danger had to be judged by each nation for itself, since "no one nation has a right to sit in judgment over another." Nations were, however, still subject to "the tribunal of our consciences, and that also of the opinion of the world." These tribunals, he suggested, would "revise the sentence" each nation would pass in its own case, and as "we respect" the tribunals of conscience and world opinion, "we must see that in judging ourselves we have honestly done the part of impartial and vigorous judges."[20]

Having conceded some right of a nation to consider itself free of its treaty obligations, Jefferson proceeded to explain the principles that limited this right. "Reason," he suggested, bestows on nations "this right of self-liberation from a contract in certain cases." Reason, too, however, "has subjected" that same right "to certain just limitations." Jefferson identified three. In the first place, the "danger which absolves us must be great, inevitable, and imminent." Yet this was not the case in relation to our treaties with France. What exactly, Jefferson asked, is the danger to be apprehended from the treaties? Was America to fear that France's revolution might terminate in a "military despotism," and that therefore the persistence of our alliance with France would "taint us with despotic principles"? At the time of our alliance with it, Jefferson argued, the government of France was "a perfect despotism," both "civil and military." The treaties having been made with a despotic power, the danger of its reversion to despotism could "furnish no just cause" to abrogate America's obligations. Could America fear – as Jefferson believed that Hamilton feared – that the French Revolution might "issue in a republic" and therefore that our alliance would "too much strengthen" America's "republican principles?" This, Jefferson held, was no matter of "dread" but rather of "hope" on the part of "the great mass of our constituents," who did "not look with longing to the happy mean of a limited monarchy." Or was the fear, as Hamilton had contended, of the incalculable character of the great change France was undergoing? Were we to break off the treaties because the French Revolution could "end in something we know not what, and bring on us danger we know not whence"? Even if this were a reasonable fear, Jefferson argued, it would not justify America in throwing off the treaties before such a danger had in fact materialized as truly imminent. When such a danger was really present, then we might justifiably avoid it "by renouncing our ancient friends," but not before. A party is not rightly absolved from a contract by the mere "*possibility*

[20] Jefferson, *Writings*, 424.

of danger," according to Jefferson. Such dangers always existed in possibility in relation to every contract, and if they were made a justification for the evasion of contractual duties "there never could be a valid contract." "Obligation is not suspended" until "the danger" has become "so imminent that we can no longer avoid decision without forever losing the opportunity to do it." The French treaties caused no such danger. The perils discussed so far had not taken shape and could not be defined, did not exist at the present moment and might never come to exist. Such dangers – or rather possibilities of dangers – could not be judged to be so imminent that there would be no later opportunity of avoiding them and therefore could not be invoked as grounds for throwing off the obligations of America's treaties with France.[21]

Jefferson then turned to a less hypothetical and better defined danger: that the guarantee clause in America's treaty of alliance with France might draw war upon the United States. Is the "danger apprehended," Jefferson asked, that if the treaties remain "valid" then the "clause guaranteeing" France's "West India islands will engage us in the war"? Even here, however, no imminent threat confronted America. The United States had not been called upon, and might never be called upon, by the government of France to defend its West Indies possessions. Jefferson questioned whether France could rightly make such a call before the islands were actually "invaded" or at least "imminently threatened." Even in that case, France might not be able to call on America if the French were able to save the islands by their own exertions. Moreover, he continued, even if France were to call on the United States, the call itself would not oblige an immediate American entry into the war. In such a case, America would be free to try "peaceable negotiations" with France's enemies and could also delay entry into the war because of its inability at present to prosecute a war. Jefferson had, after all, admitted that impossibility excused from performance of an agreement. He accordingly suggested here that America might not have to perform the guarantee if it lacked the power to save the islands for France: "If we cannot save them are we bound to go to war for a desperate object," he asked? Finally, he observed, America had for ten years forborn to call on France to guarantee American posts, which would "entitle us to some indulgence" if we did not immediately respond to any call of theirs to guarantee their islands. On the basis of all these doubts, Jefferson concluded that the danger of war was "not yet certain enough to authorize us in sound morality to declare, at this moment, the treaties null."[22]

War might arise, however, not only through the treaty of alliance but also, perhaps, through the treaty of commerce. Article 17 of the latter agreement permitted "French ships of war and privateers to come and go freely, with prizes made on their enemies," while denying their enemies these privileges. There was no real danger here either, Jefferson contended. None of France's

---

[21] Jefferson, *Writings*, 424–25 (Jefferson's emphasis).
[22] Jefferson, *Writings*, 425.

enemies in the present war could justly complain of such a principle, since they had themselves acknowledged it in other contexts. Article 22 of the commercial treaty might appear to impair American neutrality by forbidding "the enemies of France from fitting out privateers" or "selling their prizes" in American ports. Nevertheless, Jefferson pointed out, nothing in the treaty forbade the United States from denying the same things to France, which, Jefferson noted, the government ought to do "on principles of fair neutrality."[23]

Next, Jefferson addressed Hamilton's fear that an unqualified reception of the French Minister would implicitly concede that the treaties were still in force, thus impeding the government's ability to declare them null later if the nation's safety required it. Jefferson began by noting a certain incoherence in Hamilton's position. To receive Genet at all, which Hamilton had been in favor of doing (although reluctantly), admitted the legitimacy of the French government. If the "qualifications" that Hamilton desired were intended to "deny that legitimacy," the procedure would constitute a "curious compound" that would "admit and deny the same thing." In any case, Jefferson denied that the reception of the French minister had "anything to do with the treaties." The treaties said nothing about the question of sending or receiving ministers, which had instead been done between France and America according to "the common usage of nations." Therefore, receiving the French minister did not, as Hamilton feared, have the effect of either continuing or annulling the treaties. Moreover, Hamilton was wrong to fear that continuing the treaty was the same thing as making a new treaty in a time of war, and thus an infraction of neutrality. Hamilton had not, after all, argued that the treaty was in fact already void, only that America had a right to declare it void. To make it void would require America to do an affirmative act, while to let it continue would require only that America "do nothing" – "and doing nothing" could "hardly be an infraction of peace or neutrality." Finally, Hamilton was mistaken to fear that any acknowledgment of the treaty now, either implicit or even explicit, would rob the United States of its right to throw it off later if doing so was necessary to America's safety. Not even "the most explicit declaration made at this moment that we acknowledge the obligation of the treaties could take from us the right of non-compliance at any future time when compliance would involve us in great and inevitable danger." Jefferson summed up that few of the "sources" of possible peril about which Hamilton had fretted actually threatened "any danger at all," and none threatened anything that was "inevitable." Accordingly, he concluded that none of these circumstances gave America "the right at this moment of releasing" itself from its treaty obligations.[24]

Jefferson then turned to the second limitation on a nation's right to release itself from its treaty obligations. Here he contended that a nation could not rightly use the danger from some part of its engagements to free itself from all of them and that its decision to liberate itself from any of those engagements created certain reciprocal rights for its treaty partner. If danger justified the voiding of some part of a treaty, Jefferson argued, it could not justify a nation's releasing itself from the "residue" of the treaty. Self-liberation from any part might indeed end up voiding the whole treaty, but, Jefferson noted, citing Vattel, that was up to the other party to the treaty, who could declare the whole void in light of the first nation's decision not to comply with some part of it. Since in the present case the guarantee clause was the only portion of the French treaties that could threaten the United States with danger, it was the only portion of the treaties that the United States could, under the right circumstances, decide not to honor. In such an event, France would then be free to decide whether the rest of the treaty should continue in force or not.[25]

Finally, Jefferson examined the third limitation on the right of a nation to self-liberate from the obligations of treaties. Here he argued, citing the authority of Vattel and Wolff, that even when "necessity or danger" truly justified non-compliance with a treaty, the nation would still be "bound to make compensation" to its partner "where the nature of the case admits" of it. If France were to call on America's aid under the guarantee clause, and if America were to refuse, even for good reasons, it would still be a question whether America could excuse itself from giving France some "compensation" for its failure.[26]

Jefferson concluded this portion of his argument by pointing out that Hamilton's approach, which intended to keep America out of war, actually carried with it a danger of involving America in war. If Hamilton feared that the guarantee clause might end up making America the enemy of France's enemies, he should also have considered that reneging on America's obligations to France might make America France's enemy. If America were to deny compliance without a just cause or without compensation, then it would "give to France a cause of war, and so become associated in" the present conflict "on the other side." While Hamilton understandably feared putting America on the side of France against the whole rest of Europe, Jefferson emphasized that there were dangers, too, in offending France. "An injured friend in the bitterest of foes," he observed, and France had not shown "either timidity" or much "forbearance on late occasions."[27]

The Obligation of Treaties and the Writers on the Law of Nations
Although Jefferson held that American obligations could be determined by a simple appeal to reason and morality, he also sought to engage Hamilton on his own ground. He therefore proposed "to examine the principal authority"

[25] Jefferson, *Writings*, 427.
[26] Jefferson, *Writings*, 427.
[27] Jefferson, *Writings*, 427.

to which Hamilton had appealed in trying to establish an unjust "latitude" for "the right of self-liberation" – namely, Vattel. Before turning to the acknowledged authorities on the law of nations, however, Jefferson first offered a brief treatment of how their authority was to be received. That authority was good only insofar as it harmonized with our own sense of right and justice. "Questions of natural right," he observed, "are triable by their conformity with the moral sense and reason of man." Therefore, the writers of "treatises of natural law" could "only declare what their own moral sense and reason" told them in the cases about which they wrote. Those writers who happened "to have feelings and a reason coincident with those of the wise and honest part of mankind" were "respected and quoted as witnesses of what is morally right or wrong in particular cases." Among them Jefferson named "Grotius, Puffendorf, Wolff, and Vattel." Where such writers agreed, Jefferson said, their "authority" was "strong," but where they differed, as they often did, then we would have to "appeal to our own feelings and reason to decide between them."[28]

Jefferson then examined these four authorities with a view to showing that the weight of opinion was against the view Hamilton had pulled from Vattel. "Grotius, Puffendorf, and Wolff" all agreed, said Jefferson, that "treaties remain obligatory notwithstanding any change in the form of government," except in the narrow case – not relevant in the present controversy – in which the very aim of the treaty was the preservation of a particular form of government. In this case, Jefferson noted, the treaty lapsed not because of the decision of one of the parties but instead by the "evanishment" of the treaty's object. Vattel, indeed, had laid down "the same doctrine, that treaties continue obligatory, notwithstanding a change of government by the will of the other party, that to oppose that will would be a wrong, and that the ally remains an ally notwithstanding the change." To that extent Vattel agreed with Jefferson and the other traditional authorities. Then he added the passage to which Hamilton had appealed: that if the change in government made "the alliance *useless*, dangerous, or *disagreeable*" to the other party, then it was "free to renounce it."[29]

Jefferson focused on the question of uselessness and disagreeableness, since danger could excuse a nation from its obligations in any case, irrespective of a change in government, as he had already admitted and explained. In suggesting that "we are free to renounce" a contract merely because it has become "*useless* or *disagreeable*," Vattel placed himself in "opposition to Grotius, Puffendorf, and Wolff," who admitted "no such license against the obligation of treaties," but also "in opposition to the morality of every honest man, to whom we may safely appeal to decide whether he feels himself free to renounce a contract the moment it becomes merely useless or disagreeable to him."[30]

---

[28] Jefferson, *Writings*, 428.
[29] Jefferson, *Writings*, 428–29 (Jefferson's emphasis).
[30] Jefferson, *Writings*, 428–29 (Jefferson's emphasis).

Indeed, in maintaining this doctrine that Hamilton had tried to appropriate, Vattel contradicted even himself because much of his work emphasized the sacred character of faith between governments. Jefferson therefore appealed to other parts of Vattel's work where he could "not be misunderstood" and generally to his reputation "as one of the most zealous and constant advocates for the preservation of good faith in all of our dealings." Vattel had contended, for example, that "simple lesion" – a category of Roman law referring to the loss suffered by selling an item for less than half of its value – and other forms of "disadvantage" accompanying a treaty did "not suffice to render it invalid." Such invalidation could only arise if the treaty involved such "inconveniences which would go to the ruin of a nation." Elsewhere Vattel had gone on in the same vein, contending that mere lesion could not "render a treaty invalid." It was the duty of one who entered into engagements, he had admonished, "to weigh all things before" concluding the agreement. He was free to dispense with his property, his rights, and his advantages as he thought proper, and the other party was under no obligation to learn his partner's motives or to "weigh" the "just value" of what was being exchanged. This principle, Vattel had argued, was essential to any kind of stable order among nations. "If we could free ourselves from a compact because we find ourselves injured by it, there would be nothing firm in the contracts of nations."[31]

Elsewhere, Vattel had reasoned on these questions just as Jefferson had, by referring to the simple and widely understood principles of natural justice and reason. It was clear in the "natural law," Vattel argued, that one who made a promise to another conferred on the latter "a perfect right to require the thing promised." Therefore, failure to perform a promise was a violation of another's right and was as "manifest injustice as to plunder" anybody of any right. "All the tranquility, the happiness and security of mankind rest on justice, on the obligation to respect the rights of others," Vattel had observed. The security of one's possessions depended on a general respect for our "rights of domain and property," just as the security of goods that could not be delivered or executed immediately depended on a general respect for "the faith of promises." There could be "no security" and no "commerce among men" if they believed themselves "not obliged to preserve faith" or "to keep their word." Accordingly, Vattel concluded that this obligation was "necessary," "natural and indubitable" – not only among men but also among "nations who live together in a state of nature, and who acknowledge no superior on earth" – in order to "maintain order and peace in their society." Governments were therefore obliged to keep their promises, and while this principle was "too often neglected in practice," it was nevertheless "generally acknowledged among all nations," as evidenced by their use of the reproach of "perfidy" against governments that broke faith.[32]

[31] Jefferson, *Writings*, 429, 432.
[32] Jefferson, *Writings*, 432.

Treaties, Vattel elsewhere contended, were the foundation of order in international relations. Treaties imposed "rules on the pretensions of sovereigns," caused "the rights of nations to be acknowledged," and secured "their most precious interests." Since sovereigns acknowledged no superior power above themselves, treaties among them were the only way of establishing a just order among them, "the only means of adjusting their different pretensions, of establishing a rule," permitting us to "know on what to count, on what to depend." Treaties, however, would be nothing more than "vain words" if governments did not understand them to be binding, as "rules, inviolable for sovereigns and sacred through the whole earth." Keeping of faith was therefore "holy and sacred" among nations because it was essential to their "safety and repose"; and out of a prudent regard for their own interests nations should "load with infamy whoever violates his faith."[33]

In light of "evidence so copious and explicit" of Vattel's "respect" for the "sanctity of treaties," it was rather surprising, Jefferson noted, that Hamilton would try to invoke his authority for a "wanton invalidation" of treaties "whenever they should become merely *useless* or *disagreeable*." "We should hardly have expected," Jefferson continued, that Hamilton, "rejecting all the rest of" Vattel's "book," would have "culled" this one "scrap" and "made it the hook whereon to hang such a chain of immoral consequences." Given its incongruity with Vattel's other remarks on the sanctity of treaties, the passage to which Hamilton appealed could not be given the authority that he attributed to it. If that passage had "accidentally met our eye," a more natural reaction would be to think that "it had fallen from the author's pen under some momentary view, not sufficiently developed to found a conjecture" about "what he meant." In any case, Jefferson argued, one could "certainly affirm that a fragment" such as the one to which Hamilton had appealed could not overrule the "authority of all other writers," the "uniform and systematic doctrine" of the rest of Vattel's work, and the "the moral feelings and reason of all honest men."[34]

Finally, Jefferson argued that even if the Vattel remark on which Hamilton had relied were true, it would still not justify America in nullifying the treaties with France. Supposing that one could abrogate treaties when they became useless or disagreeable, how, Jefferson wondered, could any American regard the treaties with France in that light? Here he laid special emphasis on the grounds Vattel had given for his claim of a right of self-liberation from obligations to a nation that had changed its government. In that case, he held, the other party could "say with truth that it would not have allied itself with this nation if it had been under the present form of its government." The American republic had allied itself to France when it was "under a despotic government," Jefferson observed. Since then France had thrown off despotism, declared an intention

[33] Jefferson, *Writings*, 433.
[34] Jefferson, *Writings*, 433.

to establish a republic, prepared "a form of republic extremely free," and was now "governing herself as such" a republic. Hamilton, then, was proposing that America should "declare the treaties void" because it could "say with truth that it would not have allied itself with" France "if it had been under the present form of its government." What American, Jefferson asked, could "say with truth that he would not have allied himself to France if she had been a republic, or that a republic of any form would be as *disagreeable* as her ancient despotism."[35]

Conclusion

Jefferson's *Opinion on the French Treaties* made a powerful argument against abrogation, and it did so, moreover, in terms Hamilton was bound to respect. From the *Report on Public Credit* to his 1792 critique of Jefferson, the secretary of the treasury had presented himself as a champion of strict observance of the public faith. Governments, Hamilton had insisted repeatedly, were just as bound as individuals to fulfill their contracts. Yet, as Hamilton had noted in the *Federalist Papers*, treaties are "contracts with foreign nations which have the force of law but derive it from the obligations of good faith."[36] Jefferson might have said that Hamilton's argument for abrogation of the treaties had placed him in opposition to the opinion of all honest men, including even himself, as he had appeared in other controversies.

Despite the apparent strength of his general position, however, Jefferson's argument involved several difficulties. The secretary of state had to strain to make it appear that Hamilton regarded the treaties as disagreeable because he regarded the republicanism of the new French government as disagreeable. Here Jefferson raised in the context of a foreign policy dispute the concern that had animated his criticism of Hamilton's domestic policy: his fear that Hamilton was not a true republican and that he hankered after monarchy. Such a conclusion, however, did not follow from the position Hamilton had staked out on the treaties. Hamilton had not said that a treaty with France was disagreeable because of the nation's new republican government but instead because that government was unsettled and its future incalculable.

Indeed, even a good republican might have found a connection to France disagreeable not because the nation was now under a republic but instead because it was under a republic led by political terrorists who had demonstrated a tendency to get embroiled in wars with other nations. Such a country might well end up a pariah state, and a due respect to American interests could therefore counsel against maintaining any connection with it. Such considerations suggest how Hamilton and Jefferson's disagreement about the character of the French Revolution influenced their foreign policy thinking.

---

[35] Jefferson, *Writings*, 423–34 (Jefferson's emphasis).
[36] Hamilton, Madison, and Jay, *The Federalist*, 504.

For Hamilton, the excesses of the Revolution were grounds on which a reasonable nation could find a connection with it disgraceful. This was less likely to occur to Jefferson because, as we have seen, he could not bring himself to think that any tactics could discredit a truly republican cause. In any event, Hamilton's concerns about maintaining a connection with France were, contrary to Jefferson's insinuations, consistent with the view that France should be shunned not because of but despite its republicanism. Indeed, a republican statesman in Hamilton's position might even have concluded that the very cause of republicanism could be better served by keeping clear of France. It was not beyond the realm of possibility, after all, that the wildness of its rulers would lead the French republic to collapse. In that event, America would be left as the only example of a republic in the world, and its reputation – and hence republicanism's reputation – for sobriety of policy would depend on its having eschewed too close a connection to France.

Also, while Jefferson could have accused Hamilton of a certain inconsistency in promoting the public faith in some contexts while downplaying it in others, the secretary of state himself was subject to a similar charge. At first sight, Jefferson's insistence on the irrevocability of treaties might seem to be in tension with his commitment to self-government. Could a nation make a law that could not be repealed? Certainly not, on Jefferson's understanding, or almost any understanding. Then why, we might wonder, may a nation not throw off a treaty, which has the force of law, when it seems no longer in its interests? This approach to the question is admittedly too superficial, however, since treaties are not just ordinary laws but, as Hamilton pointed out, laws having the character of a contract with another nation. Nevertheless, even with this important qualification, Jefferson's argument on the French treaties appeared to contradict his theoretical musings elsewhere, for he had held – as Hamilton had noted scornfully – that the present generation has no authority to bind its successors. That principle would not invalidate the treaties at issue here, which had been made less than a generation previously, but neither could it sustain Jefferson's general insistence that treaties are irrevocable except by the consent of both parties.

The *Opinion on the French Treaties* also suffered from a certain internal inconsistency. Jefferson insisted that treaties continue to bind the parties irrespective of any changes of government because treaties are commitments on behalf of the nation. On this view, the American and French nations were still linked by their treaties despite the fact that both had undergone changes in government. At the same time, however, Jefferson held that France's old government was a complete despotism. How, then, one might wonder, could any of its acts, including the treaties it signed, be considered acts of the nation? Jefferson might have been right to say that a mere change in government could not destroy a nation's treaty obligations, but his account of Louis's government called into question whether the treaties could have been understood as the will of the French nation in the first place.

Moreover, the authorities that Jefferson cited – Grotius, Puffendorf, and Wolff – did not in fact support his position as clearly as he contended. According to Jefferson, each of these experts on the law of nations held that treaties between nations are always binding irrespective of a change in government. A review of the extracts that Jefferson himself provided in the text of his *Opinion*, however, shows that these thinkers had in fact expressed themselves in narrower terms. Each had said that a treaty made by a free people or by a republic would remain in force even if that people subsequently established a monarchy. In such a case there could be no doubt that the nation itself had consented to the treaty originally and that its free decision to establish a monarchy could not be construed as undoing its earlier commitments.

In view of Grotius, Puffendorf, and Wolff's comparative guardedness on this question – as well as Vattel's sobriety about the seriousness of treaty obligations elsewhere in his writings – it would have been more reasonable for Jefferson to have been less dismissive of the "scrap" of Vattel on which Hamilton had tried to capitalize. In fact, Vattel's position – and Hamilton's – was not as strange or immoral as Jefferson had suggested. The argument was not that treaties could be abrogated whenever they became useless, disagreeable, or dangerous, as Jefferson had so strenuously denied. It was instead that they could be abrogated when one of the parties changed its government – a momentous step with potentially far-reaching implications – and that change in turn rendered the treaty useless, disagreeable, or dangerous. Here, Hamilton argued, one party to a treaty made a decision, for its own reasons, that carried a whole train of potentially serious consequences that the other party might rightly say it had not counted on when making the agreement. This was a key argument in Hamilton's own opinion, which is examined in Chapter 13.

13

Faith among Nations II

Hamilton's Opinion on the French Treaties

Hamilton presented his opinion on the French treaties to Washington on May 2, 1793.[1] Unlike Jefferson, who had gone straight to the question of the status of the treaties themselves, Hamilton began with the related question of whether the United States should receive the French minister with or without qualifications. He argued that the reception of Genet should be "qualified by a previous declaration" reserving America's right to determine the status of the treaties at a later time. The message was to be friendly but firm. On the one hand, Hamilton recommended an expression of America's "cordial wishes for the happiness of the French nation," its disposition to "maintain" with France an "amicable communication and intercourse," and its lack of hesitation to receive the French minister. On the other hand, while the government should not confront France with the possibility of a complete renunciation of the treaties, it should make clear to the French minister – "in a spirit of candid and friendly procedure" – that it found it "advisable and proper" to "reserve to future consideration and discussion" whether the treaties should be "temporarily and provisionally suspended," "lest silence on the point should occasion misconstruction."[2]

Hamilton's Review of the "Material Facts"

Hamilton then proceeded to elaborate the "grounds" of his opinion, turning first to the circumstances surrounding France's recent changes in government. Where Jefferson had emphasized the welcome transition from

---

[1] The opinion was submitted as coming from both Hamilton and Secretary of War Henry Knox, but it was in Hamilton's handwriting and was signed only by Hamilton. See *PAH*, 14: 367, n. 1.
[2] *PAH*, 14: 368.

despotism to republicanism, Hamilton stressed a step that Jefferson's opinion had omitted: the transition from constitutional monarchy to republicanism, in which French republicans had taken steps of at least doubtful legitimacy. "The treaties between the United States and France were made," Hamilton observed, "with His Most Christian Majesty, his heirs and successors." The French government that had entered into those treaties was later replaced by a "new constitution, formed by the representatives of the nation, and accepted by the king." So far, Hamilton's argument implied, the political changes in France did not offer grounds on which America could question the continuation of the treaties. Subsequent events, however, called into question the legitimacy of the present French government. After a period of time under its new constitutional monarchy, a "sudden" and "tumultuous rising took place" as a result of which "the king was seized, imprisoned, and declared to be suspended by the authority of the National Assembly." This institution, however, had been delegated only the "legislative functions of the already established government" and was "in no shape authorized to divest any other of the constituted authorities of its legal capacities or powers." To that extent, Hamilton concluded, the overthrow of the constitutional monarchy involved a "manifest assumption of power," which gave it an air of irregularity and dubious legitimacy.[3]

It might seem strange that an American would make such an argument, for America owed its own origins to measures that might have been similarly impeached from the standpoint of strict legality. America had thrown off its own king by the act of a Congress that had been created by colonial legislative bodies who themselves had no legal power to dissolve the nation's connection to the British Crown. Was this not, to use Hamilton's own words, a "manifest assumption of power"?

Although he did not explicitly address this difficulty, Hamilton's subsequent argument implied an awareness of it. He tacitly conceded that such steps could be justified by a grave enough cause, but he also suggested that such a justification had to be subjected to a critical examination. This approach, moreover, can be reconciled with the proceedings of the American Revolution. The "manifest assumption of power" by the Second Continental Congress, after all, had not been done simply at the will of the Congress or the nation but had been justified by the experiences of abuse detailed in the *Declaration of Independence*. Some similar cause would be required to justify what the National Assembly had done in France.

The French revolutionaries had indeed invoked such a cause. In order to "justify" deposing the king, they claimed it was "necessary for the safety of the nation," to "prevent the success of a counter-revolution" that was "mediated or patronized by the king." Hamilton did not deny that such a fact could justify what the National Assembly had done. He expressed doubt, however, about

---

[3] *PAH*, 14: 368–69.

whether the allegation was really a fact or merely a pretext invented to bring down the constitutional monarchy. After all, there was no sufficient proof of the charges against the king, and there were those in France who contended or implied "that the whole transaction" had been "merely the execution of a plan" long ripened by the republican party "to bring about an abolition of the royalty and the establishment of a republican government."[4]

We encounter here a difference between Hamilton and Jefferson both as to principles and as to facts. In relation to principles, we have seen already in Jefferson's *Opinion on the French Treaties* the claim – more radical than that made in the *Declaration of Independence* – that a people may change their government whenever they please. Here, in contrast, Hamilton effectively insisted on a more conservative interpretation of the right to revolution, holding that it could be justified only by the threat of some grave abuse. In fairness to Jefferson, however, it is necessary to add that, while his words to Washington had expressed a lower standard for revolution that he had put into the *Declaration*, he did think that as a matter of fact such a grave threat did exist and therefore did justify what the French revolutionaries had done. Jefferson, as we have noted, accepted the Jacobin claim that the revolution had reached a point at which the government would either revert to despotism or progress to pure republicanism. Hamilton, however, was more inclined to view this as a bogus justification for a step the revolutionaries wanted to take for their own reasons.

Hamilton continued his review of the recent course of the Revolution, emphasizing both the doubtful legitimacy of what had been done and the unsettled state and uncertain future of the present government. After deposing the king, the National Assembly had called upon the country's "primary assemblies" to elect deputies to a convention that would establish a provisional government to manage the nation's affairs until a new constitution could be made. Although taken outside the ordinary course of law, these steps sound so far like an effort at rational self-government. Hamilton suggested, however, that a cloud of illegitimacy hung over the proceedings because of the methods to which the revolutionaries had resorted. The National Convention had indeed voted the "abolition of royalty." Yet the elections by which the deputies were chosen had been held in "circumstances not free from precipitation, violence, and awe." Indeed, the initial deposing of the king had been followed by "the massacre of a great number of persons in different parts of France . . . who were known to be attached either to the ancient" monarchy or to the constitutional monarchy that had followed it. Moreover, after the elections, but before the Convention had met, the Jacobins had "entered into measures with the avowed object of *purging* the Convention" of those supporters of the monarchy "who might have escaped the *attention* of the *primary assemblies*." Finally, the Convention had tried, condemned, and executed the king, the justice of which step,

[4] *PAH*, 14: 369.

Hamilton indicated, was at least as problematic as the original suspension of his powers.[5]

As a result of these events, "almost all of Europe" was, or was likely to be, "armed, in opposition to the present rulers of France – with the declared or implied intention of restoring if possible the royalty, in the successor of the deceased monarch." The war itself, then, in which the government of France might call upon the aid of the United States, turned upon the very question: "what shall be the future government of France? Shall the royal authority be restored in the person of the successor of Louis, or shall a republic be constituted in exclusion of it?"[6]

This review of the "material facts," Hamilton concluded, was not intended to establish "a definitive opinion concerning the propriety of the conduct of the present rulers of France." It did show, however, that the Revolution had been "attended with circumstances" that operated "against a full conviction of its having been brought to its present *stage*, by such a *free, regular* and *deliberate* act of the nation, and with such a spirit of justice and humanity, as ought to silence all scruples about the validity of what" had "been done, and the morality of aiding it, even if consistent with policy." Here, Hamilton suggested that morality, and not only questions of policy expediency, ought to play some role in a nation's foreign policy deliberations. Where Jefferson had emphasized the immorality of seeking to get out of the nation's treaty obligations, Hamilton suggested that there was something morally troubling about aiding a government such as that at present ruling France. His argument suggested two considerations on the basis of which one could question the "validity" of the Revolution at its present stage and therefore the morality of aiding it. First, given the atmosphere of political violence in which the new developments had taken place, it could be difficult to say whether they really did represent the will of the French nation. Was the utter destruction of the monarchy what the people of France really wanted, or were they cowed into accepting this step by the willingness of the Jacobins to destroy the leading royalist figures? Second, Hamilton's appeal to the "justice and humanity" that ought to have been observed suggested that even a truly popular revolution could be discredited by a departure from these principles. Even granting that the people had a right to change their form of government, they had no legitimate power to authorize departures from justice and humanity in the means that were used to that legitimate end. On the basis of these factors, Hamilton was unwilling to affirm the legitimacy of the present French government – something he emphasized in the sequel by carefully referring to it as "the actual governing powers of the French nation," a locution that emphasized the reality of its power without acknowledging the legitimacy of its authority.[7]

[5] *PAH*, 14: 370–71 (Hamilton's emphasis).
[6] *PAH*, 14: 370–71.
[7] *PAH*, 14: 371–72 (Hamilton's emphasis).

The Right of Revolution and the Obligation of Treaties

Hamilton then linked these considerations to the "great and important question" at hand: the status of America's treaties with France. The United States, he suggested in opposition to Jefferson, was not "bound by the laws of nations" to consider the treaties as "in present force and operation." On the contrary, America could rightly choose to "consider the operation of the Treaties as suspended" for the present and could even go so far as to "renounce them" completely if "such changes" had occurred "in the political affairs of France" as could "*bona fide* be pronounced to render a continuance" of the treaties as "disadvantageous or dangerous" for America."[8] Although Hamilton had introduced this idea to the cabinet by invoking Vattel, in his written defense of it he turned first, like Jefferson, not to the authority of writers on the law of nations but instead to an examination of basic moral principles.

Hamilton framed his argument as a response to two objections that might be made to his position. First, he addressed the point – which Jefferson had emphasized in his own opinion – that "a nation has a right, in its own discretion, to change its form of government."[9] Hamilton conceded that the "truth" of this "proposition ought to be admitted in its fullest latitude." He denied, however, that the principle in fact supported Jefferson's conclusion: that the change in government could not impair the obligations of the treaties. Any nation certainly had a "right to manage its own concerns as it thinks fit, and to make such changes in its political institutions as itself judges best calculated to promote its interests." It "by no means" followed, however, that such a nation therefore possessed a "right to involve other nations, with whom it may have had connections, *absolutely* and *unconditionally* in the consequences of the changes" it may have made in its own government. Such a principle would "give to a nation or society not only a power over its own happiness but" also "a power over the happiness of other nations or societies." This would "extend the operation of the maxim" – that each nation has a right to change its government – "much beyond the *reason* of it – which is simply that every nation ought to have a right to provide for its *own happiness*." Therefore, Hamilton concluded, when a nation changes its government in such a way as to make its treaties "useless or dangerous or hurtful" to its partner, "it is a plain dictate of reason that the *latter* will have a right to renounce those treaties." The partner, after all, "also has a right to take care of its own happiness, and cannot be obliged to suffer" that happiness "to be impaired" by the changes in government made by the other party, which had been "adopted for its own advantage" and not with a view to the well-being of its ally.[10]

---

[8] *PAH*, 14: 371–72 (Hamilton's emphasis).
[9] *PAH*, 14: 372.
[10] *PAH*, 14: 374–77.

This led Hamilton to the second objection to his position. One might contend that a nation was obliged to "submit to the inconveniencies" arising from its treaty partner's revolution by the principle that "real treaties bind nations, notwithstanding the changes which happen in the forms of their governments." Here Hamilton referred to the distinction between "real" and "personal" treaties. The latter were understood to be with a given nation's monarch, while the former were understood to be contracts between the nations themselves. Although Hamilton had earlier referred to the French treaties as having been contracted with Louis and his successors, he did not in fact deny that the treaties were real rather than personal in character. He also did not deny the general principle that real treaties remained in force irrespective of changes in government. He contended, however, that this principle had to be understood as operating only within a certain scope. "All general rules," he argued, "are to be construed within certain reasonable limitations." Changes in forms of government did not of themselves automatically annul real treaties. Such changes could, however, permit the party that had not changed its government to renounce the treaty for a "just" or "good and sufficient cause" – specifically, that the change in government had made the treaties "useless or materially less advantageous, or more dangerous than before." Hamilton noted a limit, too, on the scope of this exception: nations could not "in good faith" renounce their treaties even after a change in government by their partner if they could not make a reasonable claim that this change really had rendered the treaties less advantageous. That is, nations should not invoke Hamilton's exception on spurious grounds. Nevertheless, he did depart from Jefferson's insistence on strict adherence to treaties regardless of changes in government. What Jefferson presented as an inflexible rule Hamilton presented as a general principle that admitted of an exception.

Hamilton adduced reasons for this exception. Even a real treaty, he observed, could be contracted between nations on the basis of considerations that included their existing forms of government. Two republics, for example, might "contract an alliance" the main "inducement to which" could be the "similarity" of their "constitutions," which they believed would produce a "common interest to defend their mutual rights and liberties." Conversely, two monarchies might become formally allied the better to defend themselves against a powerful neighboring republic. In either case, a change in the form of government of one of the partners could "destroy" the "inducement" to the alliance and eliminate the "main link of common interest" that had been an important presupposition of the agreement in the first place. Such developments, he argued, could "render it prudent for the other ally to renounce the connection, and seek to fortify itself in some other quarter."[11] Even when the form of government was not the principal cause of a treaty, Hamilton continued, it could still be an important consideration underlying the contract. Two countries

[11] *PAH*, 14: 377.

might ally themselves because "each has confidence in the energy and efficacy of the government of the other." A revolution in one of them, even if it did not result in a different kind of regime, might nonetheless create a government "feeble, fluctuating, and turbulent, liable to provoke wars and very little fitted to repel them."[12]

Furthermore, Hamilton contended, a change in government might materially alter the consequences of an alliance not by directly damaging the quality of the government that had undergone revolution but by depriving it of allies that it had enjoyed at the time the treaty was made. The "connections of a nation with other foreign powers may enter into the motives of an alliance with it." If a change in government caused a nation to lose some of its allies, the "external political relations of the parties" might become so different from what they had been as to render the alliance no longer beneficial to the other party.[13]

The "maxim" under consideration held that real treaties remain in force even when one of the parties had changed its government. Hamilton insisted, however, that "reason" was the "touchstone" of all such maxims, capable of discerning the exceptions to the general rule. In the cases he had sketched, reason "would dictate" that the nation whose government had not changed had a "right" to "declare its connection" to the other nation "dissolved," if the former had a "bona fide conviction that the change" in the latter's government would render the connection "detrimental or dangerous." Hamilton, like Jefferson, held that a treaty "*pernicious* to the state is of itself void," even where there had been no change in the government of either party. Unlike Jefferson, however, he concluded that there was an even "stronger reason" to hold that a treaty was "*voidable*, at the option of the other party, when the voluntary act of one of the allies has made so material a change in the condition of things as is always implied in a radical revolution of government."[14] Contrary to what Jefferson charged, then, Hamilton did not defend the view that a nation could renounce its treaty obligations whenever they became useless or dangerous through *any* change in circumstances – a doctrine that Jefferson correctly noted would destroy the very idea of good faith among nations. Hamilton instead contended for a more narrowly defined exception: that a nation had a right to renounce a treaty when its partner's *own conduct* had rendered the agreement dangerous or even only useless to its partner.

As we have seen, Jefferson had insisted in his own opinion that the same rules of morality applied to both nations and individuals. Hamilton had expressed a similar view in a different context – in his 1792 criticisms of the Jeffersonians as insufficiently committed to the public faith. He did not understand himself as departing from it in the present case. "Contracts between nations as between

---

[12] *PAH*, 14: 378.
[13] *PAH*, 14: 378.
[14] *PAH*, 14: 378 (Hamilton's emphasis).

individuals," he observed, "must lose their force where the considerations fail."[15] Hamilton did not explain what he had in mind, but it is possible to suggest a likely account of his thinking, and of how it departed from that of his cabinet colleague. Jefferson had held, and Hamilton would no doubt agree, that a promise between individuals must fail if the execution of it proved impossible or destructive to the life of one of the parties. Hamilton also went further than Jefferson, however, and indicated that other factors might also void a contract between individuals. This suggestion is consistent with what Hamilton had argued explicitly in the *Report on Public Credit*. There, Hamilton had admitted that one could find that a party to a contract was not a fair purchaser, and that the contract was accordingly void if that purchaser had himself caused the distress that impelled the seller to part with his property at a loss. By similar reasoning, it would seem, one could conclude that – in a case where no property had yet changed hands, but in which there was a promise of some future performance – when one party had taken steps that rendered the agreement useless or detrimental to the other party, the contract was no longer binding. And by the same reasoning again one could find that the same freedom existed among nations as among individuals.

Next, Hamilton explained a "further limitation" to the "maxim" that real treaties bind nations irrespective of changes in government. For such a real treaty to be considered in force, he argued, the nation undergoing the change in government needs to have gotten to the point at which it has established a stable new government and not still be in a state of revolutionary flux. In Hamilton's words, the "revolution" must be "*consummated*," the "new government" must "be *established* and recognized among nations," there must "be an *undisputed* organ of the national will, to claim the performance of the stipulations made with the former government." Where the nation had not achieved this political stability, insistence that the treaty must be in force would compel the allied nation to choose which of the two contending sides really represented the nation. Hamilton argued, however, that it was "not natural to presume that an ally" could be obliged to lend support to either side "where the war involves the very" question "what shall be the government of the country" – especially when being forced to choose sides might require it to work "against the very party with whom" the treaty had been contracted in the first place. It was "more natural to conclude" that in such an unsettled case the ally should either aid the party with whom the treaty had been contracted or "consider the operation of the alliance as suspended." "The latter" course, he added, was "undoubtedly" a duty "where the nation" seemed "to have pronounced the change" in government.[16]

The "contrary doctrine" – a strict refusal to admit the right to suspend a treaty while a nation was still undergoing a revolution – could involve a

[15] *PAH*, 14: 378.
[16] *PAH*, 14: 378–79 (Hamilton's emphasis).

government in "an opposition of moral duties" and in "dilemmas of a very singular and embarrassing kind." A nation might "owe its existence or preservation" to the support it had received from some monarch who at the time had been the "lawful organ" of his people's "national will." Furthermore, the country "indebted" to the monarch for such "good offices" might have "formed" an "alliance" with him and his successors, "stipulating future cooperation and mutual aid." Suppose further, Hamilton continued, that this monarch were, "without any particular crime on his part," removed from his office and expelled from the country "by his nation, or by a triumphant faction" gaining a temporary power to "direct the national voice." Such a monarch might then find support from other countries in his effort to "reinstate himself." At this point, the "ruling powers of the nation" over which this unfortunate monarch had formerly reigned, might "call upon the country which had been saved by his friendship and patronage to perform the stipulations expressed in the alliance made with him and embark on a war against their friend and benefactor," contending that "the treaty being a *real* one the actual rulers of the nation have a right to claim the benefit of it."[17] If there were no "option" to consider the treaty suspended, Hamilton argued, there would be "a most perplexing conflict of opposite obligations": on the one hand, the "abstract theoretic proposition" that real treaties continue to bind despite a change in government and, on the other hand, "the faith supposed to be plighted by the treaty" to the man with whom it had been concluded, as well as "justice and gratitude towards a man from whom essential benefits had been received" and who could appeal to "the formal and express terms of the contract," which had named him as a party to it. Hamilton questioned whether in such a case "genuine honor" and "true morality" would "permit" a government to take "a hostile part against the friend and benefactor" who was "at the same time the original party to the contract."[18]

Indeed, later in his opinion, Hamilton noted that there was a very real possibility of such conflicts of duty in the present case. In the course of the present war, a French island might be "taken by Great Britain or Holland with the avowed intention of holding it for the future king of France, the successor of Louis the XVI." Such an event could trigger the guarantee clause of the treaty of alliance, and the present government of France might then demand America's assistance in reclaiming that island. Could it be possible, Hamilton asked, "that a treaty made with Louis the XVI should *oblige*" the United States "to embark in the war to rescue a part of his dominions from his immediate successor?" Hamilton doubted whether "the national integrity or delicacy" would "permit" such a course, and whether the United States should "involve" itself "in a dilemma of this kind."[19] Yet such difficulties were

---

[17] *PAH*, 14: 379 (Hamilton's emphasis).
[18] *PAH*, 14: 379.
[19] *PAH*, 14: 392 (Hamilton's emphasis).

inseparable from Jefferson's insistence that the treaties could not be suspended, and were for Hamilton a further reason Jefferson's view should be rejected.

Writers on the Law of Nations

Having made his own appeal to moral reason, Hamilton next examined "the opinions of writers" on the law of nations, which, he contended, supported his understanding of the maxim in question, at least as far as they took up the question. Besides reiterating his appeal to Vattel, Hamilton also sought support from Grotius and Puffendorf, thus challenging Jefferson's claim that these authors unequivocally supported his side in the dispute. Grotius, to be sure, insisted that real treaties were binding despite changes in government. Nevertheless, he also admitted the very "qualification" on which Hamilton had "insisted": he explicitly excepted from the general rule cases in which the "motive to the treaty was 'peculiar to the form of government, *as* when free states enter into an alliance for the defense of their liberties.'"[20] This was something, although not as much as Hamilton suggested: Grotius seemed to have in mind a treaty that was clearly intended to preserve a certain form of government, not one in which the form of government might merely have gone into the calculations for entering into the agreement.

Hamilton found something better, however, in Puffendorf's response to another opinion of Grotius's. Grotius had contended – "with too much latitude," in Hamilton's judgment – that a "'league made with a king'" would remain in force even though the "'king or his successors be expelled from the kingdom *by his subjects*; for though he has lost his possession the right to the crown still remains in him.'" This was clearly correct, Puffendorf held, if the treaty were a personal one, that is, if its terms "'expressly mention and intend the defense of the prince's person and family.'" In such a case, he concluded, the ally should assist him "'in the recovery of his kingdom.'" The obligation was not so clear, however, if the treaty had been made not for the king himself but for the "'*public good* only.'" In that case, Puffendorf held, it was "'a disputable point, whether the exiled prince' could 'demand assistance in virtue of his league.'" On the one hand, his ally could rightly claim that the league had been formed in order to protect the kingdom against foreign enemies and was not intended for the present case of rebellion. On the other hand, however, the league left the ally at "'*liberty* to assist a *lawful prince* against an *usurper*.'" Here, then, was a case in which Puffendorf held that a nation might have an option to consider even a real treaty as suspended because of a change of government, for his opinion amounted to the view that the ally might be free to refuse help to either the former king or the new government that sought to take his place. There was an important "difference," Hamilton concluded, between holding – as Jefferson's principles seemed to do – that an ally was

---

[20] *PAH*, 14: 382 (Hamilton's emphasis).

"bound at all events to assist the nation" against its former king because a real treaty remains binding despite a revolution in government, and holding – as Grotius did – that it was a "disputable point" whether the "ally of a dethroned prince" was obliged by a real treaty "to assist him against" his own "nation."[21]

The Perils of the French Connection

Hamilton turned next to another objection: that even if there were a right to renounce the treaties for a "sufficient cause," still the present case of a change in the French government presented no such "sufficient cause" for renunciation, and the mere "possibility" of such a cause arising later "in the progress of events" did not justify "resorting to the principle in question" at the present time. Hamilton responded by appealing to the unsettled state of French politics. There really was at present, he contended, no French government in place of the one that had been "pulled down." The French themselves admitted that the "existing political powers" were "provisional" and were to be followed by a new "constitution" yet "to be established." It was thus "impossible to foresee what the future government of France will be." In such a state of "uncertainty," Hamilton argued, the right to renounce a treaty necessarily implied a right to suspend its operation. "If there be a right to renounce when the change of government prove to be of a nature to render an alliance useless or injurious," then there must also be "a right, amidst a pending revolution, to wait to see what change will take place." To deny a right to suspend, and to insist that the treaty must continue in force during a revolution until some clear evidence emerged that the obligations had become useless or hurtful, would involve the "inadmissible" consequence that the nation's duties might "fluctuate indefinitely" with the progress of the revolution, being "one thing today" and "another tomorrow." Besides, he argued, "the right to consider the operation of the treaties as suspended" arose from the fact that "during a *pending revolution* an ally in a real treaty is not bound to pronounce between the" parties "contending" over who should rule the nation.[22]

If such an option existed, Hamilton continued, there were serious reasons to exercise it: to protect America's character and its interests. America's character, or its international reputation, Hamilton argued, might be compromised by its maintaining a connection with the French revolutionary government. In the first place, America's previous relationship with Louis XVI might make it appear unseemly for her to side with those who had deprived him of his office and his life. America had received from Louis the support that had been so important in establishing her own liberty, and she had contracted with "him, his heirs, and successors" the "engagements" by which she had "obtained" his assistance. America did no wrong in respecting France's right to change its

---

[21] *PAH*, 14: 383–84 (Hamilton's emphasis).
[22] *PAH*, 14: 385 (Hamilton's emphasis).

government, and thus in receiving the new government's ambassador, maintaining friendly relations and performing "every good office not contrary to the duties of a real neutrality." To go further, however, to "throw" America's "weight" into the scale in support of the revolutionary government would "be considered by mankind as" inconsistent "with a decent regard to the" past "relations" between America and Louis," with "a due sense of the services" he had performed, and thus with "national delicacy and decorum."[23]

In the second place, Hamilton emphasized the danger to America's reputation from being allied with a French revolutionary government that had stained itself with crime. Apart from whatever embarrassment might arise from America's peculiar relationship with the former king, Hamilton also suggested that any decent government should hesitate to be associated with the present French rulers. He conceded the legitimacy of the end the Revolution had in view. "A struggle for liberty," Hamilton observed, "is in itself respectable and glorious." Hamilton immediately went on to insist, however, that this end could not justify a resort to just any means, that the worthiness of a revolutionary movement had to be judged not only by its ends but also by the means it was willing to use. Such a struggle for liberty "ought to command the admiration of every friend to human nature," but only when it was "conducted with magnanimity, justice, and humanity." If such a movement was instead "sullied by crimes and extravagancies," it lost "its respectability." Success in the end might "rescue it from" absolute "infamy," but it still could not win "much positive merit or praise" from "the sober part of mankind." And if it should fail, it must be attended with "a general execration."[24]

Here, as in Hamilton's *Report on Public Credit*, we encounter a kind of echo of Machiavelli. Here as before it is worth considering both the similarities and the differences in order to understand Hamilton's position more accurately. In Chapter 18 of *The Prince*, Machiavelli – reflecting on the same issues as Hamilton, the end of establishing a new state and how the means to that end might be judged – had written:

And in the actions of all men, and especially of princes, where there is no court to appeal to, one looks to the end. So let a prince win and maintain his state: the means will always be judged honorable, and will be praised by everyone. For the vulgar are taken in by the appearance and outcome of a thing, and in the world there is no one but the vulgar."[25]

Hamilton was certainly not a naïve moralist, and he went part of the way with Machiavelli, admitting that a successful conclusion might save even a crime-stained political movement from absolute infamy. He did not go so far,

---

[23] *PAH*, 14: 386.
[24] *PAH*, 14: 386.
[25] Niccolo Machiavelli, *The Prince*, trans. Harvey Mansfield (Chicago: University of Chicago Press), 71.

however, as to say that success could make such a movement actually reputable or praiseworthy. Moreover, he suggested, its failure in praiseworthiness is not just an abstract moral judgment, or the practically ineffective judgment of the powerless moral philosopher. Rather, this failure of respectability has a significant impact in the real world on the movement's reputation. Hamilton could posit such an impact because he saw a force at work in the world that Machiavelli denied. Where the Florentine held that, at least for all practical purposes, there is "no one but the vulgar" who are taken in by appearances and outcomes, Hamilton attached some influence to the opinion of "the sober part of mankind," who are apparently able to withhold their praise even from a successful effort to establish a new state.

Hamilton thus feared that the French revolutionaries had behaved so badly that there was considerable risk to America's reputation in choosing to maintain a relationship with the government they had established. Given the tactics to which the revolutionaries had resorted, there was little chance that America's reputation would be "promoted" even by a "successful issue." And if the revolution were to fail, it was likely "that a sentence uncommonly severe" would "be passed upon it" and that America might share to some extent in its disgrace. These possibilities, Hamilton concluded, suggested "very serious considerations to a mind anxious for the reputation of the country – anxious that it may emulate a character of sobriety, moderation, justice, and love of order"[26]

Proper solicitude for the "*interest* of the United States" also suggested suspending the treaties and keeping the French government at least temporarily at arms-length. America had not only an interest in maintaining a decent international reputation but also an interest in remaining at peace, which the continued operation of the French treaties tended to imperil. Those treaties included stipulations that America was to provide military support to France in cases that were, in Hamilton's judgment, "likely to occur." If America had – as he had contended – a legitimate right to choose to consider the treaties as not in operation, then its decision to forego that right – or to consider them as in operation – "would be the equivalent of making new treaties" containing the same obligations. This, however, would be a departure from the neutrality that the United States was determined to observe because it was a "well settled point," Hamilton urged, that entering into such stipulations with a war pending is "a departure from neutrality." This departure in turn threatened the peace of the United States. There was, after all, no way to tell in advance to what extent France's enemies would use this departure as a justification (or a pretext) for treating the United States as an enemy. Their decision whether to do so would "probably be regulated by their views of their own interest." And if France's enemies thought it was in their interest to make war on the United States, Hamilton warned, they were unlikely to be restrained by the

[26] *PAH*, 14: 386.

fact that America was merely a formal ally of France but had not yet taken an "active part" in the war. Suspension of the treaties, then, was to Hamilton an important step in limiting the possibility of dangerous collisions with France's numerous and powerful allies.[27]

What, then, of the danger on the other side? Hamilton did not agree with Jefferson's assessment that suspension of the treaties raised a serious prospect of provoking France to make war on the United States. On the contrary, Hamilton surprisingly suggested, suspension of the treaties was useful with a view to maintaining good relations with France herself. There was general agreement, Hamilton observed, that America "ought not to embark in the war." If, then, the French islands were attacked and France called upon America to fulfill its guarantee, America would have to refuse in order to maintain its neutrality. What could it say in defense of such a refusal if it had admitted that the treaties were still in force? Its only options would be to contend that the alliance was a defensive one, and that the present war was in fact an offensive one on France's part, so that the present case did not come within the operation of the treaty. Alternatively, America could plead that its assistance would be useless to France – because the United States did not have the forces required to secure the islands – and so dangerous to America that we could "not afford" to perform the guarantee. Hamilton doubted that either of these justifications would be "satisfactory to France." The first claim would be positively displeasing, and the second would be at least not pleasing. Moreover, he later observed, the second had the added disadvantage of formally making the United States a party to the war as France's ally, which would in turn authorize France's enemies to regard the United States as an enemy.[28] Hamilton thus concluded that, given the government's determination to actually remain neutral, keeping the treaties in operation was no more likely to avoid France's displeasure than declaring them suspended.[29]

In light of France's uncertain political future, Hamilton suggested, calculations about America's relationship with it would have to take into account the possible restoration of the monarchy as well as the possible establishment of a permanent republic. In view of the first possibility – not to be dismissed, since most of Europe was armed precisely with a view to that object – a decision to consider the treaties as in force was also dangerous to the United States' relationship with France. If the revolution should fail and the monarchy be reestablished, what, Hamilton asked, "would be our situation with the future government of that country? Should we not be branded and detested by it, as the worst of ingrates?" The danger of such an animosity was heightened, Hamilton suggested, by the fact that a restored French monarchy would probably owe its position to the help of Great Britain. If America maintained its

---

[27] *PAH*, 14: 387.
[28] *PAH*, 14: 391.
[29] *PAH*, 14: 387–90.

connection with the revolutionary government and the revolution ended up failing, then, America could find itself alienated from both of these powerful nations. However, if the revolution should succeed in establishing a republic, America's decision to suspend the treaties would not be terribly damaging to her relations with France. In that event, Hamilton observed, America could still give to the new French republic "better claims to friendship than any other power," since America would have acknowledged that government at an early date by receiving its ambassador and would have not "taken side with her enemies." Indeed, Hamilton expected that once such a republic were established – and "tranquility, moderation, and sober reflection" had been restored – the "reasons" America had for declaring the treaties suspended would "justify us even to France herself." The secure establishment of a republic in France, Hamilton apparently assumed, implied the presence at its head of serious and responsible leaders who would understand that America had decided to suspend the treaties during a time of great tumult and uncertainty, on the basis of a reasonable and just concern for its own security. If there was, as Jefferson had suggested, danger that suspension would lead to immediate hostilities with France, Hamilton took this as further evidence that any connection to its government was to be shunned. Such a danger, he contended, could not be "supposed" without also "supposing such a degree of intemperance on the part of France as will finally force us to *quarrel* with her or *embark* with her." If that was her "temper," then, given America's determination not to embark with her, "a fair calculation of hazards" would indicate that we might as well "risk her displeasure in the first instance."[30]

As Hamilton's argument for a right to suspend drew to a close, he introduced a kind of pragmatic appeal to a government's need to maintain a reasonable latitude of action in the face of serious and incalculable dangers. "In national questions," he observed, "great weight" must be accorded to "the general conduct of nations." In the present crisis, he implied, America could not afford to be governed only by its treaty obligations but also needed to take into account how the rest of the world was in fact behaving. At present, "all Europe" was or was likely to be "armed in opposition to the authority of the present government of France." In such a perilous situation, it would be "carry[ing] theory to an extreme" to hold that the United States was "under an absolute indispensable obligation, not only to acknowledge respectfully" France's government, but also "to admit the immediate operation of treaties" which would make America France's ally.[31]

Finally, Hamilton contended that if the government were not to go so far as to declare the treaties suspended, then prudence at the very least counseled that it explicitly reserve the question of their future operation, so that "further reflection and a more complete development of circumstances may enable us to

[30] *PAH*, 14: 390–91 (Hamilton's emphasis).
[31] *PAH*, 14: 392–93.

make a decision both *right* and *safe*." This could be accomplished by receiving Genet with qualifications, so as to avoid the "fixing of our relations to France beyond the possibility of retraction," which Hamilton viewed as "putting too suddenly too much to hazard." It might be objected – as Jefferson had in fact objected – that an unqualified reception of the French minister would not necessarily preclude America's later suspension or renunciation of the treaty. Hamilton admitted that this *might* be the case, but he added that there was "no satisfactory guide by which to decide the precise import and extent of such a reception," or by which to affirm that it would not oblige us to the future operation of the treaties. There was good reason, he suggested, to consider the reception of the minister as the proper time at which to explain the government's understanding of its relationship to France, and therefore silence on the question of the treaties might be interpreted as a belief in their continued validity. Surely France would want to view the matter in that light, and so for America to "raise the question" later "would lead to complaint, accusation, ill humor." For Hamilton, it seemed "most candid and most safe" to frankly say that we were not determined as to the future operation of the treaties, so as "not to risk the imputation of inconsistency." Moreover, and just as important, such a course would permit the United States to tell France's enemies that by "receiving the minister of France, we have not acknowledged ourself its ally" but "have reserved the point for future consideration."[32]

Jefferson had suggested that such a reception would be self-contradictory, as both admitting and denying the legitimacy of the French government. Hamilton did not think so. "The acknowledgement of a government by the reception of its ambassador," he explained, was "different and *separable* from" the "acknowledgement" of such a government "*as an ally*." In making this point, Hamilton actually agreed with Jefferson, who had stressed that the treaties had nothing to do with the sending and receiving of ambassadors, so that one could receive France's minister without saying anything at all about the treaties. Nevertheless, Hamilton held that merely receiving an ambassador, where a "connection before existed between two nations," might well "imply" reception of him as an ally if nothing to the contrary was said. Such an "implication" could be "repelled," he noted, by a simple "declaration" that this was not the intention.[33]

Conclusion

Hamilton's argument in this opinion placed him in a somewhat paradoxical position. During his time in the Washington administration, he had often presented himself as the defender of the public faith, of a strict performance of the public's obligations. That, at least, had been his position when it came to

---

[32] *PAH*, 14: 393.
[33] *PAH*, 14: 394 (Hamilton's emphasis).

paying the government's debts and observing the arrangements it had entered into with regard to property. Here, however, he appeared to take the opposite side, contending that the nation might find a way to escape from its treaty obligations. Hamilton's opinion on the treaties concluded by making a distinction that suggested he saw no inconsistency in the positions he had taken.

The last objection Hamilton considered to his call to hold the treaties suspended, or at least to reserve the question, held that it was too late to do so, because the government had already admitted that "all engagements to the former Government" of France were "to be fulfilled" to its present government." This it had done, the objection ran, by continuing debt payments to the new government. In response, Hamilton argued that the two things – "a debt in money," on the one hand, and "a treaty of Alliance," on the other – had "no necessary connection," being "governed by considerations altogether different and irrelative." "The payment of a debt," Hamilton contended, "is a matter of perfect and strict obligation. It must be done at all events," and it "ought to be done with precise punctuality." "In the case of a nation," he continued, whoever got "possession of its political power," or whoever became the "master of its *goods*," was obliged to "pay all the debts which the government of the nation" had "contracted." Similarly, the "sovereign in possession" of a nation's political power was to "receive the debts due to the government of the nation." Such "debts are at all events to be paid," Hamilton contended, and the mere "possession" of the nation's political authority was in itself a sufficient "guide as to the party to whom they are to be paid." Accordingly, nations were obliged to pay each other their debts totally irrespective of any changes in government, and therefore no one "could doubt that the debt due to France is at all events to be paid, whatever *form* of government may take place in that Country." The difference between the two cases, Hamilton suggested, was that debt involved property. "Questions of property," he observed, "are very different from those of *political connection*." Political connections, or treaties between nations, were "capable of being affected by a great variety of considerations, casualties and contingencies." The forms of government might easily be one of these relevant factors. Therefore, a revolution in government could "vary the obligations of parties." Hamilton thus concluded that "the payment of a debt" to a nation's government did "not imply an admission of the present operation of political treaties. "It may so happen, that there is a strict obligation to pay the debt, and a perfect right to withdraw from the treaties."[34]

On another issue, however, Hamilton and Jefferson's debate over the treaties replayed in familiar terms an argument they had had several times before in the context of domestic policy: Jefferson wanted the government tied down as much as possible by a clear and strict rule, while Hamilton sought greater leeway. They agreed that treaties are not absolutely irrevocable, despite their

[34] *PAH*, 14: 395 (Hamilton's emphasis).

implications for the country's security. Both held that a treaty that threatened the very life of the nation was for that reason void. Jefferson would leave it at that, however, while Hamilton defended a further exception that gave the government greater freedom of action: treaties could also be abrogated when one of the parties had undergone a change in government and the change rendered the treaty useless, disagreeable, or dangerous to the partner.

Jefferson prevailed in this confrontation. Washington decided that the treaties remained in effect and that he would receive Genet unconditionally. This decision, however, did not end all conflict between the secretaries of state and treasury over American foreign policy. They continued to wrangle over the details of neutrality policy, with Jefferson generally leaning in a pro-French and Hamilton in a pro-British direction. More important for the purposes of this study, however, Washington's decision did not preclude further debate over matters of high principle. Hamilton shortly took to the public prints to defend the neutrality proclamation, at the same time offering an interpretation of it, and of the Constitution, that Jefferson found highly objectionable and that he enlisted James Madison to refute. We turn next, then, to the celebrated debate between Pacificus and Helvidius.

14

The Constitutional and Political Theory
of Hamilton's *Pacificus* Papers

By 1792, Hamilton and Jefferson had developed a political enmity of the most serious kind. Each man now believed not only that the other was mistaken in his approach to domestic policy but in fact that the other represented a threat to the preservation of the American regime. Hamilton opened his first *Pacificus* essay by placing this charge, if not directly at Jefferson's feet, then at the feet of his partisans in the public papers, whom Hamilton regarded as the instruments of the secretary of state. Public criticism of the neutrality proclamation, said Hamilton, manifested a spirit "not very friendly to the Constitution" of the United States. Some "objections" to the proclamation had been "urged in a spirit of acrimony and invective," which proved "that more was in view than merely a free discussion of an important public measure." Rather, the fierceness of the criticism pointed to "a design of weakening the confidence of the people in the author of the measure." And this effort to diminish public support for the president in turn aimed to "remove or lessen a powerful obstacle to the success of an opposition to the government" itself. This was the radical aim to which the Republican critics of the administration "adhered," and which they "pursued with persevering industry," even though they modified their approach to it as circumstances required.[1]

Hamilton therefore sought to defend the government and the Constitution by replying to these criticisms of the proclamation. Hamilton arranged the principled objections "under" three "heads," embracing constitutional, legal, and moral considerations. First, it was held that "the proclamation was without authority," or that the president is constitutionally unauthorized to issue such a proclamation. Second, the proclamation was said to be "contrary to our treaties with France." Third, it was held that the proclamation was "contrary to the

---

[1] *PAH*, 15: 33–34.

gratitude which is due" from America to France, "for the succors rendered to us in our own revolution."[2]

The President's Constitutional Authority in Foreign Policy

Hamilton aimed in the first *Pacificus* essay to reply to the first objection and thus to vindicate the president's constitutional authority to issue a proclamation of neutrality. This vindication required as a preliminary step an examination of the "nature and design" of such a proclamation. The point of such a document, Hamilton contended, is to *"make known"* that the country of the government issuing the proclamation is at "peace with the belligerent parties, and under no obligations of treaty to become an *associate in the war* with either," and that it intends to conduct itself accordingly by performing the "duties of neutrality" toward each of the combatants. Such a document aims to communicate these facts to two distinct audiences: "the powers at war" and "the citizens of the country" issuing the proclamation. To the latter in particular, the proclamation serves as a warning "to abstain from acts that shall contravene" the duties of neutrality, "under the penalties which the laws of the land (of which the law of nations is a part) annexes to acts of contravention."[3]

Hamilton went on to note the limited scope of such a proclamation, implicitly acknowledging that Washington's did not in fact reflect the position for which Hamilton had contended in the cabinet. Hamilton had sought a suspension of the treaties in their entirety, possibly with a view to their eventual renunciation, on the grounds that France's change in government permitted the United States to dissolve its link with France. Washington, however, did not follow this advice, and the neutrality proclamation did not go so far. Accordingly, Pacificus admitted and even emphasized that the proclamation left undisturbed almost all of America's treaty obligations toward France. A proclamation of neutrality does not imply that the nation issuing it will not fulfill its ordinary treaty obligations, ones that "can be performed without rendering it an *associate* or *party* in the war." Thus Washington's proclamation in no way meant that America was completely repudiating its connections with France. Its treaties required the United States to make "certain distinctions" between France and England, and these distinctions were to be observed to the extent that they did not actually involve America in the war.[4]

Nevertheless, the facts of the case compelled Hamilton to admit that the proclamation seemed inconsistent with a specific provision of America's treaty of alliance with France, for the "clause of guarantee" of the "11th article" of

---

[2] *PAH*, 15: 34. Hamilton also considered a fourth "head": criticism that the proclamation was untimely and unnecessary. That argument is not examined here, since it does not go as directly as the others to matters of political principle.

[3] *PAH*, 15: 34.

[4] *PAH*, 15: 34–35.

that treaty called for the United States to come to the aid of France as a partner in war. Here, Hamilton chose his words with great care. He did not say that the proclamation violated the treaty, or even that it appeared superficially to do so. He rather admitted that "execution of the clause of guaranty," which would certainly involve America in the war, would be "contrary to the sense and spirit of the proclamation." In other words, Hamilton suggested that while *execution* of that provision would certainly be incompatible with American neutrality, whether or not it *ought* to be executed was an open question. Accordingly, he held that the proclamation was "virtually a manifestation of the sense of the government that the United States" was, "under the circumstances of the case, not bound to execute the clause of guarantee." The proclamation, in other words, was an authoritative interpretation of the treaty on the part of the government of the United States.

This brought Hamilton to the objection that the president had "stepped beyond the bounds of his constitutional authority and duty" by issuing such a proclamation. He began by stipulating two points that he took to be beyond reasonable dispute. First, American foreign policy is entrusted to the federal government. Second, a neutrality proclamation is a "*usual* and *proper* measure" when a nation is "at liberty" and intends to stay out of a "war in which other nations are engaged." Accordingly, there could be no constitutional question about whether the proclamation was a measure within the authority of the federal government. The only question was "what department" of the federal government has authority to issue a "declaration of neutrality" when such a step is permitted by the nation's "engagements" and demanded by its "interests." The "correct and well informed mind," Hamilton held, will immediately see that this power "can belong" to neither the legislature nor the judiciary but "of course must belong to the executive."[5]

Hamilton first argued by way of exclusion. The "legislative department," he contended, "is not the *organ* of intercourse between the U[nited] States and foreign nations." It neither makes nor interprets treaties, and therefore it is "not naturally that organ of the government" appropriate to the task of announcing the nation's relationship to "foreign Powers" or to admonishing "the citizens of their obligations and duties founded upon" that relationship. "Still less," he added, is the legislature responsible for "enforcing the execution and observance" of the "obligations" and "duties" that arise from our relationship to other nations.[6]

The act of issuing a neutrality proclamation, Hamilton continued, is similarly "foreign" to the character of the judicial department. The province of the courts is "to decide litigations in particular cases." This function admittedly includes the interpretation of the laws, and therefore of treaties as well, but only "where contending parties" bring "a specific controversy" before the

[5] *PAH*, 15: 36–37 (Hamilton's emphasis).
[6] *PAH*, 15: 37–38 (Hamilton's emphasis).

judiciary. This judicial power of interpretation, however, "has no concern with pronouncing upon the external political relations of treaties between government and government." By exclusion, then, the power of issuing a declaration of neutrality must "of necessity belong to the executive department."[7]

Hamilton then proceeded to identify the positive aspects of the executive department that support its authority to issue a neutrality proclamation. To a considerable extent these positive arguments mirror the negative ones of the preceding paragraphs. Unlike the legislature, the executive *is* "the organ of intercourse between" America and "foreign nations." Unlike the judiciary, the executive *is* the "interpreter" of the nation's treaties in cases that arise not between individuals but "between government and government." Moreover, unlike either the legislative or judicial departments, the executive "is charged with the execution of the laws, of which treaties form a part," and with "the command and application of the public force." It would seem, then, that deciding whether to proclaim neutrality in a war, and interpreting whether the nation's treaty obligations permit such a step, belongs properly to the executive. This, Hamilton suggested, is the "natural and obvious" view of the matter, and one "analogous to general theory and practice."[8]

Here, as in his earlier interpretation of the legislative power in his *Opinion on the Constitutionality of a National Bank*, Hamilton was guided by certain general theoretical considerations. There, he had begun his inquiry with reflections on the nature of sovereignty and the needs of all governments. Here, he considered the nature of the executive power and the common practice of existing governments as useful to determining the scope of the executive authority. Nevertheless, it is equally the case here as earlier that Hamilton could not treat such general considerations as determinative of the question. The United States had chosen to not merely establish governing institutions and leave the scope of their power to general reasoning about the nature of government but had instead established them by means of a written constitution that also specified their powers and the limits on those powers. Hamilton accordingly turned next to the Constitution itself to see if any of its "particular provisions" cast any "doubt" on the conclusions to which his general reasoning pointed.[9]

Hamilton began this inquiry with Article II of the Constitution, which establishes the executive department of the government. This article begins, Hamilton observed, with the "general proposition" that the "executive power shall be vested in a president of the United States of America." In subsequent sections, the Article "proceeds to designate particular cases of executive power." Hamilton identified not all of these but only those he deemed relevant to the question at hand. Thus, he noted the specifically enumerated power of the president to "be commander in chief" of American military forces; the

---

[7] *PAH,* 15: 38.
[8] *PAH,* 15: 38.
[9] *PAH,* 15: 38.

"power by and with the consent of the senate to make treaties"; the "duty to receive ambassadors and other public ministers"; and finally the obligation "to take care that the laws be faithfully executed."[10]

The constitutional text confronted Hamilton with a problem: it says nothing one way or the other about a power to issue proclamations of neutrality. This was, of course, also a problem for the critics of the neutrality proclamation who wished to contend that the power belongs to the legislature instead. Hamilton, for his part, chose to solve this problem by means of an expansive interpretation of the executive power that proved just as intolerable to his opponents as his earlier expansive reading of the legislative power.

The foundation of this expansive reading of the executive power is Hamilton's treatment of the first sentence of Article II not as a mere introduction to the subject matter of the article but instead as an actual grant of authority. As we have seen, Hamilton thought that a recurrence to general principles revealed a neutrality proclamation to be in its nature an executive act. If we understand the first sentence of Article II as a "general grant" of executive power, then it will follow that it implicitly includes the authority to issue a neutrality proclamation as well as the authority to do any other thing that essentially belongs to the executive power, whether or not it is included in the subsequent enumeration of particular executive powers.

This brings us, however, to another difficulty: if the first sentence of Article II really is intended to be a "comprehensive grant" of executive authority, as Hamilton contended, then what is the purpose of the subsequent more specific grants of power? Why list particular instances of the executive power as belonging to the president if the first sentence has already vested *all* executive power in his office? Mindful of this objection, Hamilton attempted to answer it as follows. The "rules of sound construction," he contended, suggest that the "enumeration of particular authorities" in Article II should not be understood to "derogate[e] from the more comprehensive grant contained in the general clause, further than" as the enumeration carries with it "express restrictions or qualifications" on the president's authority. Two considerations, he suggested, support his view that the opening clause is in fact a general grant of authority. He appealed in the first place to the nature of constitution-writing: it would be, he held, unreasonable to expect the document to include a complete list of executive powers. "The difficulty of a complete and perfect specification of all the cases of executive authority would naturally dictate the use of general terms" and at the same time "would render it improbable" that a later "specification of certain particulars" was intended as a "substitute" for the general terms already used.[11]

In the second place, Hamilton argued from the constitutional text itself, which he believed confirms the general reasoning sketched above. He noted here

---

[10] *PAH*, 15: 38–39.
[11] *PAH*, 15: 39.

the "different mode of expression employed in the Constitution" in relation to the legislative and executive powers. Article I, which establishes the legislative power, opens with the statement that *"All legislative powers herein granted shall be vested in a Congress of the U[nited] States."* In contrast, Article II begins, as noted earlier, with the claim that "The executive power shall be vested in a president of the U[nited] States."[12] Hamilton did not here spell out in detail why this difference of wording supports his understanding of the beginning of Article II as a comprehensive grant of authority. We can, nevertheless, offer the following plausible lines of argument. The language of Article I clearly suggests that the Constitution does not intend to invest Congress with a comprehensive legislative power. It instead speaks of legislative powers in the plural and suggests that it is conferring *some* of them on the government of the United States, and then that *all* of these are to be vested in the Congress. Congress possesses all of the legislative powers that the Constitution grants to the federal government, but the Constitution does not grant all conceivable legislative powers to the federal government. Such an understanding is, indeed, essential to the commonly accepted view of the federal government as one of limited powers delegated by the Constitution. The Constitution could not confer "the legislative power" comprehensively on the Congress without implicitly denying that the state governments still possessed substantial legislative power by which to govern their own affairs.

In contrast, Article II's opening language speaks of "the executive power" as a single, unified entity placed entirely in the hands of the president of the United States. Here, we might add, a comprehensive grant of power involves none of the difficulties mentioned in the case of the legislative power. It is less problematic to make a comprehensive grant of executive power because the executive power in its nature is not as expansive as the legislative power. The latter has a more active character and broader scope than the former, which is in its nature to a large extent a servant of the latter: the executive executes laws enacted by the legislature. Accordingly, the scope of the executive power is in an important respect confined by the scope of the legislative power. In a constitution for the government of the United States, a simple, unqualified grant of "the legislative power" to Congress would doubtless imply an authority to legislate in all areas, even those that had been the domain of the states. But under a constitution acknowledging the existence of state governments, no one would think that a grant of "the executive power" to the president would confer authority to execute state laws as well as federal ones.

On Hamilton's understanding, then, the purpose of the subsequent enumeration of executive powers is not to provide a complete list of such powers, and thus to disallow whatever is left unmentioned, but instead, "by way of greater caution, to specify and regulate the principal articles implied in the definition of executive power" while "leaving the rest to flow from the general grant

---

[12]   *PAH*, 15: 39 (Hamilton's emphasis).

of that power, interpreted in conformity to other parts" of "the constitution and to the principles of free government." As Hamilton had already admitted, however, some "other parts of the Constitution" – such as certain passages in Article II – do undeniably assign executive functions to actors other than the president. Thus, the purpose of the enumeration is really twofold: not only to make explicit the important executive powers that already flow implicitly from the general grant of power but also to identify certain important exceptions to the general vesting of the executive power in the president. Hamilton thus concluded that the "general doctrine of our Constitution" is that "the executive power of the nation is vested in the president, subject only to the *exceptions* and *qualifications*" that are "expressed" in the Constitution.[13] Hamilton also sought to lend support to this view by observing that it was not his alone, that he was not the first to have suggested it, but that one of the other departments of government had already acted upon it. Here, he referred specifically to the debate in Congress over the removal power of the president. The Constitution is silent on the question of whether the president has a power to remove subordinate executive branch officers, yet Congress concluded that he does indeed possess such a power, since it appears to be in its nature an executive function, and nothing in the constitutional text explicitly deprives him of it. Thus, Hamilton suggested, Congress had, through its "formal acts," done on the basis of "full consideration and debate," already "recognized" the "mode of construing the Constitution" for which he was now contending.[14]

Returning to the immediate practical question, Hamilton's understanding of Article II solves the aforementioned problem of the Constitution's silence on the matter of neutrality proclamations. That silence is in fact not a problem because we should not expect to find most specific instances of the executive power listed in the Constitution anyway, since they flow by implication from the general grant of authority with which Article II begins. Put another way, and using Hamilton's own language, the only way the text of the Constitution could cast "doubt" on his assertion that neutrality proclamations, as exercises of the executive power, belong to the president would be if it stated in plain terms that such a power in fact belongs to some other actor. The text, however, does not do this. As Hamilton noted, the "participation of the Senate in the appointment of officers" and in the "making of treaties" and the "right of the legislature 'to declare war and grant letters of marque and reprisal" are the only specific exceptions to the general rule that the executive power belongs to the president. Apart from these clearly stated exceptions, "the executive power is completely lodged in the president." Therefore, "since upon general principles

---

[13] *PAH*, 15: 39 (Hamilton's emphasis).
[14] *PAH*, 15: 40. For an extended discussion of Hamilton's thinking about the removal power, see Jeremy Bailey, "The New Unitary Executive and Democratic Theory: The Problem of Alexander Hamilton," *American Political Science Review* 102 (2008): 453–65.

for reasons already given, the issuing of a proclamation of neutrality is merely an executive act," the president's decision to issue one "is liable to no just exception on the score of authority."[15]

At this point Hamilton had to respond to another objection. He had just admitted that the text of the Constitution explicitly grants to Congress the power to declare war. Would it not then follow that this "power naturally includes the right" of judging whether or not the country is under any "obligations" to make war?[16] A treaty might include an express provision that the nation come to the aid of an ally in the event of war. It might go so far as to provide in terms that the nation "join" in the war against the ally's enemies or that that nation "make war" on the ally's enemies. Nevertheless, because of the Constitution's equally explicit vesting of the power to declare war in the Congress, it would surely fall to that body to determine whether or to what extent such treaty obligations were to be honored. It would, that is, fall to Congress to decide the nation's status as belligerent or neutral.

Hamilton conceded the force of this reasoning, yet at the same time held that it does not necessarily undermine his claim for a similar power on the part of the president within his own sphere. The "division of the executive power" in the Constitution, he contended, "creates a *concurrent* authority, in the distributed cases," such that Congress may have a right to judge whether the nation is obliged to make war, which right nevertheless does not exclude "a similar right of Judgment" in the president in the "execution" of his "own functions."[17] Hamilton illustrated his understanding by means of a detailed account of how the specific powers of the executive and the legislature create an overlapping authority not only over foreign policy in general but also over particular issues that might arise in foreign policy. The president, he observed, possesses the "right" to "receive ambassadors and other public ministers." This right in turn includes a further right of "judging, in the case of a revolution of government in a foreign country, whether the new rulers" should or should not be "recognized" as "competent organs of the national will." The president's authority to receive foreign officials also includes a power not to receive them, not to recognize them as actual representatives of their country, at least in cases in which a serious doubt could be entertained on this score. Moreover, the use of this presidential power can result in a kind of determination of whether the nation is obliged to enter into war, for if a "treaty antecedently exists between the U[nited] States" and a nation that has recently undergone a political revolution, the president's decision whether to receive that nation's public ministers, and hence whether to recognize its new government, inescapably includes the "power of giving operation or not to such a

[15] *PAH*, 15: 39–40.
[16] *PAH*, 15: 40.
[17] *PAH*, 15: 42, 40 (Hamilton's emphasis).

treaty." "For until the new government is *acknowledged*, the treaties between the nations, as far at least as regards *public* rights, are of course suspended."[18] If, moreover, the treaty in question includes a provision obliging the nation to join in its ally's war, then the president's decision to receive its ambassadors and recognize its government will amount to an executive determination that the country is obliged to enter into war. Applying this reasoning to the "case of France," Hamilton contended that if the American treaty with France created an offensive and defensive alliance, the president's decision to acknowledge the new government "would have put the U[nited] States in a condition to become an associate in the war in which France was engaged – and would have laid the Legislature under an obligation, if required, and there was otherwise no valid excuse, of exercising its power of declaring war." Thus the American "executive" possesses "in certain cases" a right to "determine the condition of the nation" in regard to its foreign obligations, even though the exercise of the right may carry consequences that "affect the proper or improper exercise of the power of the legislature to declare war."[19]

In keeping with his understanding that we are here operating in a realm of "concurrent" authorities, Hamilton immediately added that the executive "cannot control the exercise" of the legislative power to declare war – or at least no "further" than by the use of his veto power, his "general right of objecting to all acts of the legislature," subject to "being overruled by two thirds of both houses of Congress." Thus, while the president's decision to recognize a foreign government may place in active operation a treaty obligation to enter into war, this use of his own "constitutional powers" can only create an "antecedent state of things" that the legislature ought to weigh in making its own determination but cannot bind the legislature to a similar determination. Rather, it leaves the legislature "free to perform its own duties according to its own sense of them."[20] Hamilton's understanding of the concurrent authority in relation to such obligations thus envisions the possibility that the president and the Congress might disagree in the same specific case whether the nation is or is not in fact obliged to enter into war.

If there is an area of concurrent power in regard to foreign affairs, however, it does not follow that the departments of government are equal in this field of policy. On the contrary, Hamilton closed this portion of his constitutional argument with the admonition that the president's power, while not exclusive, is nevertheless predominant. This understanding follows from his earlier claim that there is a general executive power and that it is, with certain limited exceptions, vested entirely in the president by Article II of the Constitution. Treaties, he observed, "can only be made by the president and Senate" but the "president alone" may decide whether their "activity" is to be "continued or

[18] *PAH*, 15: 41 (Hamilton's emphasis).
[19] *PAH*, 15: 41–42.
[20] *PAH*, 15: 42.

suspended." Similarly, while Congress alone may take the important foreign policy step of declaring war, it "belongs" to the president "to do whatever else the laws of nations cooperating with the treaties of the country enjoin, in the intercourse of the U[nited] States with foreign powers." In Hamilton's view, the constitutional grants of executive power to actors other than the president stand only for themselves and cannot legitimately be invoked to imply any further authority. The role of the Senate in making treaties, he argued, and the role of Congress in declaring war "are exceptions out of the general 'Executive Power' vested in the president." They are therefore "to be construed strictly – and ought to be extended no further than is essential to their execution."[21]

We noted earlier that the silence of the Constitution on the power to issue a neutrality proclamation creates a kind of problem for Hamilton's argument. Here we might observe that the Constitution creates that problem not only by omission but also by what it says explicitly in the subsequent enumeration of executive powers in Article II, for that enumeration includes instances in which the executive power is given to non-presidential actors, such as the Senate or the whole Congress. Assuming that a neutrality proclamation is a valid exercise of national power, we would be at a loss, if we relied only on these specific grants of authority, to determine to which department of government this essential power belongs. Hamilton tried to overcome this difficulty, again, by his claim that the opening sentence of Article II vests the president with the whole executive authority of the government, subject only to exceptions specifically enumerated in the Constitution.

Up to this point, Hamilton's defense of the constitutionality of the neutrality proclamation had relied on his claim that foreign relations is to be understood as an aspect of the executive power, which is largely vested in the president. Before concluding his constitutional defense, however, he ventured a second, and considerably shorter, line of argument. Although he had found it "advisable to vindicate the authority of the executive" on the "broad and comprehensive ground" already covered, "it was not absolutely necessary to do so." He might instead have relied "alone" on a "simple" argument based on the "clause of the Constitution which makes it" the president's "duty to 'take care that the laws be faithfully executed.'" This passage, Hamilton suggested, makes the president the "constitutional executor of the laws." Yet our "treaties and the laws of nations form a part of the law of the land" that the president is constitutionally obliged to execute. Moreover, the official charged with executing the laws "must first judge for himself of their meaning." That is, before enforcing the laws the president must first interpret them and discern what they intend in the relevant circumstances. Thus the president has a right to issue a neutrality proclamation as an exercise of his authority to interpret the nation's legal obligations under its treaty with France. "In order to the observance of that conduct which the laws of nations combined with our treaties

[21] *PAH*, 15: 42.

prescribed to this country, in reference to the present War in Europe, it was necessary for the president to judge for himself whether there was anything in our treaties incompatible with an adherence to neutrality." And if he found no such incompatibility, and was convinced that the nation's interest required it, he had a "duty as executor of the laws to proclaim the neutrality of the nation, to exhort all persons to observe it, and to warn them of the penalties which would attend its non-observance."[22]

Consistent with his claim that the neutrality proclamation could be justified as an exercise of the president's duty to see that the laws be faithfully executed, Hamilton concluded with an admonition that it would be a mistake to suppose, as some critics had, that the proclamation established some new legal situation. "The proclamation has been presented," he observed, "as enacting some new law." To some, apparently, it had seemed that by issuing the proclamation the president had *created* a state of neutrality between the United States and the warring nations of France and England. Indeed, Hamilton's own choice of words might invite such an interpretation. He had already suggested, after all, that in some cases the president has authority to "determine the condition of the nation" in relation to foreign powers.[23] This view of the proclamation, Hamilton nevertheless insisted, was "entirely erroneous." The proclamation created no new law but only announced a *"fact"* about the *"existing state* of the nation." To be sure, it threatened with punishment those who failed to observe neutral conduct. Yet those punishments were not ultimately authorized by presidential power but by the authority of the preexisting laws that he was determined to enforce according to his interpretation of them. The proclamation thus simply "inform[ed] the citizens of what the laws previously established require[d] of them" in a neutral state and "warn[ed] them that these laws" would "be put in execution against the infractors of them."[24] Although the Proclamation announced the president's decision to pursue a line of policy, the original source of that decision was not so much his own will as his perception of the will of the community as it was expressed in its already-enacted treaties. Put another way, the "determination" the president made in such a case was not a substantive determination but an interpretive one: he did not so much determine what is good for the nation as what its treaties required.

This understanding of the proclamation as an executive rather than a legislative act is also consistent with Hamilton's earlier presentation of it as an exercise of the president's general foreign policy authority. His well-known formulation held that if "the legislature have a right to make war on the one hand – it is on the other the duty of the executive to preserve peace" until "war is declared."[25] Similarly, he later suggested that "the right of *changing*" the

[22] *PAH*, 15: 43.
[23] *PAH*, 15: 41.
[24] *PAH*, 15: 43 (Hamilton's emphasis).
[25] *PAH*, 15: 40.

state of neutrality and *"declaring war* belongs to the legislature." Finally, he concluded his argument based on the president's foreign policy power with the observation that it is "the province and duty of the executive to preserve to the nation the blessings of peace," while the "legislature alone can interrupt those blessings, by placing the nation in a state of war."[26] Even in relation to the foreign affairs power, then, the neutrality proclamation did not create a new state of things but simply affirmed an existing state of things.

Hamilton's Interpretation of the French Treaties

In the second and third *Pacificus* letters, Hamilton turned to the "second & principal objection" to the neutrality proclamation: that it was "inconsistent with the treaties between the United States and France." Having vindicated the authority of the president to issue a formal interpretation of those treaties, he still had to respond to the claim that the interpretation was erroneous. Hamilton began by recalling his earlier observation that the neutrality proclamation was in no way inconsistent with the vast majority of the provisions of the treaties with France: the United States was still bound to perform all "stipulations" that would not render it "an associate or party in the war."[27] Nevertheless, Hamilton again had to confront the problem of the "clause of guarantee" in the treaty of alliance, which might appear to oblige the United States to take France's part. Here he was once again careful with his choice of words so as not to concede the reality of such an obligation in the present case. He admitted "that the declaration of neutrality exclude[d] the idea of an execution of the clause of guarantee." He asked, then, "whether the United States would have a valid justification for not complying with it" if France called for its execution. In other words, Hamilton did not deny that the guarantee clause imposed an obligation on the United States. Rather, his language implied that the obligation did not come into operation in the present case because the proper conditions were not present to justify "execution" of the clause. The treaty obviously did not intend to bind America to France in a perpetual state of war but only to trigger the obligation to make war on behalf of France in certain circumstances. Hamilton had already contended that it belongs to the president constitutionally to determine whether or not the circumstances exist that would call such a clause into operation. Now he contended that the president was correct in his judgment that those circumstances were not present and that the clause therefore should not be executed. There were, he suggested, "very good and substantial grounds" for such a view.[28]

According to Hamilton, the "alliance" the treaty created "between the United States and France" was only a "defensive" one. The defensive character

---

[26] *PAH*, 15: 42 (Hamilton's emphasis).
[27] *PAH*, 15: 55–56.
[28] *PAH*, 15: 56.

of the alliance was evident in the words used in the treaty itself, both in its "caption," which referred to the document as "a treaty of alliance eventual and *defensive*," and in the body of the treaty, which held that the "direct end of the present defensive alliance is to maintain effectually the liberty, sovereignty, and independence absolute and unlimited of the United States, as well in matters of government as of commerce." The nature of the alliance, he suggested, must inform the interpretation of all of its specific provisions. Since the "predominant quality" of the alliance was defensive, "the meaning, obligation, and force of every stipulation in the treaty" was to be "tested and determined by that principle," except in those provisions, if any, in which "express negative words" excluded such "implication." The "nature and effect" of a "defensive alliance," however, is that it is called into operation when one of the "allies is *attacked*, when war is made upon him," but "not when he makes war upon another." In other words, a defensive alliance requires that the "stipulated assistance" be given only when "the ally" is "engaged" in a "*defensive*" and not in an "*offensive* war." To claim, then, that the clause of guarantee had to be executed, or that the government of the United States was "bound to assist France" in the war, would be "to convert our treaty with her into an alliance offensive and defensive, contrary to the express and reiterated declarations of the instrument itself."[29]

This argument suggested that France's present war was in fact offensive in character. That this was the case was evident, Hamilton contended, from an examination of the facts in light of the relevant principles. The relevant principles, he suggested, were provided not by ordinary conceptions of what is offensive or defensive conduct but instead by the "laws of nations" as expounded by the authoritative "writers." Hamilton leaned especially on the authority of Burlamaqui, who had "accurately laid down" the proper "principle." The treaty was a legal document, and one of its key terms, "defensive alliance," relied on legal terminology that had a precise and settled meaning. Hamilton's reliance on the technical terminology of customary international law required him to address the "incorrectness of ideas" of those who might judge the character of France's war according to more commonplace but less appropriate standards. Such observers might contend that France's war was defensive – and therefore that the clause of guarantee must come into operation, and that the neutrality proclamation is accordingly a violation of the treaty – because the enemies of France had given "the first provocation" or committed the "first injury," which led to the war. Such considerations, Hamilton insisted, were irrelevant. According to the proper principles, the "cause or occasion of the war," on the one hand, and "the war itself," on the other, are "things entirely distinct." Accordingly, whether a war is offensive or defensive is to be determined not by who did what to whom in relation to "the causes leading to" the war but by which nation "*first declares*" or "*actually begins*" the war. Yet there

---

[29] *PAH*, 15: 56–57.

could be no doubt, Hamilton concluded, that "France first declared and began the war against Austria, Prussia, Savoy, Holland, England, and Spain."[30] On its part, therefore, the war was offensive in character and therefore did not call into play America's guarantee in the treaty. Thus, the president could issue the neutrality proclamation without violating the treaty.

As Hamilton was at pains to clarify, as terms of art in international law, "offensive" and "defensive" war did not correspond necessarily to the moral categories by which one might evaluate wars. Those categories might have their own validity, but they were not determinative of the issue at hand because they are not ordinarily employed in treaties, and certainly were not employed in the treaty in question. In other words, "offensive" and "defensive" are legal concepts that do not necessarily correspond to the moral concepts "just" and "unjust." An offensive war is not necessarily an unjust war, and a defensive war is not necessarily a just war. The justice of the case depends, Hamilton suggested, on the causes of the war, while its offensive or defensive character depends simply on who started it. Thus, he contended, using Burlamaqui's words, if "we take up arms to revenge" an "unjust act, we commence" a war that is both *offensive* and *just*; while if we have done "injury and will not give satisfaction," we may make a war that is *defensive* yet "unjust." Whoever is "the first" to resort to "arms, whether *justly* or *unjustly*, commences an *offensive* war, while "he who opposes him, whether with or without reason, begins a defensive war."[31]

Moreover, Hamilton contended, it is entirely proper for the nation's treaty obligations to be decided only with reference to such clear legal conceptions, rather than on the basis of considerations of justice, which, however important they may be, are too murky to serve as a reliable guide to our conduct in such a case. He recognized that those "disposed to justify indiscriminately everything" in France's "conduct" might respond to his argument thus far by holding that France's war was offensive only "in point of form" but defensive "in point of principle." It was, in other words, "a mere anticipation of attacks meditated against her, and was justified by previous aggressions of the opposite parties." Hamilton responded that such considerations are altogether "too vague, too liable to dispute, too much a matter of opinion to be a proper criterion of national conduct." Indeed, the question of justice is ordinarily so uncertain that "when a war breaks out between two nations," all others, "in regard to the positive rights of the parties and their positive duties toward them are bound to consider it equally just on both sides." Accordingly, when a nation has entered a defensive alliance, it is legally bound "to fulfill the conditions stipulated on its part" when its ally is attacked, "without inquiry" into the question of whether the ally's cause in the war is just, or whether it unjustly provoked the war that has now been justly commenced against it. Similarly,

---

[30] *PAH*, 15: 57.
[31] *PAH*, 15: 58 (Hamilton's emphasis).

there is no obligation to join a defensive ally's offensive war, however just its cause may be. The "doctrine" on which he here insisted, Hamilton concluded, is founded on "the utility of clear and certain rules for determining the reciprocal duties of nations – that as little as possible may be left to opinion and the subterfuges of a refining or unfaithful casuistry."[32]

At first glance, Hamilton's doctrine here might appear amoral. He has said, it would seem, that when war breaks out between two nations, other nations are to regard the war as "equally just on both sides." This impression is perhaps strengthened later in *Pacificus* II, when he refers to questions about the justice or injustice of the causes of war as mere "metaphysical niceties."[33] This seems as much as to say that the question of the justice of a war should not enter into other nations' reasoning about how to conduct their own foreign policies. More careful consideration of Hamilton's words, however, reveals that this is not his intention. His point is not that the justice of a war, or considerations of justice in general, is irrelevant in foreign policy. It is rather that such considerations cannot change, and ought not to be the basis for determining, the legal obligations that exist between nations. Moral considerations are not unimportant, but neither can they alter the "positive rights" and "positive duties" that have been "stipulated" in written agreements among nations.[34] Nothing that Hamilton said denies that governments may, and perhaps should, take justice into account as they judge the proper posture toward nations at war, but he does insist that their freedom to act on their judgments about the justice of the matter must be constrained by the treaties to which they have consented.

The next steps in Hamilton's argument afford further evidence that he did not intend to reject the role of moral considerations in the conduct of foreign policy. He implicitly acknowledged a distinction between wars in which the justice of the matter is questionable and those that involve obvious injustice. And he was willing to entertain the possibility, although he did not commit himself to it, that the latter sort of war excuses allies from their obligation to give assistance. "Some writers indeed of high authority," he noted, have held that "it is a tacit condition of every treaty of alliance that one ally is not bound to assist the other in a war manifestly unjust." At the same time, "other respectable authorities" had questioned this proposition precisely on the grounds Hamilton had already laid out – namely, the importance of having clear rules for determining the obligations of nations. Even if we were to concede that cases of manifest injustice excuse allies from their obligations, however, this introduction of moral considerations into our reasoning would in no way impeach Washington's neutrality proclamation, for while some writers of high authority may hold that the "manifest injustice" of a war is "a good cause for

[32] *PAH*, 15: 58–59.
[33] *PAH*, 15: 62.
[34] *PAH*, 15: 58.

not executing the formal obligations of a treaty," Hamilton claimed that he had "nowhere seen it maintained that the justice of a war is a consideration which can *oblige* a nation to do what its formal obligations do not require."[35] Clear injustice may excuse a nation from its formal obligations, but not even clear justice can create such obligations where they have not been consented to. And since America's alliance with France was defensive in character, the United States had no formal obligation to come to its assistance in its offensive war, even if justice was on its side.

The relevance of morality to foreign policy is further suggested by the next step in Hamilton's argument, in which he evaluated the justice of the French cause. Even if one rejected Hamilton's doctrine that the justice of the dispute is not the basis on which treaty obligations are to be determined, he contended, it would still be the case that France would have no claim on America's support in its war with the European powers, for "an impartial examination would prove" that in relation to some of the nations in question France was "not blameless in the circumstances which preceded and led to the war; that if she received she also gave causes of offense, and that the justice of the war on her side is in those cases not a little problematical."[36] This discussion is also important insofar as it brings to light Hamilton's understanding of the standards of justice by which the conduct of nations is to be judged.

He began his critique of the French revolutionary government's policy by noting a rather clear-cut French violation of international law that implies a rather ordinary and defensible standard of justice, both among nations and individuals: namely, keep your contracts. "France," Hamilton observed, "committed an aggression upon Holland" by "declaring free," or "open to all nations," the "navigation of the Scheldt" river, and then by acting in accord with that declaration. This conduct was a violation of "treaties" in which France had "explicitly acknowledged and even guaranteed the exclusive right of Holland to the navigation of that river."[37]

Hamilton devoted much more attention, however, to an indictment of France's efforts to meddle in the affairs of other nations and to undermine their existing governments. This discussion, too, implies a simple standard of justice that is often good for both individuals as well as nations: mind your own business, or do not molest your neighbors. France violated this principle of international justice when the National Convention issued its decree of November 19, 1792, which it "ordered to be printed in *all languages.*" By this decree, France declared that it would "grant *fraternity* and *assistance* to every people who *wish* to recover their liberty." It further ordered the nation's "executive power to send the necessary orders to *the generals* to give assistance

[35] *PAH*, 15: 59 (Hamilton's emphasis).
[36] *PAH*, 15: 59.
[37] *PAH*, 15: 59.

to such people, and to *defend those citizens who may have been or who may be vexed for the cause of liberty.*"[38]

This decree was an act of injustice on at least two counts, Hamilton's argument suggested. In the first place, by issuing it France was holding other nations to standards different from those to which it held itself, for the decree "amounted exactly to what France herself" had "most complained of – an interference by one nation in the internal government of another." In the second place, France's decree was unjust in the sense that it ran counter to the traditional understanding of the "liberty" and "independence of nations." Drawing on Vattel, Hamilton noted the customarily recognized "consequence" of this principle: "That it does not belong to any foreign power to take cognizance of the administration of the *sovereign* of another country, to set himself up as a judge of his conduct or to oblige him to alter it." In addition, Hamilton reminded his readers that this traditional principle of the law of nations was to be respected not merely because it was long established, but also because it tends to secure what anyone would have to concede is an important good: namely, peace and harmony among states. Avoidance of war may not be the highest kind of justice, but it is hardly an inconsequential consideration. Thus Hamilton, relating these ideas to the case at hand, observed that France's decree "had a natural tendency to disturb the tranquility of nations, to excite fermentation and revolt everywhere." Accordingly, it "justified neutral powers who were in a situation to be affected by it in taking measures to repress the spirit by which it had been dictated."[39] France's openly stated and publicized willingness to assist in the overthrow of established governments made the latter's war on France a just war – or at least made it impossible to say that justice was simply on France's side.

Hamilton's argument, however, raises an implicit difficulty. He here appealed to a traditional "liberty" of nations, their freedom to be governed without the interference of outsiders. But no American could be ignorant of or insensitive to the importance of other kinds of liberty: the liberty of a people to govern themselves, or at least to have a government that respects their rights. Why should we consider these liberties, which France sought to champion, as subordinate to the older liberty of nations, a liberty that recognizes and protects the authority – or the supposed authority – of governments to deny the liberty of their own subjects? Hamilton defended, as we have just seen, the sensible view that justice is what preserves peace among nations. But is there not a higher justice among nations, one that must take into account whether the subjects of other countries are governed justly by their own governments? France's aid to America in the course of its own revolutionary struggle with England might be seen as a violation of the very principles for which Hamilton

[38] *PAH*, 15: 59–60.
[39] *PAH*, 15: 60 (Hamilton's emphasis).

was here contending. Yet most Americans, including Hamilton himself, welcomed that aid and raised no complaint that it was a violation of the law of nations or an irresponsible disturbance of the peace.

Hamilton was aware of these difficulties, and he attempted to reconcile respect for the traditional law of nations, on the one hand, with a foreign policy in defense of an oppressed people's liberty, on the other. This reconciliation worked by way of a distinction: Hamilton tried to show that what France did for America during the latter's revolution was different from what France was now trying to do to other nations in the wake of its own revolution. The difference, he suggested, is between assisting a revolution that has gotten underway on its own power, which Hamilton thought defensible, and inviting revolution where there is none, which he thought indefensible. "When a nation has actually come to a resolution to throw off a yoke, under which it may have groaned, and to assert its liberties," Hamilton argued, it is not only "justifiable" but even "meritorious" for another nation "to afford assistance to the one which has been oppressed and is *in the act* of liberating itself." It is not, however, "warrantable for any nation *beforehand*," in the absence of revolution, "to hold out a general invitation to insurrection and revolution by promising to assist *every people* who may *wish* to recover their liberty, and to defend *those citizens* of every country *who may have been or may be vexed for the cause of liberty*."[40] Yet this is what France had done. For Hamilton, then, governments may intervene on behalf of liberty where they find a revolution in pursuit of liberty, but they may not foment revolution, even with a view to liberty, where they find tranquility and good order. A nation that adopts the latter course should not be surprised, and cannot reasonably claim to be the victim, when established governments treat them as hostile and make war on them.

Hamilton pressed his indictment of French policy further by noting other instances in which France expressed its intention to interfere in the domestic politics of neighboring nations. He did not, however, merely add items to a bill of particulars. Rather, the subsequent examples reveal the French posture as even more aggressively ideological than was indicated by the aforementioned decree on which Hamilton had based his argument up to this point. He began by observing that France made subsequent statements applying the decree to Great Britain in particular. Shortly after the promulgation of the original decree, the National Convention responded to two "addresses" from British subjects sympathetic to French revolutionary principles. In its answers to these

---

[40] *PAH*, 15: 60 (Hamilton's emphasis). As Nathan Tarcov notes, Henry Clay later advanced the same distinction as Hamilton made here. Clay held that he "would not 'disturb the repose of a detestable despotism,' but he would aid an oppressed people who 'will their freedom' and seek to establish or have established it." "The Spirit of Liberty and Early American Foreign Policy," in *Understanding the Political Spirit: Philosophical Investigations from Socrates to Nietzsche* (New Haven, CT: Yale University Press, 1988), 148.

addresses, the convention expressed the expectation that it would soon be able to "*bring congratulations to the National Convention of Great Britain.*" That is, the Convention had anticipated with approval a regime change in Britain, a replacement of Parliament with some new and unheard of legislative body. As the answer proceeded, it revealed in an even clearer light the French intentions. It pointedly referred to France and England as "the two republics," and then went on to add that "*thrones*" would be consumed by the "*devouring fire*" of declarations of "*rights,*" and that European "*royalty*" had been or was about to be destroyed "on the ruins of feudality." Such language, Hamilton noted, amounted to an open call for revolution in a neighboring country, which "was unquestionably an offense and injury to the nation to which it related." France, moreover, had made a similar declaration in relation to, and hence gave "cause of offense" to, the rest of the nations of Europe, for in another decree, of the 15th of November, it pronounced that the "*French nation*" would "*treat as enemies the people who, refusing* or *renouncing* liberty and equality, *are desirous* of preserving their *prince* and *privileged casts* – or of *entering into an accommodation with them.*" "This," Hamilton noted, "was little short of a declaration of war against all nations having *princes* and *privileged classes*" – or against all the nations of Europe.[41]

What do these additional complaints add to Hamilton's indictment, besides piling up additional examples of the same kind of misconduct? Careful attention to the language of the subsequent proclamations Hamilton examined shows that their tendency was even more troubling than the one with which he began his argument, that of November 19th, which called for France to assist all peoples that wished to recover their liberty. In the first place, both the statements about Britain in particular, as well as the more general decree of November 15th, increased considerably the demands that France was presuming to place on the governments of other nations. The "liberty" that France had first promised to support might have been understood merely as protection for individual rights, perhaps the Lockean rights to life, liberty, and property that all Americans would have agreed ought to be respected by any government. The other statements, however, took a very large and, in Hamilton's view, very irresponsible step further. They suggested that the governments of Europe not only must respect the natural rights of their people but that they must be "republican" in character. Indeed, some of the rhetoric regarding Britain – which noted that "principles are waging war against tyranny, which will fall under the blows of philosophy" – seemed to imply that the problem with Europe was not so much that there were tyrannical kings as that kingship is by its nature tyrannical.[42] In other words, the "liberty and equality" that France demanded was not only an equality of protection for natural rights by a just government but rule by the people. In the second place, while the initially

[41] *PAH*, 15: 60 (Hamilton's emphasis).
[42] *PAH*, 15: 61.

examined declaration suggested an invitation to revolution, the latter expressed more of an insistence on revolution: peoples who refused to throw off their kings and privileged classes were held to be in the wrong, even if their own experience may have been that their kings and privileged classes had behaved considerably more responsibly than those of France.

It is in light of remarks such as these that we can understand Hamilton's claim that, whatever "partiality" one might have for "the general object of the French Revolution," any "well-informed or sober-minded man" would have to "condemn" France's conduct as "repugnant to the general rights of nations, to the true principles of liberty," and to "the freedom of opinion of mankind."[43] In Hamilton's argument, we might say, French policy was offensive both to older or more conservative conceptions of justice as well as to more modern or liberal ones. As we have seen, Hamilton had something of the conservative in him, insofar as he was willing to embrace institutions and principles that experience appeared to have endorsed, even when the experience was that of somewhat pre-modern, pre-liberal, and non-democratic societies. This conservatism was also displayed in the present critique of France's foreign policy. Hamilton began that critique with an appeal to the established law of nations, a law that was developed gradually from the experience of nations governed by aristocratic classes but that Hamilton still took as an authoritative guide, defending it as wise in its principles and benevolent in its effects. It is this older sense of justice that comes to mind most immediately when Hamilton concludes that French policy has been "repugnant to the rights of nations" – that is, to the traditional rights of sovereigns to rule their subjects without outside interference.

Nevertheless, the expression "the rights of nations" may also have a more modern meaning. It can as easily call to mind the political theory of the *Declaration of Independence*, with its modern emphasis on the rights of individuals and of peoples. That Hamilton intended to invoke this more modern conception as well is rendered clear in the sequel, in which he added that French conduct was also "repugnant" to "the true principles of liberty" and the "freedom of opinion of mankind." In what sense, we may wonder, was the French instigation to, and even insistence on, republican revolution contrary to the *Declaration of Independence* and the Lockean teaching informing it? Hamilton did not spell out his thinking here, but it is possible to offer some reasonable speculations. First, we might observe that the *Declaration*, while it embraces the people's right of revolution, equally teaches that this right must be mediated by prudence. It is possible, the *Declaration* teaches, to have a government that fails to respect rights fully but that nevertheless is to be tolerated precisely because of the uncertainty of whether those rights would be better protected by whatever new government is established or of what violations they might suffer in the course of the revolution itself. Whether revolution is justifiable is a judgment for the people to make according to their best calculations of their own best

43 *PAH*, 15: 62.

interests, presumably uninfluenced by the enticements, to say nothing of the threats, of foreign powers. To the extent that France offered such enticements and made such threats, it interfered with the "liberty" and "freedom of opinion" of others even on modern standards. Second, France also trampled on this "freedom of opinion" by insisting that other nations adopt a specifically *republican* form of government. The *Declaration* – again, following Locke – implicitly recognized the right of the people to consent to a non-republican form of government if they believed such an arrangement would be consistent with the security of their rights. France imperiously demanded that all peoples reject their princes and privileged classes, but even on American and Lockean principles any people would have a right to conclude that their rights were sufficiently protected even by a political system that included princes and privileged classes.

French conduct, Hamilton concluded, "threatened the independence of all other countries" and therefore gave "to neighboring neutral powers the justest cause of discontent and apprehension."[44] "It is a principle well agreed and founded on the best reasons," he argued, that whenever a state "adopts maxims of conduct contrary to those generally established among nations," and "calculated to disturb their tranquility and to expose their safety, they may justifiably make a common cause to oppose and control such nation." Therefore, the justice of France's position was "questionable enough to free the U[nited] States from all embarrassment" in refusing to assist it, even if, contrary to what was demonstrated earlier, it were "incumbent" on America to go into such an "inquiry."[45]

Hamilton then turned in *Pacificus* III to a final argument showing that the United States was not obligated to execute the clause of guarantee. Once, again, this argument takes us beyond the issue at hand and sheds light on the principles informing Hamilton's thinking about obligations among nations. Here he argued that an attempt on the part of the United States to execute the guarantee clause would involve a serious "disproportion" between the "mischiefs and perils, to which the U[nited] States would expose themselves by embarking in the war," on the one hand, and, on the other, the advantages that France was due or that she could actually expect to achieve from American support. France had little to gain, and America much to lose, from execution of the guarantee clause in the present circumstances, and this "disproportion" of interests excused America from intervention on France's behalf.[46]

The guarantee clause, Hamilton observed, referred not to the "immediate defense" of "France herself" but only to that of her "American colonies." It was doubtful, however, that the United States could provide any effective succor. France, Hamilton noted, was "engaged and likely to be engaged in war

---

[44] *PAH*, 15: 61–62 (Hamilton's emphasis).
[45] *PAH*, 15: 62.
[46] *PAH*, 15: 66.

with all or almost all Europe," and "without a single ally in that quarter of the globe." "In such a state of things," France could defend herself at home but could not effectively defend her possessions abroad. Her assistance, however, would be necessary to accomplishing anything in relation to their defense, since America had no naval power to speak of. In the prevailing circumstances, Hamilton suggested, an American execution of the guarantee clause would be nothing more than a futile gesture in support of France and therefore could not be obligatory. Moreover, Hamilton noted, loss of her "American colonies" would still leave France "a great and powerful and a happy nation."[47]

In contrast, for America the risks of trying to execute the guarantee clause were genuine and daunting. To intervene on France's behalf without the support of the French navy would be to risk the "destruction of our trade." Indeed, according to Hamilton, American intervention would put at risk not only the nation's "essential interests" but perhaps also its "very existence," for intervention would place America in a dangerously unequal contest with rival powers. She would enter the war with "the possessions of Great Britain and Spain on both flanks, the numerous Indian tribes, under the influence and direction of those powers, along our whole interior frontier, with a long extended seacoast – with no maritime force of our own, and with the maritime force of all Europe against us, with no fortifications whatever, and with a population not exceeding four millions." America, Hamilton concluded, must be "dissuaded" from such a "contest" by "the most cogent motives of self-preservation as well as of interest."[48]

Hamilton's argument raises a question: Is he suggesting, as Jefferson might have suspected, that mere self-interest can excuse a nation from performing its treaty obligations? If so, what is the point of treaties if nations are free not to observe them when self-interest forbids it? In the first place, we should remind ourselves that Hamilton's argument here is somewhat hypothetical. He had already concluded that America had no treaty obligation because the treaty created a defensive alliance while France was engaged in an offensive war. Nevertheless, he was here taking his argument further and suggesting that even if France's war were defensive America would not, in the circumstances, be obligated to execute the guarantee clause. To that extent, then, he was suggesting that considerations of self-interest and self-preservation are at least relevant to determining whether a treaty obligation should be fulfilled. Such considerations may not automatically excuse a nation from complying with its treaties, but neither does a treaty necessarily compel a nation to ignore its own interests.

Indeed, Hamilton contended that the glaring disproportion he described – execution of the guarantee could not even succeed in securing inessential French interests but would jeopardize vital American interests – provides a "valid

---

[47] *PAH*, 15: 65–67.
[48] *PAH*, 15: 65–67.

reason for not executing the guarantee." Hamilton's argument in defense of this conclusion did not reject the role of justice in international relations. Rather, it invoked principles of equitable justice similar to those his *Report on Public Credit* had recognized in thinking through the contractual rights of buyers and sellers of the public debt. "All contracts," Hamilton argued as Pacificus, "are to receive a reasonable construction." Moreover, "self-preservation is the first duty of a nation." Among individuals, this argument implies, justice would not necessarily demand rigorous enforcement of a contract if fulfillment of it impeded one of the parties from fulfilling other, more fundamental obligations that precede the contract. This principle applies among nations no less than among individuals. Because a nation's first duty is to secure its own preservation, it is unreasonable to interpret any treaty to which it has consented as requiring it to take actions that threaten its preservation. Or, at least, it is unreasonable to insist that it execute treaty provisions that *seriously* endanger its preservation. Hamilton was compelled to make this qualification because treaties pertaining to war obviously oblige a nation to take some risks. In the "performance of stipulations relating to war," he noted, "good faith requires" that its "*ordinary hazards*" must be "fairly met, because they are directly contemplated by such stipulations." Nevertheless, good faith "does not require that *extraordinary* and *extreme* hazards should be run." This is especially true, he added, when, as in the present case, the extreme dangers are faced in pursuit of an object that is merely "a *partial* or *particular* interest of the ally."[49]

Once again, Hamilton contended that his position was supported by the traditionally accepted understanding of justice among nations. He had argued that America would be excused from executing the treaty of guarantee by its inability to secure French possessions without French assistance and by the extreme dangers such an attempt would involve. Yet Vattel, "one of the best writers on the laws of nations," similarly taught that when a "state" that has "promised succors finds itself unable to furnish them, its very inability is its exemption" and that when "furnishing the succors would expose it to an *evident* danger this also is a lawful dispensation." For a "treaty" that is "*pernicious* to the state" is "*not obligatory*." On the contrary, "*every treaty*" reserves an exception when compliance involves "an *imminent danger* threatening the *safety* of the state."[50]

Hamilton concluded this portion of his argument by noting two other considerations that, in reason, tended to excuse America from fulfilling the treaty. In the first place, he again observed that the present war was to some considerable extent the result of France's own imprudent conduct. "No country," he contended, "is bound to partake in hazards of the most critical kind, which may have been produced or promoted by the indiscretion and intemperance of another." This principle is "an obvious dictate of reason, with which the

49 *PAH*, 15: 66 (Hamilton's emphasis).
50 *PAH*, 15: 67 (Hamilton's emphasis).

common sense and common practice of mankind coincide." In the second place, he suggested that the ultimate origin of the war – in the French Revolution – was outside the ordinary circumstances contemplated by the treaty and therefore absolved the United States of any obligation to execute the clause of guarantee. "Military stipulations in national treaties," he argued, "contemplate only the *ordinary* case of *foreign* war and are irrelative to the contests which grow out of revolutions of government." The French Revolution, however, was surely the "primitive source" of the present war. The restoration of the French monarchy was the "implied" or "avowed" aim of all of France's enemies. "That question then is essentially involved in the principle of the war," and it is a question "certainly never in the contemplation of that government with which our treaty was made." Accordingly, "it may thence be fairly inferred" that a war over such a question was "never intended to be embraced" by the treaty.[51]

Hamilton was not here arguing that America's treaty obligations had been voided by the revolution itself, since the government with which we partnered in the treaty no longer existed. This was not the position the United States had adopted. The Washington administration in fact received the minister of the revolutionary government and thus tacitly admitted it to be the legitimate government of France. America's claim was not that it was absolved from all obligation by the nature of France's government but that it was absolved in the present instance by the nature of the present case. The United States, Hamilton said, had "fulfilled the utmost that could be claimed by the nation of France" when it recognized the "newly constituted powers; giving operation to the treaty of alliance for *future occasions, but considering the present war as a tacit exception.*"[52]

Gratitude and Foreign Policy

In *Pacificus* IV, Hamilton turned to the final principled objection to the neutrality proclamation: that it was "inconsistent with the gratitude due to France for the services rendered to us in our revolution." He began by noting an inconsistency in the position of those who raised this complaint. Even as they decried the supposed lack of gratitude manifested by the proclamation, they at the same time "disavow[ed]" the "position" that America should enter the war

---

[51] *PAH*, 15: 67–68.

[52] *PAH*, 15: 68 (Hamilton's emphasis). Jack Rakove oversteps the mark in saying that Hamilton had as Pacificus "challenged the validity of the alliance with France." Hamilton may have pushed in that direction during the debate within the cabinet, but he did not go so far in the newspapers as Pacificus. See Rakove's *James Madison and the Creation of the American Republic* (New York: Harper Collins Publishers, 1990), 108. Later that summer, Hamilton, writing a follow-up article under the pen name "Philo Pacificus," emphasized this point in response to some critics of Pacificus. Pacificus' arguments, he noted, "turn[ed] upon an examination of the *true meaning of the engagements* contained" in the French "treaties, not upon the obligatory force of the treaties themselves." *PAH*, 15: 191 (Hamilton's emphasis).

on France's behalf. Hamilton wondered what the critics could mean by such an objection, for "if it be no breach of gratitude to refrain from joining France in the war – how can it be a breach of gratitude to declare that such is our disposition and intention?" Given the "variance" between these positions, and the consequent groundlessness of the complaint, Hamilton concluded that this argument was a mask for other, less reputable motives. Those who occupied such an incoherent position either secretly wished to involve America in the war or were grasping for a "pretext for censuring the conduct" of the president "for some purpose very different from the public good."[53]

Hamilton then acknowledged the argument by which such critics sought to evade these consequences: their objection to the proclamation, they claimed, was not that it kept America out of the war but that it put France on an "*equal* footing with her enemies" in relation to America. America did not need to enter the war, these critics contended, to show a certain partiality to France. That partiality, moreover, was required both by our treaty obligations and by our debt of gratitude for French intervention in our own revolutionary struggle. Hamilton responded, however, that such a proper "partiality" was, as he had already argued, perfectly compatible with the neutrality proclamation, which left intact all American treaty obligations to France that did not pertain to war and left to the United States the discretion to do some "kind offices" for France that it could refuse to others – again, so long as those kindnesses did not relate to the war. On this score, there was nothing in the proclamation to which such critics could reasonably object, unless, again, they really wanted the United States to be "partial" to France in some way that related to the war. In that case, however, they could not truly claim to be advocates of a policy of peace, for partiality in things pertaining to war would surely draw war upon the United States.[54]

Such arguments, Hamilton contended, were sufficient to answer the present objection to the proclamation. Nevertheless, he went further. Hamilton aimed to show that the critics had badly and dangerously misunderstood the role of gratitude in foreign policy, that their position betrayed a foolhardy sentimentality that has no place in politics. He thus offered to "indulge some reflections on this very favorite topic of gratitude to France; since it is at this shrine" that "we are continually invited to sacrifice the true interests of the country; as if '*All for love, and the world well lost*,' were a fundamental maxim in politics."[55]

This opening shot might be read to suggest that politics – or at least international politics – is guided solely by calculations of interest, that morality has no place in it. Once again, however, Hamilton was careful to avoid going that far. There is a morality proper to foreign policy, Hamilton believed, but that morality is governed not by gratitude but by "faith and justice." Realistically,

---

[53] *PAH*, 15: 82–83.
[54] *PAH*, 15: 83.
[55] *PAH*, 15: 84.

nations cannot be expected to act out of gratitude, but they should generally keep their promises and treat each other according to long established and reasonable principles of fairness. Indeed, so far was Hamilton from advocating an amoral foreign policy that he insisted that, while gratitude is of limited relevance between nations, the virtues of "faith and justice" are "sacred and unequivocal" and "cannot be too strongly inculcated nor too highly respected." "Their obligations are absolute" and "their utility unquestionable; they relate to objects which with probity and sincerity generally admit of being brought within clear and intelligible rules."[56]

The "same," however, "cannot be said of gratitude." The clarity and intelligibility with which we can think about justice and faith among nations, Hamilton held, breaks down when we begin to think about the possibility of gratitude among nations. Nations can reliably know the basis and the extent of their obligations in justice. They need only consult existing treaties, the traditional law of nations, and the established principles of interpretation. However, it can rarely be said "with certainty" that a foundation for gratitude exists between nations, and how far the obligations of such gratitude would extend is an even darker matter.[57]

Gratitude, Hamilton's argument implied, is a sense of obligation to another, an obligation that even goes so far as to require, to some extent, the "sacrifice" of one's own "interest" for the benefit of the other toward whom the gratitude is felt. What could make someone feel such a sense of obligation? We might be tempted to say that gratitude arises from a good deed done for us by another, but Hamilton held that such an understanding is too imprecise. The basis for gratitude, he contended, "is a benefit received or intended, which there was no right to claim, originating in a regard to the interest or advantage of the party on whom the benefit is or is meant to be conferred." Gratitude is not prompted by just any benefit received but by one that proceeds from a kind of unconstrained benevolence. Thus, we feel no gratitude for benefits that we are owed by right. Furthermore, Hamilton considered not only the nature of the good received – whether or not it was owed – but also the intention of the giver. Gratitude arises from a benefit that was not required by justice and that the benefactor performed primarily for the good of the party benefitted. Gratitude is a response to generosity or selflessness. In contrast, when someone does us a good turn that is not required by justice but does it in pursuit of his own interests, seeing a mutual advantage for himself and for us, we can feel no gratitude. The proper response to such services is not gratitude but at most a disposition to return a "good office" similarly rooted in *mutual* interest and *reciprocal* advantage." To feel gratitude in response to such a good deed, Hamilton observed, is unreasonable because it involves an "effect"

56 PAH, 15: 84.
57 PAH, 15: 84.

that is "disproportioned to the cause."[58] Properly bestowed, gratitude seeks a kind of reasonable equality: it wills selfless service to another because he has done selfless service to us. It would therefore be disproportionate to offer it in response to a benefit conferred by someone who was acting out of self-interest.

Thus understood, gratitude has no place in international politics – or at least a very limited place – because the kind of actions that give rise to it do not occur among nations. "Between individuals," gratitude is common because "occasion is not unfrequently given" for its exercise. Among individuals, we can find daily examples of men "conferring benefits from kind and benevolent dispositions or feelings toward the person benefitted, without any other interest on the part of the person who confers the benefit than the pleasure of doing a good action." Among nations, however, acts of selfless benevolence "perhaps never occur." Ordinarily, nations do not confer benefits out of mere kindness, expecting no gain other than the pleasure of having done a good deed. On the contrary, Hamilton laid it down as a "general principle that the predominant motive of good offices from one nation to another is the interest or advantage" of the country "which performs them."[59]

Indeed, Hamilton continued, the "rule of morality" governing the performance of good offices "is not exactly the same between nations as between individuals." Nations not only do not ordinarily act out of disinterested benevolence, they ordinarily *ought not* to act on such motives. Both nations and individuals, Hamilton suggested, have a "duty" to guide their actions in light of their "own welfare." That duty, however, rests much more heavily upon nations than upon individuals. Hamilton suggested two reasons for the disparity. In the first place, national happiness is of much "greater magnitude and importance" than individual happiness, and the effects of national conduct are much more permanent than the effects of individual conduct. The interests of millions now living, as well as those of future generations, "are concerned in the present measures of a government," while, by contrast, "the consequences of the private actions of an individual" usually "terminate with himself or are circumscribed within a narrow compass." Consequently, "an individual may on numerous occasions meritoriously indulge the emotions of generosity and benevolence; not only without an eye to, but even at the expense of, his own interest." In contrast, a "nation can rarely be justified in pursuing" such a course, and when it does it should "confine itself within much stricter bounds." The proper boundary for a nation's generosity, Hamilton suggested, was set by its obligation not to make a sacrifice of its own interests – a proposition which still permitted it to do acts of generosity that were not necessarily intended to advance its own interests. Nations need not be selfish, but neither could they rightly be selfless. Thus, Hamilton suggested that the "limits of national generosity or benevolence" were perhaps best understood to be set by good deeds

---

[58] *PAH*, 15: 84–85 (Hamilton's emphasis).
[59] *PAH*, 15: 85.

that were "indifferent to the interests" of the "nation performing them," or were "compensated by the existence or expectation of some reasonable equivalent," or which provided "an essential good to the nation to which they" were "rendered" but without any "real detriment to the affairs of the nation rendering them."[60]

In a footnote, Hamilton added a further consideration that he believed strengthened his case against a national benevolence that involved a sacrifice of national interests. "Under every form of government," he noted, the "rulers are only trustees for the happiness and interest of their nation." Therefore, unlike private individuals, rulers could not, "consistently with their trust, follow the suggestions of kindness or humanity towards others, to the prejudice of their constituent[s]."[61]

None of this, Hamilton hastened to add, was intended to "recommend a policy absolutely selfish or interested in nations." He intended only to suggest "that a policy regulated by their own interest, as far as justice and good faith permit, is, and ought to be, their prevailing one." To attribute to nations "a different principle of action," or draw from such different principles an argument for a "self-denying and self-sacrificing gratitude on the part of a nation" that had received benefits from another, was, Hamilton warned, "to misconceive or mistake what usually are and ought to be the springs of national conduct."[62] For Hamilton, then, the primary driving force of a nation's foreign policy was its own interest. This pursuit of national self-interest was qualified in different ways by considerations of justice and gratitude. Between the two principles, justice provided the more commanding restraint on self-interest. In pursuing their own good, nations were obliged to respect justice and good faith – that is, to respect the natural laws of justice among nations and to keep their solemn agreements. They were not obliged but were free to act on gratitude or benevolence, but only to the extent that they did not impair their own interests.

In *Pacificus* V, Hamilton applied these principles to the case at hand. Any gratitude America might owe France, he suggested, was strictly bounded by the limited role that benevolence had played in France's decision to aid the American cause. French aid had been important to America's success, but it had been motivated by France's pursuit of its own national interests.

Hamilton began by sketching his understanding of the background to French intervention on America's behalf. Prior to America's declaration of its independence, French aid to the colonies was "marked neither with liberality nor with vigor." It in fact "bore the appearance rather of a desire to keep alive disturbances which would embarrass" England than "a serious design to assist a revolution or a serious expectation that it could be effected." Subsequent

---

[60] *PAH*, 15: 85–86.
[61] *PAH*, 15: 85.
[62] *PAH*, 15: 86.

victories of the Continental Army, however, showed that there was a real possibility that the Americans would make good their claim to independence. These victories "established" France's "confidence" in America's ability to achieve its aims and thereby "produced the treaties of alliance and commerce." For Hamilton, it was "impossible" to see in this line of French policy "anything more" than the behavior of a political rival of Great Britain, seizing "a most promising opportunity to repress the pride and diminish the dangerous power" of that "rival by seconding a successful resistance to its authority, and by lopping off a valuable portion of its dominions." The separation of America from Great Britain "was an obvious and a very important" French "interest," and it was therefore not to be doubted that this interest "was both the determining motive, and an adequate compensation" for the aid France had given America.[63]

Indeed, Hamilton continued, sensible Americans at the time had understood French assistance to be the product not of benevolence but of a confluence of French and American interests. Expectations of French and Spanish aid had been "bottomed" on "the known competition between those powers" and Britain and on "their evident interest to reduce her power and circumscribe her empire," and not on the belief that those countries had any disinterested "regard" for or "attachment" to America and American interests. Anyone who had put forward the latter motives "as the grounds" on which to expect French and Spanish help "would have been justly considered as a visionary, or a deceiver," and anyone at the present time who attributed "such motives" to France and Spain "would not deserve to be viewed in a better light." Hamilton therefore concluded that such help as America had received was not an act of disinterested benevolence and therefore was no basis on which to found the "enthusiastic gratitude" that was demanded by "those *who love France more than the United States.*"[64]

None of this was to deny, Hamilton hastened to add, that America owed France her "*good will.*" In truth, France had treated America well. She had not tried to take "advantage of" America's situation to "extort" any "humiliating or injurious concessions." French conduct was "certainly dictated by policy," yet "it was an honorable and magnanimous policy." It was to that extent entitled to the "approbation and esteem of mankind," as well as to "the friendship and acknowledgment" of the nation that had been benefitted. These "sentiments," however, would be properly "satisfied" by America's "sincere good wishes for the happiness" of France and her "cordial disposition to *render all good and friendly offices*" that could "*be rendered without prejudice*" to America's "*own solid and permanent interests.*" To go any further – to ask America "to make a sacrifice of substantial interest; to expose itself to the jealousy, ill will, or resentment of the rest of the world; to hazard in an eminent degree its

[63] *PAH*, 15: 90–91.
[64] *PAH*, 15: 91 (Hamilton's emphasis).

own safety, for the benefit" of France – was, Hamilton insisted, "to ask more than the nature of the case demands, more than the fundamental maxims of society authorize," and "more than the dictates of sound reason justify."[65]

As his turn as Pacificus drew to a close, Hamilton added two more arguments on the question of gratitude, arguments that conditionally admitted its role in foreign policy but then tried to show that the circumstances between the United States and France could not bring it into play. In the first place, he observed that if gratitude were due for the French assistance rendered during the revolution, it would seem to be due to the king and not to the nation itself. Louis's authority at the time was such that he and he alone had made the decision of whether or not to support America in its aspirations. "It belonged to him to assist us or not, without consulting the nation; and he did assist us, without such consultation." Therefore, "if there was any kindness" in the decision that called for "a return of kindness from us, it was the kindness of Louis XVI – his heart was the depository of the sentiment."[66]

Here, Hamilton might appear to contradict himself. Had he not denied the importance of gratitude in foreign policy in order to avoid an obligation to the French nation, and then gone on to admit the role of gratitude in foreign policy in order to claim that such an obligation must exist in relation to the former king of France and not to the people who had overthrown him? In other words, was he consistent in aim only – the aim being to deny any obligation to the present French government – while making use of contradictory arguments to enforce his basic claim?

Hamilton might repel such a charge of inconsistency by noting that this last argument was hypothetical in character: *if* gratitude plays a role in international politics, then we owe gratitude to Louis and not to the French revolutionaries. Hamilton's subsequent argument in *Pacificus* VI, however, provides further grounds on which to conclude that the inconsistency suspected here is more apparent than real. Hamilton's argument against gratitude in foreign policy was not, after all, an argument against *any* feelings of good will toward foreign nations. On the contrary, Hamilton admitted that governments and nations sometimes performed acts of benevolence within the bounds appointed by their own self-interest, and that it was natural and just to return the good will expressed in such acts. Most accurately understood, then, his argument was not against gratitude but against a self-sacrificing gratitude, one that would subordinate the nation's interests to a supposed duty to repay benefactions performed by a foreign government. While Hamilton indicated – both in *Pacificus* and in his opinion on the French Treaties – that America owed something to Louis XVI for the support he had provided for the revolution, he never argued that it owed him anything contrary to American interests. Thus, in his opinion on the French Treaties, he merely argued that America should not seek

---

[65] *PAH*, 15: 92 (Hamilton's emphasis).
[66] *PAH*, 15: 93 (Hamilton's emphasis).

gratuitously to align herself with Louis's enemies when such an alignment was also dangerous to America. Similarly, in *Pacificus*, he merely suggested that America's sense of obligation to Louis should lead it to stay out of a contest between his former subjects and his heir. A "just estimate" of the requirements of "gratitude" in relation to France, he suggested, would lead us to conclude "that we ought not to take part against the son and successor of a father, on whose *sole will* depended the assistance" that America had received in its own struggle for independence, and at the same time we ought not take part with that son "against the nation whose blood and whose treasure had been, in the hands of the father, the means of" that "assistance."[67]

Finally, Hamilton argued that even if one conceded the existence of some debt of gratitude to France, the great difference in the relevant situations – the American Revolution and the present war – strictly limited the reach of that gratitude. France had aided America as a "great and powerful nation" with ample force to meet any dangers it might incur in doing so. The general disposition of Europe was in favor of the American cause, so that Britain was alone in the struggle and likely to remain alone, and France had a "great and persuasive interest" in separating Britain from her colonies. In stark contrast, France at present was at war alone with "the greatest part of Europe." Moreover, her "internal affairs" were "in serious disorder." For its part, America was a young and comparatively weak nation with no "direct interest in going to war" and the "strongest motives of interest to avoid it." In sum, France took part in America's struggle "with *much to hope* and *not much to fear*," whereas America would have "incomparably more to apprehend than to hope" from being allied with France in the current war. "This contrast of situations and inducements," Hamilton concluded, "is alone a conclusive demonstration, that the United States are not under an obligation from gratitude to join France in the war." The total "disparity between the circumstances of the service *to be rendered*, and of the *service received*, proves, that the one cannot be an adequate basis of obligation for the other. There would be a want of equality and consequently of reciprocity."[68]

Conclusion

Hamilton thought and wrote well under the pressure of crisis. Two of his greatest productions – his contributions to the *Federalist* and his *Opinion on the Constitutionality of a National Bank* – had been written in support of crucial public measures whose fate was hanging in the balance. He rose to the occasion once again as Pacificus, and in later years he remained pleased with his work. As his biographer Ron Chernow notes, Hamilton had his *Pacificus* essays "incorporated...into an 1802 edition of *The Federalist*, proudly telling

[67] *PAH*, 15: 102.
[68] *PAH*, 15: 103 (Hamilton's emphasis).

the publisher that 'some of his friends had pronounced them to be his best performance.'"[69]

However definitively Hamilton had tried to answer the neutrality proclamation's critics, he did not succeed in putting an end to the argument. He rather provided material for further disputation. The *Pacificus* essays advanced ideas that Thomas Jefferson regarded as politically heretical and in need of a strong public correction, which he implored James Madison to provide. Thus was born Madison's *Helvidius* series, which is examined in the next chapter.

[69] Chernow, *Alexander Hamilton*, 442.

15

Jefferson, Madison, and Helvidius' Critique of Pacificus

Hamilton's turn as Pacificus provoked a spirited rejoinder in the form of five essays published under the name of Helvidius. Today, the Pacificus-Helvidius exchange is still taken as one of the great debates of the founding era and certainly as the great post-ratification debate over the scope of the executive power, especially in relation to foreign policy. A study of Hamilton's account of these issues in his *Pacificus* series is, it would seem, incomplete without an examination of Helvidius' response.

Here, however, we encounter an apparent problem. James Madison, not Thomas Jefferson, penned the *Helvidius* essays. How, then, does an examination of Helvidius' arguments fit into a study of the debates between Hamilton and Jefferson? This difficulty is more apparent than real, for while Jefferson did not write the *Helvidius* essays, he was certainly involved in their production. Moreover, it is fair to say that they represent, at least in an approximate way, his own view of the issues at stake.

Jefferson did not write the *Helvidius* essays, but he induced Madison to write them. After the first *Pacificus* paper appeared, Jefferson wrote to Madison calling it to his attention and expressing his concern that Hamilton's "heresies . . . should pass unnoticed and unanswered" – or at least that they would get no adequate answer. "For," as he observed to Madison, "none but mere bunglers and brawlers have for some time taken the trouble to answer any thing."[1]

Needless to say, Jefferson did not regard Madison as a mere bungler or brawler. It is therefore not surprising that he shortly struck upon the idea that Madison himself was the very man to take up the task of refuting Hamilton's Pacificus. Thus, after the second and third *Pacificus* essays appeared, Jefferson wrote to Madison with greater urgency, famously imploring him: "For god's sake, my dear sir, take up your pen, select the most striking heresies, and cut

[1] *PTJ*, 26: 403–04.

him to pieces in the face of the public. There is nobody else who can and will enter the lists with him."[2] Madison reluctantly agreed.[3]

Jefferson did more than just plant the seed of the *Helvidius* papers in Madison's mind. He consulted with his fellow Virginian on the project from beginning to end. As Madison began his "notes toward a discussion" of the *Pacificus* series, he asked Jefferson to provide him with information useful with a view to framing his counter-arguments, including information about the cabinet's deliberations, the president's views, and communications from foreign governments.[4] Jefferson complied with these requests to the extent that he thought appropriate.[5] Madison, indeed, sought not only information but advice from Jefferson. Before publishing the *Helvidius* essays he showed them to Jefferson, seeking his guidance about points that might require revision.[6]

Moreover, Jefferson clearly shared the basic position that Madison defended in the *Helvidius* series: that Hamilton had as Pacificus read the executive power too expansively. To be sure, Jefferson could be a spirited defender of the executive power as he understood it. To this extent he surely did not reject every claim that Pacificus had made on behalf of the presidency. In the spring of 1790, for example, Washington had sought Jefferson's counsel on whether the Senate had the right to reject the grade or rank that the president might assign to a representative of the United States to a foreign country. In his written opinion prepared for Washington, Jefferson held that the Senate had authority only to reject the person the president might nominate, and that any attempt on its part to reject the rank – to say, for example, that a particular nominee should be only a consul and not an ambassador – would carry it beyond the limits of its constitutional authority. Jefferson here affirmed some points that Hamilton would later make as Pacificus. The secretary of state based his claim about the limits of the Senate's power in this area on the observation that the "transaction of business with foreign nations is executive altogether" and that it "belongs then to the head of that department, *except* as to such portions of it as are specially submitted to the Senate." Jefferson then went on to make

---

[2] *PTJ*, 26: 444.

[3] *PTJ*, 26: 549. These origins indicate the inaccuracy of the commonplace suggestion that the *Helvidius* papers were intended as an attack on Washington's proclamation. They were rather intended as an attack on Hamilton's argument as Pacificus, which in turn was provoked by attacks on the proclamation. See, for example, Harvey Mansfield, *Taming the Prince: The Ambivalence of Modern Executive Power* (New York: The Free Press, 1989), 275–76; and Chernow, *Alexander Hamilton*, 443. Madison did have objections to the proclamation itself. See Tucker and Hendrickson, *Empire of Liberty*, 52. He did not voice these, however, in the *Helvidius* essays.

[4] *PTJ*, 26: 549 and 585.

[5] See his letter to Madison of August 3, 1793. Regarding Madison's request for information about what "concessions" had "been made on particular points behind the curtain," Jefferson replied, "I think it is better you should not know them." *PTJ*, 26: 606.

[6] See Madison's letters to Jefferson of August 20 and 22, 1793, and Jefferson's letter to Madison of September 8, 1793. *PTJ*, 26: 729 and 741, and Volume 27, 61.

the exact same point about such exceptions as Hamilton would later make as Pacificus: that they were "to be construed strictly."[7] The Senate, then, could claim no power in relation to the country's business with foreign nations except what was explicitly assigned to it by the Constitution.[8]

Nevertheless, Jefferson's thinking on this question also foreshadowed his later conflict with Hamilton. One might try to reason from the passages noted above to something like the position defended by Hamilton as Pacificus. Jefferson had admitted that the "transaction of business with foreign nations is executive altogether" and that exceptions to it were to be construed "strictly." Surely, one might then continue, treaties are a form of business transacted with foreign nations and therefore belong primarily to the executive power. Since exceptions from that power are to be construed strictly, the Senate's authority to ratify treaties implies no further power beyond itself, such that the interpretation of treaty obligations remains with the president. This, however, was not how Jefferson saw the matter. Instead, in a later effort to grapple with the problem of the Senate's claim of a power to reject the grade assigned to foreign ministers, Jefferson embraced the position that would later be defended by Helvidius. In January 1792, Jefferson prepared a draft of a possible presidential message to the Senate. After objecting to any Senate pretensions to reject the grade of the president's nominees for foreign missions, Jefferson added a passage noting that "nothing" in the message was "meant to question" the Senate's "right to concur in making treaties: this being considered not as a branch of executive but of legislative powers, placed by the constitution under peculiar modifications."[9] Jefferson, it would seem, already held the position that Helvidius would later defend, that the treaty power was legislative and not executive in its character.

Jefferson's differences with Hamilton's understanding of the executive power were also evident in his letters to Madison as the neutrality crisis developed. In late March, before the cabinet had met to deliberate about America's posture toward the warring powers, Jefferson opened his mind to his fellow Virginian regarding the proper line of policy, and in so doing also revealed his thinking about the executive's role in the decision of whether or not to go to war. If the naval powers at war with France were to "prohibit supplies even of provisions to that country," he wrote, then he supposed that Congress would

---

[7] *PTJ*, 16: 378 (Jefferson's emphasis). In an editorial note, the editors of Jefferson's papers indicate that Washington also sought advice on this question from James Madison and John Jay, both of whom agreed with Jefferson's position. *PTJ*, 16: 380.

[8] In later years, Hamilton noted that Jefferson was in his own way a defender of a robust executive authority: "It is a fact which I have frequently mentioned, that while we were in the administration together, he [Jefferson] was generally for a large construction of the executive authority and not backward to act upon it in cases which coincided with his own views." Quoted in Gary J. Schmitt, "Jefferson and Executive Power: Revisionism and the 'Revolution of 1800,'" *Publius* 17 (1987): 11.

[9] *PTJ*, 23: 18.

be called, because such conduct would constitute "a justifiable cause of war." The proper executive response to such foreign conduct, he suggested, was to summon Congress, because "as the executive cannot decide the question of war on the affirmative side, neither ought it to do so on the negative side by preventing the competent body from deliberating on the question."[10] Jefferson's reasoning here in effect construed the executive's role in the war power strictly and thus implied that this power is legislative in its character.

In light of these statements, it is not surprising that later that summer Jefferson denounced as heretical Hamilton's suggestion that the president could prejudge the question of war or peace for Congress by making a declaration of neutrality that amounted to an official interpretation of the nation's treaty obligations. In his letter to Madison about the first *Pacificus* paper, Jefferson objected to "three heresies" in particular that Hamilton had advanced in the cabinet and that he was now proclaiming in the public prints. Hamilton, in the first place, asserted the "right of the *executive* to declare that we are *not bound to execute the guarantee*" of the treaty of alliance with France. Hamilton had also held that while the Congress had a right to judge whether or not the country was obliged to make war, this did not exclude a similar right of judgment of the executive in the exercise of its own functions. Finally, Hamilton had claimed that the treaties could be considered as suspended until the new government of France was recognized. Jefferson had resisted all of these claims during the cabinet debate. The executive, he had argued, "had no authority to issue a declaration of neutrality, nor to do more than declare the actual state of things to be that of peace." In other words, for Jefferson the president could not rightly declare, in the sense of deciding, that the country's posture was one of neutrality but could only affirm that the country was in fact at peace because Congress had not acted to take it to war. An executive declaration of neutrality, he suggested to Madison, was objectionable because it would "respect the future" or would prejudge the issue in conflict with Congress's right to decide it at the proper time. As far as one could tell from the cabinet deliberations, Jefferson suggested, nobody but Hamilton intended the executive proclamation as an authoritative interpretation of the treaties, and Jefferson had understood his objections to such an apparent exercise of executive authority to have been accommodated by the cabinet's agreement to not to use the term "neutrality" in the proclamation.[11]

---

[10] *PTJ*, 25: 442. Although Jefferson here hoped Congress's right to deliberate the question of war or peace would be respected, he did not in fact want Congress to declare war. He instead hoped that Congress would adopt a policy of commercial punishment of the nations that committed the "aggression" of cutting France off from American provisions. This line of conduct, he told Madison, would "furnish us a happy opportunity of setting another precious example to the world, by showing that nations may be brought to do justice by appeals to their interests as well as be appeals to arms."

[11] *PTJ*, 26: 403 (Jefferson's emphases). Although Jefferson had succeeded in dissuading the president from using the word "neutrality" in the proclamation, and although his complaint was

In view of all these considerations, it is reasonable to consider Madison's *Helvidius* papers as a kind of explication of the Jeffersonian understanding of the errors of Pacificus, and hence of the true understanding of the executive power's role in war and foreign policy. Jefferson encouraged the project from beginning to end, and his first letter to Madison about Pacificus laid down the outline of the critique of Hamilton that Madison would develop in detail as Helvidius.[12] We may turn now to that detailed critique.

Helvidius I

Madison's rhetoric in the introductory passages of the first *Helvidius* paper showed that the collapse of respect and goodwill between the Hamiltonian and Jeffersonian parties so evident in 1792 had only been worsened by the foreign policy developments of 1793. Hamilton's performance as Pacificus, Madison suggested, was both noxious and dishonest. The *Pacificus* series, he indicated, was of such a character that it had been received with "singular pleasure and applause" primarily by "the foreigners and degenerate citizens among us, who hate our republican government and the French revolution."[13] One might expect that so flagrant a performance would pose no danger of corrupting or confusing public opinion. Unfortunately, however, this was not the case. The doctrines of Pacificus, Madison contended, surely would have been "rejected by the feelings of every heart" if they had been "nakedly presented to the public." Hamilton, however, had cleverly "disguise[d]" these doctrines

---

therefore primarily with Hamilton's presentation of the proclamation rather than with the proclamation itself, Jefferson did register some dissatisfaction with the wording of the president's statement. The proclamation's "declaration of the *disposition*" of the United States to follow a friendly and impartial line of conduct toward the warring powers was, Jefferson told Madison, "certainly officious and improper," although it could "hardly be called illegal." Jefferson gave a similar account of these issues regarding the proclamation in another letter to Madison of August 11, 1793. *PTJ*, 26: 649–50.

[12] It is clear from their correspondence about the *Helvidius* series that Jefferson and Madison's quarrel with Hamilton went beyond his presentation of the executive power. Jefferson's alarmed call for Madison to take up his pen in opposition to Hamilton came in a letter noting the appearance of the second and third *Pacificus* papers, in which Hamilton moved beyond the question of executive authority and launched his actual interpretation of the French treaties, as well as his argument that the war was offensive on the part of France. In his letters, Madison indicated an intention to respond to Hamilton's arguments on these questions and to his argument about the role of gratitude in the conduct of nations. In the end, however, Madison confined the *Helvidius* series to the questions of executive power that Hamilton had raised. He seems to have given up the more extensive critique in part because of a lack of time and in part because of his sense of the delicacy of the issues. See *The Papers of Thomas Jefferson*, Volume 26, 403, 443, and 585, and Volume 27, 16.

[13] Madison later regretted the tone he had taken as Helvidius, judging it to have been "of no advantage either to the subject or to the author." Quoted in Lance Banning, *The Sacred Fire of Liberty: James Madison and the Founding of the Federal Republic* (Ithaca, NY: Cornell University Press, 1995), 377.

"in the dress of an elaborate dissertation" and had "mingled" with them some truths, as well as "professions of anxiety for the preservation of peace, for the welfare of the government, and for the respect due" to the president. As a result, the friends of republicanism had paid insufficient attention to Pacificus's dangerous principles, and there was some peril that the clever presentation might ensnare some readers. Madison had therefore taken up the task of a careful examination of the first *Pacificus* entry in order to show that, "under color of vindicating an important public act" of a beloved "chief magistrate," Hamilton had put forward "principles...which strike at the vitals" of the country's "constitution."[14]

Madison began by summarizing the Hamiltonian arguments he intended to confute. "The substance of the first" *Pacificus* essay could be stated as follows. The "powers of declaring war and making treaties are in their nature executive powers." Accordingly, to the extent that the Constitution vested these powers in other departments, these assignments of authority were "to be considered as exceptions out of the general grant to the executive department" and were to be "construed strictly," so that any powers not included in those specific grants were understood to "remain with the executive." Moreover, since the executive was "the organ of intercourse with foreign nations, and the interpreter and executor of treaties," it was "authorized to expound all articles of treaties," including "those involving questions of war and peace," and thus "to judge of the obligations of the United States to make war or not, under any casus federis or eventual operation of the contract relating to war," and to "pronounce the state of things resulting from the obligations of the United States, as understood by the executive." From these more general propositions, Hamilton had concluded that "the executive had authority to judge" whether the United States was bound, by the mutual guarantee with France, to "engage" in the present war, and that the executive had in fact decided there was no such obligation and had expressed that decision in the neutrality proclamation.[15]

The foundation of this chain of reasoning, Madison contended, was the claim that the war power and treaty power were "in their nature executive" and were "therefore comprehended in the general grant of executive power" where they were "not especially and strictly excepted out of the grant"[16] – a "doctrine" that Madison found so "extraordinary" and "extravagant" that it

---

[14] James Madison, *The Papers of James Madison*, ed. Thomas A. Mason, Robert A. Rutland, and Jeanne K. Sisson, Volume 15 (Charlottesville: University Press of Virginia, 1985), 66. In subsequent citations, Madison's papers will be abbreviated as *PJM*, followed by the volume and page numbers.

[15] *PJM*, 15: 67.

[16] As Madison's formulation makes clear, his quarrel was with Hamilton's presentation of the theoretical nature of the executive power, the constitutional consequences that Hamilton drew from it, and the further dangerous consequences that Madison saw as following from Hamilton's position. Contrary to Hamilton's biographer Jacob E. Cooke, Madison did not as Helvidius accuse Hamilton of "claim[ing] that the president possessed inherent powers to unilaterally

was hard to believe that it had been publicly "hazarded at so early a day in the face of the public." Madison proposed to "examine this doctrine" in the light of three standards. Any "countenance" that could be found for Hamilton's position, he contended, would have to be discovered either in authoritative writers "on public law," in "the quality and operation of the powers to make war and treaties," or "in the constitution of the United States."[17]

Madison turned first to the authoritative writers on public law, although even as he did so he admitted that he thought it "of little use to enter far" into their understanding of the question at hand. He suggested instead that "our own reason and our own Constitution" would be "the best guides." Moreover, he frankly doubted whether "the most received jurists" had been in a position to understand separation of powers accurately. A "just analysis and discrimination of the powers of government, according to their executive, legislative, and judicial qualities" was not, Madison said, "to be expected" in the works of men who had written "before a critical attention was paid to those objects" and who had had "their eyes too much on monarchical governments, where all powers are confounded in the sovereignty of the prince." Despite these limitations, however, Madison found that these writers – and "particularly Wolfius, Burlamaqui, and Vattel" – had at least spoken "of the powers to declare war, to conclude peace, and to form alliances as among the highest acts of sovereignty." Madison suggested that even this much, however, seemed to undermine Hamilton's position. Madison noted that "the legislative power must at least be an integral and preeminent part" of the sovereignty.[18] He thus implied that, contrary to Hamilton's assertion, the war and treaty powers could not be exclusively executive in their character, according to the implications of the thinking of these old writers on public law.

One might expect something more promising from writers like Locke and Montesquieu, since they had addressed themselves "more particularly" to "the principles of liberty and the structure of government." Yet Madison contended that even they were inadequate, for they, too, had labored "under the same disadvantage, of having written before these subjects" had been "illuminated by the events and discussions" of "a very recent period." Moreover, the thinking of both had been "evidently warped by" their "regard to the particular government of England, to which" Locke "owed allegiance" and for which Montesquieu "professed an admiration bordering on idolatry." Madison did not bother to examine Montesquieu on the question at hand, noting that the Frenchman had "distinguished himself" more by developing the reasons for

---

make treaties and wars." Hamilton had made no such claims, which would have flatly contradicted the text of the Constitution. Madison rather feared that such consequences could eventually follow from an uncritical acceptance of Hamilton principles. Jacob Ernest Cooke, *Alexander Hamilton* (New York: Charles Scribner's Sons, 1982), 129.

[17] *PJM*, 15: 67–68.
[18] *PJM*, 15: 68.

and importance of separation of powers than by "enumerating and defining the powers which" properly belonged "to each particular" department of government. In Locke, Madison found some glimmer of support for his critique of Hamilton, although it was obscured by errors arising from Locke's excessive attachment to political institutions of his own place and time. Despite the disadvantages of the "early date of his work on civil government, and the example of his own government before his eyes," Locke was able to discern that the powers in question – which Locke called "*federative*" powers – were in fact "*distinct*" from the "*executive*" power. Madison found here only limited support for his own view, however, because Locke had gone on to hold that these powers, though distinct from the executive power, were nevertheless "almost always united with it, and *hardly to be separated into distinct hands.*" Again, Madison attributed this error to Locke's supposed inability to think beyond the confines of his own regime and time. "Had he not lived under a monarchy, in which these powers were united; or had he written by the lamp which truth now presents to lawgivers," Madison held, this "last observation would probably never have dropped from his pen." Similarly, in a footnote, Madison added that Locke's "chapter on the prerogative" demonstrated "how much the reason of the philosopher was clouded by the royalism of the Englishman."[19]

Madison had, it would seem, gained very little of use to his argument from his examination of the authoritative writers on public law. He had tried to suggest that the thought of Wolfius, Burlamaqui, and Vattel implicitly supported his view by pointing out that they held that the war and treaty power were "among the highest acts of sovereignty," and he then added his own observation that the legislative power must be "an integral and preeminent part" of the sovereign power. Nothing helpful to his position necessarily followed from these observations, however. A given action could be among the highest acts of sovereignty and still not be part of the legislative power, even if the legislative power was itself an important part of the sovereignty. Moreover, his examination of Montesquieu and Locke tended, if anything, to support Hamilton's position. Montesquieu had praised the British government as free, despite the fact that at the time he examined it the war power and the treaty power had belonged to the monarch. And Locke had treated the foreign policy powers as conceptually different from the executive power but almost always in practice united to it. In view of the respectability of these sources, it would seem that even if Hamilton had erred, Madison had little ground on which to accuse him of having put forward an "extraordinary" or "extravagant" doctrine.

Concluding that an investigation of the respected writers on public law was "more likely to perplex" than to "decide" the question at hand, Madison then turned to the second standard by which he proposed to judge Hamilton's argument: "the nature and operation of the two powers to declare war and

---

[19] *PJM*, 15: 68 (Madison's emphasis).

to make treaties." Here, he indicated, the issue could be brought to "tests of which it will prove more easy to judge." The "nature and operation" of these powers, Madison contended, showed that they could "never fall within a proper definition of executive powers." The executive's "natural province" was "to execute laws," just as the legislature's was "to make laws." Accordingly, all of the executive's acts that were themselves "properly executive" in their character had to "pre-suppose the existence of laws to be executed." Neither the treaty power nor the war power, however, could be understood as properly executive acts on this understanding of things. "A treaty," Madison observed, was "not an execution of laws" and did "not presuppose the existence of laws." On the contrary, a treaty had the "force of a law" and was "to be carried into *execution*, like all *other laws*, by the *executive magistrate*." To hold, as Hamilton had, that "the power of making treaties, which are confessedly laws, belongs to the" executive "department" was to say "that the executive department naturally includes a legislative power." This, Madison declared, was "an absurdity" in "theory" and "a tyranny" in "practice." "The power to declare war," he continued, was "subject to similar reasoning." A declaration of war was "not an execution of laws," did not "suppose preexisting laws to be executed," and was "not, in any respect, an act merely executive." It was instead "one of the most deliberative acts" that could "be performed," and "when performed" it had "the effect of *repealing* all the *laws* operating in a state of peace, so far as they are inconsistent with a state of war" and at the same time of "*enacting*, as a *rule for the executive*, a *new code* adapted to the relation between the society and its foreign enemy." Similarly, Madison observed, "a conclusion of peace *annuls* all the *laws* peculiar to a state of war, and *revives* the general *laws* incident to a state of peace." In addition, Madison observed, treaties in general, but especially "treaties of peace," sometimes not only changed "the external laws of the society" but also operated "on the internal code" of the nation, which was "purely municipal, and to which the legislative authority of the country is of itself competent and complete."[20]

None of this was to say, Madison noted, that the executive had no role whatsoever in these matters. The executive was a "convenient organ of preliminary communications with foreign governments" on matters pertaining to war and treaties, as well as the "proper agent for carrying into execution the final determinations of the competent authority" on these questions. Nevertheless, Madison added, it was "evident" from the previous chain of reasoning comparing the "nature" of the treaty and war powers to the "nature of the executive trust," that the executive could "have no pretensions" to the "essential agency" that could give "validity to such determinations." In other words, the substantive question of whether to go to war or whether to enter into a treaty was a legislative one and not an executive one.[21]

[20] *PJM*, 15: 69 (Madison's emphasis).
[21] *PJM*, 15: 69.

Madison also conceded the possibility of ambiguity on these questions, although not so much as to conclude the question in Hamilton's favor. Perhaps, he suggested, the war and treaty powers might not be "purely legislative" in their "nature." Nevertheless, they partook so much more of the legislative character than of any other "that under a constitution leaving them to result to their most natural department, the legislature would be without a rival in its claim." And if the war and treaty powers were "substantially of a legislative" and "not an executive nature," then the "rule of interpreting exceptions strictly must narrow, instead of enlarging, executive pretensions on those subjects."[22]

Finally, Madison turned to the third standard by which to judge the character of the war and treaty powers: the Constitution of the United States. Since the instrument contained no explicit statement on the issue, Madison's inquiry turned to whether Hamilton's understanding could be fairly inferred from the Constitution. Here, Madison advanced two lines of argument. The first examined whether the "actual distribution of powers among the several branches of the government" supported Hamilton's claim that the war and treaty powers were executive in their nature. Madison observed that the Constitution "expressly vested" the power to declare war in the Congress, "where every other legislative power" was "declared to be vested." To this extent, the Constitution "clearly" indicated that the war power "is of a legislative, and not an executive nature."[23]

"This conclusion" became "irresistible," Madison added, when one recalled the theory of separation of powers that had informed both the making of the Constitution and the debate over its ratification. One could not reasonably suppose that the Constitution had placed "any power legislative in its nature entirely among" the "executive powers," or, alternatively, "any power executive in its nature entirely among" the "legislative powers." Such a supposition was inadmissible, Madison argued, because it implicitly charged the Constitution "with that kind of intermixture and consolidation of different powers which would violate a fundamental principle in the organization of free governments." Any such intermixture, he added, had been denied both when the Constitution was "originally vindicated" and in its subsequent exposition.[24]

The constitutional distribution of authority did not so straightforwardly settle the question of the nature of the treaty power, which was "vested jointly" in the executive and in one branch of the legislature, the Senate. "From this arrangement merely" no solid inference could be drawn that "would necessarily exclude the power from the executive class." Nevertheless, Madison found "sufficient indications" elsewhere that the Constitution "regarded" the treaty

[22] *PJM*, 15: 69.
[23] *PJM*, 15: 70.
[24] *PJM*, 15: 70.

power as "materially different from mere executive power, and as having more affinity to the legislative than to the executive character." He first appealed to the constitutional procedure by which the Senate gave its consent to treaties. "In all other cases," he noted, "the consent of the body is expressed by a majority of voices," but for treaties the Constitution required ratification by a two-thirds vote. This supermajority requirement, he held, was intended "as a substitute or compensation for the other branch of the legislature, which, on certain occasions, could not be conveniently a party to the transaction." Be that as it may, Madison held that the "conclusive circumstance" indicating the legislative nature of the treaty power was that treaties were admitted "to have the force and operation of *laws*," were as much as any other laws "to be a rule for the courts in controversies between man and man," and were even "emphatically declared by the constitution to be 'the supreme law of the land.'"[25]

Having found the constitutional distribution of powers to be "precisely in opposition" to Hamilton's "doctrine," Madison next turned to a second line of argument regarding the Constitution. Here he asked whether there was "any fair analogy between the powers of war and treaty," on the one hand, and the "enumerated powers vested in the executive alone," on the other.[26] In other words, could any of the powers explicitly vested in the president imply that the war and treaty powers were executive in their nature? Some of these powers – such as the power to make recess appointments – Madison passed over as obviously irrelevant to the present inquiry. Among those that might possibly lend support to Hamilton's view, he began with the president's power as commander-in-chief. This power had "no relation worth examining" to the "general power of making treaties." Moreover, it was not only not "analogous to the power of declaring war," it in fact "afforded a striking illustration of the incompatibility of the two powers in the same hands." "Those who are to *conduct a war*," Madison contended, "cannot in the nature of things, be proper or safe judges whether *a war ought* to be *commenced, continued*, or *concluded*. They are barred from the latter functions by a great principle in free government, analogous to that which separates the sword from the purse, or the power of executing from the power of enacting laws."[27]

Madison turned next to the constitutional requirement that the president "take care that the laws shall be faithfully executed." Seeing to the faithful execution of the laws, Madison commented, is "the essence of the executive authority," but it had no just relation to the "power of making treaties and war, that is, of determining what the *laws shall be* with regard to other nations." These powers, he suggested, were utterly distinct in their character – executive on the one hand and legislative on the other. Accordingly, the relevant principle,

[25] *PJM*, 15: 70–71.
[26] *PJM*, 15: 70.
[27] *PJM*, 15: 71 (Madison's emphasis)

one which "forbids a coalition of the powers in the same department," actually worked against Hamilton's claim.[28]

Finally, Madison inquired into the consequences of an already-acknowledged implied power of the presidency: "the power of removal from office," which had been "adjudged to the president by the laws establishing the executive departments." Pacificus had attempted to "press" this power "into his service," but Madison denied that it could lend any real support to Hamilton's position. Any "inference" from this power "favorable" to Hamilton's argument would require showing that "the powers of war and treaties are of a kindred nature to the power of removal, or at least are equally within a grant of executive power." Nothing of this kind had been attempted or probably would be attempted, Madison observed. "Nothing" could "in truth be clearer," he averred, "than that no analogy or shade of analogy" could "be traced between a power in the supreme officer responsible for the faithful execution of the laws to displace a subaltern officer employed in the execution of the laws, and a power to make treaties, and to declare war, such as these have been found to be in their nature, their operation, and their consequences."[29]

Madison concluded *Helvidius* I by pivoting to the offensive. Since Hamilton's understanding was not supported by the respected writers on public law, by the nature of the powers in question, or by the Constitution, Madison wondered from where he could have "borrowed it." There was, he held, "but one answer to this question. The power of making treaties and the power of declaring war, are *royal prerogatives* in the *British government*, and are accordingly treated as *executive prerogatives* by *British commentators*." Madison thus found in *Pacificus* further evidence in support of his and Jefferson's fear that Hamilton was a monarchist at heart and that he was determined to interpret the Constitution in such a way as to transform it into a government on the British model.[30]

The "necessity" of this conclusion was "confirmed," Madison suggested, by turning to the period when the Constitution was being debated before the public and "satisfying ourselves" that Pacificus could not have derived his understanding of the war and treaty powers from "our own commentators on our own government." Madison contented himself with a single example, one that was chosen to emphasize Hamilton's inconsistency, and perhaps even his neglect of constitutional faith in defending the document in one way when it was being debated and then interpreting it in another in the course of its implementation: *Federalist* 75, which had been written by Hamilton himself. Hamilton had written as follows:

Though several writers on the subject of government place that power [*of making treaties*] in the class of *executive authorities*, yet this is *evidently* an *arbitrary disposition*.

[28] *PJM*, 15: 71–72 (Madison's emphasis).
[29] *PJM*, 15: 72.
[30] *PJM*, 15: 72 (Madison's emphasis).

For if we attend *carefully* to its operation, it will be found to partake *more* of the *legislative* than of the *executive* character, though it does not seem strictly to fall within the definition of either of them. The essence of the legislative authority is to enact laws; or, in other words, to prescribe rules for the regulation of the society: while the execution of the laws and the employment of the common strength, either for this purpose, or for the common defense, seem to comprise *all* the functions of the *executive magistrate*. The power of making treaties is *plainly* neither the one nor the other. It relates neither to the execution of subsisting laws, nor to the enaction of new ones, and still less to an exertion of the common strength. Its objects are contracts with foreign nations, which have the *force of law*, but derive it from the obligations of good faith. They are not rules prescribed by the sovereign to the subject, but agreements between sovereign and sovereign. The power in question seems therefore to form a distinct department, and to belong properly neither to the legislative nor to the executive. The qualities elsewhere detailed as indispensable in the management of foreign *negotiations*, point out the executive as the most fit agent in those transactions; while the vast importance of the trust, and the operation of treaties *as laws*, plead strongly for the participation of the whole or a part of the *legislative body*, in the office of making them.[31]

This passage was of limited but nonetheless real use in Madison's attempt to show Hamilton's inconsistency and his departure from American principles. Hamilton here as Publius had said nothing at all about the character of the war power, and neither had he admitted that the treaty power was legislative in its character. Still, Madison pressed with some justification that any discussion of the war power had surely been omitted because it had been "arranged with such obvious propriety among the legislative powers" and that Hamilton had denied that the treaty power was executive in its nature, contrary to what he was now contending as Pacificus.[32]

Helvidius II

In the second *Helvidius* paper, Madison moved to an examination of the "inferences and consequences" of the constitutional positions Hamilton had defended as Pacificus. These implications, Madison held, posed a dire threat

---

[31] *PJM*, 15: 73 (Madison's emphases).

[32] *PJM*, 15: 73. Madison laid such emphasis on Hamilton's departures from his earlier presentations of constitutional powers because Madison viewed them as abuses not only of the constitution but also of the spirit of republicanism. Hamilton, Madison believed, was interpreting the Constitution in a sense different from that which had been held by the public that consented to it, and, as Colleen Sheehan observes, for Madison this procedure "struck at the very philosophical basis of republican government." "Madison v. Hamilton: The Battle over Republicanism and the Role of Public Opinion," *American Political Science Review* 98 (2004): 414. In later life, Madison continued to hold that Hamilton had tried "to administer the government . . . into what he thought it ought to be; while I, on my part, I endeavored to make it conform to the Constitution as understood by the Convention that produced and recommended it, and particularly by the state conventions that adopted it." Quoted in Stephen F. Knott, *Alexander Hamilton and the Persistence of Myth* (Lawrence: University Press of Kansas, 2002), 12.

to the Constitution, both as it sought to establish free government and as it sought to establish self-government. "No ramparts in the constitution," he claimed, "could defend the public liberty, or scarcely the forms of republican government," if Hamilton's principles were embraced. Hamilton, again, had held that the treaty and war powers were executive in nature and that "so far as they are not by strict construction transferred to the legislature, they actually belong to the executive." From this it followed, according to Madison, that all other powers that were "not less executive in their nature" than the treaty and war powers could also be "claimed by the executive" if they were not overtly "granted to the legislature," and, if they were granted to the legislature, they had to be construed "*strictly*, with a residuary right in the executive" or "perhaps" even "claimed as a concurrent right by the executive." Accept these principles and their consequences, Madison warned, and "no citizen could any longer guess at the character of the government under which he lives," and "the most penetrating jurist would be unable to scan the extent of constructive prerogative."[33]

Seeking to justify these claims, Madison began with Hamilton's treatment of the power to declare war. Pacificus had admitted that "the right of the legislature to declare war *includes the right of judging*, whether the legislature be under obligations to make war or not." He denied, however, that from this it followed that the executive "is *in any case* excluded from a *similar right* of judging in the execution of its own functions." According to Madison, Hamilton erred in his application of this doctrine by "shrinking from its regular consequences." If he had "stuck to his principle in its full extent, and reasoned from it without restraint," he would not have conceded to the legislature this right to judge whether the nation was obliged to go to war. After all, Madison reminded his readers, Hamilton had contended that the constitutional right of the legislature to declare war was "*to be taken strictly*," since the power was really executive in its nature.[34]

Madison continued that the Constitution's delegation of the right to declare war to the legislature must carry with it the right to judge of the nation's obligations to make war, while excluding any similar right in the executive. Even if, as Hamilton contended, the legislative right to declare war were "an exception out of the general grant" of executive power to the president, the president would still have no right to judge the nation's obligation to go to war. In truth, Madison held, "everything included in the right must be included in the exception" and therefore must be "excluded from the grant" of executive power to the president. Moreover, Madison contended, Hamilton could not "disentangle himself" from these difficulties by "considering the right of the executive to judge as *concurrent* with that of the legislature." This would lead to obviously unacceptable consequences. Since the right to judge the nation's

33 *PJM*, 15: 80–81.
34 *PJM*, 15: 81 (Madison's emphases).

obligation to go to war is "included in" and "is in fact the very essence of" the right to declare war, one could not claim a "concurrent right" to judge for the executive without also claiming a concurrent right to declare war for the executive.[35]

Nor, Madison continued, could Hamilton successfully "creep out of the difficulty" by emphasizing the qualification that the president has a right to judge the nation's obligation to go to war "in the execution of its" own "functions." While some "difficulties" might well "arise in defining the executive authority in particular cases, there could be none in deciding on an authority clearly placed by the Constitution in another department." Here, Madison continued, the Constitution had "decided" that the power to declare war was "not to be deemed an executive authority" but had instead explicitly made it "a legislative function." As a result, the right of "judging of the obligations to make war" had to be "admitted to be included as a legislative function." Therefore, when the question arises "whether war shall be declared, or whether public stipulations require it, the question necessarily belongs to the department to which those functions belong – and no other department" could "be *in the execution of its proper functions*" if it took upon itself to "decide such a question."[36]

The only possible "refuge" from "this conclusion," Madison held, was to be found in Hamilton's "pretext of a *concurrent* right in both" the executive and the legislature "to judge of the obligations to declare war." This was "the ground on which the ultimate defense" of Hamilton's position had "to be made." Accordingly, Madison proposed to "give its strength a fair trial," emphasizing what he took to be the unacceptable consequences of this Hamiltonian doctrine of concurrence. If, he observed, the executive possessed a "concurrent right with the legislature to judge" the nation's "obligations to declare war," and if "the right to judge" was "essentially included in the right to declare," then Hamilton's position would imply, whether he acknowledged it or not, that the executive "must" also have a "concurrent right to declare" war along with its concurrent right to judge. This was not all. By a similar "analogy," Madison continued, the executive must have "the same right to judge of other causes of war" besides those to be found "in a public stipulation." Madison concluded that "whenever the executive, *in the course of its functions*," met with such "cases, it must infer either an equal authority in all, or acknowledge its want of authority in any."[37]

The former alternative, Madison added, could be "embraced" by only by those "who overlook or reject some of the most obvious and essential truths in political science." The authority to "judge the causes of war" was "involved in the power to declare war" and was therefore "expressly vested," like "all other legislative powers," in Congress. This power had thus been "determined by the

---

[35] *PJM*, 15: 81 (Madison's emphasis).
[36] *PJM*, 15: 81–82 (Madison's emphasis).
[37] *PJM*, 15: 82 (Madison's emphases).

constitution to be a *legislative power.*" Laying aside any questions about how a "compound power" might be "partly legislative" and "partly executive," and thus "vested" partly in one department and partly in the other, or "*jointly* in both," Madison emphasized instead that "the same power" could not possibly "belong, *in the whole* to *both* departments, or be properly so vested as to operate *separately* in *each.*" It was even more "evident," he added, that "the same *specific function or act*" could not "belong to the *two* departments, and be *separately* exercisable by *each.*"[38]

At this point, Madison hastened to clarify that his argument did not absolutely condemn any mixing and blending of powers or prohibit all forms of concurrent power under the Constitution. The executive might enjoy some participation in legislative acts, as by possessing a veto power, just as the legislature might have some share in executive acts, as by possessing an authority to consent to appointments to executive offices. While such "arrangements" were "familiar" both in "theory" and in "practice," what Hamilton had suggested was utterly outlandish, according to Madison. Hamilton's theory carried with it the possibility of "an independent exercise of an *executive act* by the legislature *alone*" and the converse possibility "of a *legislative* act by the executive *alone.*" Both were implied by his suggestion that the "same act" was "exercisable by each," and indeed the second possibility was the one that Hamilton seemed to be urging in the present case. Such things, Madison insisted, were "contrary to one of the first and best maxims of a well-organized government, and ought never to be founded in a forced construction" of the Constitution.[39]

Madison also conceded that the various departments of government, in the course of exercising "their functions," might "interpret the constitution differently" and thereby "lay claim each to the same power." The "inconvenience" of such a "difference of opinion," Madison admitted, could not be escaped "entirely" under America's system of government. The possibility of such clashes arose from a "*concurrent* right to expound the Constitution." This kind of concurrence, however, differed "obviously and radically" from that defended by Hamilton. Madison's understanding of a concurrent power to interpret only supposed that the Constitution had assigned the power at issue "to one department only" and only conceded a "doubt" as to "which" one it had "been given." Hamilton's theory went further in assuming the power in dispute "to belong to both" branches and to be capable of being "exercised by either or both, according to the course of exigencies."[40]

Hamilton's "concurrent authority in two independent departments to perform the same function with respect to the same thing," would, Madison continued, be "as awkward in practice" as it was "unnatural in theory." After all,

---

[38] *PJM*, 15: 82 (Madison's emphases).
[39] *PJM*, 15: 83 (Madison's emphases).
[40] *PJM*, 15: 83 (Madison's emphasis).

if both the legislative and executive departments possessed "a right to judge of the obligations to make war," it would inevitably happen at some times that they would "judge differently." Under Hamilton's theory, today the president might decide that the United States is under no obligation to make war and, in executing his "functions, proclaim that determination to all the world," and tomorrow the Congress might take up the same question, in the execution of its functions, decide differently, and declare war, thus setting up a clash between the executive's "*constitutional proclamation*" and the legislature's equally "*constitutional declaration.*" Here we would have the country "speaking through two different organs, equally constitutional and authentic, two opposite languages, on the same subject, and under the same existing circumstances." "In what light," Madison asked, would such a situation "present the Constitution to the people who established it," or the "nation" to "the world."[41]

Madison then argued that Hamilton's doctrine was in fact a threat to the whole system of separation of powers that the Constitution had so carefully established because the consequences of Hamilton's principles could not be confined to the particular powers and departments to which he had applied them in the present case. If the executive had a right, in performing its own functions, to exercise a power vested in the legislature, then why should it not have a similar right, under similar conditions, to exercise a power vested in the judiciary? And why should not the judiciary and the legislature have a similar right, in the exercise of their functions, to perform acts entrusted to the executive? Madison feared that "occasions and pretexts" for such "interference" would be "frequent." He thus concluded that Hamilton's doctrine undermined the "partition" of "powers" that the Constitution had "so carefully made among the several branches," throwing them into an "absolute hotchpot" and exposing them "to a general scramble."[42]

Hamilton had also argued that the executive has a right to judge the nature of the public obligations in the course of fulfilling its duty to preserve peace until the legislature has declared war. Madison found this argument to be full of contradictions. Hamilton began by conceding the right of the legislature to make war and by asserting the duty of the executive to preserve peace until war has been declared. He then went on, however, to claim on the basis of this duty to preserve peace an executive right to judge "the nature of the obligations which the treaties of the country impose on the government." This amounted, Madison contended, to saying that "in fulfilling" its "*duty to preserve peace,*" the executive "must necessarily possess the right to judge whether *peace ought to be preserved,*" or "in other words, *whether its duty should be performed.*" Here was a case of flat contradiction: the duty Hamilton asserted could not imply the right he had deduced but rather had to exclude it. Hamilton had

[41] *PJM*, 15: 83–84 (Madison's emphases).
[42] *PJM*, 15: 84.

gone on and held that, when the executive found that there was nothing in the public obligations inconsistent with neutrality, it was its "province and its duty to enforce the laws incident to that state of the nation." But if it had, as Hamilton had contended, the right to judge the public obligations, then the executive might, Madison observed, come to the conclusion that those obligations were not consistent with neutrality, or that the United States was obliged not to be neutral in a foreign conflict. If one were to say – based on the supposed duty of the executive to preserve peace until war was declared – that the executive nevertheless still had a duty to enforce the laws incident to neutrality, then one would "destroy the right to judge" on which Hamilton had insisted. At the same time, if one were to hold that in such a situation the executive was bound to enforce the laws incident to the state of non-neutrality that it had discerned in the public obligations, then one cancelled the executive's "duty to preserve peace" until "war is declared."[43]

One possible way out of this contradiction was to hold that the executive's authority to judge whether war was obligatory was "absolute and operative" while its "duty to preserve peace" was "subordinate and conditional." This would, however, posit a power in the executive to decide, based on the nation's treaties, that the country was obliged to adopt a non-neutral stance or even to wage war. This Madison was at pains to deny. For him, the executive could have no business judging whether treaties did or did not affect the nation's neutrality, because the nation must in any case be neutral and in a state of peace until the legislature actually declared war. "Neutrality," Madison affirmed, "means peace, with an allusion to the circumstance of other nations being at war." It had "no reference to the existence or nonexistence of treaties or alliances between the nation at peace and the nations at war." Until war was "duly authorized by the United States" – that is, by a declaration of war by the Congress – the country was in fact at peace in relation to other nations at peace and neutral in relation to other nations at war. The existence of a treaty, he held, even a treaty of alliance, could not change the country's neutral status, even when the circumstances to which the alliance looked had in fact emerged. Such a change required the positive act of Congress in declaring war. Such *"eventual engagements,"* Madison held, "can only take effect on the declaration of the legislature" and therefore "cannot, without that declaration, change the actual state of the country."[44]

One might suppose otherwise, Madison continued, and hold that the "existence" of treaty "obligations to join in war" were in themselves, prior to a congressional declaration, "inconsistent with neutrality." In that case, would the executive be obliged to execute those laws "incident to war" even before the legislature had given effect to the nation's "obligations" by declaring war? Madison believed that Hamilton's principles tended "strongly" to this

[43] *PJM*, 15: 84–85.
[44] *PJM*, 15: 85.

conclusion, but that such consequences would not be "avowed" by him. But
if one rejected this consequence and held instead that until war was actually
declared by the legislature the executive was bound to execute the laws of
neutrality, then, contrary to what Hamilton had argued, the executive really
had no authority to judge the public obligations and was absolutely obliged to
preserve peace until war was declared. As far as the executive was concerned,
Madison indicated, treaty obligations that changed the nation's neutral status
were not in fact operative until the legislature acted.[45]

Madison concluded *Helvidius* II by examining one more of Pacificus' arguments, which Hamilton had expressed as follows:

The executive is charged with the execution of all laws, the laws of nations as well as
the municipal law which recognizes and adopts those laws. It is consequently bound, by
faithfully executing the laws of neutrality when that is the state of the nation, to avoid
giving cause of war to foreign powers.[46]

According to Madison, Hamilton's first sentence here was true but irrelevant to the point at issue; and his second sentence was "*partly true* in its proper
meaning, but *totally untrue*" in the meaning Hamilton had intended. Madison
understood Hamilton to mean that the executive had a substantive duty to
avoid giving a cause of war to foreign powers, which in turn suggested that the
executive bore some substantive responsibility for whether the nation was on a
neutral or a war footing. For Madison, this was not the case. Rather, the executive was bound to faithfully execute the laws of neutrality because Congress
had determined that those were the laws in place, and the consequences of the
execution of those laws was not something about which the executive could
properly concern himself. The executive was indeed "bound," Madison contended, to "faithfully execute the laws of neutrality, while those laws continue
unaltered by the competent authority." This duty arose, however, not from any
obligation of the executive "to avoid giving cause of war to foreign powers."
It arose rather from the "nature" of the executive "trust" as well as the "sanction of its oath," which obliged the executive "to the faithful execution of" all
"laws internal and external." The executive was duty-bound to execute these
laws "even if turbulent citizens should consider it as a cause of war at home,
or unfriendly nations should consider its so doing as a cause of war abroad.
The duty of the executive to preserve external peace can no more suspend the
force of external laws than its duty to preserve internal peace can suspend
the force of municipal laws."[47] It was "certain," he observed, "that a faithful
execution of the laws of neutrality" could in some cases tend just as much to
provoke war from some countries as to avoid war from others. Regardless of
those potential consequences, the executive's duty was to "execute the laws of

---

[45] *PJM*, 15: 85–86.
[46] *PJM*, 15: 86 (Madison's emphasis removed).
[47] *PJM*, 15: 86 (Madison's emphases).

neutrality while in force, and leave it to the legislature to decide whether they ought to be altered or not." In these matters the executive had no "discretion" other than to call Congress and provide it with information. That done, "the trust of the executive is satisfied, and that department is not responsible for the consequences." This conclusion was a necessary consequence of the system of separation of powers, for the executive "could not be made responsible for" such consequences "without vesting it with the legislative as well as with the executive trust."[48]

Helvidius III

In *Helvidius* III, Madison turned to two more arguments Pacificus had deployed in support of an executive right to "exercise" what Madison held to be "the legislative power of judging whether there be a cause of war in a public stipulation." According to the first of these arguments, the executive's obligation to enforce a treaty implied an authority to interpret it. It was, Hamilton had held, the "right and duty of the executive to judge of and interpret" the provisions of the treaties that gave certain privileges to France, "*in order to the enforcement*" of those very "*privileges*." From this claim, Hamilton then went on to derive the supposed right of the executive to judge whether there was a cause of war in a treaty to which the United States was a signatory.[49]

Madison responded by way of "a very obvious distinction." The "first right" – to interpret the treaty with a view to its execution – was indeed, Madison conceded, "essential to the execution of the treaty *as a law in operation*," and to that extent it "interfere[d] with no right vested in another department." The second right – the one at issue, the executive right to determine whether there was a cause of war in a public stipulation – was "not essential to the execution of the treaty or any other law." This was so, Madison held, because the executive could not rightly consider the treaty as a law in operation until there was a declaration from Congress to that effect. The treaty article Hamilton was claiming a right of the executive to interpret, Madison contended, "cannot, as has been shown, from the very nature of it, be *in operation* as a law without a previous declaration of the legislature." Therefore, until such a declaration should take place, "all the laws to be enforced by the executive remain" just "the same, whatever be the disposition or judgment of the executive."[50]

The second Hamiltonian argument to which Madison now turned sought to derive an executive power to determine whether a treaty was operative from the president's constitutional authority to receive public ministers. The latter power, Hamilton had suggested, included "the right of deciding, in the case of a revolution, whether the new government sending the minister ought to

---

[48] *PJM*, 15: 86.
[49] *PJM*, 15: 95–96 (Madison's emphases).
[50] *PJM*, 15: 96 (Madison's emphases).

be recognized or not." This in turn included an executive "right to give or refuse operation to preexisting treaties." Madison contended in response that the executive power on which here Hamilton relied was more ceremonial than substantive and that his effort to "magnify" it "into an important prerogative" was improper, more especially since the effort was made in order to "abridge" the rights of another department, which had been assigned "in one of the most express and explicit parts of the constitution": namely, the "power of the legislature to declare war and to judge of the causes for declaring it."[51]

Madison began from the words of the Constitution: The president "shall receive ambassadors, other public ministers, and consuls."[52] Where Hamilton saw here a substantive presidential authority to decide whether or not to recognize a foreign government, Madison saw instead a largely ceremonial function in the performance of which the president had very little discretion. The clause intended "little, if anything, more" than "to provide for a particular mode of communication, *almost* grown into a right among modern nations; by pointing out the department of the government most proper for the ceremony of admitting public ministers, of examining their credentials, and of authenticating their title to the privileges annexed to their character by the law of nations."[53]

Here, Madison once again recurred to the *Federalist* in order to show Hamilton's inconsistency. In *Federalist* 69, Hamilton himself had argued against those who sought to magnify the power at issue. "The president," Hamilton had written,

is also to be authorized to receive ambassadors and other public ministers. This, though it has been a rich theme of declamation, is more a matter of *dignity* than of *authority*. It is a circumstance, that will be *without consequence* in the administration of the government, and it is far more convenient that it should be arranged in this manner than that there should be a necessity for convening the legislature or one of its branches upon every arrival of a foreign minister, though it were merely to take the place of a departed predecessor."[54]

In 1788, Hamilton had insisted that the executive's role in receiving public ministers would be "*without consequence* in the administration of the government." Now he contended that it effectively empowered the president to decide "on the validity of revolutions in favor of liberty," to put "the United States in a condition to be an associate in war," and even to lay "the *legislature* under an *obligation* of *declaring* war." Borrowing Hamilton's own words from *Federalist* 24 to use against him in this context, Madison suggested that the 1788 "advocates of the Constitution," had they been confronted with such an

---

[51] *PJM*, 15: 96.

[52] *PJM*, 15: 96. The text of the Constitution at this point actually mentions only ambassadors and other public ministers. Madison erroneously included "consuls" in his restatement of the provision – no doubt because the three terms (ambassadors, other public ministers, and consuls) are yoked together in other provisions in Article II and Article III.

[53] *PJM*, 15: 96 (Madison's emphasis).

[54] Quoted in *PJM*, 15: 97 (Madison's emphases).

interpretation of presidential power, would have regarded it as "'an experiment on public credulity dictated either by a deliberate intention to deceive or by the overflowings of a zeal too intemperate to be ingenuous.'"[55]

Recognition of a foreign government, Madison suggested, was primarily a factual determination about whether or not a given government actually governed a nation, not a right to pass judgment on whether that government possessed legitimate authority. According to Madison, when a "foreign minister presents himself" to the government of the United States, "two questions immediately arise: Are his credentials from the existing and acting government of his country? Are they properly authenticated?" These rather mundane questions fell "of necessity" to the executive, but the bigger question of whether the government in question had a "right" to govern belonged only to the "nation" under that government's power. The questions the executive confronted in receiving ministers were merely factual, and he would have exactly the "same right," or be under exactly the "same necessity," of making the decision if the executive "function was simply to receive *without any discretion to reject* public ministers."[56]

This was not to deny, Madison added, that there were times when one government might be justified in refusing to recognize another. In such cases, however, the right to determine the proper stance of the nation did not belong to the president. Some "cases" might arise "in which a respect to the general principles of liberty, the essential rights of the people, or the overruling sentiments of humanity might require a government, whether new or old, to be treated as an illegitimate despotism." These cases, however, were "great and extraordinary" and, Madison added, "by no means submitted to so limited an organ of the national will as the executive of the United States." They "were "certainly not to be brought by any torture of words within the right to receive ambassadors."[57] Since such questions seem clearly beyond the competency of the judiciary, it would seem that Madison believed they were entrusted to the legislature.

As we have seen, Washington had followed Jefferson rather than Hamilton on the question of whether the treaties should be declared suspended. Accordingly, Hamilton's Pacificus presented the neutrality proclamation as an official interpretation of the treaties rather than as a declaration of their suspension. Nevertheless, Pacificus did suggest that the executive possessed an authority – not used in the present case – effectively to suspend the operation of a treaty

---

[55] *PJM*, 15: 97 (Madison's emphases). See Hamilton, Madison, and Jay, *The Federalist*, 154. Hamilton had used this language to describe Anti-Federalist efforts to stir up fears about a standing army.

[56] *PJM*, 15: 97 (Madison's emphasis).

[57] *PJM*, 15: 98. Jefferson, as president, and Madison, as his secretary of state, seem to have acted according to a different understanding of the executive power when they refused to recognize the revolutionary government of Haiti during Jefferson's administration. See Tim Matthewson, "Jefferson and the Non-Recognition of Haiti," *Proceedings of the American Philosophical Society* 140 (1996): 22–48.

after a revolution by refusing to recognize the new government. Madison turned next to his refutation of this claim.

According to Madison, Hamilton had contended that "the executive has a right to give or refuse activity and operation to preexisting treaties." Madison rejected this claim with arguments similar to those employed by Jefferson in his *Opinion on the French Treaties.* Like Jefferson, Madison observed that any nation has a right to "abolish an old government and establish a new one." Like Jefferson, he linked this right to the idea that treaties are binding on nations as such and that their obligations could not be escaped or denied because of a change in government. Since a "change in government makes no change in the obligations or rights of the party to a treaty," then clearly the "executive can have no more right to suspend or prevent the operation of a treaty on account of the change than to suspend or prevent the operation, where no such change has happened." The executive, Madison added, had no "more right to suspend the operation of a treaty in force as a law than to suspend the operation of any other law."[58]

One might object to Madison's position on the grounds that cases could arise in which there is legitimate doubt whether a government exists, or which of two contending governments really is the government of the nation. Surely here the executive would inevitably possess some authority to refuse recognition and thus suspend the operation of some treaty rights. Madison, however, insisted that this was not the case that had been put by Pacificus. Rather, Hamilton's argument had supposed that there is an existing but new government that the executive might refuse to recognize. In any case, Madison continued, the "full reply" to this objection could be found in arguments he had already brought forward. Such questions concerned mere matters of fact. They were entrusted to the executive only as questions of fact, and they would equally belong to the executive even if he were required by the Constitution to receive public ministers "without any discretion to receive or reject them." Where the fact appeared to be that there was no government, the consequent "suspension" took place "independent of the executive." Where the fact appeared to be that a government did exist, the executive was bound to be "governed by the fact" and could "have no right or discretion, on account of the date or form of the government, to refuse to acknowledge it, either by rejecting its public minister or by any other step taken on that account." If the executive did refuse on such grounds, the "refusal" would be "a wrongful act," and could "neither prove nor illustrate a rightful power."[59]

Helvidius IV

In *Helvidius* IV, Madison examined the dangers posed by Hamilton's understanding of the executive power. These dangers, he suggested, were obscured

[58] *PJM,* 15: 98.
[59] *PJM,* 15: 101.

by the fact that Hamilton had not brought to light all of the implications of his doctrine and probably would have "disavowed" them if he had been confronted with them. Hamilton had emphasized the executive's duty to preserve peace until Congress declared war. Nevertheless, his argument, by asserting an executive authority to judge the causes of war, implied an executive power to involve the country in war with or without a Congressional declaration. Even if Hamilton were to repudiate such consequences, Madison observed, we would be wise to "regard it as morally certain" that to the extent that Hamilton's principles were accepted by the public, "every power" that could be "deduced from them" would in fact be deduced and "exercised sooner or later by those" with "an interest in so doing." Our knowledge of "human nature" and of "the history of government in all its forms," Madison observed, attested to this "danger." Therefore, any people "so happy as to possess the inestimable blessing of a free and defined constitution" could not be "too watchful against the introduction, nor too critical in tracing the consequences, of new principles and new constructions" that tended to "remove the landmarks of power."[60]

If Hamilton's executive "prerogative" were permitted "to usurp the public countenance" even "in its most limited sense," it would probably not be long, Madison argued, before someone would contend that if the power meant anything, it must include a "right to judge and conclude" not only that the nation's treaty obligations "permit peace" but also that they "impose war." Those making this claim would contend that it is surely "fair reasoning" to hold that "if the prerogative exists at all" it ought to possess an "operative" and not merely "an *inert* character." In defense of such claims, they would appeal to various considerations such as Hamilton had adduced in the present controversy: the executive's role as the "organ of intercourse" with foreign nations," its authority "as the interpreter of national treaties," its obligation to see to "the execution of the laws, of which treaties make a part," and its responsibility for the "*command and application of the public force.*" Moreover, Madison continued, it would be argued in defense of this prerogative that "the executive is as much the *executor* as the *interpreter* of treaties," that it accordingly is authorized not only to "judge of the *obligations* of treaties" but also to "carry" them "into *effect.*" On this basis, the partisans of presidential power would conclude that if there is a treaty requiring the "military cooperation" of the United States, and if an American military force should be in existence, the executive would "have the same right, as *executor of public treaties*, to *employ* the public force, as it has in quality of *interpreter of public treaties*, to decide whether it ought to be *employed.*"[61]

Indeed, Hamilton's doctrine opened the door to the possibility that the executive could use even a treaty of peace as a tool by which to involve the nation in war. Every treaty, Madison observed, included, implicitly or explicitly, the

---

[60] *PJM*, 15: 106–07.
[61] *PJM*, 15: 107 (Madison's emphases).

"condition" that "an infraction" of "an important article" by one party "extinguishes the obligations of the other." Moreover, a "restoration of a state of war" is "the immediate consequence of a dissolution of a treaty of peace." In view of all the claims that Hamilton had made on behalf of the executive, it would not be hard in some future circumstance for the executive to "plunge the nation into war" on the grounds that "a treaty of peace" had been "infringed." After all, Madison noted, once Hamilton's principles had been accepted, "any pupil of political casuistry" could justify such an executive action by arguing that it did not involve an illegitimate executive declaration of war but rather a simple *"relapse* into a war that *had been declared"* previously by Congress.[62]

Madison went even further. According to Hamilton's principles – or at least to their unacknowledged but, to Madison's mind, inevitable implications – the executive could revive a state of war without even bothering to claim a violation of the peace treaty by the other nation. After all, if that nation had changed its form of government, the executive could simply refuse to receive a minister from the new government, as a result of which the treaty of peace would be suspended and "the state of war" would resume as a matter "of course."[63] Such were the consequences that would follow if one "swallowed the gross sophistry which wrapped up the original dose" of Pacificus' reasoning. Therefore, Madison admonished his readers to adhere strictly "to the simple, the received, and the fundamental doctrine of the constitution," according to which the war power is a legislative power and only a legislative power.[64]

Madison then turned to an examination of the practical "wisdom" underpinning this constitutional dispensation, emphasizing the dangers to peace that arose from entrusting the war power to a single individual. According to Madison, "the trust and the temptation would be too great" for "any one man." He acknowledged – perhaps with Washington's greatness in mind – that such danger need not exist in the case of a man of extraordinary integrity, "such as nature may offer as the prodigy of many centuries." This danger was very real, however, in the case of such men "as may be expected in the ordinary successions of magistracy." Temptation would come, Madison expected, because war was generally in the interests of the executive. "War," he observed, "is in fact the true nurse of executive aggrandizement." War meant the creation of a military force, which would be directed by the executive; the appropriation of vast sums of money, which would be spent by the executive; and the multiplication of honors and offices, which would be awarded by the executive. Moreover, war opened a path to glory, which would be won by the executive. "The strongest passions and most dangerous weaknesses of the human

---

[62] *PJM*, 15: 107–08 (Madison's emphases).
[63] *PJM*, 15: 108.
[64] *PJM*, 15: 108 (Madison's emphases).

breast" – such as "ambition, avarice, vanity," and "the honorable or venial love of fame" – all conspired "against the desire and duty of peace." As a result, Madison concluded, it had become an "axiom" of sound political thinking that "the executive is the department of power most distinguished by its propensity to war" and had accordingly become the "practice of all states, in proportion as they are free, to disarm this propensity of its influence."[65]

Madison closed *Helvidius* IV by examining one more instance of Pacificus' departure from the doctrine of the *Federalist* and by using this departure as an occasion to revive, implicitly at least, Jefferson's charge that Hamilton was angling to transform the government into a monarchy on the British model. According to Madison, the Constitution also manifested a prudent caution about the abuses to which the executive was prone by withholding from it "the *sole* power of making peace." Treaties, even treaties of peace, could not be made by the executive alone but only by the executive in cooperation with the Senate. "The trust" here, just as in the power of making war, "would be too great for the wisdom, and the temptations too strong for the virtue, of a single citizen."[66] Hamilton, Madison noted, had very ably set forth the reasons for this limit on the president's power over foreign affairs in *Federalist* 75. There was little danger in placing the entire treaty power in the executive, Hamilton had observed, when the executive was a hereditary monarch. After all, such a ruler generally had "personally too much at stake in the government to be in any material danger of being corrupted by foreign powers." This was not the case, however, in an executive, like the president of the United States, elected to hold office only temporarily. Such an executive, being "obliged" at the end of his term "to return to the station from which he was taken, might sometimes be under temptations to sacrifice his duty to his interest, which it would require superlative virtue to withstand." Under such circumstances, an ambitious man might "betray the interests of the state" for the sake of his own power, just as an avaricious man might do so in order to enrich himself.[67]

Hamilton's argument as Publius, Madison suggested, undercut his later argument as Pacificus. The Constitution did not allow "the executive *singly* to judge or conclude that peace ought to be made," Madison observed. From this "circumstance alone" one could conclude that the Constitution "never meant to give" the executive the "authority *singly* to judge and conclude that war ought not to be made." The "trust" in question was "precisely similar and equivalent" in both cases. The executive right to conclude a peace treaty, or the "right to say that war ought not to go on," was, Madison contended, "no greater than the right to say that war ought not to begin." Similarly, the temptation was equivalent in both cases. "Every danger of error or corruption incident to such" an executive "prerogative in one case is incident to it in the

[65] *PJM*, 15: 108–09.
[66] *PJM*, 15: 109 (Madison's emphasis).
[67] Quoted in *PJM*, 15: 109 (Madison's emphasis).

other." Therefore, because the Constitution had "deemed it unsafe or improper in the one case, it must be deemed equally so in the other case."[68]

Moreover, Madison saw a tendency in the conjunction of Hamilton's different arguments as Publius and Pacificus to move the nation toward hereditary monarchy. As Hamilton had observed as Publius, the hereditary status of the executive provided the necessary security against abuse when the executive was entrusted with the entire power to make treaties and thus to regulate its relations with the rest of the world. Therefore, Madison concluded, every addition to the American executive's power over such questions constituted "an increase in the dangerous temptation to which an *elective* and *temporary* magistrate is exposed." These dangers in turn provided "an *argument* and *advance* toward the security offered by the personal interests of an *hereditary* magistrate."[69] The tendency of Pacificus' argument, Madison suggested, was to create the kind of executive power that could only be trusted if it were hereditary.

Helvidius V

In his fifth and final installment as Helvidius, Madison turned to Pacificus' treatment of the neutrality proclamation itself. Much of Pacificus' argument had been dedicated to defending the executive's authority to interpret treaties and determine that the nation was neutral in relation to warring powers. Madison considered that in his first four numbers he had refuted these pretensions and shown "that the executive has no constitutional right to interfere in any question whether there be or be not a cause of war." Hamilton's arguments on this score, however, supposed that the neutrality proclamation needed to be defended as an exercise of such an authority because it *was* an exercise of such an authority. Madison undertook to challenge Hamilton here, as well. It was not really true, he contended, that "the proclamation of the executive" had "undertaken to decide the question" whether the "article of guaranty" in the French treaty of alliance created a "cause of war" and had thereby "exercised the right" which Hamilton had "claimed for that department."[70]

Because this argument does not raise the issues of constitutional and political principle important in the rest of the Pacificus-Helvidius debate, we need not examine it here. Nevertheless, before turning to this argument about the character of the neutrality proclamation, Madison dedicated a few more remarks to the constitutional implications of Pacificus' argument to which we should attend. Here Madison took issue with what he called the "novelty of the phraseology" employed by Pacificus. Such an inquiry, he suggested, was useful both with a view to understanding the origins of Hamilton's doctrines as well as to bringing to light their problematic tendency. With regard to the latter concern,

[68] *PJM*, 15: 15, 110.
[69] *PJM*, 15: 110.
[70] *PJM*, 15: 113.

Madison noted that "words often have a gradual influence on ideas, and, when used in an improper sense, may cover fallacies which would not otherwise escape detection." Here Madison was particularly concerned with Hamilton's "application of the term *government* to the *executive authority alone.*" Pacificus had used the terms practically interchangeably. Over and over again, Madison noted, Hamilton had spoken of the neutrality proclamation as an act of "the government" rather than as an act of "the executive" or "the president." The "singularity" of this "style," Madison contended, showed "either that the phraseology of a foreign government" was more familiar to Pacificus "than the phraseology proper to our own, or that he wishes to propagate a familiarity of the former in preference to the latter." Madison considered this matter far more than "trivial." In the United States, Madison observed, "the government unquestionably means" not merely the "executive part" but "the whole government." It took on the former meaning only "in a monarchy." Until the present argument, Madison suggested, the term had always been used in America in its "proper sense" in "official proceedings, in public discussions, and in private discourse." Since it was just as easy, and less liable to misunderstanding, to use an expression like "the executive" or "the president," Madison thought that Pacificus' use of "the government" could not have been dictated by considerations of "necessity, propriety, or perspicuity." Hamilton's "marked" and unusual "fondness" for the term therefore merited the "notice" Madison had taken of it.[71]

Conclusion

As Helvidius, Madison gave expression once again to a complaint that Jefferson had been making about Hamiltonianism since his critique of the bank bill.[72] Both Jefferson and Madison desired a federal government confined by strict and clear delineations of power. In the controversies over the bank and the *Report on Manufactures*, Jefferson had decried the tendency of Hamilton's constitutional reasoning to obscure – and even, he thought, to overthrow – the

---

[71] *PJM*, 15: 113–14 (Madison's emphases).

[72] George Thomas contrasts a "political constitutionalism" of separate branches checking each other through the exercise of concurrent powers with a more legalistic approach that "sees the Constitution as a set of legal rules enforced by courts." He contends that Hamilton's thinking about the executive power is "best characterized as political constitutionalism" and adds that Madison shared this approach, not only as Publius but also even in the context of the Pacificus-Helvidius debate. In contrast, I would say that, as Helvidius, Madison moves in the direction of a more legalistic constitutionalism, at least to the extent that his argument emphasizes not the concurrent authority of the executive and legislature but instead his desire for clearly defined delineations of authority – even though his approach is not so legalistic as to suggest that the courts should be involved in adjudicating the dispute. See Thomas's "The Limits of Constitutional Government: Alexander Hamilton on Extraordinary Power and Executive Discretion," in *Extra-Legal Power and Legitimacy: Perspectives on Legitimacy*, ed. Clement Fatovic and Benjamin Kleinerman (New York: Oxford University Press, 2013), 99–100.

constitutional limits on the federal government's domestic powers. In 1793, Jefferson believed that Hamilton was now obscuring the limits on the executive power in foreign policy by obscuring the constitutional distribution of authority among the departments of the federal government. And in James Madison, Jefferson possessed a formidable ally who could give detailed expression to this critique.

For his part, Hamilton did not think that his arguments posed a threat to limited government because he did not understand limited government in the same way as Jefferson and Madison. That is, he did not understand the constitutional grants of power as establishing the kind of clear and narrow limitations that Jefferson and Madison thought essential. He had defended his domestic program by observing that, in between what is clearly constitutional and what is clearly unconstitutional, there is a considerable gray zone of doubtful but also plausible constitutionality, and that the most one could say is that by enacting his policies Congress had chosen to occupy part of that territory.[73] Similarly, his presentation of the executive power in the *Pacificus* papers recognized a kind of gray area with regard to foreign policy by arguing that both the executive and the legislature had considerable pretensions in that field. Both could claim a legitimate power to interpret the country's treaty obligations. Hamilton seems to have believed that a concurrent power like this posed no threat to constitutional government so long as both powers existed and were capable of checking each other.

Who, then, had the better part of the present argument? To begin with, one must observe that some of Madison's specific arguments against Hamilton were rather strained. For example, Madison had held that Hamilton's constitutional reasoning was a threat not only to separation of powers but also to the "forms of republican government."[74] Supposing that by "republican government" Madison meant a government in which the people rule through elected representatives, it is difficult to see how such a charge could be maintained. After all, even if Hamilton had gone so far as to call openly for the treaty and war powers to be *entirely* vested in the executive – which he certainly had not done – such an arrangement, though questionable in many ways, would not amount to a betrayal of republican government so long as the president was an elected official. It is true that Madison argued that Hamilton, by expanding the executive's power in relation to treaties, had moved the country in the direction of the kind of executive power that would be safer in the hands of a monarch. Nevertheless, Hamilton's point in the *Federalist*, which Madison echoed as Helvidius, was that monarchy provided the necessary safety where the treaty power was *entirely* vested in the executive. As Pacificus, however, Hamilton had not argued that the treaty power belonged exclusively to the president, and there was no reason based on what he had written to suspect that he intended

73 *PAH*, 12: 251.
74 *PJM*, 15: 80–81.

to push the power that far at some later time – a project that, indeed, seems fantastic given the Constitution's clear assignment of a participation in the treaty power to the Senate.

In other passages, too, Madison seemed determined to refute not what Hamilton had said but the supposed implications of what Hamilton had said – implications that Hamilton had not affirmed but that Madison labored mightily, but not always persuasively, to insist were inevitable. In *Helvidius* IV, Madison contended that the Constitution held that it was unsafe to allow the president alone to make a treaty, and thus that it was unsafe to allow the president alone to make peace. It followed, Madison said, that it was equally unsafe to hold that the president may alone conclude that war ought not to be made.[75] Here, however, he ruled out a position that Hamilton had not in fact embraced, for Pacificus had made clear that the president's authority to declare his judgment that a treaty did not oblige the United States to make war did not preclude Congress from exercising its own judgment independently, reaching a different conclusion, and in fact declaring war. Whatever else one may think of Hamilton's arguments as Pacificus, they involve no question of the president singly concluding that war ought not to be made. Again, Madison attempted to show that this was really the bearing of Hamilton's argument, whether he wanted to admit it or not. Thus he said that if Hamilton had really stuck to the principles he had laid down he would have to deny that the legislature has any power to judge the nation's obligations to go to war. After all, Hamilton had insisted that the war and treaty powers are executive in their nature, and that any sharing in them by the legislature is to be interpreted strictly.[76] Surely Madison here sought to press the principle of strictly interpreting exceptions – which, as we have seen, Jefferson also affirmed – much too far, farther than Hamilton, or probably any reasonable person, could have intended. As Madison himself noted as his argument proceeded, even if one conceded both that the powers in question are executive in their nature and that exceptions are to be construed strictly, it would not follow that Congress had no right to judge the nation's treaty obligations because, in the relevant case, Congress could not decide whether to declare war without also deliberating about whether the treaty in question obliged it to do so. That is, even if the assignment of the power to declare war to the legislature was an exception, a power to judge its proper use would be inseparable from it. This point can be clarified by considering an easier case in which the same principles are in play. The president's veto power is clearly legislative in its nature, and it follows that it must be construed strictly. Obviously, however, one could not say on this basis that a strict interpretation of this power would forbid the president from exercising his own judgment about whether some public principle requires him to exercise it or not.

---

[75] *PJM*, 15: 110.
[76] *PJM*, 15: 81.

As Helvidius, Madison certainly succeeded in showing the inconsistencies or changes in Hamilton's thinking over the previous half decade. Pacificus' presentations of the treaty power and the power of the president to receive ambassadors differed noticeably from what Hamilton had said as Publius in 1787–88. Madison's own argument, however, revealed similar inconsistencies on his part.

In the first place, Madison's narrow reading of the executive power seems somewhat incompatible with the supposed advantages of separation of powers. Helvidius insisted that the executive's only duty was to execute the laws, without taking account of or being responsible for the consequences. Contrary to what Hamilton had suggested, Madison denied that the executive had any substantive responsibility to avoid giving cause of war: he was obliged to execute the laws even if they did give cause of war to other nations.[77] On this view, apparently, the president is in no position to make his own substantive judgments about the common good, which have been made for him and for the country by Congress, and which he only need carry into effect. According to a common understanding of separation of powers, however, one of the key advantages of that arrangement is its tendency to impede tyranny. If the legislature, for example, is captured by a tyrannical impulse, the executive can mitigate the effects of its tyrannical laws in the execution.[78] This advantage demands, however, that the executive make his own substantive judgment about the common good. Mitigating the operation of tyrannical laws requires that the executive have some discretion in the execution of the laws and that discretion has to be informed by the president's own judgments about what is tyrannical and what is just. One of the most important advantages of separation of powers cannot emerge if the president considers himself as nothing more than the servant of the laws. If this is true in domestic policy, it is hard to see why it would not also be true in foreign policy as well, where presumably the president would exercise some discretion, informed by his own judgments about what is in the country's interests, when giving execution to the nation's treaties – especially where the execution might lead to war. Madison, to be sure, has a point: there must be some limit to the president's discretion, otherwise it would be impossible to say, as the Constitution does, that he has an obligation to see to the faithful execution of the laws. On the other hand, it seems impossible, consistent with the advantages we are supposed to derive from separation of powers, to limit that discretion as much or as clearly as Madison desires. It seems that Madison and Jefferson wish to treat such questions as legal ones: they expect there is a domain of executive authority beyond which the president may not take a single step. In contrast, one senses that Hamilton would consider such questions political in their nature.

---

[77] *PJM*, 15: 86.
[78] Consider Montesquieu's statement in *The Spirit of the Laws*, quoted by Madison in *Federalist* 47. Hamilton, Madison, and Jay, *The Federalist*, 326.

The president has a considerable discretion, but there must be some limit to it if we are to have rule of law. That limit cannot be precisely identified, but as long as we have a Congress capable of checking – and, indeed, impeaching – the president, such limits can be maintained consistent with the executive discretion that is necessary to the common good.

Indeed, if Hamilton as Pacificus defended different interpretations of the treaty power and power of the president to receive foreign ministers than he had as Publius, it would seem that Madison, too, defended as Helvidius a different understanding of separation of powers than he had as Publius. In *Federalists* 47 and 48, Madison had contended, in response to Anti-Federalist fears, that separation of powers was compatible with a certain mixing and blending of powers among the various departments, and even that such mixing and blending was necessary if the departments were to check each other. Hamilton's position as Pacificus – which emphasized that the executive and the legislature shared the authority to interpret the nation's treaties and, hence, the authority to judge the nation's obligation to make war – would seem to be generally consistent with the understanding of separation of powers that Madison had defended in the *Federalist*. In his effort to condemn Pacificus, Madison was forced as Helvidius to put forward a stricter version of separation of powers than the one he had developed as Publius.

According to Madison's Helvidius, Pacificus's claim that the power to make treaties belongs by its nature to the executive said in effect that "the executive department naturally includes a legislative power." This, Madison held, was "an absurdity" in "theory" and "a tyranny" in "practice."[79] As Publius, Madison seems to have been less exacting. In *Federalist* 47, appealing to Montesquieu's authority in defense of the Constitution's scheme of separation of powers, he held that tyranny appeared not when one department held a power that in its nature belonged to another but when one department swallowed up another's power completely. Having reviewed the ways in which the British Constitution, which had been Montesquieu's model, mixed powers among the various institutions, he concluded that the great Frenchman had only meant "that where the *whole* power of one department is exercised by the same hands which exercise the *whole* power of another department, the fundamental principles of a free constitution are subverted." Indeed, in *Federalist* 47, Madison noted that the king possessed the "prerogative of making treaties with foreign sovereigns" – the very point on which he now said Hamilton had gone so far and so dangerously wrong – without in any way suggesting that such an arrangement was tyrannical.[80]

Some of Helvidius' claims were also inconsistent with – or at least in tension with – the Constitution itself. Madison held that the president's power as commander-in-chief can convey no power over the substantive question of

---

[79] *PJM*, 15: 69 (Madison's emphasis).
[80] Hamilton, Madison, and Jay, *The Federalist*, 525–26.

whether to engage in war. "Those who are to *conduct a war*," he insisted, "cannot in the nature of things, be proper or safe judges, whether *a war ought* to be *commenced, continued*, or *concluded*. They are barred from the latter functions by a great principle in free government, analogous to that which separates the sword from the purse, or the power of executing from the power of enacting laws."[81] Madison here effectively accuses the Constitution itself of having dangerously botched the distribution of powers. Even if one concedes Madison's claim that the commander-in-chief power gives the president no authority over the question of whether to engage in war, it is nevertheless the case that the Constitution also assigns the president a role in the making of treaties. And by sharing in the treaty power, the president, who as commander-in-chief is also entrusted with the power of conducting war, will clearly in some instances be in a position to participate in the judgment of whether a war ought to be continued or concluded. The "great principle" that Madison invoked requires that the power to execute the laws be separated from the power to make the laws. The Constitution nevertheless assigns the president a limited share in the lawmaking power by giving him a qualified veto. It is therefore difficult to see why that great principle – at least as it is understood by the Constitution itself – would be violated by holding that the president, who conducts war, has some limited power to judge whether the nation should or should not make war.

This leads us to a point that Hamilton had made only in passing as Pacificus, and of which Madison seems to have taken no notice, but which has serious implications for the validity of the positions he had defended as Helvidius. In the first *Pacificus* paper, Hamilton had claimed that the president cannot "control" Congress's power to declare war "further than" through the use of his "general right of objecting to all acts of the legislature, liable to being overruled by two thirds of both houses of Congress." In other words, Hamilton believed that the president has the authority to veto a congressional declaration of war. It is not clear whether this view is correct, but it is clear that either answer to the question poses a serious problem for Madison. If the president does have a power to veto a declaration of war, then the Constitution is opposed to Madison's claim that the president must have no share in the judgment of whether or not to make war. However, if the president has no power to veto a declaration of war, then such a declaration must be somehow different from an ordinary exercise of the legislative power, in which case the power to declare war is not as purely legislative as Madison has insisted that it is.

Madison's treatment of the president's power to receive public ministers presents another set of problems. As we have seen, Hamilton suggested that this power implies a right in the president to refuse recognition to a foreign government by refusing to receive its representatives. Madison, in response, contended that the presidential power in question was purely formal and that

---

[81] *PJM*, 15: 71 (Madison's emphases).

it therefore gave the president no discretion not to receive the representatives of foreign nations. Madison went on, however, to admit that in some cases it might be necessary to refuse to recognize a foreign government, to treat it as an "illegitimate despotism." He insisted, however, that such a power was certainly not entrusted to so "limited an organ of the national will as the executive of the United States."[82] But why not? Much of Madison's argument against the president's authority to determine the obligations of the nation in relation to war depended on his assertion that the war and treaty powers were clearly legislative in their character. Whatever the merits of that contention, the same cannot be said of the power to receive foreign ministers.

Indeed, Madison's position here seems inconsistent with Jefferson's argument about the president's power to *send* ministers to foreign governments. Jefferson had said that the "transaction of business with foreign nations is executive altogether, and that it belongs to the president "except as to such portions of it as are specially submitted to the Senate" by the Constitution.[83] Surely, however, receiving the ministers of foreign governments is as much the "transaction of business with foreign nations" as sending American ministers to such governments. If so, then the question of whether or not to receive belongs to the president, and the Senate's power to approve the foreign representatives the president chooses must be interpreted strictly as giving it no further say in the transaction of such business with foreign governments.

In any case, following Madison's argument here to its logical conclusion seems to lead to anti-constitutional results. By denying that the power to treat a foreign government as an illegitimate despotism rests with the president, Madison is surely suggesting that it belongs to the legislature. From this it would seem to follow that Congress could pass a law forbidding the president to receive the representatives of whatever government it regards as unworthy of recognition. This consequence of Madison's thinking, however, seems obviously inconsistent with the Constitution's placement of the right to receive the representatives of foreign governments in the president's hands.

Finally, Madison condemned what he took to be the unacceptable consequences of Hamilton's arguments as Pacificus. Hamilton had argued that the president has an authority to interpret the nation's treaties and find that they included no cause of war. As Madison rightly pointed out, this argument surely proved more than Hamilton was willing to acknowledge in the present controversy. If the president possessed such an authority, it must also include the right to find, if such be the case, that the nation's treaty obligations *do* include a cause of war. Hamilton had prudently – or, Madison might have said, misleadingly – couched his argument in terms of the president's obligation to preserve

---

[82] *PJM*, 15: 15, 98.
[83] *PTJ*, 16: 378 (Jefferson's emphasis).

peace until Congress declared war, but that could not be the whole story, as Madison discerned, if the president really has the authority to interpret treaties that Hamilton claimed.

Madison was correct to draw this out as an implication of Pacificus' argument. However, it is not clear that this implication is as evidently unreasonable as Madison suggests. Here, a distinction is in order. One may imagine a treaty that obliges the United States to declare and wage war on behalf of an ally. Madison would surely be correct to hold that such a stipulation could not take effect until Congress had actually declared war. At the same time, one may also imagine a treaty framed somewhat differently. Such a treaty might simply oblige the United States to provide certain specified forms of military assistance in the event of the ally being drawn into war. A treaty drawn in this way might well, on Hamilton's argument, authorize or even require the president to use military force – in effect to wage war – without waiting for a congressional declaration. This is an admittedly grave consequence of Hamilton's position but not an obviously unacceptable one. The Constitution, after all, holds unmistakably that treaties are "the supreme law of the land." The Constitution also clearly charges the president with the faithful execution of the laws, including, presumably, the nation's treaties. In ordinary cases of domestic legislation the president executes existing law without awaiting further congressional permission to do so, and it is not clear why his obligation would be different in relation to an existing treaty that called for the government to perform certain specified actions, even if they involved using force. Nor need such a situation be understood as requiring the president to take upon himself the substantive decision whether to involve the nation in war. It would be consistent with Hamilton's argument to hold that in such a situation the president was instead simply giving effect to the preexisting law – in this case a treaty – that had already been established by the competent authority – in this case the president and the Senate.[84]

One might hold that such a theory seems to trespass upon the Congress's undoubted right to declare war. This need not be the case, however, if the president's right to use military force is in some cases distinct from Congress's power to declare war. In any case, insisting on the strict Madisonian view simply creates other tensions with the constitutional text – namely, the aforementioned problem of a treaty that is to be regarded as law but that, unlike any other law, is not to be executed without further Congressional action beyond that explicitly required to ratify a treaty. In view of these difficulties on both sides, it is hard to say that Madison's position is decisively superior to Hamilton's.

Perhaps we can go further and say that it is easier to conclude that Hamilton's position is superior to Madison's. This is the easier conclusion because

---

[84] On this point, see also Walling, who observes that when "Congress makes an alliance" it can be understood as having "promise[d] to provide aid to an ally in the future without deliberating" further "about the matter." *Republican Empire*, 148.

Hamilton had staked out the more qualified, and therefore the more defensible, position. Madison argued for a legislative power in relation to the decision to make war that excluded all executive pretensions. Hamilton, in contrast, merely argued for an executive power in this realm that acknowledged Congress's concurrent authority. Madison was correct that a simple, unchecked power of the executive to make war would present intolerable dangers. This was not, however, what Hamilton had defended. On the other side, Madison had insisted on the opposite position, that the executive should simply be excluded from the decision of whether or not to make war, and had in the course of defending this position overlooked that it involved its own dangers. It is in truth unsafe to assert absolutely that the executive may only act pursuant to a previous declaration of war by Congress before using military force or doing what in effect is waging war. Nobody would deny, for example, that when the United States is attacked by a foreign power the president may rightly use military force to repel the attack, and without awaiting a Congressional declaration of war. Once this is admitted, however, it becomes impossible to overlook that the executive authority in this area can and must be pushed even further because if the president may use force to repel an attack without a declaration of war, then surely he can use force without a declaration of war to interdict such an attack before it can be consummated. Any other position would seem inconsistent with the nation's security and therefore presumably not what the Constitution intends.[85] Once this much is admitted, however, it also becomes hard to see why we must deny, with Madison, that a president could be authorized to use force promised by a treaty already in existence, as failure to perform such stipulations might also involve serious dangers to the state, and, again, in performing them the president would not be making his own determination of policy so much as executing a law already enacted by the competent constitutional authority.

According to Madison's complaint, Hamilton's argument implied that the war power could somehow "belong to both" the legislative and executive departments and was capable of being "exercised by either or both, according to the course of exigencies."[86] Madison was correct that Hamilton's argument implied this. But Hamilton's is not an evidently unreasonable or foolish interpretation of the Constitution, in view of the ambiguities of the constitutional text and the kind of "exigencies" that the nation may encounter in foreign policy.

---

[85] Later, in the first of his *Examination* essays, Hamilton developed these kinds of concerns in response to Jefferson's presentation of the war power as president. *PAH*, 25: 453–57.

[86] *PJM*, 15: 83 (Madison's emphasis).

16

Conclusion

The intra-cabinet contest over the status of the French treaties and the public argument between Pacificus and Helvidius over the scope of the executive authority mark the end of Hamilton and Jefferson's major conflicts during their service together in the Washington administration. Jefferson resigned as secretary of state effective the last day of 1793.[1] Hamilton remained in the cabinet for another year and one month, laying down the office of secretary of the treasury on January 31, 1795.[2]

Although neither man could approve the other's contribution to the new republic, Washington could approve both. "I cannot suffer you to leave your station," the president wrote to Jefferson, "without assuring you that the opinion which I had formed of your integrity and talents, and which dictated your original nomination, has been confirmed by the fullest experience; and that both have been eminently displayed in the discharge of your duties."[3] In his reply to Hamilton's resignation, Washington told his departing secretary of the treasury: "In every relation which you have borne to me, I have found that my confidence in your talents, exertions, and integrity has been well placed. I the more freely render this testimony of my approbation because I speak from opportunities of information which cannot deceive me and which furnish satisfactory proof of your title to public regard."[4] As we noted at the beginning of this study, by his own admission, Hamilton's public service was motivated by the love of fame or a desire to win "individual reputation."[5] Perhaps he could

---

[1] Dumas Malone, *Jefferson and the Ordeal of Liberty* (Boston: Little, Brown, and Company, 1962), 161.
[2] *PAH*, 18: 241.
[3] Malone, *Jefferson and the Ordeal of Liberty*, 161.
[4] Chernow, *Alexander Hamilton*, 479.
[5] Hamilton, *Writings*, 573.

take some satisfaction in knowing that in Washington's judgment he had truly earned it.[6]

Hamilton and Jefferson's political disagreements would continue through the 1790s and beyond. As he departed as secretary of state, Jefferson left behind a report that condemned British trade policy toward America as discriminatory and called for American commercial retaliation. Hamilton regarded such a policy as dangerous, and he assisted congressional Federalists in constructing an extensive critique of Jefferson's recommendations.[7] In 1795, Jefferson condemned the Jay Treaty as strongly as Hamilton approved it, and in 1798, Jefferson denounced the Alien and Sedition Acts, which Hamilton defended. Moreover, Jefferson's opposition to those laws led him to author the Kentucky Resolutions, which manifested a spirit that Hamilton believed would, if not checked, "destroy the Constitution of the U[nited] States."[8] Although Hamilton worked to see Jefferson elected to the presidency instead of Aaron Burr, Hamilton also later penned an extensive critique of Jefferson's actual conduct of the presidency.[9]

None of these subsequent disagreements, however, took place at such close quarters, as it were, or with such clarity, as those that Hamilton and Jefferson prosecuted while they served together under Washington. Their position in the cabinet repeatedly required them to respond not only to the same events and policies but also to respond directly to each other's arguments. These cabinet clashes, therefore, provide not only the earliest but also the most illuminating account of their deeply different views about how to set the new government in motion, about how to execute its powers in a way that would serve the nation well while also remaining faithful to its founding principles.

What lessons, then, can we learn from this examination of Hamilton and Jefferson's debates from 1790 to 1793? We learn first and most obviously that there are no easy or simple lessons. Although it is understandable that Americans would wish to turn to the founders for political guidance, and it is even essential to the maintenance of the regime's fundamental character that they should do so, the Hamilton-Jefferson disputes show us that we cannot always find a straightforward answer by turning to the founders.

We see this, first, in relation to questions of government policy. Should the government intervene in the economy with a view to fostering the kind of economic development that public policy makers think is most in the country's interests, or should it simply enforce neutral rules designed to protect everyone's rights, leaving the economy to grow in whatever direction is dictated by the private choices of individual actors? Those who oppose such intervention

[6] Indeed, Hamilton replied to Washington: "As often as I may recall the vexations I have endured, your approbation will be a great and precious consolation." *PAH*, 18: 253.
[7] Chernow, *Alexander Hamilton*, 458–59.
[8] Hamilton, *Writings*, 913.
[9] Chernow, *Hamilton*, 648.

today are tempted to claim – and often succumb to the temptation – that the founders would never have approved of such governmental efforts to influence the economy. Yet we can see that some important founders, such as Alexander Hamilton, actually defended this role for the government. Hamilton's proposals for government support of manufacturing, and even his national bank, were efforts to use the government to promote a particular kind of economic development. Moreover, as we have seen, Hamilton thought of these policies not as merely desirable but as actually essential to completing the founding. Accordingly, we cannot pretend that Hamilton's advocacy of such policies had nothing to do with his understanding of himself as a founder, or that they were merely an idiosyncratic departure from his earlier work as a founder. At the same time, those on the other side of this dispute, those who favor government intervention in the economy, cannot simply appeal to Hamilton's treasury program as evidence that such intervention is the way of the founders because, as we have seen, these policies were deeply controversial from the beginning. And the arguments that men like Jefferson made against them – that they were not really informed by a desire to advance the public good but were instead only a way to advance the interests of certain influential segments in the society – are as suitable for use today by the opponents of intervention as Hamilton's are for its defenders.

Following Senator Arthur Vanderburg, most Americans want "politics" to "stop at the water's edge." This desire is often defeated by contemporary politics, however, so we might try to turn to the founding to find an example of foreign policy made wholly on the basis of shared principles. The Hamilton-Jefferson debates, however, caution us that even in this arena we cannot turn to the founders for a simple resolution of our differences. Politics did not stop at the water's edge for them any more than for us. Some Americans today think that the primary purpose of American foreign policy should be to promote America's national interests and that we should cooperate with whatever nations can assist us in this endeavor, regardless of their regime or form of government. Others think that America, as the world's leading democracy, should especially befriend and defend the other democracies of the world. Proponents of the former view can find some support in Hamilton's thinking about foreign policy, but proponents of the latter view can find some support in Jefferson's. Neither side could truly succeed in painting the other's approach as a betrayal of a monolithic founding approach to foreign affairs.

The Hamilton-Jefferson debates reveal the absence of easy answers not only in the realm of prudence and policy but also at a deeper level of constitutional and political principle. After all, politics could not stop at the water's edge for Hamilton and Jefferson not so much because they differed on what would be the safest practical course for America in the face of the French revolutionary wars – both thought neutrality was necessary – but because they could not agree on the proper interpretation of the constitutional powers of the executive and the legislature in relation to foreign policy. Our own disagreements over this question to a considerable extent reflect theirs, so that we cannot resolve our disputes simply by turning to them for answers.

This is also true in the realm of domestic policy. No question has agitated American politics more vigorously (or more angrily) over the last several years than the scope of the powers of the national government. No question has generated more efforts to turn to the founders for a solution. Yet the Hamilton-Jefferson debates caution us that no simple answer to this question is to be gleaned from the founders. Disagreement about the constitutional extent of the national power was present almost from the moment the Constitution was created, and among figures of the highest authority. The disagreement, moreover, was not a trivial one, over mere matters of detail. Rather, both parties to the founding era dispute believed that the government itself was at stake. Jefferson thought that Hamilton's capacious approach to the national power would effectively destroy the Constitution as a charter of limited government. Hamilton thought that his approach was necessary to the effective operation of the government and that Jefferson's narrower interpretation would return the government to the imbecility of the Articles of Confederation, which would in turn threaten the very life of the Union. Hamilton and Jefferson had the same argument we are having now, and they understood the principles at stake to be at least as fundamental as the ones over which we have been contending. They cannot be our referees because they are themselves competitors in the same contest.

To say that the founding can offer us no easy lessons in these disputes, however, is not to say that it can offer us no positive lessons at all. To affirm the latter claim would involve grave and unwelcome consequences. America's character as a political community is inseparable from its sense that it has a founding with which it intends to live in continuity and a Constitution to which it intends to be faithful. We must be able to derive something positive from the founding, even where we find the founders disagreeing deeply, if these commitments are to have real substance, if they are to be more than formal and empty aspirations. Fortunately, then, there is something of positive value to take from a study even of Hamilton and Jefferson's profound disagreements.

We can learn, in the first place, from Hamilton and Jefferson's great seriousness about the principles over which they disagreed so frequently and so vehemently. To follow their arguments is to get a lesson in the importance of earnestness about principles to constitutional – as opposed to merely pragmatic – statesmanship. Fundamental constitutional and political principles were never far from their minds, or absent from their arguments, as they grappled with the tasks thrust upon them by the conduct of the public's business. The purposes and security of the regime itself always informed their approach to even the most seemingly ordinary concerns, such as the management of the nation's finances or its dealings with foreign governments. They always, in other words, weighed the influence of present policy on the ability of the government to maintain its character and fulfill its duties well into the future. If our own approach to politics is often oriented around more partial, shorter-term, or lower considerations, we find Hamilton and Jefferson united in calling us to a more principled and far-sighted statecraft.

This is not to say, of course, that Hamilton and Jefferson were perfect purists of political principle, that their statesmanship was guided by nothing but an unmixed reverence for the Constitution. On the contrary, their example shows the difficulty – probably the practical impossibility – of a purely disinterested constitutionalism. Put another way, their careers show that our interpretations of the Constitution are apt to be influenced by a certain spirit of partisanship. By partisanship here I don't mean anything necessarily low and unworthy but instead our opinions about what makes for sound policy, or what best suits the needs of the community that the Constitution is designed to serve. Hamilton and Jefferson could not keep these factors out of their deliberations, and neither can we. In his attack on the constitutionality of the bank, Jefferson could not help intruding his policy judgment that a paper currency is not the advantage that Hamilton believed it to be. And in defending the constitutionality of the bank, Hamilton at one point simply appealed to practical experience, holding that anybody who had to run the treasury for a week would be convinced of the bank's constitutionality.

Hamilton and Jefferson's constitutional debates reveal a higher kind of partisanship as well. Here they permitted political considerations external to the Constitution to shape their interpretations of it, although they did so with a view to preserving the Constitution itself. Jefferson, as we have seen, thought the natural tendency of things was for the government to grow ever more centralized, for the national government to grow more and more powerful and to lean in the direction of monarchy. This belief surely influenced his insistence on a strict or narrow interpretation of the national powers, which is certainly not required by the words of the Constitution itself. Hamilton saw an opposite threat, that the power of the states would undermine the national government and threaten the Union, and he openly admitted that this concern had led him to advocate a "liberal construction of the powers of the national government."[10]

Moreover, a purely disinterested constitutionalism is not only impossible; it is not even desirable. The task of the statesman, after all, is not just to preserve the nation's founding principles inviolate but to deal adequately with the challenges the country faces. The task is twofold and must involve considerations of both principle and expediency: the aim is to address successfully the issues the community confronts in a way that is also guided by its fundamental principles. Here, again, Hamilton and Jefferson's example is impressive. They were practical men of business, high-ranking administrators, and so the nation's

[10] *PAH*, 11: 443.

practical needs were always before their eyes. Yet, again, they never divorced their thinking about how to address these needs from a genuine respect for constitutional principle. If their sense of those needs influenced their constitutional thinking, they had too much constitutional seriousness to let it simply determine their conclusions. Hamilton admitted that his fear of state power contributed to his preference for a liberal construction of the national power, but he added that he had never advocated any interpretation that he could not judge to be "consistent with constitutional propriety."[11] There is no reason to doubt that Jefferson strove to maintain a similar integrity in his own constitutional reasoning.

Hamilton and Jefferson's example here is not only edifying but also instructive. They were not just very earnest but also very intelligent. They did not just *want* to judge the policies of the moment in light of their distant consequences, or to evaluate them in relation to the fundamental principles of the regime; rather, they were *able* to do so in a way that is impressive for its intellectual rigor. Accordingly, working through their arguments over the issues on which they squared off provides not just a moral lesson in the importance of respect for principle but an intellectual training in how to apply principle to practice. Following their debates, tracing the play of their minds on the issues of their day, is an education in the kind of reasoning that is essential to enlightened statesmanship – even if the fact of their disagreements means that we cannot get from them ready-made answers to all of our questions.

Furthermore, the education we receive from thinking along with Hamilton and Jefferson is not merely an abstract training in political reasoning such as we could get from following the arguments of intelligent statesmen in any regime. It is, rather, truly an education in American political thought at its best – an education, that is, in applying America's fundamental principles to the concrete problems that American statesmen have faced. The Hamilton-Jefferson debates can provide such instruction because the protagonists, despite their important disagreements, really were reasoning within the context of a shared set of principles. The differences between Hamilton and Jefferson were deep, but they did not go all the way down.[12]

No question divided Hamilton and Jefferson more emphatically than the scope of the powers of the national government. Jefferson thought that Hamilton's approach to these powers betrayed the Constitution by abolishing all limits on the national government. Hamilton thought that Jefferson's approach would cripple the government and throw the nation's affairs into chaos. These

---

[11] *PAH*, 11: 443.

[12] As Lance Banning puts it, speaking more broadly, the "parties" that Hamilton and Jefferson represented "were partly right but mostly wrong about the other. Each was truly, from the other's point of view, a fundamental threat to the sort of nation they desired. But Federalists were never, as the opposition thought, the enemies of a republic; and Republicans were never enemies of union." *Conceived in Liberty*, 3.

are serious differences, but our study of their debates and our knowledge of their public conduct shows that they were not in fact fundamental. Whatever Jefferson may have suspected and feared, Hamilton clearly did not want to be an advocate of an unlimited federal power. Even as he defended a broad interpretation of congressional authority in his *Opinion on the Constitutionality of a National Bank* and his *Report on Manufactures*, Hamilton was also at pains to identify limits to that authority.

On the other side, later developments – especially Jefferson's own presidency – showed that Jefferson, whatever Hamilton may have feared, would not in fact allow his narrow interpretation of the national power to cripple the government when he believed it had to act in the public interest. Hamilton may have been correct later to think that Jefferson's scruples over the constitutionality of the Louisiana Purchase were silly. Nevertheless, Jefferson's willingness to go forward with it show that he was unwilling to hold the public interest hostage to the narrow interpretation of the national power that he had often preached.

Hamilton did not believe that the kind of limited government that Jefferson advocated – one characterized by a narrow and legalistic reading of the national power – was possible or desirable. He did, however, believe in limited government. Jefferson did not believe in the kind of energetic government that Hamilton advocated, but his own conduct as a statesman responsible for the nation's affairs showed that he was not simply an enemy of energetic government.

Similarly, Hamilton and Jefferson's disputes over the public faith, as contentious as they were, point to a common ground that both occupied. When it came to the government's obligation to honor contracts regarding property, Hamilton was certainly more of a stickler than Jefferson. Hamilton may have been correct that Jefferson's theoretical musings, pressed to their logical conclusion, would threaten the public faith and the rights of property and that Jeffersonian denunciations of the debt could only undermine the public's sense of its duty to pay it. Nevertheless, Jefferson as a statesman did not press his theoretical musings to their logical conclusion or act out all of his earlier moralistic denunciations of Hamilton's policies. Even during the Washington administration, Jefferson admitted to the president that not everything Hamilton had accomplished could be repealed consistent with the public faith. And although he may have mused on repealing the irredeemable quality of the debt and the national bank, Jefferson attempted neither of these things when, as president with a congress dominated by his own party, he had an opportunity to do so.

A similar common ground can be discerned as well in their debate over keeping faith with the nation's treaty commitments. Here, the positions are reversed. Jefferson was more scrupulous about the binding quality of treaties, but, at the same time, Hamilton's more relaxed approach cannot reasonably be presented as a mere Machiavellian rejection of the obligations of treaties.

Jefferson was scandalized that Hamilton would suggest that treaties could be rendered void merely by becoming useless or disagreeable. There might well be a fundamental difference between them if Hamilton had advanced such a position, but he had not in fact done so. He had instead argued that when a nation changes its form of government – a momentous step that it takes for its own good and not with a view to the interests of its friends – its treaty partners have an option to nullify the treaty if that change in government has rendered the treaty useless or disagreeable. Even if Hamilton's position were too lax, it was hardly, given the rareness of revolutions, calculated to undermine all faith among nations. For that matter, Jefferson himself admitted that treaties were no longer binding when they were truly dangerous to the state. In the end then, despite their differences, Hamilton and Jefferson actually agreed on the following general propositions: one nation's faith pledged solemnly to another is ordinarily to be respected, but certain rare circumstances create exceptions to this general rule. They agreed on the general rule but disagreed on the nature and extent of the exceptions.

Finally, there is a common area of consensus underlying Hamilton and Jefferson's disagreement over the importance of republican government. Although Jefferson surely carried too far his suspicions that Hamilton was an enemy of republicanism who aimed to establish a monarchy on the British form, there was nevertheless a real difference between the men in how they valued republican government. Jefferson, as we have seen, was more inclined to view it as a matter of natural right and a requirement of reason, while Hamilton tended to view it as a noble and beautiful thing where it could be established consistent with the rights of society. Put simply, Jefferson thought of republicanism as more fundamentally obligatory than Hamilton did.

These theoretical differences, however, did not preclude both men from being practically committed to the success of the American experiment in republican government. Hamilton, after all, evidently believed that there was a good chance that – in America, at least – republicanism could be made compatible with the rights of society, and he dedicated his considerable talents to establishing the kind of energetic republican government that could secure those rights. For Hamilton, the rights of society were primary, and republican government was secondary, but this did not prevent him from viewing republican government as a genuine good that should be pursued and defended where possible, even if it did not lead him to insist on republican government in the way that Jefferson seemed to do. It is possible, moreover, that even this formulation overstates their real differences. As we have seen, Jefferson was too much the practical statesman to make a fetish of his narrow interpretation of the national power when departing from it was necessary to securing some important public advantage. He was also probably too much the practical statesman, and too much the Lockean, to continue to insist on republican government if experience had really proven it to be incompatible with the rights of society. Jefferson, in other words, was too committed to the individual rights doctrine informing the founding to hold to his republicanism if republican government had turned out to be hostile to the individual's secure enjoyment of his rights to life, liberty, and property. Hamilton and Jefferson's differences over republicanism, in the end, may have been less a difference over fundamental principles and more a difference in perceptions of republican government's actual ability to secure rights.

Of course, although Hamilton and Jefferson's differences did not go all the way down, they often talked as if they did. Here, their debates provide another useful lesson, one in the dangers of principled constitutional statesmanship. Again, that kind of statesmanship is one to which we should aspire, but it also carries its own paradoxical perils. To maintain the regime the founders established, it is essential to keep fundamental principles in view and to argue in light of them. However, keeping such principles in view, and striving to treat them with proper respect, can tempt us to think that those who dissent from our policy prescriptions either do not understand or do not respect those principles. Recurrence to fundamental principles in political debate can foster the impression in each party that the other is perverting or abandoning those principles. The danger of such principled political argument, then, is that it can lead us to think that our political opponents are not just erring but in fact enemies of the regime, with the effect that trying to keep an eye on what unites us on a fundamental level leads us to think that we are divided at a fundamental level. Such a danger is inseparable from politics in a regime like America's in which political debate can never be confined to questions of expediency.

Fortunately, however, the study of the Hamilton-Jefferson debates also points to the possibility of overcoming this danger. That possibility appears in the prudence and moderation of George Washington, who, as we have seen, could duly value both Hamilton's and Jefferson's contributions to the new constitutional republic, as different as they were. Washington was not, of course, a political thinker of Hamilton and Jefferson's caliber, nor would he have claimed to be. It does him no injustice to observe that he could not have written the state papers that they wrote for him. Nevertheless, Washington's ability to praise both men shows not superficiality but real wisdom. He had the practical good sense to see that, despite the differences that tended to blind Hamilton and Jefferson to each other's merits, both were committed to the same fundamental principles and were laboring in the service of the same noble project.

The American project requires an intelligent effort to reconcile diverse political goods that do not fit together unproblematically. Americans today, like the founders, want a government that is both energetic and limited, that observes principles of justice among nations while safeguarding American interests, and that is republican in character while also respecting individual rights. Hamilton and Jefferson sought all these things as well, and they argued about how best to secure them with a seriousness and rigor that has only rarely been achieved in the history of American statesmanship. We can therefore learn from them how to be more thoughtful about these aims, even if disagreement persists about how to achieve them. In studying the Hamilton-Jefferson debates, we learn how to be better constitutionalists and better Americans, even if some of us will still choose to be Hamiltonians and others to be Jeffersonians.

Index